PROMISING
LANGUAGE

PROMISING LANGUAGE

Betrothal in Victorian Law and Fiction

RANDALL CRAIG

State University
of New York
Press

Published by
State University of New York Press, Albany

Production by Susan Geraghty
Marketing by Dana Yanulavich

Cover illustration of **Das Wert-Paket/"The Important Package,"** 1939, 858
(UU 18) 45, 5 × 32, 7/33, 3cm; coloured paste and pencil on paperM
Kunstsammlung NordrheinWestfalen, Dusseldorf, by Paul Klee. Copyright
© 1999 Artists Rights Society (ARS), New York/VG Bild-Kunst, Bonn.

Printed in the United States of America

For information, address State University of New York
Press, State University Plaza, Albany, N.Y., 12246

Library of Congress Cataloging-in-Publication Data

Craig, Randall, 1951–
    Promising language : betrothal in Victorian law and fiction /
    Randall Craig.
        p.   cm.
    Includes bibliographical references and index.
    ISBN 0-7914-4425-2 (alk. paper). — ISBN 0-7914-4426-0 (pbk. :
alk. paper)
    1. English fiction—19th century—History and criticism.
2. Betrothal—Law and legislation—Great Britain—History—19th
century. 3. Legal stories, English—History and criticism. 4. Love
stories, English—History and criticism. 5. Betrothal in
literature. 6. Courtship in literature. 7. Marriage in literature.
8. Promises in literature. I. Title.
PR878.B47C73 1999
823′.809355—dc21   99-22478
                                                                          CIP

10 9 8 7 6 5 4 3 2 1

For

G·R·A·H·A·M

CONTENTS

FOREWORD

Cross Your Fingers . . .

This study explores the linguistic implications and social ramifications of promising as a verbal practice, especially as depicted in novels by Charlotte Brontë, George Eliot, Anthony Trollope, George Meredith, and Henry James. While the emphasis ultimately falls upon critical analysis of the fiction, my intention throughout is to limn the interconnections of several emergent nineteenth-century discourses: the science of language (notably etymology and philology), utilitarian social theory and jurisprudence (especially freedom of contract), and the aesthetics of the novel (predominantly realism). The introduction, using *Far from the Madding Crowd* as an example, prepares for this project by locating promising precisely at the intersection of these discourses: as speech act, as social practice and legal contract, and as structural principle and topos.

Because my focus is upon the linguistic dimensions of promising, and specifically of promising marriage, chapter 1 examines nineteenth-century thinking about language. It is only with a sense of the pervasive attitudes concerning words and how they work that the importance of a particular—and a particularly consequential—verbal practice can be appreciated. After discussing the impact of John Locke's *An Essay Concerning Human Understanding*, I turn to representative early and mid-century figures, primarily John Horne Tooke, Samuel Taylor Coleridge, John Stuart Mill, Richard Chenevix Trench, and Max Müller, in order to document the tradition of relativism in British linguistic thought and to explain the new emphasis upon the historical and comparative analysis of language. Shifts in interest from the origin to the development of language and from theoretical grammar to vernacular practice are reflected in the practices of novelists themselves. Thus, while Mrs. Garth "in a general wreck of society would have tried to hold her 'Lindley Murray' above the waves" and Elizabeth-Jane Henchard searches for answers to the puzzle of social class in "grammar-books and dictionaries," modern scholars might find *Middlemarch* and *The Mayor of Casterbridge* themselves to be of greater interest and significance.[1]

Chapter 2 discusses the Victorian ethos of promising in the contexts of betrothal and breach of promise law. I draw upon Hume on promising, as well as upon Victorian jurists and legislators, in order to delineate the contexts in which novelists worked and to suggest the ways in which they both practice and challenge what philosophy preaches and the legal system promulgates. The abstractions of the former and the technicalities of the latter often seem incapable either of explaining or regulating premarital promissory practices. This difficulty becomes increasingly obvious throughout the nineteenth century as more and more women turn to the courts to settle disputed betrothals. While the adversarial model of legal ethics and the oppositional method of the political system typically result in coherent and compelling narratives, these stories tend to be one-dimensional and mutually exclusive. They neither fairly represent nor adequately resolve the nuances and complexities of actual promissory practices. To get a better sense of these practices, that is, of how Victorians actually conform to, circumvent, and modify the conventions of betrothal, we can do no better than turn to the fiction of the day. Freed from the pragmatic objectives and generic requirements of judicial and political debate, novelistic representations of promising are both more supple and more subtle than those of either plaintiffs and defendants or partisan Members of Parliament.

Chapter 3 relies upon various meanings of the term "legal fiction" to bridge the linguistic, legal, and social concerns of the preceding chapters. The concept of narrative itself provides a link between the otherwise dissimilar stories of broken promises issuing from the mouths of lawyers and flowing from the pens of novelists. The common demands of narratibility—such things as coherence, continuity, and completeness—establish a structural connection between novels, in which breach of promise trials typically do not appear, and courtrooms, in which novels are equally out of place (unless perchance they are the physical means of murder or mayhem). Each of the first three chapters maintains a dual interest in intellectual, social, and cultural contexts, on the one hand, and fictional texts, on the other. *The Mill on the Floss* serves as the exemplary text in chapters 1 and 2, *The Pickwick Papers* and *An Old Man's Love* in chapter 3.

Chapters 4 through 8 focus on single novels that represent promising in the context of courtship and that show novelists' reconceptions of betrothal. I have selected works in which the practice of promising raises fundamental questions about the nature and social function of language. In each, the central male character makes at least two proposals of marriage, and the central female character receives offers from at least two men. While multiple and competing promises may seem to be the stuff of comedy, the resulting strain upon language is not rendered in the comic fashion that these plots might otherwise suggest since each novel, with the exception of *The Wings of the Dove*, ends with at least one and sometimes several marriage(s). Throughout these analyses, my concern is less with the ethics than the pragmatics of using language and making promises. Again, the focus is double: first, upon what words actually do and how they are used (as opposed to what they mean or how they are defined), and, second, upon the dynamics of promising itself as a verbal act and a social practice whose consequences extend beyond questions of manners or law.

The emphasis of chapters 4 through 8 changes gradually from language to breach of promise, roughly following the sequence of the first three chapters. In *Jane Eyre*, the focus is on a general mistrust of language, in *Adam Bede* on standard English, and in *The Egoist* on figurative language. The nature of promising is considered in each of these novels; however, beginning with Meredith and continuing in *Can You Forgive Her?* and *The Wings of the Dove*, the emphasis shifts more squarely to betrothal and broken engagements—without losing sight of underlying linguistic issues related to promising.

Jane Eyre offers a virtual anatomy of logophobia. A series of courtships and pseudo-courtships leads to the conclusion that what Blanche Ingram calls "trailing" (and what we might call "leading someone on") may in fact characterize all speaking. Since the misuses of language are always present—even when unintended—and often undetectable, Brontë proposes the dark possibility that to promise is to lie. *Adam Bede* stages several rustic symposia in order to examine the social function of language. Eliot points to a curious similarity between seemingly unrelated verbal acts: harvest speeches, marriage proposals, and Protestant sermons. In the process, she raises the possibility that to promise is not merely to affirm but further to hallow. *The Egoist* portrays a society entirely devoted to talk, one in which figurative speaking is invariably taken as a sign of deceit. Meredith, however, reconfigures promises in precisely the terms that he questions. To promise, he suggests, is to trope. *Can Your Forgive Her?* intertwines political with romantic promises in a common-sense criticism of empty rhetoric. Trollope, like Meredith, unexpectedly redefines promises in the terms previously criticized. He combines two tropes—oxymorons and rhetorical questions—to formulate what might be called the "rhetorical promise." For Trollope, to promise is to speak rhetorically. *The Wings of the Dove* anatomizes secrecy in the context of betrothal and terminal illness. Promising and death are shown to be related in that each may have liberating consequences. Furthermore, the logic of promising is not simply that of a contractual exchange. Instead, a "promissory surplus" is produced, making promises less significant for what they commit an individual to than for what they free him or her from. James hypothesizes that to promise is to liberate—which (as Brontë knows full well) may also be to lie.

Thus the discussion begins and ends with works presenting a rather dark view of the possibilities and consequences of using words and making promises. Between Brontë's sense that language can never be fully trusted and James's that promises mean anything but what they profess are found the varied efforts of Eliot, Meredith, and Trollope, if not to recover Adamic language, then at least to redefine the potential of postlapsarian promises. Each reconceives promises in the terms that are cast into greatest doubt: religious oratory, poetic language, and political rhetoric. Their efforts reflect a deeply felt Victorian need to address encompassing fears about that which is felt to be distinctly and definitively human: the capacity to speak and to shape words into promises, in other words, into surrogate selves possessing the ability, as well as the reliability, to act in the world.

Doubts about this ability mean that promises must always be made with fingers crossed, that is, in a gesture of fervency and with the hope that against whatever odds and despite whatever accidents they can and will be kept. Promises are sometimes made, however, with fingers covertly crossed, that is, with a secret sign of insincerity. These contingencies—definitional and individual—are compounded when it comes to affairs of the heart and promises of marriage. The attitude noted in Plato's *Symposium* guarantees that promising love is at best an uncertain enterprise: "What is strangest of all is the popular conviction that a lover, and none but a lover, can forswear himself with impunity—a lover's vow, they say, is no vow at all."[2] If not, then what is a lover's vow, what might it mean, and how does it work? To these and related questions, I turn in the following pages . . . with fingers crossed.

ACKNOWLEDGMENTS

Whatever the implicit promise of this project, I have accrued a number of explicit debts in completing it, and I am grateful for the chance to acknowledge them. Over the last several years and in a number of different places, a nourishing—in several senses of this term—working environment has been provided for me: in Marin County, California, by Sheila and Michael Rolfer; in the Capital District of New York by Barbara and Jeffrey Berman, Lana Cable and Eshi Motahar, Boba and Michael Werner, Betty Jane and John Leschen, and Richard Goldman; in Würzburg, Germany, by Uschi and Peter Stahl, Karin Köhne and Michael Will, and Christine and Freimut Löser; and in each place by Noel Grunwaldt. That I have at last settled in the Northeast, finding both a home and a climate in which to finish this book owes a great deal to my family—to Graham, David, Kristin, Jennifer, Ellen, and Cheryl Craig—and most of all to Jane Patterson Craig, who has given substance and significance to that most elusive word, "promise."

I would like to acknowledge the colleagues at Albany and elsewhere who have been generous and careful readers of this work-in-progress: Hans Aarsleff, Sheila Berger, Jeffrey Berman, David Craig, Diva Daims, Robert Donovan, Jennifer Fleischner, Elizabeth Gemmette, Richard Goldman, Christopher Knight, and William Vitek. I am also pleased to acknowledge the assistance of Marianne Simon of Computing Services and Dina Anthony of the English Department, who at crucial moments circumvented the unexpected obstacles presented by recalcitrant computers and entrenched bureaucracies. The secretarial staff of the English Department has been a continual source of practical and emotional support, and it is a pleasure to recognize Carline Davenport, Rose Marie Di Camillo, and Annette Roberts. I would also like to thank James Peltz of SUNY Press who with grace and goodwill carefully shepherded this manuscript into print. I am especially grateful to the three anonymous reviewers who provided astute and consistently helpful criticism. I have tried to make the final work equal to their critique and to their confidence.

Chapters 6 and 7 are revised versions of essays originally appearing in *ELH*: "Promising Marriage, *The Egoist*, Don Juan, and the Problem of Language" (53:897–921) and "Rhetoric and Courtship in *Can You*

Forgive Her?" (62:217–35). They are reprinted courtesy of the Johns Hopkins University Press.

Chapter 4 is a revised version of an essay originally appearing in the *Journal of Narrative Technique*: "Logophobia in *Jane Eyre*" (23:2). It is reprinted courtesy of the *Journal of Narrative Technique*.

Four lines from "Law like love" are reprinted from *W. H. Auden: Collected Poems*, edited by Edward Mendelson. Copyright 1940 and renewed 1968 by W. H. Auden. Reprinted by permission of Random House, Inc.

The cover illustration, Paul Klee's *Ohne Titel (Das Wertpaket)*, is reproduced with the kind permission of Kunstsammlung Nordrhein-Westfalen, Düsseldorf, Germany and the Artists Rights Society. The photograph is by Walter Klein of Düsseldorf, Germany.

Finally, I gratefully acknowledge the financial support of United University Professions, the University at Albany, and the National Endowment for the Humanities.

ABBREVIATIONS

A	An Autobiography
AB	Adam Bede
AM	The Amazing Marriage
AW	Alice in Wonderland
BH	Bleak House
BL	Biographia Literaria
BQR	British Quarterly Review
CW	Collected Works of Jeremy Bentham
CYFH	Can You Forgive Her?
DC	The Duke's Children
DCW	Diana of the Crossways
DD	Daniel Deronda
DP	The Diversions of Purley
E	The Egoist
ED	The Eustace Diamonds
EE	An Eye for an Eye
ELH	English Literary History
FMC	Far from the Madding Crowd
FLW	French Lieutenant's Woman
HKHWR	He Knew He Was Right
JE	Jane Eyre
KD	Kept in the Dark
L	Logic
LA	Lady Anna
LC	Life of Cicero
M	Middlemarch
MC	The Mayor of Casterbridge
MF	The Mill on the Floss
NA	Nightmare Abbey
NLH	New Literary History
OED	Oxford English Dictionary
OF	Orley Farm
OML	An Old Man's Love
PC	The Princess Casamassima
PF	Phineas Finn

PM	*The Prime Minister*
PP	*The Pickwick Papers*
PR	*Phineas Redux*
QS	*The Question of Our Speech*
SHA	*The Small House at Allington*
SL	*A System of Logic*
TD	*Tess of the d'Urbervilles*
TL	*Tales of Love*
TS	*Tristram Shandy*
VF	*Vanity Fair*
WAD	*Wives and Daughters*
WD	*The Wings of the Dove*

INTRODUCTION

Promising:
Language/Narrative/Law

The appearance of three books in 1861 symbolizes the overlapping concerns of this study. The first is a series of lectures given by Max Müller, attended on one occasion by Queen Victoria and subsequently published as *The Science of Language*. The second is Sir Henry Sumner Maine's *Ancient Law: Its Connection with the Early History of Society and Its Relation to Modern Ideas*. Both are highly influential and surprisingly popular works advocating—but not always exemplifying—historical, scientific, and comparative methods.[1] Müller utilizes comparative philology to advance the familiar, biblically sanctioned claim that language divides humans from animals: "Language is our Rubicon, and no brute will dare to cross it."[2] Maine enlists comparative jurisprudence to reach an analogous conclusion concerning evolving social structures. His famous assertion that the "movement of the progressive societies has hitherto been a movement *from Status to Contract*" establishes contractual relations as a definitive feature of advanced social and legal systems.[3]

The evolutionary bent of both works suggests a connection between the study of language and of law that is confirmed by a third work of 1861, Anthony Trollope's *Orley Farm*. In this novel, Lucius Mason, facing the perennial problem of what to do with his life, rejects a legal career on the grounds that "all lawyers are liars."[4] Instead, he proposes devoting himself "to philology and the races of man. Nothing considerable has been done with them as a combined pursuit" (*OF* 23). He naively believes that etymology holds the key to human evolution and "that by tracing out the roots of words he could trace also the wanderings of man since the expulsion of Adam from the garden" (*OF* 24). Trollope mildly satirizes this optimism, but it does reflect growing Victorian interest in natural history and the emerging human sciences. In *An Essay on the Origin of Language* (1860), for example, Frederic W. Farrar announces that his discipline would accomplish what neither history nor archaeology had been able to: "we toilfully examine the unburied monuments of extinct nations, and are rewarded for years of labour if we can finally succeed in gaining a feeble glimpse of their his-

tory by deciphering the unknown letters carved on the crumbling fragments of half-calcined stone; but in language we have the history not
only of individuals but of nations; not only of nations but of mankind."[5]
Farrar's confident assertion is overstated; Lucius Mason's youthful
enthusiasm is short-lived. Both, however, typify British attitudes toward
language around 1861.

For my purposes, the fleeting reference in *Orley Farm* to linguistics
and anthropology is significant because it suggests that fiction might
provide a common ground upon which to examine Victorians' understanding of themselves in relation to language and to evolving social and
legal practices. If so, then perhaps a "missing link" between Müller's linguistic and Maine's sociolegal interests, that is, between language and
contract, on the one hand, and the fictional concerns of writers like
Trollope, on the other hand, is to be found in the concept of the
promise. In the form of "a gentleman's word of honor," promising is a
cardinal principle of Victorian society; in the form of betrothal, it is an
integral aspect of its preferred literary form, the novel of courtship and
marriage. Marriage, too, is a Rubicon, as the *Examiner* of January 21,
1871, points out when likening the promise to marry to "a pause, during which those who are entering matrimony may reflect before they
cross the Rubicon."[6] But, as George Eliot points out, the Rubicon "was
a very insignificant stream to look at; its significance lay entirely in certain invisible conditions" (*M* 803). This study is concerned less with the
unseen dangers guaranteeing that "the course of true love never did run
smooth" than with the "invisible conditions" of promises to marry.
Such promises are obscure, if not invisible, for several reasons: by circumstance, because they typically occur in private and without the official witnesses present at weddings (a particularly vexing issue for the
legal system); and by nature, because they are indeterminate, existing
both prior to and as part of the process of traversing the marital Rubicon. If marriage is a river, then engagement is both a riparian and an
aquatic activity. This ambiguity means that "invisible conditions" are
often undetected, their consequences, therefore, unforeseen. Betrothal,
defined as no more than a "pause," is a contradictory and self-defeating
practice: a promise that need not be kept. Furthermore, this view effectively transforms engagement from a promise into a promise to make a
promise, raising questions about the nature and force of such self-reflexive language.

Approaching the issues of language and promising from the dual
perspective of law and fiction constitutes my version of the "combined
pursuit" proposed but not pursued by Lucius Mason. This pursuit
requires crossing several disciplinary boundaries, and I want to begin by
outlining at least some of the relations among these four terms.

LANGUAGE AND THE NOVEL

Novelists taking up the pen in Victorian England face a double jeopardy. The first danger derives from the long and distinguished tradition of skepticism concerning language itself. Elaborating upon book III of Locke's *Essay*, John Horne Tooke sets the skeptical tone for the century to follow in *Winged Words, or the Diversions of Purley* (1798). This widely read study emphasizes that language invariably occasions unintended flights of meaning, therein producing muddled thinking and confused communication. Tooke's warning amplifies those of Hobbes, Bacon, and Locke and resonates widely among the Victorians. For example, both Farrar and Müller discuss Tooke and cite Bacon's observation that "although we think we govern our words . . . yet certain it is that words, as a Tartar's bow, do shoot back upon the understanding of the wisest, and mightily entangle and pervert the judgment."[7] The suspicion that the wings of language belong to Satan and not to Hermes leads beyond skepticism to fear, especially with regard to highly figurative or "merely" literary language. The novelists considered here, however, typically turn this skepticism against itself, suggesting that even the most potentially untrustworthy forms of speech—for example, political oratory (*Can You Forgive Her?*) and figurative language (*The Egoist*)— can, in their very riskiness, revivify language and heighten expressiveness. They take inspiration from Coleridge, who substitutes "living" for "winged" in Tooke's formulation in order to emphasize that language possesses "vital & idea-creating force."[8] These novelists depict popular language fears not to show that they are baseless but to reveal that the risks of language use are complemented by its creative potential.

The second liability confronting novelists is that, even from within the perspective of the arts, fiction is stigmatized as a distant and disreputable relation of established genres like drama and poetry. Many hold the view expressed in the *British Quarterly Review* (*BQR*, 1866) that novels ought to be "simply read as a relaxation to minds wearied with more important studies, not looked upon as substitutes for such."[9] Precisely because of this marginalization, however, the novel provides a rich source of attitudes toward and experimentation with language. While Wordsworth may have announced to the nineteenth century that the "language really used by men" is an appropriate medium for poetry, the novel seems better able to accomplish this objective, precisely because it is comparatively unconstrained by either literary tradition or stylistic convention.[10] Novelists are free not only to depict the function of words in everyday circumstance but also to articulate the relations between language as the object and the means of representation. Both factors contribute to linguistic variety and innovation in fiction, making it possible to argue in opposition to the *BQR* essayist and along with Bakhtin: "Studying other genres is analogous to studying dead languages; studying the novel, on the other hand, is like studying languages that are not only alive, but still young."[11] Nowhere is that vitality more apparent than in fictional representation of promising, especially betrothal. The marriage of a dubious genre and an overdetermined social practice (engagement) produces works of fiction in which assumptions about the meaning of promises are challenged and fundamental ideas about language and how it works are reshaped.

Novelists' self-reflexive interest in language is given considerable impetus in the nineteenth century by the "still young" science of philology, which influences—both progressively and conservatively—Victorian thinking about language and social development. While Continental philology is not always warmly received in nineteenth-century Britain, it does incite a new preoccupation with the English language: with its history, evidenced by the interest in Anglo-Saxon studies and the popularity of etymological analysis; and with its lexicon, demonstrated by the massive effort culminating in the publication of *The Oxford English Dictionary* (1884–1928).[12] Popular interest in the nature and history of the English language is further generated by works such as Richard Chenevix Trench's *On the Study of Words* (1851) that make etymological and ethnographic approaches to language widely accessible. Etymology may have been of particular interest to writers and readers of fiction since a "natural history" of language transforms words and phrases into potential narratives in and of themselves and renders every eccentricity of speech into a possibly significant anthropological or sociological datum. Max Müller suggests as much in his 1888 work, *Biographies of Words*: "Our poets make poems out of words, but every word, if carefully examined, will turn out to be itself a petrified poem. . . . Each word has its biography, beginning with its birth, or at least with its baptism. We may speak of its childhood, its youth, its manhood and old age, nay, even of its death, and of its heirs and successors."[13] The affinity between stories of words (etymology) and stories with words (novels) lies in their common plot: words no less than literary characters assume the shape of human lives. In this regard, the effect of etymology as a means of linguistic analysis coincides with that of realism as a fictional mode: words and language practices resonate with significance beyond questions of semantics alone. The confluence of linguistic and literary concerns encourages the use of colloquial dialects in fiction and transforms the novel into a record of established speaking and writing practices. Even more significant than verbal mimesis, however, is *poiesis*—the novel's creative challenge to linguistic boundaries and active experimentation with new forms of verbal expression.

LANGUAGE AND PROMISING

The pronounced skepticism confronting novelists applies *a fortiori* to the makers of promises. Promises are, first and foremost, a matter of words—an instance of what speech act theorists describe as performatives, that class of utterance by which something is accomplished merely by saying it.[14] As such, promising can be isolated and analyzed both as an indication of the power of words alone to accomplish specific ends and as evidence of the unreliability or potential misuse of that power. Promising, in fact, seems calculated to augment the increasingly prevalent view since Locke that words are active, often subversive, agents and not simply passive, *a posteriori* vehicles of expression. In making promises, speakers self-consciously subject themselves to the agency of words, irrespective of non-linguistic contingencies, and in so doing face the double jeopardy of an unreliable medium and an uncertain future. Especially when "winged words" are associated with Cupid, doubts about language and promises are intensified and insinuated into the very basis of the Victorian social order. After all, a vessel of mere words is unlikely to instill confidence in those making the risky crossing into married life.

Anxieties of this nature are heard, for example, in the antonymic echoes of a common expression for betrothal: plighting one's troth. "To plight," according to the *OED*, is "to endanger or compromise" as well as "to warrant or assure." The contradictory meanings sound an ominous reminder: the very act of promising, with the intention of guaranteeing that something will be done, necessarily raises the possibility that it will not. These dichotomous strains are rendered even more dissonant by the realization that "troth" means "truth" or "faith," therefore, that "plighting troth" might be interpreted as "compromising truth" or "endangering faith." The etymological echo of the sacral nature of engagement is a faint but persistent reminder of the inescapable tension between the sacramental (and sentimental) character of betrothal, on the one hand, and its mercantile (and sexual) aspects, on the other. The danger in promising to marry is not simply a matter of forfeiting truth or honor if the engagement is broken; the risks are not limited to the social, legal, and financial ramifications of betrothal. The plight of promising is the plight of language itself. Promising epitomizes (and is a synecdoche for) the perilous human circumstance of having to take others at their word.

Paul de Man presents the culmination of this skepticism when he claims that promises are characterized by a double discrepancy—the first, linguistic and theoretical, the second, temporal and phenomenological. All language, he claims, entails a fundamental contradiction:

"the logic of grammar generates texts only in the absence of referential meaning, but every text generates a referent that subverts the grammatical principle to which it owed its constitution."[15] Verbal promises are no less unstable than other utterances in this regard; in fact, they are more so because promises are further characterized by a temporal disjunction. The locutionary moment of promising is in the present, but its illocutionary force is "future-oriented and prospective, . . . every promise assumes a date at which the promise is made and without which it would have no validity." As a result, "the present of the promise is always a past with regard to its realization."[16] The nineteenth century may not have reached this deconstructive impasse, yet an awareness of the contradictions inherent in promising not only informs thinking about betrothal but also explains why the creative resources of the novel might play an important role in reinterpreting the predicament of promising. From its doubly dubious status as a verbal and an artistic construct, the novel raises the possibility that "winged words" are not the exclusive property of Hermes, Satan, or Cupid; they might also belong to Daedalus, the figure of the craftsman/author used by Joyce to represent escape from the labyrinth of language by means of language itself.

PROMISING AND THE NOVEL

Focusing on the place of promising in fiction emphasizes that both are verbal practices engaging the logic as well as the mechanisms of contract and performance. Each is a dialogical process, requiring the mutual consent of those involved but depending ultimately upon the willingness of promisees and readers alike to accept words for deeds, or at the very least, uncertainties for certainties. Nietzsche suggests that promising depends more upon forgetting than upon remembering. We have to remember in order to keep promises, but we must forget in order to make them—and what we ignore are all those things that make promising such an unlikely and uncertain venture into the future.[17] Those engaged in promising willingly forget that words cannot substitute for things or actions in the present, let alone the future; they actively disregard the fact that no promissory guarantee can be unconditional and that any number of unforeseen circumstances might prevent promises from being kept. Analogously, readers of literature must, in Coleridge's words, willingly suspend disbelief. What Nietzsche characterizes in terms of promissory forgetting, Coleridge defines as poetic faith: "that *illusion*, contra-distinguished from *delusion*, that *negative* faith, which simply permits the images presented to work by their own force."[18] His references to disbelief and to faith invoke, in a new context, the concept of plighting troth. Readers ignore the unreality of fiction and fully consent to an illusory wor(l)d. Novels, no less than promises, are linguistic entities/actions whose efficacy requires that their purely verbal existence be forgotten. Promises, no less than novels, exemplify words "work[ing] by their own force."

Writing fiction and making promises are connected not only by structural analogy but also by mutual implication. Tellers of stories make implicit promises (the promise of narrative), just as the makers of promises tell explicit stories (the narrative of promise). The promise of meaning inheres in any communicative act or work of literature—a circumstance described by Derrida as "the performative structure of the text in general *as* promise."[19] By the "promise of narrative," I allude to this general circumstance but more specifically to the expectations raised when writers employ conventions that signal to readers the presence as well as the nature of narrative. Such generic "promises" may be subject to negotiation—the rules of storytelling can be stretched or broken—but they cannot be entirely avoided.[20] The author of prose fiction necessarily agrees to such a contract, even though it may entail unwelcome conditions, which, for the nineteenth century, might include a mandatory love plot, preferably with multiple and varied betrothals, culminating in at least one and optimally several wedding(s). The ways in which writers fulfill and finesse this promise are necessarily a concern of this study, although at this point I want only to indicate the ways in which telling stories and making promises are themselves wedded together.

The "narrative of promise" describes more than a story about problematic engagements inevitably leading to marriage. It refers more significantly to the fact that all promises contain a narrative component. Promisers in effect write a script, or construct a plot, that is motivated and articulated by the promise itself. The three factors that Greimas identifies as characterizing the narrative situation—contract, performance, and recognition—are also structural elements of promising: promises are made (or not), kept (or not), and their (non)performance acknowledged and acted upon.[21] Peter Brooks's account of narrative desire closely correlates to promises that are, like the plots of novels, "intentional structures, goal-oriented, and forward-moving." Both have meaning "always *in terms of* the impending end."[22] In its syntagmatic as well as its symbolic dimensions, therefore, promising is linked to narrative by temporality. Novels are permeated by promise: from without by the promise of narrative, from within by the narrative of promise.

LAW AND THE NOVEL

The analogical and implicatory links between novels and promises are also to be found between novels and law, and once again the connections are grounded in narrative. Seeking a metaphor for the practice of the novelist, George Eliot turns to a jury trial:

> my strongest effort is . . . to give a faithful account of men and things as they have mirrored themselves in my mind. The mirror is doubtless defective; the outlines will sometimes be disturbed, the reflection faint or confused; but I feel as much bound to tell you as precisely as I can what that reflection is, as if I were in the witness-box, narrating my experience on oath.[23]

This trope carries both negative and positive force. On the one hand, Eliot dissociates her fiction from the practice of romancers, whose "arbitrary pictures" (*AB* 174) are derived from artificial literary conventions and driven by wish-fulfillment fantasies. On the other hand, she associates *Adam Bede* with the scrupulous testimony of witnesses, who add to the implicit promise of narrative an explicit promise to tell the truth.[24] By acknowledging that even the most accurate reflections are subjective, however, Eliot raises a possibility that she does not pursue, specifically, that the "truth" itself may be multiple and conflicting and that juries may be hung. By associating her narrator with the sworn witness, she affirms that which the act of narrating itself implies: the truth of its representations and the fairness of its verdicts.

Eliot's metaphor has come to be definitive of Victorian realism. In his pioneering study *The Rise of the Novel* (1957), Ian Watt uses this trope to describe the narrative method of the new literary form. A "circumstantial view of life," Watt maintains, is common to mimetic fiction and courtroom proceedings:

> The novel's mode of imitating reality may therefore be equally well summarised in terms of the procedures of another group of specialists in epistemology [the first is philosophers], the jury in a court of law. Their expectations, and those of the novel reader coincide in many ways: both want to know "all the particulars" of a given case—the time and place of the occurrence; both must be satisfied as to the identities of the parties concerned . . . ; and they expect the witnesses to tell the story "in his own words."[25]

The potential relativism implied by Eliot's image of a faulty mirror is here intensified (although again not developed) and in two ways: first, by the emphasis placed upon the individual stories and words of witnesses, as opposed to the unitary vision and voice of Eliot's narrator, and, second, by the acknowledgment that: "Formal realism is, of course, like the rules of evidence, only a convention."[26] The latter admission raises the possibility of discursive relativism in addition to the epistemological skepticism implied by Eliot. Above and beyond the subjectivity of individual perception—and irrespective of the "circumstantial" compatibility between novelistic and legal views of life—the possibility must now be admitted that the conventions of truth-telling in one medium do not necessarily correspond to those of another. Hence, to the skepticism about language generally must be added the particular fear that, even with a single language, different discourses will isolate speakers from one other and from communal understandings of truth or reality. A conclusion, drawn neither by Eliot nor Watt but subsequently posited by poststructuralists and asserted by the critical legal studies movement, is that such understandings, whether depicted in fiction or constituted by law, are necessarily shaped by linguistic and narrative codes. The senses of "the real" are constructed and confirmed according to agreed upon sets of procedures or rules, whether artistic or evidentiary. This argument accentuates a previously unarticulated aspect of Eliot's metaphor: the explicit association of truth with narrative, therefore, with rhetoric.[27] Readers and jurors must be persuaded of the truth, a truth that depends upon—in fact, is constituted by—them. In law, no less than in literature and in promising, words "work by their own force." In the case of a jury's verdict or a judge's decision, for instance, it is quite clear that saying makes it so. Thus what is perhaps obviously the case with novels—that the methods and criteria of truth reside in narrative conventions (the law of narratives)—is no less the case with courtroom proceedings and in the law generally (the narratives of law).

The "law of narratives" describes the circumstance in which the realism of any story, whether of fictional characters or actual people, depends upon its conforming to the conventions of narrativity—to those historically and culturally specific practices that signify telling the truth about the world outside of language. This principle explains, for example, why the truth might be stranger than fiction and why coherence is an important criterion of truth. The theoretical groundwork for the law of narratives is laid by Hayden White:

> Common opinion has it that the plot of a narrative imposes a meaning on the events that make up its story level by revealing at the end a structure that was immanent in the events all along. What I am trying to establish is the nature of this immanence in any narrative account of real events, events that are offered as the proper content of historical [and I would add, legal] discourse. These events are real not because they occurred but because, first, they were remembered and, second, they are capable of finding a place in a chronologically ordered sequence. . . . It is historians themselves who have transformed narra-

tivity from a manner of speaking into a paradigm of the form that reality itself displays to a "realistic" consciousness. It is they who have made narrativity into a value, the presence of which in a discourse having to do with "real" events signals at once its objectivity, its seriousness, and its realism.[28]

What counts as "narrativity," of course, varies: across ethnic and cultural boundaries, from period to period, and among disciplines and discourses. What remains constant amidst this diversity, however, is the function of narrative itself in signifying objectivity and truth.

An example of the "immanence" of narrative accounts to which White alludes can be derived from Watt's thesis that formal realism is a defining characteristic of the novel. Novels, Watt maintains, differ from previous genres in their dependence upon categories of experience not usually associated with literature: such things as particularized characters, settings, and plots; temporality; causation; and so on. Mimesis, however, is not simply a matter of correspondence to perceived notions of how the world works; it also depends upon the formal conventions and aesthetic strategies that are recognized as representing the real. Insofar as representation is a function of formal considerations, the logic of mimesis is counterpointed by an alternative logic of poiesis according to which, for instance, common sense notions of cause and effect may be reversed.[29] Eliot's *Daniel Deronda* illustrates how the contradictory logic of life and art may yield identical conclusions. Daniel learns of his Jewish birth only after he has already dedicated himself to Judaism. Taking Hans Meyrick's flippant comment about "the present causes of past effects" seriously, Jonathan Culler suggests that the secret of Daniel's birth is "the product of the demands of signification":

> Instead of the revelation of a prior deed determining meaning, we could say that it is meaning, the convergence of meaning in the narrative discourse, that leads us to posit this deed as its appropriate manifestation. . . .
> One could argue that every narrative operates according to this double logic, presenting its plot as a sequence of events which is prior to and independent of the given perspective on these events, and, at the same time, suggesting by its implicit claims to significance that these events are justified by their appropriateness to a thematic structure.[30]

The narrative moves relentlessly forward to the revelation of Daniel's Jewish past—the decussated temporal and causal sequences of birth/identity and identity/birth finally coalescing in the verdict whose immanence is the product of its being narrated as much as its having happened.

When the "law of narratives" is applied to actual events, specifically, to legal proceedings, "the narratives of law" are the inevitable result. At every stage of legal process—from attorney-client conferences, to courtroom proceedings, to judicial opinions, to legal scholarship—the business of law is carried on by means of stories. Recent legal scholarship has been increasingly inclined to see the law as constituted by, functioning according to the logic of, and subject to the same considerations as, storytelling.[31] Reversing tenor and vehicle of Eliot's metaphor, Ronald Dworkin turns to literature to suggest that the law be understood according to an "aesthetic hypothesis."[32] Legal decisions are like chapters in a collective novel, written successively by different authors with the aim of constructing the best possible work of art, that is, of law. The ramifications of this paradigm shift are dramatic and varied, including, for example, the understanding of what it means to apply rules to particular cases. In legal matters, the double logic of deed and meaning (in Culler's terms) or the present cause of a past effect (in Hans Meyrick's) offers little comfort to those seeking an objective basis for justice in foundational principles and preexisting rules. Conventional logic holds that the law works by adjudicating disputes according to the rules that may apply to them. Disagreements may arise concerning how a particular rule is to be interpreted or which rules apply in the first place, but the process itself is typically not questioned. When the thinking of legal positivism is supplemented by that of the "narratives of law," however, there can be no "first place"—no rule that stands outside of narrative according to which narratives might be judged. Foundational principles are simply another narrative form or genre. In an argument analogous to Culler's, Bert C. Van Roermund suggests that subsequent cases give meaning to preexisting rules rather than vice versa:

> What we grasp in following a rule is how to carry on in new situations. When, however, we hesitate in a certain case and someone would say "but don't you *see* . . . " the rule is of no use. On this level, the rule is what is explained, not what does the explaining. The expressions in which the rule is framed, are explained by the values, i.e. the facts of the matter in question, not the values by the rule.[33]

Put in specifically narrative terms, this argument implies that all stories begin at their endings, which shape and give meaning to the incidents leading up to them; applied to jurisprudence, it suggests that the phrase "legal fiction" describes all workings of the law.

Narrativity establishes a structural ground subtending discursive and disciplinary partitions. It interconnects and entangles language, promising, novels, and law—threatening to transform a "combined pursuit" into an impossibly multiple one. But it also points to the different impulsion of fiction and law with regard to language and promising.

The novelist is more likely to see the unreliability of language and the problem of promising as opportunities to explore new modes of expression and social behaviors; the lawyer more likely to see in them the need to police language and to regulate betrothal. Robert Cover describes fictional narratives as "jurisgenerative"; they are multiple and multivalent, contradictory and competing. Legal narratives, on the contrary, are "jurispathic"; judges "[c]onfronting the luxuriant growth of a hundred legal traditions . . . assert that *this one* is law and destroy or try to destroy the rest."[34] The conventions of fiction are far less constricting than the forms of legal action. The novelist's "verdict" is seldom unequivocal; the jury's is almost always definitive—the amount of damages providing the only latitude for qualifying an otherwise categorical edict. In novels, betrothal may be treated as a process; from a legal perspective, it is an entity whose existence must be either proved or disproved. In fiction, the promises exchanged by lovers are frequently a means of social negotiation; in litigation, negotiation has already come to an end, and the court adjudicates rather than mediates. These differences mean that beyond merely representing promissory practices, Victorian novelists reconsider what it might mean to make a promise.

A TEST CASE: *FAR FROM THE MADDING CROWD*

Thomas Hardy's fiction exemplifies the differences between legal and artistic interest in the practice of promising. In *The Mayor of Casterbridge*, for instance, Henchard's sale of his wife clearly violates British law.[35] It complicates his subsequent promise to marry Lucetta but does not affect his marital status: from a legal perspective, marrying Susan a second time is supererogatory. Hardy, however, is more vitally interested in the social and psychological ramifications of the sale than in whatever legal complexities it might generate. These personal and moral conundrums are suggested by Elizabeth–Jane's comment, "It wants a Pope to settle that" (*MC* 133), when Lucetta asks whether she should marry Henchard, to whom she is engaged, or Farfrae, whom she loves. A judge in possession of the facts could provide the legal advice, but neither pope nor magistrate can alleviate the burden of Lucetta's predicament. The question confronting her—and typically preoccupying novelists—is, as Stein says in *Lord Jim*, "not how to get cured, but how to live. . . . How to be."[36] Hardy frequently explores this quandary in the context of lovers or spouses who are separated and reunited in changed circumstances—a temporal disjunction analogous to the interval between making and keeping promises. The double discrepancy analyzed by de Man in intellectual terms is dramatized by Hardy in existential terms, not only in *The Mayor of Casterbridge* but also in *Tess of the d'Urbervilles*. Perhaps the best example of the complexities of promising in Hardy—and a good introduction to the concerns of this study—is *Far from the Madding Crowd*. By the time that Bathsheba Everdene even thinks of turning to a solicitor for help, the book is virtually over. The novel reveals how characters live with rather than litigate their promises. Bathsheba's romantic history entails an elaborate sequence of promissory kinds and consequences whose ironic effect is to delay and ultimately to defeat the purported objective of marriage. In detailing this history, Hardy includes themes central to the Victorian experience of promising: the conflict between principle and practice, the uncertain relation of cause and effect, the relative importance of intention and expectation, the contrasting views of betrothal in economic and romantic terms, and the different gender roles of men and women. This novel is particularly interesting because it includes both implied and conditional promises, special forms accentuating the impossible project of all promises, that is, the wedding of the contingent and the categorical.

The promissory sequence begins with Bathsheba's double-voiced valentine, which is purchased for little Teddy Coggan but sent to Farmer Boldwood. Its "large red seal," with the "extraordinary . . . motto . . . 'Marry me,'" resonates beyond the day and outside the boundaries of innocent play.[37] The valentine may not constitute a legal promise of marriage, but it does lead to one. Boldwood understandably but mistakenly assumes that the "letter must have had an origin and a motive. . . . The same fascination that caused him to think it an act which had a deliberate motive prevented him from regarding it as an impertinence" (*FMC* 80). Even Bathsheba admits the reasonableness of his deduction, describing his proposal of marriage as "the natural conclusion of serious reflection based on deceptive premises of her own offering" (*FMC* 100). She has not learned the lesson of a previous misunderstanding with Gabriel Oak. He, too, interprets her behavior as a sign of romantic interest, indeed as tantamount to acceptance of his proposal. His mistake leads to a conclusion with which Boldwood must sympathize: the "cabala of this erotic philosophy seemed to consist of the subtlest meaning expressed in misleading ways. Every turn, look, word, and accent contained a mystery quite distinct from its obvious import" (*FMC* 97–98). Bathsheba's behavior with both suitors confirms the narrator's observation that "[m]aterial causes and emotional effects are not to be arranged in regular equation. The result from capital employed in the production of any movement of a mental nature is sometimes as tremendous as the cause itself is absurdly minute" (*FMC* 93). In matters of the heart, no conclusion is natural. Whether deducing causes from perceived effects or inferring intentions from observed actions, suitors should be forewarned that their interpretations are not reliable. Bathsheba's two offers of marriage prove this theorem and question the adequacy of the view that promises of love can be, like written contracts, matters of conscious control and intention—or even that promised actions are the effects of the promises that reputedly cause them.

One reliable aspect of the Victorian ethos of promising, however, is that promises should be kept and that the obligation to do so results from the expectations they raise in others. Bathsheba's efforts to rectify the consequences of her mock proposal reveal the extent to which she has inculcated this principle. Having raised Boldwood's expectations, she feels obligated by them no matter how unreasonable they become. Mortified at the upshot of her joke, she attempts a counter-promise: "If you will only pardon my thoughtlessness, I promise never to—" (*FMC* 101). Boldwood, however, preempts her, not allowing her to reject the advances that she herself has invited. Renewing his suit, he is assured that: "I have every reason to hope that . . . I shall be able to promise to be your wife. . . . But remember this distinctly, I don't promise yet" (*FMC* 125). Although explicitly withholding "a solemn promise" (*FMC* 125), Bathsheba virtually promises to promise to marry him. The postponed promise establishes a kind of prepromissory suspension, one that anticipates betrothal in the same way that betrothal anticipates marriage. Thus her later assertion, "Mr. Boldwood, I promised you nothing" (*FMC* 158), is perhaps technically true, but it does not seem to be substantially so, and it is certainly not pragmatically so. Boldwood exclaims, "How nearly you promised me!" (*FMC* 158), and he seems justified in feeling that her nonpromise has a certain promissory force. Sensing, though, that the status of being "engaged to be engaged" is not particularly secure, he seeks reassurance from Gabriel concerning Bathsheba's "implied promise" and is told: "I won't answer for her implying. . . . That's a word as full o' holes as a sieve" (*FMC* 277)—as is "promise" itself. Whether the origin of this advice is experiential or linguistic, and whatever is implied of Bathsheba personally, Gabriel's cautionary wisdom acknowledges that which no promise—hers or another's, implied or otherwise—can eliminate: the uncertainty of the future. Boldwood may have, as Bathsheba says, "every reason to hope," but he has even more reason to doubt.

The renewal of Boldwood's proposal after Sergeant Troy's disappearance is not surprising—nor is Bathsheba's temporizing. He asks for "only a little promise—that if you marry again, you will marry me!" and he receives yet another conditional promise: never to "marry another man whilst you wish me to be your wife" (*FMC* 271). Pressed even further, Bathsheba makes two proleptic promises: to become engaged at Christmas and to marry six years after that. To the quizzical nature of conditional promises must now be added that of proleptic promises. What does it mean to promise (now) to promise (at Christmas) to marry (in six years' time)? Are promises, like the images on a Quaker Oats box, endlessly and invariably repeatable? Despite Bathsheba's intended meaning ("I do not want to marry you"), can her promise to promise ("I will marry you if . . . and when . . . ") be substantially different from the promised promise itself ("I will marry you")? By putting her reluctant acquiescence to Boldwood's proposal in conditional terms, Hardy makes patent that which is willfully obscured by the custom of promising: its necessarily accidental nature.

The mixed message of Bathsheba's betrothal allows Hardy to address another conflict lying at the heart of courtship and engagement: that between romantic and commercial views of marriage. Apart from the specific issues of conditional and implied promises, and in addition to the inescapable difficulty of what Boldwood calls "unexpected accidents," the betrothed must negotiate the difference between seeing themselves as partners in love and partners in a joint-stock venture. Calculatedly absent from Boldwood's final proposal, for example, is any hint of sentimental ideology and romantic rhetoric. This scene is an amplified echo of Gabriel's earlier proposal to Bathsheba, when he is "content to be liked" (*FMC* 29) and she considers marriage in largely comic terms: "I shouldn't mind being a bride at a wedding, if I could be one without having a husband" (*FMC* 81, 80). Boldwood does not go so far as to dispense with the bride, but he ignores the conventional requirement of affection. As "the strategic lover" (*FMC* 256) feigning indifference, Boldwood contends that their engagement will be a "mere business compact . . . between two people who are beyond the influence of passion" (*FMC* 286). This misrepresentation of his own feeling is ironically apt, however, coming as it does from the man who twice offers Sergeant Troy money to marry. Given the opportunity to take the moral high road, Troy grandiloquently spurns the offers: "Bad as I am, I am not such a villain as to make the marriage or misery of any woman a matter of huckster and sale" (*FMC* 181). Troy, however, not only rejects the woman he professes to love in order to marry a woman of wealth but also subsequently reclaims his abandoned wife because she now has "plenty of money, and a house and farm, and horses, and comfort, and here am I living from hand to mouth—a needy adventurer" (*FMC* 281). His behavior indicates, therefore, that he is far from impervious to commercial considerations and that he is far less loving than the unloved Boldwood.

Gabriel describes Bathsheba's promise to marry in six years as "an uncommon agreement for a man and woman to make" (*FMC* 272). He does not, however, object to the engagement, telling Bathsheba that her

> want of love seems . . . the one thing that takes away harm from such
> an agreement with him. If wild heat had to do wi' it, making ye long
> to overcome the awkwardness about your husband's vanishing, it mid
> be wrong; but a cold-hearted agreement to oblige a man seems differ-
> ent, somehow. The real sin, ma'am, in my mind, lies in thinking of ever
> wedding wi' a man you don't love honest and true. (*FMC* 272)

On one level, the advice not to marry without love is consistent with the
popular sentiment about marriage, but it is ironic given Gabriel's willingness to marry despite Bathsheba's not loving him. On another level,
Gabriel's ability to act and speak differently (he would accept in his own
marriage what he criticizes in hers) as well as to offer contradictory
advice (the "want of love" both "takes away harm" and constitutes "the
real sin") amply prove his own confused feelings; they also point to the
uneasy coexistence of incompatible conceptions of marriage in his society. Both factors, in turn, underscore the uncertain role of promises in
accommodating these antipodal values. While it is clear that promises
have a place in commercial relations, they seem uncongenial to
romance. Plighting troth occupies a nebulous area at the intersection of
competing values and spheres: public and private, commercial and
romantic, male and female. This murkiness is compounded by the difference between promises to marry and vows of marriage. Marriage
possesses a clearly defined legal and social status, but betrothal remains
rather penumbral, both in practice (occurring in private and alluding to
the future) and in law (resembling a promise to promise rather than an
oath or contract).

Related to the conflict of romance and finance is the tension
between freedom and constraint. Boldwood clearly plays upon
Bathsheba's senses of personal responsibility and social duty in begging
her to marry him. In saying that she must "repair the old wrong to me"
and that "you owe me amends" (*FMC* 270), he asserts that she is
responsible for the state of his affections because of her gratuitous valentine (*FMC* 157). In so doing, he exploits a familiar social narrative that
might be titled, to borrow from Aphra Behn, *The Fair Jilt*. Bathsheba's
guilt inheres in her gender, which is, so the story goes, fickle and flighty
by nature. Having already experienced what he calls "a woman's privi-
leges in tergiversation" (*FMC* 156), Boldwood seeks advice:

> "Does a woman keep her promise, Gabriel?"
> "If it is not inconvenient to her she may."
> "—Or rather an implied promise. . . . does a woman keep a
> promise, not to marry, but to enter on an engagement to marry at some
> time? Now you know women better than I—tell me."
> "I am afeard you honour my understanding too much. However,
> she may keep such a promise, if it is made with an honest meaning to

repair a wrong. . . . It seems long in a forward view. Don't build too much upon such promise, sir. Remember, you have once be'n deceived. Her meaning may be good; but there—she's young yet." (*FMC* 277)

The privilege to which he alludes is in practice a curse, for it means that women can only tergiversate and that their promises are, as Gabriel implies, merely a matter of convenience. Furthermore, it means that the always anticipatory nature of promising carries a paradoxical significance for women: regardless of age, they will be imprisoned in a childish past. Bathsheba may be "young yet," but she will always be female and always, therefore, subject to promissory suspicion. Women, as women, are viewed as inconstant and incapable of keeping their word; hence, they will always be too young to make promises. Bathsheba's double-voiced valentine, therefore, is bitterly ironic, because ultimately it speaks with the unified but the nonserious voice of youth. It is finally appropriate only for the person to whom it is not sent: little Teddy Coggan.

When the time for betrothal arrives, Christmas Eve, Bathsheba is still reluctant to make the unequivocal commitment demanded of her. She never actually says that she will marry Boldwood, at least not without conditions: "But I give my promise, if I must. I give it as the rendering of a debt, conditionally, of course, on my being a widow" (*FMC* 286). Boldwood urges her to name the day—or at least the year:

> "But surely you will name the time, or there's nothing in the promise at all?"
> "O, I don't know, pray let me go. . . . I am afraid what to do! I want to be just to you, and to be that seems to be wronging myself, and perhaps it is breaking the commandments. There is considerable doubt of his death, and then it is dreadful; let me ask a solicitor, Mr. Boldwood, if I ought or no!" (*FMC* 286)

Bathsheba's call for a lawyer is a wish for a *deus ex machina* wearing a wig and judicial robes. The arrival of solicitors, if not on the scene then in the conversation, symbolizes the end of the romantic ethos of marriage. Her frantic wandering from the sacred to the profane, from the commandments to common law, heralds an age in which legality takes precedence over morality. Similarly, the cry to "Send in the solicitors!" signals a boundary between literature and law, between novelistic and legal narratives.

Bathsheba herself sounds like something of an attorney when she seeks refuge from her dilemma in a legal fiction: "we are not engaged in the usual sense" (*FMC* 287). The dramatic increase in breach of promise actions between 1850 and 1900 indicates that "engaged in the usual sense" is exactly what many women claim to be, even as the circumstance of being a plaintiff in a civil trial suggests otherwise.[38] One conclusion to be drawn from these circumstances is that "the usual sense" is becoming uncommon and that "uncommon agreements" are becoming usual. The words and ways of engagement are the primary topics of the following chapters, beginning with discussions of language in the nineteenth century, promising in Victorian culture and literature, and narratives of broken engagements in Victorian legal practice and fiction. Subsequent chapters are devoted to single novels in which unusual engagements are prominently featured. Brontë, Eliot, Trollope, Meredith, and James emphasize the pragmatics of promising as much as, if not more than, promissory ethics, and each reconceives the nature and dynamics of promising not only in response to the limitations imposed upon all speakers by language but also in reaction to the anomalies and inconsistencies of Victorian social and legal thinking about betrothal.

CHAPTER 1

Language and the Victorians

In an essay written in 1835 and republished in the year of *The Origin of Species* (1859), Reverend Richard Garnett makes an observation that might be taken as a bellwether of Victorian considerations of language: "The knowledge of words is, in its full and true acceptation, the knowledge of things, and a scientific acquaintance with a language cannot fail to throw some light on the origin, history, and condition of those who speak or spoke it."[1] In one sense, Garnett exhibits a kind of updated Adamicism when he asserts that the knowledge of words is tantamount to the knowledge of things; however, the thrust of his remark is more anthropological than theological. He not only evinces the optimism voiced by Farrar (and Lucius Mason) but also anticipates two of the primary preoccupations of Victorian language study. The first is a philosophical interest in the relation of words to the world, and, the second, a linguistic concern with scientific and historical methods, especially as they might illuminate larger issues of human evolution and social development.

Although the focus of this chapter is exclusively on language, both points are relevant to the subsequent consideration of promising: the former, because the gap between words and things is precisely what those engaged in promising agree to overlook. Indeed, insofar as promisers assert that present words are directly translatable into future actions, they exhibit a form of Adamicism distinctly out of step with their skeptical age. The latter is important because of the general significance accorded to promises as a vehicle of civilized progress, for example, by scholars like Sir Henry Sumner Maine. As language is increasingly understood to be part of a living and evolving process, it becomes easier for writers to envision promising as a flexible and variable use of words rather than as a reifying and reified social institution. The evolutionary turn of language studies thus provides an intellectual context for novelists' representations of and experiments with the language of promising.

Three pairs of language scholars—Locke and Tooke, Coleridge and Mill, and Trench and Müller—are used to establish key attitudes concerning the efficacy and limitations of language. These otherwise diverse figures are linked by three general motifs: linguistic relativism and the recognition that language is a fractious and unreliable medium; skepticism about words in general and intense mistrust of figurative language and rhetoric in particular; and insistence that linguistic meaning is established pragmatically, not theoretically, and that the knowledge of language is best served by empirical methods directed toward historical objectives. Whereas the first two points are quite familiar both in and outside of the philosophy of language, their connection to the third is particularly suggestive with regard to novelists' representations of language. If words are invariably subjective and frequently unreliable, then it is understandable that verbal communication must be studied (or depicted) in fairly specific contexts. While an empirical bias is common to both language studies and literary realism, novelists can do more than map dialects or describe sound changes. They do, of course, reflect prevailing attitudes, such as the desires of Mrs. Garth and Elizabeth-Jane Henchard to speak socially prestigious dialects, but they are also free to depict language working in "nonstandard" or new ways. Their versions of the vernacular, therefore, may challenge such "languages" as the promissory code of the Tullivers in *The Mill on the Floss*, the example with which this chapter ends.

THE STUDY OF LANGUAGE IN VICTORIAN ENGLAND

Throughout the nineteenth century, considerations of language shift gradually from the theoretical to the scientific, from the philosophy of language to linguistics. The British philosophical approach to language is characterized by linguistic relativism and a growing suspicion that the babel of human languages applies to individual speakers no less than to entire nations. Many trace this position to John Locke's *An Essay Concerning Human Understanding*.[2] Turning from philosophy to etymology, John Horne Tooke nevertheless builds directly upon Locke in *EPEA PTEROENTA or the Diversions of Purley* (1798), announcing to the new century that words are the active agents of thought and not simply the passive vehicles of expression—an ominous augury for the Victorians because it implies that speakers may be at the mercy of their own language. Through the "contrivances" of language in Tooke's terms (or "fictions" in Jeremy Bentham's), which are useful but misleading conventions of ordinary discourse, words deceive us about the world that they purportedly reflect.[3] The most benign consequence of this view, even for those who stop short of Tooke's ironic observation that Hermes "put out the eyes of Argus: and I suspect that he has likewise blinded philosophy" (*DP* 15), is an uneasy yet persistent consciousness of language itself. This awareness explains why both Coleridge and

Mill, fearing myopia if not blindness, find that philosophical inquiry is impossible without a preliminary and extensive consideration of language.

The scientific approach to language study is characterized by historicism and the belief that language acquires meaning in use and, as a consequence, must be studied empirically. The turn to history is stressed by Max Müller, perhaps the most influential and widely known of Victorian linguists, who unfavorably contrasts the "mere theorizers" of the past with the comparative philologists of his own scientific age: "Such systems [as were erected by Locke, Voltaire, and Rousseau], though ingenious and plausible, and still in full possession of many of our handbooks of history and philosophy, will have to give way to the spirit of what may be called the *Historical School* of the 19th century."[4] Müller doubtlessly overestimates the scientific consistency and rigor with which the historical school conducts its research; nevertheless, from the mid-nineteenth century on, linguistic analysis is typified by the general reconsideration of language from empirical perspectives and in pragmatic terms—a reconsideration evidenced by the formation of groups like the Etymological Society at Cambridge (1832) and the Philological Society of London (1842). Tooke is an important forerunner of this historicism, which finds eloquent partisans in Richard Chenevix Trench on etymology and Müller himself on philology.

Whether philosophically or scientifically oriented, language study in Victorian England reflects the larger intellectual controversies of the period. The new philology introduced by Bopp, Rask, and Grimm gradually gains widespread acceptance and generally eclipses, without entirely effacing, the romantic linguistics of Herder and Humboldt. Foucault summarizes this linguistic revolution in *The Order of Things*, which traces the broad outlines of an encompassing epistemic shift in Western culture during the nineteenth century. In linguistics, the new episteme produces a fundamental reconception of language, which is now "ceasing to be transparent to its representations because it is thickening and taking on a peculiar heaviness."[5] This generalization, however, can be qualified in two important, if seemingly contradictory, ways. It both underestimates and exaggerates the epistemic shift, at least insofar as it is manifest in England: the former, because elements of the modern episteme are heard well before the nineteenth century, and, the latter, because acceptance of the new language theories is anything but universal, even by their proponents.

The change located by Foucault in the nineteenth century can be seen in embryonic form much before this time. Bacon, Hobbes, and Locke all famously warn of the dangers of opaque language and the muddy thinking it occasions. Müller prefaces his 1861 *Lectures on the*

Science of Language with this quotation from Bacon: "Men believe that their reason is lord over their words, but it happens, too, that words exercise a reciprocal and reactionary power over our intellect"—a view that sounds very much like Foucault's description of the modern episteme: "men believe that their speech is their servant and do not realize that they are submitting themselves to its demands."[6] Indeed, part of the attraction of scientific methods and historical research to Müller and his contemporaries is the promise that they hold of escaping the linguistic relativism associated with British empirical philosophy and symbolized by Locke. In his study of language and law, Peter Goodrich acknowledges that "the nineteenth century as a whole was dominated by historical linguistics" and goes on to point out that the

> concept of science at work in this early nineteenth-century philology was strongly influenced by the highly successful models of natural science, especially those of mechanistic physics and latterly Darwinian evolutionary theory. A set of universal, deterministic, laws drawn from the highly successful studies in philology, and especially Indo-European phonetics, could provide a set of regularities, a protolanguage, which naturalistic abstraction could explain away all individual variations and irregularities.[7]

The comfort of a rational explanation of language and the promise of fixed and stable verbal meanings do not come without a cost, however, for philology poses a new threat to human autonomy. The power of language over the intellect can no longer be understood as "reciprocal and reactionary," as in Bacon's formulation; rather, it has become radical, rational, and relentless. Laws take over where doubts reigned before, and determinism becomes a no less troubling philosophy than skepticism. Even the most progressive scholars, therefore, are as likely to resist as to embrace the new science of language and to search for a compromise between human skepticism and scientific certainty, between individual freedom and ineluctable law.

As a result, the change described by Foucault in monolithic terms occurs at best fitfully throughout the period. Whereas comparative philology does initiate a revolution, it is important to recognize that Victorian linguists like Trench and Müller not only promulgate but also resist, modify, and occasionally co-opt the new linguistic science for more conservative agendas. Language study in nineteenth-century Britain is both impelled to consider the new philology, with the possibility that language is a self-enclosed system whose workings can be described by uniform principles, and repelled by the possibility that something so personal as language is blindly driven by laws, phonetic and otherwise, that are not subject to individual control. In *The Lan-*

guages of Paradise: Race, Religion, and Philology in the Nineteenth Century, Maurice Olender points out that many linguists "joined romanticism with positivism in an effort to preserve a common allegiance to the doctrines of Providence":

> [t]hough they cast aside the old theological question, they remained attached to the notion of a providential history. Although they borrowed the techniques of positivist scholarship, took inspiration from methods perfected by natural science, and adopted the new perspective of comparative studies, they continued to be influenced by the biblical presuppositions that defined the ultimate meaning of their work.[8]

The nineteenth century thus constitutes a crossroads in linguistic theory, one that looks ahead to Saussure but also back to Adam. *Genesis*, in fact, provides the one account with which all subsequent theorists, including Locke, must contend, and it is to Locke that I first turn in order to gain further insight into Victorian thinking about language.

LOCKE AND TOOKE

While decrying the absence of "inductive research" among his forebears, Müller nevertheless acknowledges Locke in particular as one of the few who "have so clearly perceived the importance of language in all the operations of the human mind, [and who] have so constantly insisted on the necessity of watching the influence of words on thought." He concludes: "there are no books which, with all their faults—nay, on account of these very faults—are so instructive to the student of language as Locke's *Essay*, and Horne Tooke's *Diversions*; nay there are many points bearing on the later growth of language which they have handled and cleared up with greater mastery than even those who came after them."[9] Although Tooke's philosophy is tainted by his linguistic shortcomings (many of his etymological proofs are more speculative than scientific), Locke remains the dominant influence upon the philosophy of language in nineteenth-century England.

Locke casts the biblical account of language in a distinctly secular light. He asks readers to imagine Adam "in the State of a grown Man, with a good Understanding, but in a strange Country, with all Things New, and unknown about him; and with no other Faculties, to attain the Knowledge of them, but what one of this Age has now" (III.vi.44).[10] This Adam is an Everyman, who confronts problems of communication not essentially different from those facing Locke and his contemporaries (III.vi.51). Posing the problem in profane rather than sacred terms enables Locke to make an argument that will lead directly to Victorian fears about language and indirectly to the (post)modern paralysis articulated by Foucault. Of course, Foucault's conclusions about the new episteme go well beyond the practical objectives of Locke's *Essay*. The seventeenth-century reminder that "the very nature of Words, makes it almost unavoidable, for many of them to be doubtful and uncertain in their significations" (III.ix.1) seems modest compared to the twentieth-century insistence that "we are already, before the very least of our words, governed and paralyzed by language."[11] While Locke hopes to improve communication by exposing the dangers to which speakers are subject, Foucault rejects the notion of language as a communicative tool fully under human control. Words are elements of a self-referential system that functions primarily in relation to itself. Despite the obvious contrast with the argument and objective of the *Essay*, this view follows from Locke's association of words with ideas rather than with things. The rerouting of linguistic reference from things to ideas of things detaches language from external reality and prevents words from simply providing a map of Creation. Once language is channeled through individual minds, dubious directions, detours, and dead ends are the inevitable result. To understand what language can do and how it might be improved, Locke foregoes the search for the first language and turns to the verbal behavior of latter-day Adams.

Locke does not begin the *Essay* with the intention of considering language. He soon realizes, however, that language and understanding are so intricately related that it is impossible to consider the latter without taking up the former, and he concludes, first, "that unless their [words'] force and manner of Signification were first well observed, there could be very little said clearly and pertinently concerning Knowledge," and, second, "that they interpose themselves so much between our Understandings, and the Truth, which it would contemplate and apprehend, that like the *Medium* through which visible Objects pass, their Obscurity and Disorder does not seldom cast a mist before our Eyes, and impose upon on Understandings" (III.ix.21). The repeated association of language with mist (e.g., III.x.6 and 13) makes it obvious that speech cannot be understood simply as the transparent or neutral medium of thought. Locke does not suggest that thinking depends upon language, or that words speak us, but he does make it impossible not to consider the impact of words on ideas and their communication. His mistiness and obscurity are not quite the thickness and loss of transparency that Foucault attributes to language in the modern episteme; nevertheless, Locke does make language itself an epistemological problem. He makes words visible. Truth can be approached only through the distorting mists of words, and thought becomes visible only in the misrepresentations of language.

While the *Essay* examines the nature and use of language with the intention of making it a more reliable medium of philosophical thought and a more sound base for social intercourse, this effort to free speakers from verbal entanglements has ironic consequences. First, it inextricably connects thought with language, and, second, it leads to a compelling argument for the irremediable weakness of words. Locke ultimately concludes that language is characterized by a number of "inconveniences" (III.ix.6) that are treated in separate chapters "On the Imperfection of Words" (III.ix) and "On the Abuse of Words" (III.x). The former describes "the Imperfection that is naturally in Language"; the latter elaborates the *"wilful Faults and Neglects*, which men are guilty of" (III.x.1); their combined effect is a legacy of suspicion and skepticism whose impact is fully felt by the Victorians.

Words are unreliable in Locke's view because they are active; they do more, therefore often accomplish less, than speakers intend. One reason for this liability lies in the power of names to abbreviate and to generalize—a power that makes discourse functional and communication possible but that also raises the possibility of mistaken meanings. Locke compares the names of complex ideas to knots that tie together bundles of associated ideas.[12] While necessary to expedient and efficient communication, these names, or knots, are prone to unintended entanglements. A single name may tie together so many different ideas that an individual cannot be aware of all of them. When ideas, words, speakers, and interlocutors proliferate, such names are likely to become Gordian. Even the most vigilant speakers cannot help but find themselves entangled in "a curious and unexplicable Web of perplexed Words" (III.x.7).

Both the opacity and the unreliability of speech lead Locke to consider not what language ideally should be but how it functions as an actual and flexible set of social practices.[13] He looks to common usage as the basis of meaning, reminding readers that most words "received their Birth and Signification, from ignorant and illiterate People, who sorted and denominated Things, by those sensible Qualities they found in them" (III.vi.25). Meanings may change, but they remain a function of ordinary use. "Words," Locke writes, are "no Man's private possession, but the common measure of Commerce and Communication" (III.xi.11). And, although quotidian speech is the source of a great many errors and is typically used with even less care than philosophical discourse, Locke reluctantly admits that ordinary language should be consulted in cases of semantic confusion: "'Tis true, *common Use*, that is the Rule of Propriety, may be supposed here to afford some aid, to settle the signification of Language; and it cannot be denied, but that in some measure it does" (III.ix.8). This vernacular turn in Locke's philosophizing explains the importance that he places upon a scholarly project that he himself is understandably unwilling to undertake—one that is not begun for another two centuries and that once started will take almost a half a century to complete, *The Oxford English Dictionary*.

When Locke stresses the need for a natural history of language, he anticipates a central element of Victorian scholarship: "*to define their Names right, natural History is to be enquired into*; . . . we must, by acquainting our selves with the History of that sort of Things, rectify and settle our complex *Idea*, belonging to each specifick Name" (III.xi.24). Lacking such a dictionary, "we must content our selves with such Definitions of the Names of Substances, as explain the sense Men use them in" (III.xi.25). This emphasis upon ordinary language anticipates the importance of etymology in subsequent linguistic theory and of dialect in literature. It might be said with some justification that the nineteenth century is virtually ushered in with an appeal to a poetics of ordinary usage (Wordsworth's "Preface") and that its dominant literary form, the novel, is characterized by verisimilar dialogue and conversational narration.

Locke's call for a "natural history" of words acknowledges the inevitability of unstable meaning and expresses a desire for a lexical standard with which to limit subjective usage. "Common Use," he admits, is "a very uncertain Rule" and "a very variable Standard" (III.xi.25). Furthermore, because words and ideas are often confusingly connected by individual speakers, speech might conform to accepted usage as well as to grammatical principle and still generate confusion. As Locke points out, "Men speaking the proper Language of their Country, *i.e.*, according to Grammer-Rules of the Language, do yet speak very improperly of Things Themselves" (III.xi.25). Idiosyncratic speech cannot be restricted to national languages or even regional dialects. A more radical subjectivism is apparent among speakers of the same language or dialect. Locke implies that individuals seem almost to have private languages:

> Sure I am, that the signification of Words, in all Languages, depending very much on the Thoughts, Notions, and *Ideas* of him that uses them, must unavoidably be of great uncertainty, to Men of the same Language and Country. This is so evident in the Greek Authors, that he, that shall peruse their Writings, will find, in almost every one of them, a distinct Language, though the same Words. (III.ix.21)

In this formulation, linguistic relativism takes a step toward skepticism, if not solipsism. Locke's position, amplified by Condillac and Herder in the eighteenth century, echoes resoundingly throughout the nineteenth.[14] These reverberations are the ironic result of an effort to make the language of secular Adams at least a serviceable approximation of their nominal ancestor's, and they set the tone of Victorian speculations about our human—and verbal—nature. George Eliot, for example, notes that "among the peasantry it is the race, the district, the province, that has its style; namely, its dialect, its phraseology . . . which belong alike to the entire body of the people."[15] Among the Victorians, the linguistic relativism for which Locke lays the philosophical foundation is often reformulated in terms of class, with the same potential for miscommunication. The language of Eliot's peasantry, for example, is so different from that of other social groups that, in the words of noted Victorian linguist A. J. Ellis, "real communication between class and class is impossible."[16]

There is another aspect of Locke's treatment of language that bears consequences for nineteenth-century novelists. It might be taken as significant, or at least suggestive, that Locke does not take up the subject of the arts—even as it is admitted that aesthetic questions fall outside of his primary consideration. The *Essay* is concerned with philosophy, not poetics, and with linguistic efficiency: words should express ideas "*with* as much ease and *quickness*, as is possible" (III.x.23). This utilitarian bent disinclines Locke to consider the complexities of metaphor or the difficulties of poetic style. When he does refer to literature, for instance, it is only to use Sancho Panza as an example of one insufficiently anchored in empirical reality (III.iv.11). Nevertheless, the little that is said of poetic or figurative language in the *Essay* contributes to a specific form of linguistic mistrust that will resonate among the Victorians: the fear of figurative language.

This fear is playfully exploited by Sterne in *Tristram Shandy* when the narrator insists that he uses the word "nose" literally and not as a phallic trope. Tristram, of course, encourages readers' prurient speculations by pretending innocence of them: "In books of strict morality and close reasoning, such as this I am engaged in,—the neglect [of defining terms] is inexcusable; and heaven is witness, how the world has revenged itself upon me for leaving so many openings to equivocal strictures,—and for depending so much as I have done, all along, upon the cleanliness of my reader's imaginations."[17] Sterne delights in the double entendre enabled by the nasal metaphor and employs it in a parody of the seriousness of philosophical and other discourse. Locke might agree with Tristram's sentiment that "to define—is to distrust" (*TS* 218), but he would do so with the hope of delimiting rather than expanding signification. In his view, metaphor and simile are readily turned to devious purposes by smooth talkers—or, as in the case of Sterne, turned to mischievous ends by witty authors. Furthermore, tropes, by calling attention to themselves, contribute to the detrimental opacity of language and to the proliferation rather than the clarification of meaning. Proper in its place, figurative language nevertheless adds to the tendency inherent in all language to private and multiple meanings.

Locke thus passes on to the nineteenth century not only a fear of the relativity and concomitant fallibility of language in general but also a pronounced skepticism about figurative speech in particular. The latter concern is heard, for instance, in Wordsworth, who voices his own protest against "the gaudiness and inane phraseology" of poetry, opting instead for the "real language of men."[18] His flight from figuration, however, is no protection against the associative madness exploited for comic purposes by Sterne. In the "Preface" to the *Lyrical Ballads*, for instance, Wordsworth attributes possible "defects" in the poems to the fact

> that my associations must have sometimes been particular instead of general, and that, consequently, giving to things a false importance, I may have sometimes written upon unworthy subjects; but I am less apprehensive on this account, than that my language may frequently have suffered from those arbitrary connections of feelings and ideas with particular words and phrases, from which no man can altogether protect himself.[19]

Wordsworth fears that he will be the victim of his own lexical idiosyncrasies. His anxieties may have been substantiated, since he later writes that words "hold above all other external powers a dominion over thoughts."[20] Misused—and misuse seems inescapable—language becomes a "counter-spirit," and proves to be "an ill gift; such a one as those poisoned vestments, read of in the stories of superstitious times, which had power to consume and to alienate from his right mind the victim who put them on."[21] The shirt of Nessus is not simply a mythological symbol; in linguistic terms, it is a human birthright.

The second of Locke's legacies of skepticism receives a forceful impetus at the beginning of the century, less surprisingly from a philosopher and not a poet. Jeremy Bentham claims even more insistently than Locke that all poetry is misrepresentation. Bentham warns that any use of figuration is liable to elicit "disgust" or to promote "confusion," especially when "a quality which belongs only to one of these images . . . is inadvertently ascribed to another. In this way, perhaps, before the discourse is come to a close . . . the state of things originally meant to be designated has been forgotten, and is dropt out of sight, and thus the whole become a tissue of nonsense."[22] Bentham decries a kind of "association of figures" that is potentially no less chaotic than the association of ideas that isolates characters from each other in *Tristram Shandy*.

That Locke figures so prominently in a discussion of nineteenth-century attitudes to language is partially due to John Horne Tooke. A transitional figure, Tooke builds upon the *Essay* in ways especially impor-

tant to utilitarian thinkers like Bentham and James Mill. He also anticipates the scientific approach to language of the mid- and late nineteenth
century. *The Diversions of Purley* is a direct response to Locke's *Essay*
and opens on a familiar note: "I very early found it, or thought I found
it, impossible to make many steps in the search after *truth* and the nature
of *human understanding*, of *good* and *evil*, of right and wrong, without
well considering the nature of language, which appeared to me to be
inseparably connected with them" (*DP* 12). Tooke, however, goes well
beyond Locke in attributing the actions of the mind to the processes of
language. He claims that the "business of the mind, as far as it concerns
Language, appears to me to be very simple. It extends no further than to
receive impressions, that is, to have Sensations of Feelings. What are
called its operations, are merely the operations of Language" (*DP* 51).
By making thought a function of language rather than the other way
around, Tooke raises the possibility of the anthropocentric displacement
soon to be effected by Darwin and later to be articulated in linguistic
terms by Foucault. While this aspect of Tooke's theory prompts many
including Coleridge (after initial enthusiasm) to reject it, *Winged Words*
remains an important work well into the nineteenth century.

One reason for Tooke's appeal despite his radical philosophy is the
attention he brings to language study as important not only to philosophical discourse but also to many aspects of practical life. For Tooke,
the operative principle of language formation and use is abbreviation.
Abbreviations are single terms that take the place of many other words.
They are "the *wheels* of language, the *wings* of Mercury" (*DP* 25). By
virtue of these "artificial wings" (*DP* 27), however, both philosophers
and grammarians have been misled. The failure to recognize the function
of abbreviation leads to the mistaken belief that all words refer directly
either to things or, as in Locke, to ideas. Tooke argues, on the contrary,
that "*many* words are merely *abbreviations* employed for dispatch, and
are the signs of other words" (*DP* 27). Words make sense only in relation to other bundles of words. Locke's error, therefore, has been to
attribute to thought that which is merely a function of language. Had he
understood "the inseparable connexion of words and knowledge," he

> would not have talked of the *composition* of *ideas*; but would have
> seen that it was merely a contrivance of Language: and that the only
> composition was in the *terms*; and consequently that it was as
> improper to speak of a *complex idea*, as it would be to call a constel-
> lation a complex star: And that they are not ideas, but merely *terms*,
> which are *general* and *abstract*. (*DP* 36–37)

At this point, we can see language beginning "to fold in upon itself," as
Foucault will later put it. Having found the key to Locke, Tooke turns

to etymology as the sword with which to cut through the "knots" of language, without perhaps fully anticipating etymology's Saussurean effect: signs, or words, are shown to refer only to other words. The radical implications of Tooke's philosophy, however, are avoided by his successors, in part, because his empirical turn is inconsistently and partially executed. Many of his etymologies are entirely fictional—imaginative constructions of an a priori notion of language—and provide ample ammunition with which to refute his theories.[23]

Nevertheless, he at least appears to ground the study of language in empirically verifiable fact, therefore, to elevate linguistics to the status of natural science. Tooke, for instance, compares etymology to a microscope, and as early as 1825, William Hazlitt credits him for treating "words as the chemists do substances; he separated those which are compounded from those which are not decompoundable. He did not explain the obscure by the more obscure, but the difficult by the plain, the complex by the simple. This alone is proceeding upon the true principles of science."[24] The appeal of positivism is one reason for Tooke's influence. He brings etymology to the forefront of language studies, and in the hands of his successors, it becomes a more reliable antidote to hazy speculation and abstract philosophizing.

Another reason for Tooke's importance is that he brings authority and respect to the historical analysis of modern and vernacular languages. Since he considers both early English and "common speech" as worthy of study, he contributes to the rise of Anglo-Saxon studies and is responsible, in Olivia Smith's view, for redirecting the attention of linguists to "human life and public exchanges. The value of words depends on their temporal evolution to facilitate a necessarily and strictly human exchange."[25] In stressing etymology as a practical tool, therein providing incentive for the dictionary of natural history thought impractical by Locke, Tooke opens the door to the scientific study of language and brings attention to vernacular English. The reasons for Tooke's appeal, even after his etymologies are discredited, may lie precisely in his contradictions: on the one hand, he offers a recognizable connection with the philosophical traditions of the past, and, on the other hand, he champions a scientific method for the future—one that will dispel the old uncertainties, rendering philosophical discourse more functional and ordinary language more accurate.

COLERIDGE AND MILL

The promise of rigor and precision is especially attractive to Coleridge and Mill, who otherwise represent diametrically opposed reactions to the legacies of Locke and Tooke. While Tooke translates Locke's philosophy into grammatical theory, Coleridge returns and reverses the favor by suggesting that Tooke's system itself ought to be philosophized.[26] In pursuing this suggestion, Coleridge ultimately rejects Tooke's sensualist orientation for a more idealistic conception of language. Mill, on the contrary, remains much closer to the empirical tradition, especially as expressed in the utilitarianism of Bentham and his father, James Mill. Despite this basic difference, Coleridge and Mill have important points in common with each other and with Locke. These commonalities suggest that underlying contradictory ideas of language in the nineteenth century is a set of common themes. Both Coleridge and Mill emphasize that words are active and predisposed to error. They do so in works whose ostensible purposes are quite different from linguistic analysis. Language seems almost to force its way into both Coleridge's *Logic* and Mill's *A System of Logic* and to do so for the same reason compelling Locke to address this issue in the *Essay*. Each alludes to the confusions and carelessness of everyday speaking and warns that philosophy must be ever vigilant against these errors. At the same time, however, both defend ordinary language as the true test of meaning and find themselves, like Locke, in the contradictory position of suggesting that vernacular usage cannot yet must be trusted. They recognize the need for a historical dictionary of English, and Coleridge actually begins one. Finally, both see figurative language as a threat to clarity and a source of semantic deviation—a circumstance ultimately welcomed by Coleridge and condemned by Mill.

Coleridge's *Logic* has a lengthy history leading to an ironic conclusion: it is not published in his lifetime. The work, planned in 1817 as a "practical Logic for the use of the student," evolves by 1822 into *Elements of Discourse*. Several years later, the still incomplete manuscript appears to be taking on the contours, if not the specific arguments, of Locke: it will be "one large Volume of the Power and Use of Words, including a full exposition of the Constitution & Limits of the Human Understanding."[27] The second section of *Logic* emphasizes accuracy in language use and aims at eliminating the "utter logomachy" of disputes that are essentially no more than "a mere difference of words" (*L* II.i.15). Coleridge blames such disputes less on the faulty resources of language than on the faulty thinking of those employing them (*L* II.i.21a). In addition to "logomachy," for example, he coins the term "logodaedalism" to describe "verbal sleight-of-hand and word-trickery" (*L* II.i.20). These neologisms imply that words have wings not by nature but as a result of the forgeries of latter-day Dedaluses. Thus of the two chapters devoted to language problems by Locke, Coleridge would emphasize "On the Abuse of Words" rather than "On the Imperfection of Words."

By including a commentary on language in his discourse on logic, Coleridge seeks to remedy quite practical problems. The result of this prefatory analysis, however, is once again to remind readers of the opacity of language, of its tendency to ambiguity, and of the necessity to consider it pragmatically. On several occasions Coleridge quotes Hobbes's warning: "Notice how easily men slip from improper use of words into errors about things themselves."[28] He exaggerates Locke's figurative expression for the obscurity of language—mistiness—into a virtual tempest: "Alas, what great calamities have misty words produced, that say so much that they say nothing—clouds, rather, from which hurricanes burst, both in church and state" (BL II.31). He laments the "vicious phraseology which meets us every where, from the sermon to the newspaper, from the harangue of the legislator to the speech from the convivial chair," and alludes to a future work—presumably the Logic—that will "prove the close connection between veracity and habits of mental accuracy; the beneficial after-effects of verbal precision in the preclusion of fanaticism, which masters the feelings more especially by indistinct watch words; and to display the advantages which language alone . . . presents to the instructor of impressing modes of intellectual energy . . . as to secure in due time the formation of a second nature" (BL II.22). "Watch words" for Coleridge are consciously constructed examples of what Locke would pejoratively subsume under the category of rhetoric. For instance, in the mouths of politicians, "[s]ome unmeaning Term generally becomes the Watch-word, and acquires almost a mechanical power over his frame" (L II.i.21a). This power, however, is more often the result of indolence than of intention. Careless speakers and insentient interlocutors, with "their habitual passiveness of mind to the automatic trains of the memory and the fancy" (L II.i.21a), are more responsible for linguistic confusion than are practiced logodaedalists.

Coleridge urges that everyone "think and reason in precise and steadfast terms, even when custom, or deficiency, or the corruption of language will not permit the same strictures in speaking."[29] Language itself, however, militates against such precision and steadfastness. It becomes a source of ambiguity or mistiness when, as a result of a kind of verbal conditioning, words attain subjective significance that persists despite the corrective of experience:

> For as words are learnt by us in clusters, even those that most expressly refer to Images & the Impressions are not learnt by us determinately; and tho' this should be wholly corrected by . . . experience, yet the Images & Impressions associated with the words become more & more dim, till at last as far as our consciousness

extends they cease altogether; & Words act upon us immediately, exciting a mild current of Passion & Feeling without the regular intermediation of Images.[30]

Words acquire through time and use the power to act upon consciousness. They may become, no less than human agents, a source of verbal confusion. Coleridge ultimately rejects Hartley's associative psychology along with Tooke's linguistic philosophy; nevertheless, he maintains that a verbal "second nature" plays an active and a potentially detrimental role in human experience and communication.

Following Locke, Coleridge appeals to ordinary language as a check upon winged words and logodaedalism. One means of identifying and achieving "a coincidence between the thought and the word" is to turn to "common usage" (*L* II.i.8b). The "experimental philosopher" may require more precise means and meanings than the "rude and ponderous masses," but there should be no "wantonly deviating even from the common usage" (*L* II.i.8b). This recourse to ordinary language explains his interest in projects like Locke's proposed natural history of language. Coleridge himself plans a number of dictionaries and glossaries, including the *Encyclopedia Metropolitana*, "a kind of history of English words, with citations arranged chronologically, yet with 'every attention to the independent beauty or value of the sentences chosen . . . consistent with the higher ends of a clear insight into the original and acquired meaning of every word.'"[31] For Coleridge, as for Tooke, the origin of a term provides a key to its correct meaning. Thus in *Aids to Reflection*, he writes:

> Language (as the growth and emanation of a People, and not the work of any individual Wit or Will) is often inadequate, sometimes deficient, but never false or delusive. We have only to master the true origin and original import of any native and abiding word, to find in it, if not the *solution* of the facts expressed by it, yet a fingermark pointing to the road on which this solution is to be wrought.[32]

Coleridge's reference to language as an organic product of "a People" invokes the romantic language theory of his day; nevertheless, his intimation of etymology is itself a fingermark, pointing, first, in the historical direction of language studies to come and, second, to the use of regional dialect in the novels of writers like Emily Brontë, George Eliot, and Thomas Hardy.

Perhaps the most significant aspect of Coleridge's philosophy of language to subsequent novelists lies in his emphasis upon the creative resources of language itself. He identifies two processes, neologism and desynonymization, that exhibit the creative potential of language at the same time that they dispel some of its mistiness. The former responds to the moribund circumstance of a language that is structured so as to "be impeded by its want of a verbal symbol, paralyzed by its not daring (in that formed state of language) to invent or rather to *generate* a symbol."[33] The latter reverses the direction of the former, moving back in time to distinguish two terms that have been collapsed into one, thereby eliminating the confusion occasioned by combining separate meanings in single words.[34] As we might expect of a person who is a poet as well as a philosopher, Coleridge does not share Locke's notion of figurative speech as a "perfect cheat." In literary terms, winged words represent the creativity that Joyce identifies with Dedalus rather than the deceit that Coleridge associates with politicians. While warning of the dangers inherent in language use, Coleridge also sees significant creative potential in the active force of language. Words are living entities because, beyond merely referring to the outside world, they share in the active consciousness of the speaker. In making this point, he refers to Tooke's famous work, substituting "living" for "winged" in the title.[35] The vitality of language makes *Living Words* a more apt expression, as Coleridge's amanuensis explains:

> In Coleridge's judgment it [*The Diversions of Purley*] might have been much more fitly called *Verba Viventia*, "living words," for words are the living products of the living mind and could not be a due medium between the thing and the mind unless they partook of both. The word was not to convey merely what a certain thing is, but the very passion and all the circumstances which were conceived as constituting the perception of the thing by the person who used the word.[36]

Described in these terms, language is creative, not moribund, and illuminating rather than deceiving. Indeed, the "mistiness" so antithetical to philosophy may be a virtue in poetry. Coleridge, for example, places a new twist on Tristram Shandy's distrust of definition, wondering "[w]hether or not the too great definiteness of Terms in any language may not consume too much of the vital & idea-creating force in distinct, clear, full made Images & so prevent originality—original thought as distinguished from positive thought."[37] In this regard, Coleridge differs considerably from Locke and from his contemporary, John Stuart Mill, who would very likely find in Coleridge's notion of "originality" further justification of his own life-long suspicion of novels.

However different their attitude to figurative language, Mill, like Coleridge, begins his consideration of logic with an account of language, also for quite practical reasons: "those who have not a thorough insight into the signification and purposes of words, will be under chances, amounting almost to certainty, of reasoning or inferring incorrectly."[38] For Mill, words cannot be used with "too great definiteness," and correct thinking is impossible without studied attention to exact speaking: "Language is evidently, and by the admission of all philosophers, one of the principal instruments or helps of thought; and any imperfection in the instrument, or in the mode of employing it, is confessedly liable, still more than in almost any other art, to confuse and impede the process, and destroy all ground of confidence in the result" (*SL* I.i.1). Mill's position is that language is a "help" to, but not a means of, thought. He rejects the extreme view that thought is entirely dependent on language, although he does so in qualified terms: "this opinion must be held to be an exaggeration, though of an important truth" (IV.iii.2). Recognizing this "important truth" leads Mill to focus his attention upon "any imperfection in the instrument" more than upon those using it. Mill, therefore, is more likely than Coleridge to blame language itself for logical errors, and of Locke's two chapters, he would stress "On the Imperfection of Words" rather than "On the Abuse of Words."

Mill maintains that language over time acquires a distorting opacity. He compares words to eyeglasses that fail in their intended objective to "assist not perplex . . . vision" (*SL* I.i.1). This account of verbal obfuscation suggests that, whatever the difference in emphasis, Mill's pragmatic objectives are quite similar to Coleridge's:

> When it is impossible to obtain good tools, the next best thing is to understand thoroughly the defects of those we have. . . . Philosophical language will for a long time, and popular language still longer, retain so much of vagueness and ambiguity, that logic would be of little value if it did not, among its other advantages, exercise the understanding in doing its work neatly and correctly with these imperfect tools. (*SL* I.iii.2)

An example of imperfect tools or foggy lenses is the category of general names. Mill offers as an illustration the word "civilization," which "conveys scarcely to any two minds the same idea. No two persons agree in the things they predicate of it; and when it is itself predicated of anything, no other person knows, nor does the speaker himself know with precision, what he means to assert" (*SL* IV.iv.3). Even with simple phenomena or experiences, speakers necessarily imply much more than they say: "The perception is only of one individual thing; but to describe it is to affirm a connexion between it and every other thing which is either denoted or connoted by any of the terms used. . . . An observation cannot be spoken of in language at all without declaring more than that one observation; without assimilating it to other phenomena already observed and classified" (*SL* IV.i.3). Interconnected experience, associated ideas, and ambiguous words mean that no thing can be one thing. Conceptually as well as experientially, language is inevitably expansive and militates against precision and specificity.

As with the "knots" described by Locke, Mill points out that "mere words" may launch unexpected and unintended semantic flights. "Very often, indeed," Mill writes, "when we are employing a word in our mental operations, we are so far from waiting until the complex idea which corresponds to the meaning of the word is consciously brought before us in all its parts, that we run on to new trains of ideas by the other associations *which the mere word excites*" (*SL* IV.iv.6, my emphasis). Mill, no less than Coleridge, is wary of mechanical influences of words upon people, and, no less than Locke, he holds language responsible for this "sort of Madness" (II.xxxiii.2). The tendency of words to instigate associative mayhem is most readily apparent in accounts of personal experience and in casual observations (a view that perhaps contributes to Mill's hostility to the novels, which depend so heavily on such accounts). These subjective connections result not only from the arbitrary associations of words but also from the singular experiences of individuals. In this regard, Mill emphasizes precisely the fear expressed by Wordsworth concerning *Lyrical Ballads*: singular associations will, at the least, lead to miscommunication and, at the worst, elicit derision.

The antidote to such madness is to be found, surprisingly, in nonphilosophic speech. While warning of the "trammels of every-day phraseology" (*SL* V.iii.6), Mill also insists that philosophy "must begin by recognising the distinctions made by ordinary language" (*SL* I.i.3). He repeatedly cautions against affixing new connotations to old words, insisting that "the meaning of a term actually in use is not an arbitrary quantity to be fixed, but an unknown quantity to be sought" (*SL* IV.iv.4,6)—and sought, he claims, in the history of the term's usage. This is not to say that a word's true meaning is to be found in its original meaning. He writes in *Utilitarianism*: "I am not committing the fallacy, imputed with some show of truth to Horne Tooke, of assuming that a word must still continue to mean what it originally meant. Etymology is slight evidence of what the idea now signified is, but the very best evidence of how it sprang up."[39] Meaning is a function of present and past usage. Mill thinks of language as a kind of savings bank of human history. It is "the depository of the accumulated body of experience to which all former ages have contributed their part, and which is the inheritance of all yet to come" (*SL* IV.iv.6). Conventional dictionaries being "so imperfect an exponent of . . . real meaning," informed speakers should turn to the history of a word, which is "a better guide to its employment than any definition" (*SL* IV.v.1). In addition to amplifying the call for a historical dictionary of English, Mill's *System of Logic* adds to the scientific momentum to view language as a "depository"—later a fossil—as well as to the thrust of the novel toward colloquial, regional, and class dialects.

"Real meaning" remains an elusive entity in Mill's view, and in this regard, he is closer to Locke than to Coleridge. Emphasizing the defects of "mere words" more than those of mere speakers, Mill is left with an irresolvable dilemma: how is the meaning of a word to be clarified when there are only other, possibly equally unclear, words with which to do so? Each person "is thrown back upon the marks by which he himself has been accustomed to be guided in his application of the term: and these, being merely vague hearsays and current phrases, are not the same in any two persons, nor in the same person at different times" (*SL* IV.iv.3). Individual "marks" invariably efface what Coleridge calls the "fingermarks" of original meaning. Even while setting out to improve language, therefore, Mill can ultimately be no more optimistic about the chances of overcoming its fundamental weakness than is Locke (III.xi.1).

Mill's appreciative essays on Wordsworth and Coleridge make clear that to a certain extent he overcomes the hostility to literature and figurative language initially shared with Bentham. An appreciative reader of poetry, Mill nevertheless retains narrowly circumscribed ideas of its place and purpose, and he continues to hold a strong bias against narrative literature. He exemplifies, indeed is partly responsible for, the double bind confronting novelists. Fiction, Mill maintains, panders to the appetite for storytelling so apparent in children and so valued by primitive societies. Hence "the shallowest and emptiest . . . are at all events, not those least addicted to novel-reading. . . . The most idle and frivolous persons take a natural delight in fictitious narrative."[40] Novels indulge infantile inclinations and induce insensibility in weak-minded adults. The metaphor of addiction, with the implication of narrative narcosis, expresses Mill's personal distaste and moral condemnation.[41] Hostility to the novel compounds his more general mistrust of language, and the combined effect places Victorian novelists in a doubly compromised position—they stand accused of employing an unreliable medium toward an unethical end.

TRENCH AND MÜLLER

Coleridge and Mill exemplify philosophical approaches to language; Richard Chenevix Trench and Max Müller illustrate the emergence of linguistics from philosophy and the establishment of the science of language as an independent discipline. In the second half of the nineteenth century, language studies shift in emphasis from the theoretical to the empirical—from logic to etymology and from philosophy to philology.

The work of Trench and Müller represents in a general way the Victorian effort to incorporate Continental philology into Lockean philosophy but at the same time to moderate its more radical implications. The conclusion implicit in the discoveries of comparative philologists like Grimm—that language is a self-contained system governed by phonological laws—poses new challenges to Victorian ideals of language, self, and culture. Nevertheless, to claim with Foucault that "[a]s the linguistic science of Bopp and Grimm made language visible, it simultaneously made language opaque," or to insist with Linda Dowling that Victorians possess "a new consciousness that words mean more than their representational meaning" is to take insufficient notice of the extent to which such issues are in the forefront of British thinking about language prior to the mid-nineteenth century.[42] Predisposed to think of language in precisely these terms, Victorian scholars react to the new science of language in complex ways, simultaneously accepting specific claims and rejecting threatening implications of the kind developed by Saussure and Foucault.

Richard Chenevix Trench turns to etymology with the hope of avoiding the errors leading many to dismiss *The Diversions of Purley*. Although his work is not entirely free of fanciful etymologies, Trench contributes greatly to professionalizing the study of English at a time when, according to George Sampson, etymology "was a recreation of English country gentlemen. They enjoyed the life of a word as they enjoyed the death of a fox."[43] Trench's interest, on the contrary, is far from recreational. His lectures "On Some Deficiencies in our English Dictionaries" (1857) provide the guiding principles upon which the work on the new dictionary of English will proceed.[44] He insists that lexicographers cannot confine themselves to standard usage or to moral terms. "It is," he writes, "no task of the maker of it to select the *good* words of a language. . . . The business which he has undertaken is to collect and arrange all the words, whether good or bad, whether they do or do not commend themselves to his judgment. . . . He is an historian . . . not a critic."[45]

Although a historian in matters of lexicography, Trench is very much a critic of the current state of the language. As a prominent Anglican clergyman, he has an interested reason for studying language, and more often than not he utilizes etymology to buttress conventional morality in the face of what he feels is a general ethical decline in England. In his popular works on language, "natural history" takes on a distinctly moralistic bent. He writes:

> Seeing that language contains so faithful a record of the good and of
> the evil which in time past have been working in the minds and hearts

of men, we shall not err, regarding it as a moral barometer, which indicates and permanently marks the rise or fall of a nation's life. To study a people's language will be to study *them*, and to study them at best advantage; there where they present themselves to us under fewest disguises, most nearly as they are.[46]

On the Study of Words (1851) and *English Past and Present* (1855) present mixtures of science and religion appropriate for public consumption but not always consistent with the rational spirit invoked by his age and defended by Trench himself with regard to the project for a new dictionary. *On the Study of Words* begins with acknowledgments of both Tooke and Coleridge, and with the assertion (in all likelihood borrowed from the latter's revision of the former) that "words are living powers." But even as he turns to science and away from the philosophical approaches of his predecessors, Trench owes more to the idea than to the substance of science. He approvingly cites Emerson's phrase, "fossil poetry," and asserts that language is fossil ethics and fossil history as well: there "are strata and deposits, not of gravel and chalk, sandstone and limestone, but of Celtic, Latin, Saxon, Danish, Norman, and then again Latin and French words."[47] In this way, science and history enter his work in a metaphoric form. Trench's understanding of history is paradigmatic—suggesting a static natural order—not evolutionary. His method is more rigorous and inductive than Tooke's; his objectives, however, are not as bold as his tropes suggest. Trench is unwilling, for example, to consider that language is subject to the evolutionary principles governing all natural beings, as his contemporary, Darwin, is about to argue. Trench's etymologies, therefore, are inclined to read rather like homilies. Locke's notion of linguistic failure is redefined in—and confined to—moral terms. For example, proof of the poor state of "man's natural and spiritual life" lies in the "long catalogue of words [found in dictionaries], having to do with sin." Even more damning is the testimony of colloquial and idiomatic speech. He points to euphemisms, such as "love-child" for "bastard," that in his view disguise true meaning and implicitly condone immorality.[48] Etymology in Trench's hands may be genealogical, but primarily in the sense that "the descent of man" acquires moral rather than biological significance.

A further indication of Trench's theocentrism is his reinterpretation of what Locke, Tooke, and Mill take as evidence of verbal madness. "Winged words" assume an angelic connotation when Trench finds traces of divine necessity in human accident. Language may express more that speakers are aware of, but this semantic surplus is evidence of the adroit hand of God rather than the thick tongues or lazy minds of humankind: "words often contain a witness for great moral truths—God

having impressed such a seal of truth upon language, that men are continually uttering deeper things than they know, asserting mighty principles, it may be asserting them against themselves, in words that to them
may seem nothing more than the current coin of society."[49] Trench, like
Coleridge, sees a creative power in language, but for him that power is
expressly Christian. We are more the children of Adam than we know,
mysteriously possessing *lingua Adamica* despite ourselves.

With Max Müller, language study moves more clearly from history
to science, from etymology to philology; however, he, too, ultimately
takes refuge from the assault of science in metaphor and in claims
resembling Trench's concerning the "seal of truth upon language."
Thus, whether the emphasis is upon etymology, as with Trench, or upon
comparative philology, as with Müller, the intellectual debates of the
Victorian period reveal the extent to which the new science of language
is simultaneously espoused and resisted. The equivocal role of philology
in Britain is evidenced by Müller's influential and popular lectures of
1861, attended by Mill (as well as the Queen).[50] In an 1880 preface to
this book, Müller associates the comparative analysis of language with
the comparative study of religion, announcing that "the principles that
must guide the student of the Science of Language are now firmly established. It will be the same with the Science of Religion."[51] "Science" in
this instance seems to mean no more than "study," yet Müller goes on
to claim that language is literally a physical science. Language must be
considered from the perspective of science rather than history because it
is the "production of nature" not of humankind. As the title of these
published lectures indicates, Müller, like Trench, wishes to remove the
study of language from the purview of fox-hunting squires and place it
within that of university professors. Purley is not a diversion but a profession: "In the science of language, languages are not treated as a
means; language itself becomes the sole object of scientific inquiry."[52] A
vestige of the ideal of Adamic language is retained by the new linguists,
not in the hope of discovering the original and perfect language, but in
the optimism about bringing the penetrating light of scientific method to
bear upon a heretofore stygian subject.

Physical science, however, is little more than a metaphor for Müller,
albeit a metaphor with considerable conceptual force. To embellish this
figure, Müller turns to the model of geology. Language, he insists, is to
be studied "in exactly the same spirit in which the geologist treats his
stones and petrifactions"; the comparative philologist must sift through
the "petrified strata of ancient literature" for linguistic data and "learn
to make the best of this fragmentary information, like the comparative
anatomist, who frequently learns his lessons from the smallest fragments
of fossil bones."[53] The figurative evolution of Coleridge's fingermarks

into Müller's fossils documents the difference between romantic and Victorian etymology. Words are not evocative of times past but concrete and objective remnants from them. The rhetorical force of the scientific trope pertains primarily to the methods with which verbal "artifacts" are studied; the trope itself has little basis in science. Darwin, for instance, becomes the inspiration for a redefinition of "living words" away from Coleridge's notion of verbal creativity and toward the evolutionist's understanding of survival of the fittest. Miller imagines language as part of an encompassing evolutionary struggle:

> Hence that . . . *struggle for life* carried on among these words [in ancient dialects], which led to the destruction of the less strong, the less happy, the less fertile words, and ended in the triumph of one, as the recognised and proper name for every object in every language. On a very small scale this process of *natural selection*, or, as it would better be called *elimination*, may still be watched even in modern languages.[54]

These allusions to Darwin are essentially figurative—and not very exact since the comparison of biological to verbal entities is tenuous at best. Müller's narrative, in fact, suggests a utopian rather than an evolutionary bias: names are teleological not original; true meaning is not obscured by but emerges from history.

Further suggesting that Müller's appeal to science is figurative more than substantive is his conclusion that "the Science of Language will yet enable us to withstand the extreme theories of the evolutionists, and to draw a hard and fast line between spirit and matter, between man and brute."[55] That line, or Rubicon, leads him to reject the "orang-outang" theory also summarily dismissed by Trench. All the more surprising, therefore, are the reciprocal figurative links between Müller's science of language and natural science. Darwin, for instance, approvingly cites Müller's reference to "the struggle for life [that] is constantly going on amongst the words and grammatical forms in each language," and this metaphor is also taken up by Lyell.[56] The echoing allusions and mutual citations surrounding the evolution of language speak more tellingly of changing conceptions of the past than of documented linguistic changes. The anthropomorphizing trope, evidenced by another of Müller's titles, *Biographies of Words*, cuts across intellectual disciplines, indicating both a changing perspective on the world and an effort to humanize the threatening prospects that it yields.

The fear that some brute may in fact "dare to cross" the Rubicon leads Müller from science into fiction and linguistic essentialism. He formulates a theory of roots that is entirely without scientific evidence; in fact, it epitomizes the kind of "mere theorizing" for which he criticizes Locke. Müller attributes the origin of words to a core of roots or *phonetic types* produced by a power inherent in human nature. They exist, as Plato would say, by nature; though with Plato we should add that, when we say by nature, we mean by the hand of God. There is a law which runs through nearly the whole of nature, that everything which is struck rings. Each substance has its peculiar ring. . . . It was the same with man.[57]

He hypothesizes a direct aural connection between things and their names, an idea quickly labeled by its detractors as the "ding-dong" theory. It seems clear that in positing a natural basis for language and a necessary connection between things and their names, Müller, without Trench's overt biblical orthodoxy, reverts to essentialist notions of language. His insistence upon "a proper name for every object" seems the post-lapsarian approximation of *lingua Adamica*. Linda Dowling suggests that Müller's "unreliable logic, his penchant for wordplay and speculative flights, and his succulent and sounding prose style all obscured the true object of linguistic inquiry and substituted for it a hypostatized notion of language as logos, a notion based not on 'science' or *Sprachwissenschaft* but on the much older traditions of Romantic philology and religious humanism."[58] Müller's "wordplay and speculative flights" suggest that, despite almost a century of linguistic study and theory, Tooke's theory of winged words has returned home to roost.

Müller's reference to inherent natural sounds and reliance upon the analogy of phonetic types to peculiar rings exemplify precisely the kind of figural appropriation about which he himself warns fellow Victorians under the rubric of "Modern Mythology." He argues that metaphoric usage obscures a word's root, therein concealing "true" meaning and producing "poisonous phraseology," which he labels mythology. In this meaning of the term, "mythology" is not "restricted to the earliest ages of the world"; rather, it is an ongoing process of figurative distortion: "Whenever a word is used metaphorically and without a clear notion of the stages by which it passed from its original to its metaphorical meaning, there is danger of mythology. When the steps of the process are forgotten and replaced by artificial ones, we have mythology, or, if I may put it this way, a disease of language."[59] In addition to heightening suspicions of figurative language, Müller implies that a more pervasive pathology threatens human evolution. Language becomes diseased whenever it "assumes an independent power, and reacts on the mind, instead of being, as it was intended to be, the mere realization and outward embodiment of the mind."[60] Müller's fears are familiar ones—they have been expressed in some form by each of the figures considered thus far. Like them, he hopes to minimize the pejorative influence of language upon thought, but in offering the science of language as an antidote to verbal mythology, he is unaware of his own mythologizing tendencies.

Victorian fears concerning language, amplified by philosophy and linguistics, become especially acute in part because of the success of the evolutionary metaphor. Language, which it is hoped will be a refuge as well as a Rubicon, may instead become a fossil. Müller recognizes that dictionaries record but will never impede linguistic change, and he tries to put the best face on the prospect that the Queen's English may become but a momentary stutter in the evolution of languages:

> there is a continuous change in language, it is not in the power of man either to produce or to prevent it. We might think as well of changing the laws which control the circulation of the blood, or of adding an inch to our height, as of altering the laws of speech, or inventing new words according to our own pleasure. As man is the lord of nature only if he knows her laws and submits to them, the poet and the philosopher become the lords of language only if they know its laws and obey them.[61]

Müller's optimism seems like whistling against the dark. He implies that a mastery of language is possible, but prospective lords of language, recognizing—although capable neither of impeding nor reversing—the consequences of natural selection and modern mythology may well wonder of what their kingdom consists.

LANGUAGE, PROMISING, AND *THE MILL ON THE FLOSS*

The evolutionary metaphor further explains how it is that promising becomes a key site of contested ideas concerning what it means to be human and what the future of human society might be. In *Man, The Promising Primate*, for example, Peter J. Wilson writes that the "establishment of human social relationships and the assurance of their continued existence, no matter what form they take, depend upon the exercise and imposition of the promise."[62] As a fundamental mechanism of stable social development, promising offers the Victorians a sense of security; as a purely verbal entity, it proves that language can be effectual—that it is a reliable defense against the destructive consequences and threatening implications of evolution. Promising assumes that "continuous change" can be institutionalized as its opposite: what is said of today is guaranteed to have the same meaning tomorrow. It also embodies the substitutional logic of language in general and of figurative language in particular. When I promise, my word stands for something else—not only for a promised action in the future but also for promisers themselves.

The link between language and promising is brilliantly suggested by George Eliot in *The Mill on the Floss*, which A. S. Byatt describes as a "natural history" and the work among all her novels most concerned with "record[ing] local particularities of speech."[63] Eliot introduces the subject of promising in a way that underscores its verbal character. As part of a Latin exercise, Tom Tulliver is assigned to translate a section of the *Aeneid*. He "constru[es] '*nunc illas promite vires*' as 'now promise those men'" (*MF* 317–18); whereas, a more accurate gloss is: "now put forth that strength." Tom's inexact translation not only foregrounds the issue of promising but also suggests that the energy expended under Mr. Stelling's tutelage is somewhat misdirected: Tom is a much better miller than scholar. Ironically, the correct translation, the one that eludes him, does describe him as an exemplary worker and man of business. His strengths of will and character are better exercised in reviving the family fortunes than in studying the classics. He is much more at home in the vernacular world of commerce than with the language of learning, which his father (mis)takes for the sign of a gentleman and a guarantee of social success.

Tom's misreading of Virgil reveals not only his limitations as a scholar but also Eliot's insight into the nature of promising. The different glosses of this line of Latin generate other ironies. On the one hand, Eliot's satire is both gently directed at Tom, an indifferent student of the classics who could certainly exert more energy in his studies, and harshly focused upon his father, whose efforts to educate his son are a partial result of his own litigious nature and frustrated ambition. On the other hand, the scene can be read as an instance of dramatic irony. Since the passage from the *Aeneid* that defeats Tom's limited abilities concerns ships being rowed upon the sea, it pointedly anticipates Tom and Maggie's race against the flood waters of the Floss—a race that they lose despite Maggie's "almost miraculous divinely-protected effort" and Tom's "row[ing] with untired vigour" (*MF* 654–55). Equally, if not more, suggestive than these possibilities, however, are the dialogic resonances of Tom's mistake, which encourage readers to consider the connection between making promises and exerting force. At first glance, these activities would seem to be inversely related since promises typically entail securing something that the promisers are powerless to accomplish for themselves. For instance, among the male Tullivers, promises are invoked to reinforce flagging wills or to secure the completion of unfulfilled plans. They are merely a bulwark of words mounted upon the Word. Mr. Tulliver drags out the family Bible to record the promise that he extracts from his son, and Tom will do the same to insure Maggie's loyalty to her father's spiteful intentions. Promises, however, are no more effective is restraining Maggie's heart than they are in controlling the waters of the Floss. Each promise—Tom's to his father and Maggie's to Tom—reinscribes a costly familial rivalry, and neither accomplishes more than a destructive commitment to the past.

The Latin lesson is especially relevant to Maggie, for though it is her brother who "puts forth that strength," it is she who comes to feel most acutely the impact of "promising those men." Promises to her brother, to Philip Wakem, and, arguably, to Stephen Guest constitute a large part of her dilemma and a central motivation of the plot. As with Bathsheba and Boldwood, it is unclear whether Maggie and Philip have a "tacit" or a "positive" engagement (*MF* 569–70, 620) and what the consequences of this distinction might be. In this regard, Maggie's "classical" learning is as ironically appropriate to her promissory behavior as Tom's is to his—all the more so since, as Walter Ong has pointed out, "learning Latin took on the characteristics of a puberty rite, a *rite de passage*, or initiation rite: it involved . . . the achievement of identity in a totally male group."[64] Accused by her brother of being, like all girls, "too silly" to learn Latin, Maggie argues to the contrary, offering her knowledge of "bonus" as an example. When Tom disputes her etymology, she replies: "Well, that's no reason why it shouldn't mean 'gift'. . . . It may mean several things. Almost every word does" (*MF* 214).[65] Maggie's defensive retort that words "may mean several things" is a childlike echo of the concerns of language philosophers from Tooke to Müller. Her perhaps naive sense of etymology is considerably more subtle than her brother's, and her sensitivity to polysemantic words is anything but naive. Although Maggie is "by no means that well-trained, well-informed young person that a small female of eight or nine necessarily is in these days" (*MF* 176), she "could have informed you that there was such a word as 'polygamy' and being also acquainted with 'polysyllable', she had deduced the conclusion that 'poly' meant 'many'" (*MF* 177). Her etymological knowledge may be haphazard, but its thematic reverberations are not, enabling Eliot to emphasize the polyvalence of language as well as the gap between linguistic knowledge and practical experience— for an ill-educated girl of eight or nine, to be sure, but no less so for the woman she will become. Maggie is made painfully aware of the pragmatic significance of the prefix "poly" when subjected to a quasi-polygamous situation, that is, her kissing Stephen while each is tacitly engaged to another.

For many Victorians, the promise of fixed and unitary meaning is a beacon emanating from the far shore of an uncrossable floss. Eliot suggests, however, that promising can never guarantee permanence and stability. *The Mill on the Floss* introduces the promissory equivalent of linguistic relativism. "Almost every word may mean several things," Maggie defensively claims, and in practice almost any promise may generate surplus meaning. These "bonuses" may be welcome or not, as

Henry James demonstrates in *The Wings of the Dove*, but they virtually guarantee that translating words into action will be a confusing process. Since promises, no less than words, are a matter of polysemy, those making them may "row with untired vigour" only to find that the semantic currents are not in their favor. For Maggie, the invisible conditions that change insignificant brooks into hazardous Rubicons transform Philip Wakem and Stephen Guest into Scylla and Charybdis.

CHAPTER 2

Victorian Promises

Jane Austen heroines are unlikely to find themselves afloat on the flood-waters of the Floss, but they are as likely as any George Eliot protagonist to run afoul of the language of promising. For example, in *Northanger Abbey* Henry Tilney comments ironically upon Catherine Morland's use of the expression, "promised so faithfully": "Promised so faithfully!—A faithful promise!—That puzzles me.—I have heard of a faithful performance. But a faithful promise—the fidelity of promising."[1] His stylistic snobbery accomplishes more than exposing promising as a socially significant verbal practice (he judges Catherine for how she speaks); it also reveals promising to be a linguistically significant social practice (readers may judge him for his preoccupation with standard English). The irony that Henry exercises at Catherine's expense redounds upon him, revealing unexamined prejudices of class, gender, and education. Tilney's raillery thus becomes Austen's inquiry: might the phrase "faithful promise" be neither pleonasm nor solecism? That such a usage enters the common parlance implies that the apparently oxymoronic "unfaithful promise" does, in fact, describe actual circumstances—whatever the proscriptions of prescriptivist grammarians or the protests of honorable gentlemen (another redundancy?) like Henry Tilney. His dismissal of Catherine's locution accentuates rather than suppresses it, and points to promising as an overdetermined and problematic social practice. Austen's modest questioning of and incipient challenge to the conventional wisdom of what it means to make a promise, especially in the context of courtship and marriage, become more vocal and vehement as the century progresses, leading in turn to a concomitantly vigorous defense of one's word of honor as the linchpin of all social relations.

Among the Victorians nothing is more sacred than "a gentleman's word." To illustrate the maxim that "Above all, the gentleman is truthful," Samuel Smiles quotes the Duke of Wellington: "When English officers have given their parole of honour not to escape, be sure they will not break it. Believe me—trust to their word. The word of an English officer is a surer guarantee than the vigilance of a sentinel."[2] Giving one's word is, of course, not limited to the military code of honor: it is a cornerstone of British society and a keystone of class and gender relations. The promise of a gentleman is both a symbol and a mechanism of social privilege, but it also bespeaks a condition of social limitation and dependence. Wellington's appeal, "Believe me," aptly articulates this contradiction, for it is simultaneously an assertion of authority and an admission of reliance. On the one hand, he implies that experience and status authorize speaking; on the other hand, he appeals for that which he cannot command, credence from those he addresses. He is, in a manner of speaking, no less a captive of his audience than his hypothetical English officer is a prisoner of the opposing army. This paradox of power and reliance is equally significant in that sacrosanct Victorian institution, a gentleman's word of honor.

The paradox of promising openly acknowledged by neither Wellington nor Smiles is compounded in the case of betrothal because views of marriage are so contradictory. An ongoing public debate reveals two fundamentally opposed conceptions of marriage as a domestic contract no different in kind from those of the marketplace and as a romantic union whose conventions and consequences are unique to affairs of the heart. These dichotomous positions set the terms for the meaning of betrothal, but they also inevitably muddy the waters because both the meaning of what is promised and the nature of the promise itself are indeterminate. If, for example, engagement is no more than a "pause, during which those who are entering matrimony may reflect before they cross the Rubicon," and after which they might decide to return to the secure shore of singlehood, then in what sense can the promise to marry be said to be a promise at all? But if promises to marry are binding—an interlocking not an interlude—then how can they be in essence different from wedding vows? Addressing these and related questions, the Victorians attempt with mixed success to reconcile three interconnected issues: promise as progress and prison, marriage as economic and romantic union, and betrothal as enforceable contract and non-binding agreement.

PROMISSORY PROGRESS AND IMPRISONMENT

Social theorists both before and after the Victorians seem to have resolved the progress/prison antithesis in favor of the former. The ability to make and keep promises, so the argument goes, is a fundamental condition of modern social organization. Whatever their confining effect upon individuals and however they might restrict or require certain behavior, promises serve the greater social good; therefore, they ultimately, if indirectly, serve even the interests of those who might feel imprisoned by them. Hume, for example, insists that "the freedom and extent of human commerce depend entirely on a fidelity with regard to promises."[3] They are essential "to beget mutual trust and confidence in the common offices of life. . . . The interest in the performance of promises, besides its moral obligation, is general, avow'd, and of the last consequence in life" (544). Most in the nineteenth century would emphatically agree with this view.

Promising is the fundamental principle of progressive civilizations, in the opinion of Sir Henry Sumner Maine. His analysis of the Greek and Roman judicial systems leads to the conclusion that modern societies are possible only with the change from status (one's place by birth) to contract (freely entered, legally binding agreements) as the basis of social relations. The ability of individuals freely to promise, to make and honor contracts, becomes the fundamental principle of modern social organization:

> The movement of the progressive societies has been uniform in one respect. Through all its course it has been distinguished by the gradual dissolution of family dependency and the growth of individual obligation in its place. . . . Starting, as from one terminus of history, from a condition of society in which all the relations of Persons are summed up in the relations of Family, we seem to have steadily moved towards a phase of social order in which all these relations arise from the free agreement of Individuals.[4]

The principle of "the free agreements of individuals" lies at the heart of mid-Victorian social and economic theory. Applied to promising, this concept means that individuals have the right to make virtually any private agreement that can be mutually agreed upon (and that does not infringe upon the rights or welfare of others). Once it is made, however, individual freedoms are restricted by the promise itself, which is categorically binding. Hence a principle of social organization takes on an almost religious significance. In generalizing upon the nature of social evolution, Maine concludes that a "mature civilization" goes beyond respect for social compacts, "attaching a sacredness to promises and agreements."[5]

One imagines, therefore, that many would have asserted that the problem posed by Nietzsche had already been solved—at least by the English: "The breeding of an animal that *can promise*—is not this just that very paradox of a task which nature has set itself in regard to Man? Is not this the very problem of man?"[6] Maine points to the Troglodytes as an example of "a people who systematically violated their Contracts, and so perished utterly," and he looks back with complacent condescension upon primitive, promiseless societies:

> The positive duty resulting from one man's reliance on the word of another is among the slowest conquests of advancing civilization. . . . No trustworthy primitive record can be read without perceiving that the habit of mind which induces us to make good a promise is as yet imperfectly developed, and that acts of flagrant perfidy are often mentioned without blame, and sometimes described with approbation.[7]

While this argument reveals an "affinity with the evolutionary school," as C. K. Allen points out, Maine is inclined to adapt progressive thought both to a conservative agenda (like Trench) and to a romantic notion of historical development (like Müller).[8] Thus his view of the past becomes an even more telling portrait of the present—and its fear of the future. Victorian insistence upon the trustworthiness of a gentleman's word of honor may implicitly acknowledge the processes of social change outlined by Maine, but it also explicitly defends against the threatening significance of evolution.

This nebulous fear of the evolutionary future, in addition to anxieties about social and political pressures of the present, suggests why it is that promises might become a prison as well as a proof of progress. Their confining effect entails more than the obligation to promisees, and it involves more than the fear that, if it can happen to the Troglodytes, it might also happen to the British. The circumstances of promising expose the fundamental limitations of the Victorian ethos of individuality and self-reliance; promises are necessarily reminders of the extent to which people are mutually dependent. Furthermore, promising reveals not only individual limitations but also the tenuous means by which they are overcome, that is, the mystifications of promises themselves. The promiser's, "Trust me," is very much like Wellington's, "Believe me": promises are offered as guarantees of exactly that upon which they depend in order to work in the first place. This circularity—which explains the unanswerable difficulty of Nietzsche's question—must be suppressed in order for promising to work. Victorian insistence upon the sanctity and inviolability of promises is directly proportional to their conceptual fragility and indirectly responsible for their practical frangibility.

From the seemingly secure vista of mid-Victorian prosperity, Maine's confidence in English progress is understandable but exaggerated. In fact, the continuing preoccupation of the novel with the making and breaking of promises of marriage provides one reason to believe that Maine and many fellow Britons are overly sanguine. Another indication comes from the Duke of Wellington himself, who does not prove to be an entirely exemplary man of his word, at least in domestic affairs. What he claims is true of English officers is certainly not the case with English husbands—at least insofar as his own marital history provides an indication. After his proposal of marriage is rejected by Kitty Paken-ham's family because of his relative poverty, Wellington spends nine years abroad. Returning to England no longer poor but also no longer in love, he stands by his promise of nearly a decade before: "If Kitty still wanted him, his old pledge stood and he was hers. Only the lady herself, or death somewhere on the foggy Elbe, could release him."⁹ While a promise—and apparently little else—leads Wellington into marriage, neither promises nor vigilant sentinels could keep him there. His "very susceptible heart, particularly towards . . . married ladies" (with the apparent exception of his own wife) leads to flirtations, liaisons, and rumors of criminal conversation.¹⁰

Examples such as this suggest that George Meredith's *The Amazing Marriage* (1895) is perhaps not as improbable as some critics have sug-gested.¹¹ The reluctant bridegroom in this case is Lord Fleetwood, who is "renowned and unrivalled as the man of stainless honour: the one liv-ing man of his word. He had never broken it—never would. There was his distinction among the herd. . . . But, by all that is holy, he pays for his distinction" (*AM* 192). He pays for it with a kind of verbal incar-ceration: "he was the prisoner of his word;—rather like the donkeys known as married men: rather more honourable than most of them" (*AM* 153). The Duke of Wellington, attempting to explain his own asi-nine behavior, writes: "I married her because they asked me to do it . . . in short I was a fool,"¹² and Fleetwood might say the same of himself. In a "mad freak"—precisely the term applied to Bathsheba's valentine (*FMC* 94, 160)—he offers "his hand and title to the strange girl in a quadrille at a foreign castle" (*AM* 171). He no more intends that his pro-posal be taken seriously than Bathsheba does her valentine. Resenting Carinthia Jane Kirby for taking him at his word, Fleetwood nevertheless feels compelled to carry out an engagement that he claims is contracted by "a slip of the tongue" (*AM* 191). Accepting a loveless marriage, he deserts his bride almost immediately after the ceremony, leaving readers to wonder along with the narrator: "What is a young man's word to his partner in a quadrille!" (*AM* 175). Carinthia provides a telling gloss on this exclamation when she explains the practical significance of her hus-band's ethical code: "The sadly comic of his keeping to the pledge of his word—his real wife—the tyrant of the tyrant—clothed him" (*AM* 612). Lord Fleetwood is wedded to his word, therefore, isolated in life; clothed in language, he stands naked before the world.

THE PRINCIPLE OF PROMISING

Fleetwood may be exposed, but the principle of promise-keeping that he embodies is promulgated from pulpit and podium, iterated in home and school, celebrated in periodic and popular literature—in short, it is prevalent throughout Victorian society. While self-interest and fear may be the primary motivations for the code, its pervasive influence owes a good deal to what Hume explains as "a sentiment of morals [that] concurs with interest, and becomes a new obligation upon mankind. This sentiment of morality, in the performance of promises, arises from . . . [p]ublic interest, education, and the artifices of politicians" (523). Such sentiment, resembling what Nietzsche calls the "custom of morality,"[13] overrides pure self-interest. The success of the norm of promise-keeping is evident from that fact that even dubious commitments like Bathsheba's, Wellington's, and Fleetwood's are honored, despite the compelling reasons not to do so. The public image of Wellington, along with Meredith's more critical portrait of "the man of stainless honour," demonstrates how ill-considered marriages might be transformed into (or mistaken for) signs of masculine virtue and aristocratic honor. P. S. Atiyah summarizes these processes in his study of nineteenth-century legal practice, The Rise and Fall of Freedom of Contract:

> The powerful moral force which came to be attached to truthfulness, honesty, promise-keeping, the whole code of honour associated with the concept of the 'gentleman', . . . attest to the great importance which the Victorians did place on circumstances in which reliance on others was a necessary feature of life. One had to rely on another when he gave his word, when he was a gentleman. . . . These were circumstances in which reliance was inescapable, and therefore all the more stringently protected.[14]

These protections, it should be noted, are internally enforced. The Duke of Wellington and Count Fleetwood imprison themselves in promises.

The "sentiment of morals" inculcated by the Victorians is given a systematic ethical formulation by William Paley. In The Principles of Moral and Political Philosophy (1822), Paley contends that "to allow every mistake, or change of circumstances to dissolve the obligations of a promise, would be to allow a latitude, which might evacuate the force of almost all promises."[15] The greater good requires that the doctrine of promise-keeping be adamantly maintained, regardless of individual circumstance. Paley does admit a few situations in which one might justifiably fail to keep a pledge, for instance, in cases of impossible, unlawful, or erroneous promises—promises of the kind exemplified by the marriage proposals of someone already married, like Edward Rochester in Jane Eyre, or already engaged, like Willoughby Patterne in The Egoist. "The guilt of such promises lies in the making, not in the breaking of them."[16] While exceptions of this kind are strictly delimited by Paley, other systems of ethics are even more severe, tolerating no deviations from the moral imperative of promise-keeping. Adam Smith, for instance, holds that the breakers as well as the makers of erroneous or unlawful promises are culpable. *The Theory of Moral Sentiments* (1759) emphasizes that even a promise given under duress (for instance, one given to a robber at gunpoint) cannot be broken without offense to "that part of [one's] character which makes [one] reverence the law of truth and abhor every thing that approaches to treachery and false-hood."[17] Whenever promises are "violated, though for the most neces-sary reasons, it is always with some degree of dishonour to the person who made them."[18] In this view, an aura of disgrace surrounds even such seemingly innocent promise-breakers as Jane Eyre and Clara Middleton. This ethical position, combined with the theories of many classical util-itarians and economists, leads very nearly to the position "that breaking a promise could never be best on the whole, because it could *never* cre-ate more good than keeping it."[19]

The rigidity of the principle of promise-keeping explains the mar-riages of Wellington and Fleetwood as well as their ensuing dissatisfac-tions. As unfaithful husbands, the historical duke and the fictional count indicate a double failing in the Victorian version of the "animal that *can promise*." First, the conceptual fragility of promises produces an inflexi-ble personal code of promise-keeping and, to some, a draconian system of enforcement; and, second, the inexorable ideal of promising virtually guarantees, therefore implicitly condones, the practical frangibility of promises. The former explains how a man might fulfill a promise to marry out of obligation rather than love; the latter explains how a man might compromise his wedding vows without the loss of honor that would have attended his not marrying in the first place. Both Wellington and Fleetwood accept in wholesale fashion the axiom that "a promise is a promise," with the result that their word becomes their bond—in sev-eral senses of this term. Each honors the letter of the law of promising while insulting its spirit. After his marriage, Wellington seems to have devoted himself largely to women other than his wife. Fleetwood humil-iates his wife by taking her to a boxing match to celebrate their nuptials and immediately deserting her. These weddings might justify Samuel Smiles's faith in English promises, but these marriages obviously do not. If Wellington and Fleetwood epitomize men of their word, then they also illustrate the promissory double standard according to which form is much more important than substance. Nothing illustrates this point more clearly than the Countess of Fleetwood herself, who shares her husband's code of personal honor. Carinthia's brother replies to her husband's over-tures concerning a reconciliation: "My sister received your title; she has to support it. She did not receive the treatment of a wife:—or lady, or woman, or domestic animal. The bond is broken, as far as it bears on her subjection. She holds to the rite, thinks it sacred. You can be at rest as to her behaviour. In other respects, your lordship does not exist for her" (*AM* 582–83). In form, the wife is no less wedded to her word than is the husband; in substance, the husband, if not the man, has ceased to exist.

Many Victorians have difficulty recognizing, no less admitting, the failure of their promissory code—a failure readily acknowledged by later writers. One thinks, for instance, of the marital history of Edward Ashburnham, the good soldier but unreliable husband of Ford Madox Ford's novel of 1915. Even in sounding the swan song of the Victorian gentleman, *The Good Soldier* reveals Britain's continuing preoccupation with codes of honor and promise-keeping. A more recent postmortem of the chivalric code (assuming that rumors of its demise are not premature) is found in *The French Lieutenant's Woman* (1969). Fowles's Victorian protagonist, after reneging on a promise to marry Ernestina Freeman, chooses to sign a *confessio delicti* rather than submit to the publicity and dishonor of a breach of promise trial. This document includes a particularly galling provision: "My conduct throughout this matter has been dishonorable, and by it I have forever forfeited the right to be considered a gentleman."[20] Charles's behavior violates common law, but the more serious offense is that against unwritten social laws committed by his accuser, Ernestina's father. By making explicit that which functions exclusively as a tacit code of honor, that is to say, by refusing to accept the promissory double standard enabling aristocratic freedoms, licentious or otherwise, Mr. Freeman actually loses what Charles only appears to: "the right to be considered a gentleman." Charles's jilting of Ernestina is ungentlemanly; nevertheless, he remains a gentleman. The very code by which he stands convicted also protects him from the threat to aristocratic privilege constituted by the likes of Mr. Freeman. In this regard, "[p]ublic interest, education, and the artifices of politicians"— recalling Hume's terms—all work against the entrepreneur, exposing the economic motivation and conservative force of the promissory code. Fowles epitomizes in the person and experience of Charles Smithson one of the chief inconsistencies surrounding promises of marriage in the Victorian era: what is in public invariably and unequivocally condemned is tolerated in private, depending, of course, upon the class and gender of promiser and promisee. Clearly, not everybody is imprisoned by promises—or, if so, not everybody is sentenced to hard time.

THE PRACTICE OF PROMISING

Even without the benefit of Fowles's hindsight, many Victorian novelists explore the ways in which the experience of promising complicates

Smith's and Paley's clear-cut analyses of principle. These works confirm that the nineteenth century may not have detached itself quite so neatly from a past in which, as Maine puts it, "acts of flagrant perfidy are often mentioned without blame." An unofficial practical norm concerning engagement exists among the Victorians that is in direct opposition to the principle of promise-keeping championed, for example, by Smiles. While not explicitly condoning jilting, many are inclined to look with less severity upon the breakers than the keepers of engagements. Anthony Trollope's *Kept in the Dark* (1882), for instance, illustrates the general precept that it is socially, if not ethically, preferable to break one's promise to marry than to have it broken by another. Sir Francis Geraldine, who is surprised but not very much injured when jilted by his fiancée, decides how to put the best face on things: "It was gall to him to have to think that the world of Exeter should believe that Cecilia Holt had changed her mind, and had sent him about his business. If the world of Exeter would say that he had ill-used the girl, and had broken off the engagement for mere fancy,—as she had done,—that would be much more endurable"—more endurable for him, to be sure, but less so for her.[21] Sir Francis compounds the injury of his perjurious rumor by subsequently passing it on to her husband, knowing full well that "[a]ccording to the usages of the world the lady would have less to say for herself if that were the case [that is, if she had been jilted rather than had done the jilting] and would have more difficulty in saying it" (57). Because of "the usages of the world," Cecilia no less than her former fiancé would rather be known as the breaker than the keeper of promises. She thinks to herself that "[t]o have been jilted would be bad, but to have it said of her that she had jilted when she was conscious that it was untrue was a sore provocation" (*KD* 29). Ironically, in being accused of having kept her word, she is denied a voice—she has "less to say for herself" with her husband and can say nothing to contradict the rumors circulating about her.

Moral and social value are clearly at odds in this instance—and are so in a way that indicates how the law of the market and the conventions of romance have become confusingly intertwined. In a market economy, contractual violators are liable for damages, but in romance jilts are sometimes rewarded. In the moral economy, promise-breakers are subject to the ruin of their good names, but in romance the jilted acquire the more undesirable reputations. Sir Francis, for instance, benefits from both anomalies, Cecilia from neither—not because she is the culpable party (which, in fact, she is) but because she is believed to be the innocent victim. Her subsequent marriage to Mr. Western is very nearly destroyed by her promissory past, which ironically echoes his own. Learning his wife's history, Mr. Western is reminded of his jilting by Mary Tremenhere: "Ought I not to rejoice and be thankful rather, as I think of what I have escaped? But in truth it is the poor weakness of human nature. People say that I have been—jilted. What matters it to me what people say? I have been saved, and as time goes on I shall know it and be thankful" (*KD* 34–35). "What people say," of course, matters a good deal and drowns out the solitary voice of the spurned lover. Mr. Western struggles to accept the indignity of having been jilted, but his hard earned, if not altogether convincing, equanimity is entirely denied to his wife. A version of the promissory double standard allows him to believe that "the better thing had happened to him" and at the same time to hold his wife's past against her. Cecilia is offended for a second time because it "was said truly of him, that the girl had jilted him, but falsely of her that she had been jilted" (*KD* 35). Her sense of injustice, however, merely reconfirms the social norm against which she protests. She may be more tolerant of her husband's romantic history than he is of hers, but she is less concerned with being a jilt than with being known as having been jilted.

The promissory double standard illustrated by *Kept in the Dark* is related to a general tendency to relax stringent codes of promising when it comes to romance—or at least to look fondly rather than critically upon the foibles of courtship. The strict principle of promise-keeping applying in all other circumstances is more flexible in affairs of the heart, whether those hearts are male or female, rich or poor. An indication of this difference is the phrase "at arm's length," the legal trope for the relation between signatories of a contract.[22] One readily understands the advantages of an attitude of wary detachment in business affairs, but such skepticism would not seem to be conducive to romance. Nor would a strict adherence to contractual obligations typically characterize the relationship between loved ones. Indeed, dealing with a prospective spouse literally at arm's length could present a considerable impediment to the progress of romance. Thus there seems to have been a general consensus that the complexities of courtship necessitate a certain latitude from strict truth-telling and promise-keeping.

That the difficult business of securing a spouse warrants an exemption from the general interdiction against breaking promises is suggested by the proverbial wisdom, already noted in Plato's *Symposium*, that "Jove smiles at lovers' perjuries." This figurative expression transfers a legal term, "perjury," to the seemingly uncongenial context of romance, therein suggesting that oaths and sworn professions of truthfulness simply have no place between lovers. For example, even Serjeant Bluestone, the blustery barrister with a "doggish love of fighting" in Trollope's *Lady Anna*, becomes quite kittenish when it comes to love.[23] Referring to promises that Lady Anna may have given to Daniel Thwaite, to whom she has become secretly engaged, the Serjeant says: "No doubt he has made her swear an oath, but we all know how the gods regard the perjuries of lovers" (*LA* 231). In *Phineas Finn*, Trollope's narrator also winks at the hero's disloyalty to Mary Flood Jones: "He of course was a wicked traitor to tell her that he was wont to think of her. But Jove smiles at lovers' perjuries;—and it is well that he should do so, as such perjuries can hardly be avoided altogether in the difficult circumstances of a successful gentleman's life."[24] Trollope's gentle satire is considerably sharpened by George Eliot in *Daniel Deronda*. When Grandcourt reneges on a minor promise to Gwendolyn Harleth, the narrator comments (perhaps with Grandcourt's more serious breach to Lydia Glasher in mind): "If these are the sort of lovers' vows at which Jove laughs, he must have a merry time of it."[25] Although the gods' laughter is more bitter than benign in this instance, both Trollope and Eliot allude to freedoms allowable within arm's reach but unacceptable at arm's length. At that distance, the indulgence of lovers' prevarication ceases; the drawing room is brought into the courtroom; and perjury, in its technical sense, becomes no laughing matter.

Trollope considers the potential tragedy of invoking divine risibility to cloak human paltering in *An Eye for an Eye*. Fred Neville, unexpectedly finding himself heir to the Scroope title and fortune, deserts his pregnant fiancée, Kate O'Hara. Finding a morganatic marriage unworkable, he reluctantly accepts the view of his aunt, who believes that the "breach of any such promise as the heir of Scroope could have made to such a girl as this Miss O'Hara would be a perjury at which Jove might certainly be expected to laugh. But in her catalogue there were sins for which no young men could hope to be forgiven; and the sin of such a marriage as this would certainly be beyond pardon."[26] Her assessement of mortal and venial sins is reversed by Kate's mother, herself an abandoned woman. Mrs. O'Hara murders her daughter's betrayer, pronouncing this judgment: "Yes—an eye for an eye! Death in return for ruin! One destruction for another!" (*EE* 165). If Jove is chuckling, it can only be insanely so: Mrs. O'Hara is locked up in a mental institution, and Fred's aunt is driven to "the verge of insanity" by her role in "producing the catastrophe" (*EE* 168).

Despite the catastrophic conclusion of *An Eye for an Eye*, the general sense remains that some leeway must be given to lovers, who ought not to be rigorously kept to their word. The belief that language of love constitutes a special circumstance, however, complicates the meaning of betrothal. If courtship discourse constitutes an exception to the rule of promise-keeping, then it is an especially troubling one, for it entails using one promise to obtain another, making it difficult to draw a line between "lovers' perjuries" and "lovers' vows." Once the lie has been admitted, the contagion seems uncontainable: for if a suitor's promises can be broken, why not a fiancé's; and if a fiancé's, why not a husband's? While it remains a relatively simple matter to differentiate between the white lies of Phineas Finn to Mary Flood Jones and the black deeds—in the form of broken promises—of Henleigh Grandcourt to Lydia Glasher and Fred Neville to Kate O'Hara, Victorian mores are more muddled when it comes to the gray area between them. The chromatic confusion is due, in part, to the influence of Hume.

HUME ON PROMISING

According to Hume, promising derives from "the natural and inherent principles and passions of human nature" (519). Because people are "naturally selfish, or endow'd only with a confin'd generosity, they are not easily induc'd to perform any action for the interest of strangers, except with a view to some reciprocal advantage, which they had no hope of obtaining but by such a performance" (519). He reasons that "[w]ere we, therefore, to follow the natural course of our passions and inclinations, we shou'd perform but few actions for the advantage of others, from disinterested views" (519). Promises correct this "natural course" by guaranteeing a "reciprocal advantage" in the future, therein conjoining self-interest and the interest of others. Promises are marked by "certain *symbols* or *signs* . . . by which we might give each other security of our conduct in any particular incident. After these signs are instituted, whoever uses them is immediately bound by his interest to execute his engagements, and must never expect to be trusted any more, if he refuse to perform what he promis'd" (522). To summarize Hume's position, we might say that promises are conventional in origin and symbolic in nature. They constitute a distinct motivation, or obligation, and function precisely by means of that which they are intended to regulate: self-interest.

This view is widely accepted by the Victorians.[27] Applied to betrothal, this theory creates a vexing problem: how to account for the gray area; that is, how to reconcile a practice that regulates "naturally selfish" behavior with the nature of love and the conventions of romance. For while Hume's argument may satisfactorily explain promissory relations between "strangers," one might ask how satisfactorily it accounts for freely exchanged promises to marry. An engagement is presumably more an expression of mutual love than it is a provision against "confin'd generosity." Perhaps with such instances in mind, however, Hume does allow for "disinterested commerce" between loved ones, and he seems to separate these relations from any in which "mutual advantage" is marked and guaranteed by promises: "tho' this self-interested commerce of men begins to take place, and to predominate in society, it does not entirely abolish the more generous and noble intercourse of friendship and good offices. I may still do services to such persons as I love, and am more particularly acquainted with, without any prospect of advantage" (521). In such cases, promising would seem to be virtually superfluous. If something will be done out of love, then a promise to perform that action is largely without purpose or function. As Dorothea Brooke says, "Whatever affection prompted I would do without promising" (*M 519*). Anthony Trollope's worldly, affable, but not entirely respectable gentleman, Lord George de Bruce Carruthers, delights in exposing (and one presumes in taking advantage of) this situation: "I assert that if men and women were really true, no vows would be needed;—and if no vows, then no marriage vows."[28] What Lord George says of marriage is, of course, true of betrothal, which entails in a similarly contradictory fashion the altruism of love and the self-interest of a social contract.

Hume, however, presents the contradictory components of betrothal and marriage as if they were entirely discrete. His logic is binary and mutually exclusive, leaving no possibility of a middle ground in which betrothal might be seen as possessing traits of both forms of commerce. The presence or absence of a promise itself defines the nature of a relationship. He writes: "In order, therefore, to distinguish those two different sorts of commerce, the interested and the disinterested, there is a *certain form of words* invented for the former, by which we bind ourselves to the performance of any action" (521–22). The net effect of this formulation is to reduce betrothal to a form of interested commerce. This is obviously true in some cases, for example, the proposed Smithson-Freeman alliance in *The French Lieutenant's Woman*. Charles, the relatively impoverished aristocrat, thinks: "he was now the bought husband. Never mind that such marriages were traditional in his class; the tradition had sprung from an age when polite marriage was a publicly accepted business contract that neither husband nor wife was expected to honor much beyond its terms; money for rank" (*FLW* 232). But while few would disagree that marriage may serve any number of vested interests, few would insist that it is necessarily or exclusively a matter of variously defined self-interests. Charles, however, seems incapable of considering the simultaneous presence of the two theories of marriage that he contemplates. Thus after defining hymeneal contracts from a mercenary viewpoint, he turns to a more generous and "modern" interpretation: "But marriage now was a chaste and a sacred union, a Christian ceremony for the creation of pure love, not pure convenience" (*FLW* 232). According to this evolutionary logic (the inversion of

Maine's), promises—once a sign of social progress—are now a superannuated practice, a vestige of the time when mating was exclusively a matter of barter and exchange.

Judicial history, in fact, suggests that Charles has it backwards: "business contracts" did not precede "sacred unions" in the chain of social evolution. His confusion—and his exclusive logic—is merely a reflection of the uncertain status of promises to marry in British legal history. Originally heard in ecclesiastical courts, breach of promise actions gradually come under the jurisdiction of civil courts. This transition begins with the 1651 ruling that the "engagement to marry is not merely a spiritual matter, and this action is not to compel the marriage upon the Contract, but to recover damages for not doing it . . . and here is a temporal loss and therefore a temporal action doth lie."[29] It concludes with the elimination of the ecclesiastical courts in 1857. Common law, however, is no better suited to reconcile the competing claims of the spiritual and the temporal. Charles's example, if not his logic, indicates that self-interested and disinterested commerce are invariably present in various ratios at different times whatever the venue.

This complexity discredits an overly simplistic opposition of these two forms of commerce. It both explains why trade in the marriage market is as risky as it is lively and suggests why this subject is of abiding interest to Victorian novelists. Fictional portrayals of the process of promising sometimes instantiate Hume's promissory model, but they more often than not complicate it, exploring the seams between interested and disinterested commerce. The "*symbols* or *signs*" of betrothal are familiar to all, but neither are their meanings univocal nor their consequences predictable. Engagement involves a relation that is, on the one hand, more formal and self-reflexive than an instance of disinterested commerce and, on the other hand, less contractual and adversarial than an arrangement of interested commerce. The affianced are neither single nor married; their promise is paradoxically private and public; their relationship is invested with both sentimental and mercantile significance. These tensions suggest that "the very problem of man" continues to vex the Victorians despite Hume's analysis and Maine's suggestions to the contrary.

The difficulty and mysteriousness of that problem are not entirely ignored by Hume. He recognizes that because promises "create a new motive," they necessarily change the contexts in which they are made. The existence of the promise itself, irrespective of what is promised, alters the circumstances and relationship of the promisers, establishing what Eliot might call "invisible conditions." Thus, without the benefit of deconstructionist terminology, Hume anticipates Derrida's insight:

A promise is always excessive. Without this essential excess, it would return to a description of knowledge of the future. Its act would have a constative structure and not a performative one. But this "too much" of the promise does not belong to a (promised) content of a promise which I would be incapable of keeping. It is within the very structure of the *act* of promising that this excess comes to inscribe a kind of irremediable disturbance or perversion. This perversion, which is also a trap, no doubt unsettles the language of the promise, the performative as promise; but it also renders it possible—and indestructible. Whence the *unbelievable*, and comical, aspect of every promise, and this passionate attempt to come to terms with the law, the contract, the oath, the declared affirmation of fidelity.[30]

Hume would not have been likely to describe promising as a perversion; nonetheless, he clearly recognizes the pragmatic impact of the spoken (or written) dimension of promising. A promise, he explains, is different from instances of agreement or convention that are not explicitly marked, such as rowing a boat or speaking a language. While courtship might be figuratively compared to a trial run in a rowboat or to developing a common language, there are important differences. In cases like rowing a boat, the mutual benefit is a matter of cooperative effort and action; betrothal, on the contrary, is a self-conscious and self-reflexive agreement expressed in language. In the case of speaking a language, individuals consent to general grammatical and lexical rules; in making a promise, they further and formally agree to a specific use of those rules. Thus promises to marry are overt actions by means of language that carry explicit and immediate extralinguistic consequences. By "creating a new motive," the promise itself—above and beyond the promised act—has a pragmatic effect upon those making it. This effect need not always be a "perversion," to use Derrida's terms; nevertheless, the potentially disruptive relationship of the constative and the performative is as problematic as that between the spiritual and the temporal. "It may want a Pope to settle" such tangled connections—to paraphrase Elizabeth-Jane Henchard—but in the absence of infallible pronouncements, the puzzled might do well to turn to novelists. The pragmatic, the performative, dimension of promising receives its fullest treatment in Victorian fiction.

In this regard, Hume, in addition to writers like Meredith and James, looks ahead to speech act theory, especially the dynamic tension between the rule-governed and formulaic aspects of promises and their fluid and unpredictable consequences. Betrothal is accomplished by means of an arbitrary mechanism that is both symbolic and conventional. Hume explains that "there is a *certain form of words* . . . by which we bind ourselves to the performance of any action. This form of words constitutes what we call a *promise*, which is the sanction of the interested commerce of mankind" (522). Promises are accomplished solely by repeating the form that has been agreed upon as constituting them. They come into being by virtue of the magic words, "I promise"— and "magic" does seem to be the appropriate term:

> since every new promise imposes a new obligation of morality on the person who promises, and since this new obligation arises from his will; 'tis one of the most mysterious and incomprehensible operations that can possibly be imagin'd, and may even be compar'd to *transubstantiation*, or *holy orders*, where a certain form of words, along with a certain intention, changes entirely the nature of an external object, and even of a human creature. (524)

Hume himself may be guilty of mystification, or at least of irony, yet the prestidigitation to which he alludes—called by Derrida "the *unbelievable*"—is surely a part of promises and of the seemingly insubstantial foundation upon which monumental social edifices are erected. If the power of promising inheres in an act of faith, it is nevertheless one with immense practical consequences.

LEGAL DEBATES: 1859 AND 1879

To explore some of these consequences, I would like to shift from Hume to judges and politicians, from philosophy to law. In this context, what Derrida describes as promising's "passionate attempt to come to terms with the law" might be reformulated as the law's indifferent success in coming to terms with promising. The "*certain form of words*" occupies the center stage in Victorian legal discussions but in a capacity different from what we have considered in philosophy. Legislative and juridical eyes tend to be concerned with the existence, not the pragmatic effect, of promises and with what they do, as opposed to how they do it. Nevertheless, public considerations of the promise to marry take their cue from terms that can be traced to two aspects of Hume's analysis: the form of promising (the "certain *symbols* or *signs*") and the division of interested and disinterested commerce. With regard to the former, it is to be remembered that Hume specifies both "a certain form of words" *and* "a certain intention" as necessary to promissory magic. Since determining either the intentions of alleged promisers or the expectations of alleged promisees is notoriously difficult, the justice system tends to fall back upon a principle that can be invariably applied. Proving the existence of the promise becomes tantamount to proving the obligation to keep it. Lawmakers, unable to consider the particular circumstances of every case or to foresee all consequences of a piece of legislation, can at least uniformly endorse a general principle of promise-keeping. As a consequence, insofar as promising comes under the purview of government, formalism and objectivism are the rules of the day. If the *"certain form of words"* can be proven to have been spoken, or even implied, then the promise and its provisions are enforceable. The legal system accepts as its function enforcing the ethical principles articulated by Smith, Paley, and utilitarian philosophy generally. Thus the process described in abstract terms by Hume is readily apparent in the specific practices of the English legal system a century after his death: "the will alone is never suppos'd to cause the obligation, but must be express'd by words or signs, in order to impose a tye upon any man. The expression being once brought in as subservient to the will, soon becomes the principal part of the promise" (523). In Victorian jurisprudence, the "expression" does not merely become "the principal part" of the promise; it becomes the only part.

The distinction between interested and disinterested commerce, considered synchronically by Hume and diachronically by Charles Smithson—but resolved by neither—is firmly entrenched in the legal sphere. Two foundational and competing narratives of betrothal are frequently rehearsed in public fora, one having to do with a domestic contract, the other with an expression of love—stories correlating, not coincidentally, with Hume's understanding of interested and disinterested commerce and with Fowles's depiction of "pure convenience" and "pure love." Two telling moments in the debate over the nature of marital promises occur in an 1859 trial for breach of the promise to marry and an 1879 Parliamentary session concerning these laws. *Hall* v. *Wright* focuses upon the question of whether a serious illness contracted after betrothal is a justifiable reason for breaking an engagement. The judicial opinions in the two trials of the case provide an extended commentary on the nature of marital promises, as does the debate in the House of Commons of a resolution introduced by Farrer Herschell to abolish breach of promise actions "except in cases where actual pecuniary loss has been incurred by reason of the promise, the damages being limited to such pecuniary loss."[31] These two moments of contestation in judicial and legislative history succinctly document the social divisions that make promising such a thorny issue for the Victorians. In each, the dominant narratives of marriage as interested and disinterested commerce are accompanied by diametrically opposed conceptions of engagement as an economic and a romantic agreement.

The narrative of interested commerce is presented by the plaintiff in *Hall* v. *Wright*. Her action for breach of the promise to marry follows Wright's breaking the engagement on the grounds that he is physically prevented from marrying by the onslaught of tuberculosis. Hall's attorney argues for the "strict liability" of all promises of marriage, maintaining that even were the marriage rendered impossible by an act of God, the defendant would still be liable for damages. Several judges accept this logic. According to Baron Martin, for example, the general principle raised by the case is clear, and he defends the sanctity of promises in terms reminiscent of Adam Smith:

> The law of England permits an action to recover damages for the breach of a promise to marry; although I am aware that many persons think that such an action should not be allowed. . . . The general rule upon the subject is, that, when a person by his own contract creates a duty or charge upon himself, he is bound to make it good if he may. . . . I think it very much better to adhere to the rule than to create an arbitrary exception for which, no doubt, plausible reasons may be given. To admit exceptions of this kind utterly destroys the certainty of the law, and in my opinion is inconvenient.[32]

"Inconvenient," taken out of the context of legalese, may seem understated to the point of absurdity; nonetheless, from the perspective of legal objectivists like Martin, the defendant is technically able and legally obligated to perform his promise, even though he might die in the process. In the words of Justice Crowder:

> it is not enough to show, in answer to an action upon a contract, that its performance is inconvenient or may be dangerous. The delicacy of health, alleged as an excuse, is the man's misfortune, not to be visited, beyond what is inevitable upon the woman. . . . Such a state of illness may make it a matter of the greatest prudence on his part to break his contract, and to pay such damages as a jury may award against him for the breach.[33]

The prudent course costs the defendant £100 in damages (while perhaps earning him a temporary stay of execution). Having uttered the "*certain form of words*" used in betrothal, he is bound by it. Not even the threat of death provides an escape from the obligation to keep promises of marriage or to pay for not keeping them. Only death itself terminates that obligation.[34]

To many, it might seem that the defendant, already suffering from a cruel fate, is further the victim of an unreasonable legal system. If, however, the heartlessness in *Hall* v. *Wright* is arguably the court's more than the consumptive promise-breaker's, then it is also the government's—as is shown when the debate shifts to the House of Commons in 1879. Despite public opposition to the laws under which Hall sues her lover (sentiments acknowledged by Martin's comment "that many persons think that such an action should not be allowed"), Parliament refuses to eliminate or even to modify them. The Solicitor General, Sir

Hardinge Giffard, taking the side of Baron Martin, defends the status quo and seems incredulous at the idea of restricting legal recourse to such as Miss Hall. Giffard assumes, without explicitly stating, that betrothal and marriage are contracts no different from any other. He expressly denies "that the action for breach of promise was the peculiarity it was alleged to be; the peculiarity lay in what [the bill's sponsor, Farrer Herschell] proposed. He would like to know why such an inversion of the ordinary principles of jurisprudence was to be proposed, simply because the parties were man and woman?"[35] The "ordinary principles of jurisprudence" are freedom of contract and protection by contract. This view is more bluntly articulated by Mr. Morgan Lloyd: "It was the law of the land that in cases where contracts were broken the aggrieved party had a right of action at law for damages; and he did not see why that rule should be departed from when the contract broken was a contract to marry."[36]

One imagines that the Solicitor General is both less direct and more discreet than his colleague in order to avoid associating the government with arguments offensive to the general public or to feminists. The former might object to the implication that marriage is a temporal rather than a spiritual matter; the latter to the defense of a system that defines women as inherently inferior and in need of special protection. His argument contains an interesting, if not entirely ingenuous, rhetorical stratagem. He begins by assuming the equal treatment of men and women under the law—a principle that in point of fact bears little resemblance to the policies of 1879.[37] He then uses the appeal to equity to overwrite the explicit gender bias of the narrative most frequently invoked to support breach of promise laws: women, who are otherwise without defense against heartless and unprincipled men, must be given legal protection. This chivalric narrative is repeatedly invoked during the debate, for instance, in the claim that the law acts as a "deterrent upon the minds of many men, for such were frequently to be found, who would otherwise, from mere wantonness, trifle with the affections of women. Women were much weaker than men, and in nearly all these cases, the man was the injuring party"; or again in these remarks by Sir Eardley Wilmot: "the fair sex, who were not there to advocate their own rights and speak in behalf of themselves, would find many hon. Members to fight their battle and retain an action which was valuable, chiefly as a safeguard for women."[38] Giffard's tack is different (egalitarian rather than paternalistic), his style is more subtle (pragmatic rather than heroic), but his objective is the same. Legislative conservatism reinforces judicial conservatism to guarantee that laws against breach of the promise to marry will remain on the books for almost another century.

These laws depend upon the view of promises to marry as enforceable contracts and not simply as informal agreements or pauses taken prior to the serious step of matrimony. Their defenders insist that marriage is the one commercial enterprise open to women and that barring legal redress for fraudulent behavior would both impose substantial hardship on women and sanction significant abuse by men. Wilmot, in following Giffard's tack, claims women suffer significant financial losses when engagements are broken, especially since "marriage and a settlement in life were the one object of a woman's life, whereas men had numerous engagements to occupy their time and attention, and to divert chagrin and disappointment."[39] Although he quotes Byron in this regard, Wilmot's scenario could have come directly from the pages of *Vanity Fair*. When Amelia Sedley appears to have been jilted by George Osborne, the narrator notes that she is entirely dependent upon her fiancé for a "settlement in life," while he finds "numerous engagements to occupy [his] time and attention."[40] She is, therefore, unwise to have "pledged her love irretrievably; confessed her heart away, and got back nothing—only a brittle promise which was snapt and worthless in a moment." It is better to marry "as they do in France, where the lawyers are the bridesmaids and confidantes" (*VF* 220). Amelia might have been imprudent to make this bargain, but in the eyes of the Solicitor General and his colleagues, she has the right to something more than verbal shards if George breaks his word.

In contrast to this position, the counternarrative of betrothal asserts that, whatever the case with contracts generally, promises of love cannot be construed according to the logic of interested commerce. Love is not primarily a matter of economics and should never become an object of the law. Some may willingly choose to inhabit Vanity Fair, but its mores and manners should not be imposed upon everyone. This story emanates from those on the side of Wright in 1859 and Herschell in 1879.

Hall v. *Wright*, rendered in terms of this counternarrative, might sound like this: "the defendant pledged his hand in marriage with every expectation of hymeneal happiness; however, the plaintiff held his hand at arm's length, coldly turning his misfortune into her own financial gain." The legal opinions in the case are not nearly so melodramatic, though they do produce clear and dramatically different versions of victim and villain. Wright's attorneys admit that he has broken his word but insist that this is not the issue. The engagement ended through no fault of the defendant, who, in any case, can scarcely be coerced into a conjugal embrace at the risk of death. Those judges accepting this argument tend to the opinion that if betrothal resembles a contract, it does so in a unique and flexible fashion. The strongest views in the case are those of Chief Baron Pollock, who contends that promises of marriage differ in kind from other contracts because betrothal is not simply a matter of mutual consent but also of "mutual comfort":

> a contract to marry is assumed in law to be made for the purpose of mutual comfort, and is avoided if, by the act of God or the opposite party, the circumstances are so changed as to make intense misery instead of mutual comfort the probable result of performing the contract. . . . The near approach of death by a fatal disease precludes any hope of personal comfort from cohabitation: and, if death is knowingly hastened thereby, each party, by performing the contract might incur the criminal guilt of intentionally causing death.[41]

In summing up his position, Pollock describes betrothal as "an understanding between the parties, rather than a bargain" and concludes that "a view of the law which puts a contract of marriage on the same footing as a bargain for a horse, or a bale of goods, is not in accordance with the general feelings of mankind, and is supported by no authority."[42] In this view, a contract of marriage is clearly a horse of a different color.

Even though Wright loses the case (on appeal) and even though Herschell's resolution does not become law, this estimation of "the general feelings of mankind" reflects an important mid-Victorian view of marriage. Popular sentiment would seem to favor a revision of Paley's 1822 principle that the guilt of unlawful promises "lies in the making, not in the breaking." In the eyes of a majority in the House of Commons in 1879, the fault inheres neither in making nor breaking, but in not forsaking such promises. Herschell explicitly rejects the commercial analogy. Betrothal is not "like any other contract—like one to buy a bale of wool, for instance."[43] The phrase "bale of . . . " seems almost to have become a formulaic condemnation of the market mentality of men and women in Vanity Fair. Herschell strenuously objects to the idea that "a woman earned her livelihood by performing her conjugal, social, and domestic duties":

> Earned her livelihood! He did not like the phrase, as it was impossible to admire too much the devotion, the zeal, and the unselfishness with which women performed their social and domestic duties, and endeavoured to promote the happiness of the men to whom they were united. . . . Therefore, he protested against the view that women performed those duties by way of return for board and maintenance as being as degrading as it was untrue.[44]

"Earned her livelihood," of course, is exactly the ground upon which Serjeant Buzfuz argues and wins the action against Mr. Pickwick. He tells jurors: "My client's hopes and prospects are ruined, and it is no figure of speech to say that her occupation is gone indeed" (*Pickwick*

Papers [*PP*] 563). Because Pickwick is a lodger as well as an alleged suitor, his "desertion" constitutes a double loss for Mrs. Bardell, and the symbolic significance is clear: according to the logic of the marketplace, husbands and lodgers fulfill identical functions. In Herschell's as well as Dickens's view, such thinking may enrich plaintiffs and attorneys, but it is morally bankrupt.

During the Parliamentary consideration of breach of promise laws, Serjeant Buzfuz is, in fact, alluded to as exemplifying that "certain class of lawyer" whose business is conducted "for reasons of extortion" rather than justice.[45] Mr. Rodwell, for example, opposes breach of promise actions not only because they benefit unscrupulous lawyers and their dishonest clients but also because they misrepresent the true nature of the marriage bond. Echoing Justice Pollock, he describes betrothal as a matter of "'reciprocity'. There should be a mutual return of affection . . . and when affection ceased on one side or on the other it was for the good of both parties that the engagement should cease, and that there should be an end to a state of things which, instead of leading to comfort, would lead to discomfort, and to misery instead of happiness."[46] Thus a hedonistic calculus of a different sort from that employed to urge a general rule of promise-keeping comes into play. Relying on this accounting system, Sir Henry James (not to be confused with the novelist) argues that breach of promise laws accomplish little more than "punishment on the man who refused to make two lives miserable."[47] This same calculus is advanced—also in 1879—by George Meredith in *The Egoist* (*E*). Vernon Whitford remarks on the jilting of Willoughby Patterne: "better four happy instead of two miserable" (*E* 1:100).

The debates of 1859 and 1879 demonstrate that there is little agreement upon the system of accounting to be employed in calculating the benefits and costs of promising. Rule utilitarians urge that the general good resulting from strict adherence to promises necessarily outweighs the benefits accruing to an individual as a result of waiving the rule in a particular case. Exceptions to the norm erode social and moral values, ultimately threatening the individuals they are intended to benefit. Act utilitarians, on the contrary, are willing to admit exceptions to this principle, agreeing with Vernon Whitford but stopping short of Sir Francis Geraldine in thinking that breaking an engagement might in some circumstances be preferable to keeping it. This difference is not clearly resolved, as these two moments in the continuing debate clearly document. In *Hall* v. *Wright*, all told in two trials, the judges are evenly split, with the original verdict for the defendant being narrowly overturned on appeal. The results of the Parliamentary debate are similarly inconclusive in that, although the resolution is approved by a vote of 106–65, the legislation necessary to enact the measure is not passed despite repeated attempts to do so over the next decade.[48] The House of Commons says one thing about breach of promise actions but does quite another, never enacting its officially recorded position. The diametrically opposed sides of the issue, therefore, seem, if not entirely to cancel each other out, then at least to have little direct impact upon how people actually conduct their lives.

FICTIONAL VERSUS LEGAL DISCOURSE:
THE TRIAL OF MAGGIE TULLIVER

Novelists are not constricted by the adversarial systems of legal ethics and partisan politics. Freed from the context in which narratives and counternarratives are mutually dependent but diametrically opposed, and in which practical constraints determine what judges and legislators can and must do, novelists explore alternative stories in different "languages" about how promises work. Peter Goodrich, for example, draws upon Bakhtin to contrast the language of the novel, which is "disorderly and dialogic, . . . historical and stratified" with the monologic discourse of the law, which

> actively attempts to control the language-usage, to impose "correct" meanings which are simply the assertion (though seldom the practice) of uniform meanings within the genre and to argue, in the name either of science or of professionalism, that legal language can be "exact," "objective," "logical" and "value free." The unitary language attempts to centralize and standardize meanings and in the case of legal language in particular it denies that words have other meanings or connotations, rhetorical and symbolic usages which will frequently belie or at least challenge the correct or "true" meaning as it is found by the law.[49]

On a variety of levels, including the linguistic, as argued by Goodrich, and the generic, as argued by Cover, the novelist experiences a freedom not accessible to the lawyer. In fiction, promissory practices can be represented without the contortion, sometimes the distortion, resulting from the formal and conventional requisites of courtroom testimony and political disputation, as well as from the practical demands of winning a verdict or an election. Promising can also be re-presented, that is, creatively reconfigured to suggest alternative modes of communication and conduct.

A reconfiguration of this sort, however, does not occur in *The Mill on the Floss*, which instead presents a character who is unable to find an alternative to the legalism of her family and society. Maggie Tulliver's

self-imposed guilty verdict exemplifies the internalized working of legalistic attitudes toward betrothal. She is not the subject of a courtroom
trial, but she might as well have been. In her family, attitudes about
promising seem not to have advanced much beyond the early stages of
Roman society as outlined in *Ancient Law*. Maine distinguishes between
"the crude form of Contract [and] its maturity" in this way:

> At first, nothing is seen like the interposition of law to compel the per-
> formance of a promise. That which the law arms with its sanctions is
> not a promise, but a promise accompanied with a solemn ceremonial.
> Not only are formalities of equal importance with the promise itself,
> but they are, if anything, of greater importance; for that delicate anal-
> ysis which mature jurisprudence applies to the conditions of mind
> under which a particular verbal assent is given appears, in ancient law,
> to be transferred to the words and gestures of the accompanying per-
> formance.[50]

Mr. Tulliver, for example, insists that Tom not only swear upon the
Bible but also write in it in order to pledge vengeance against the
Wakems (*MF* 357), and Tom not only demands of Maggie a solemn
vow with "your hand on my father's Bible" but also cites chapter and
verse, as it were, by "going up to the large Bible, drawing it forward and
opening it at the fly-leaf, where the writing was" (*MF* 444, 445). Invest-
ing the *ceremony* of promising with implacable force radically simplifies
the promise: contexts, such as "the considerations of mind" or mitigat-
ing circumstances, are simply irrelevant in face of the unalterable sacral
text. Maggie, in contrast to the men of the family, is as appalled by
Tom's promise as she is offended by his request, the former because an
oath of revenge seems a pact with the devil and the latter because external signs cannot compel what inner resolve has not already guaranteed.
Shunning the reductive attitudes of her family, however, immerses her in
the complications that they ignore, especially relating to ambiguous or
conflicting promises—promises neither made on nor inscribed in the
family Bible.[51]

These formalities not only simplify but also reveal the gender bias
of promising. Tom, for example, is too young for promises only because
of inexperience. When the family fortunes are at their lowest point, he
seeks help from an uncle, who "didn't quite promise me anything: he
seemed to think I couldn't have a very good situation. I'm too young"
(*MF* 318). Promises themselves are evidently a sign of maturity; only
those who have entered adult society can engage in them—or become
engaged by them. In the absence of an avuncular promise, Tom perse-
veres, restores the family reputation, and proves himself to be of the age
at which promises are both possible and superfluous. That is to say, Mr.

Deane is willing to promise help only after his nephew has shown himself to be worthy, but the very process of proving his maturity places Tom into circumstances in which his uncle's promises are no longer needed. When old enough to promise, Tom need no longer do so. Maggie, on the contrary, like Bathsheba will always be too young to promise by virtue of being a woman. She is repeatedly asked to make promises—and she is always expected to break them. Hence the paradox of gender and promising: for men, to be worthy of promising means never having to promise; for women, to be unworthy of promising means always having to promise. The "double-tensed" quality of promising (the circumstance in which "that which is not but will be has to be transformed into the 'now'")[52] is reversed for women: the present of the promise is invariably transformed into a girlish past.

There is another way in which the gendering of promises results in temporal contradiction. While still a child, for instance, Maggie promises to kiss Philip (*MF* 261, 263)—a promise kept neither upon their next meeting nor at any time during a year of clandestine assignations in the Red Deeps. During this period Maggie expresses "not the slightest promise of love towards him in her manner; it was nothing more than the sweet girlish tenderness she had shown him when she was twelve" (*MF* 403). Philip, however, finally cannot resist reminding the now adolescent Maggie of the promise that he knows she is not obligated to keep: "The recollection of that childish time came as a sweet relief to Maggie. It made the present moment less strange to her. She kissed him almost as simply and quietly as she had done when she was twelve years old. Philip's eyes flashed with delight" (*MF* 436). As different as Maggie's promise is from those of her brother and father, it has a similar consequence: a commitment to the past. Making promises may be prospective, but keeping them can be regressive. Maggie returns to the sexual innocence of her youth. She feels like a girl of twelve again, kissing Philip as she would Tom (*MF* 261), but Philip's flashing eyes reveal the sexual desire that Maggie herself will not experience until she kisses Stephen Guest.

Irrespective of the social logic according to which women may be too childlike to be fully trustworthy, the voluntary kiss of an innocently affectionate child is quite different from the contractual kiss of a marriageable woman. At Lorton, Maggie tells Philip, "I shall always remember you" (*MF* 261), and her kiss seems more elegiac than anticipatory. In the Red Deeps, however, she admits: "I should like always to live with you—to make you happy" (*MF* 437), and her kiss borders upon a promise. It is, in the words of the narrator, "one of those dangerous moments when speech is at once sincere and deceptive—when feeling, rising high above its average depth, leaves flood-marks which are never reached again" (*MF* 437). This metaphor foreshadows the final episode of the novel and figuratively links promising with Maggie's catastrophic fate. The connection, however, is more than figurative. The sincere deception of this scene inheres precisely in the temporal disjunction of promising. Maggie describes feelings that will, like flood waters, recede. Philip, however, riding the crest of these emotions, seems justified in thinking that she has promised him love—and marriage. When this pact is sealed with a kiss, Maggie finds herself in a new promissory dilemma and another temporal paradox. The similarities with *Far from the Madding Crowd* are unmistakable: both Maggie and Bathsheba make reluctant and ambiguous commitments to lovers whose ardor exceeds their own; neither Boldwood nor Philip can relinquish promises whose origins are dubious (Bathsheba's begins in childish behavior, a valentine, and Maggie's in childlike behavior, a sororal kiss), whose meaning is equivocal, and whose force is tenuous; and the love triangles resulting from the appearance of a second lover (Frank Troy, Stephen Guest) set the allegiances from the past in opposition to the desires of the present and lead, directly or indirectly, to catastrophic consequences.

Maggie's next ambiguous promise is that implied by her sailing away with Stephen. Waking from her "moment of fatal intoxication" (*MF* 590) and "partial sleep of thought" (*MF* 592), she repents her inconstancy and argues that there can be no justification for "breaking the most sacred ties that can ever be formed on earth. If the past is not to bind us, where can duty lie? We should have no law but the inclination of the moment" (*MF* 601–2). This line of thinking returns her to the promissory logic of her brother and father.[53] For while Maggie may have shown herself to be a more promising student of Latin than Tom, she has fully inculcated the gendered import of his mistranslation: "now promise those men." Ultimately, she can escape neither patriarchal promises nor masculine maxims, neither the age of promising nor fate of having those promises mistrusted. Tony Tanner points out that her return to St. Oggs reimmerses her in "the language and hence the concepts and classifications, that she had temporarily left behind. . . . Waking up, then, amounts to a reassumption of a vocabulary that effectively prescribes her own annihilation."[54] Her social death sentence is anything but fair. In condemning his sister's promissory polygamy, Tom sentences her to submersion in the past, rearticulating the very principle that has contributed in no small way to the demise of his family. In denying her love for Stephen, Maggie accepts her brother's judgment. In recalling that Philip "thought of me as the one promise of his life" (*MF* 571), Maggie comes virtually to embody Philip's hopes, in a sense, to incarnate her word. Her death, therefore, assumes the archetypal connotations of a religious sacrifice: she dies that promising might live.

Maggie's self-imposed verdict is not necessarily wrong, but "justice by a ready-made patent method, without the trouble of exerting patience, discrimination, impartiality" (*MF* 628) is wrong because it refuses to consider "the mysterious complexity" of the individual and her circumstances. The narrator comments that "moral judgments must remain false and hollow, unless they are checked and enlightened by a perpetual reference to the special circumstances that mark the individual lot" (*MF* 628). In the case of *Tulliver* v. *Tulliver*, that is, in the internal debate between Maggie's conscience and her desire, the men of maxims seem to be both judge and jury. Their opinion is well-expressed by Justice Willes in *Hall* v. *Wright* who insists that the promise to marry is "an unconditional one . . . this is not a question of sentiment."[55] Eliot maintains, on the contrary, that betrothal is very much "a question of sentiment." A principle of promising divorced from individual circumstances is repressive and destructive: "the mysterious complexity of our life is not to be embraced by maxims, and . . . to lace ourselves up in formulas of that sort is to repress all the divine promptings and inspirations that spring from growing insight and sympathy" (*MF* 628).

The Mill on the Floss does not provide readers with a new vocabulary of promising; rather, it dramatizes the destructive consequences of the old. There is, however, an important difference between Maggie's convictions and the values shared equally by her family, the men of maxims, and "the world's wife." The vocabulary that condemns her is heard in the gossip surrounding her return to St. Oggs: "Public opinion, in these cases, is always of the feminine gender—not the world, but the world's wife . . . and the world's wife, with that fine instinct which is given her for the preservation of society, saw at once that Miss Tulliver's conduct had been of the most aggravated kind. Could anything be more detestable?" (*MF* 619–20). The question is only apparently rhetorical, for Eliot implies that the one thing more detestable is the thinking of the gossips themselves. The hypocrisy of their public rectitude—a morality of convenience masquerading as social duty—is apparent in their willingness to forgive Maggie had she returned as Mrs. Stephen Guest. The matriarchal chorus, no less than the men of maxims, has nothing in common with those who possess "the insight that comes from a hardly-earned estimate of temptation, or from a life vivid and intense enough to have created a wide fellow-feeling with all that is human" (*MF* 628). The narrator's defense of fellow-feeling—of "growing insight and sympathy"—opposes flexibility to formulae and places more importance on others' suffering than on self-interest. Maggie's defense of promising may be inflexible, but it is not ready-made, emerging, as it does, from a consideration of Philip's feelings as well as of her own. Stephen, on the contrary, is thinking primarily of himself when he tries to persuade

Maggie to elope with him. Self-interest appears in the guise of natural law when he argues for the primacy of love over law: "there are ties that can't be kept by mere resolution. . . . What is outward faithfulness? Would they have thanked us for anything so hollow as constancy without love?" (*MF* 602). Maggie quickly recognizes that such appeals to natural law amount to little more than "doing what is easiest and pleasantest to ourselves" (*MF* 602). She rejects personal ease and social preservation for the moral imperative of "fellow feeling with all that is human."

This principle explains the notion of promise-keeping that distinguishes Maggie from her family. She "promises those men," with a difference, resisting the arguments of both her brother and her lover. Promises are made in the heart not on the Bible; hence, she tells Tom: "If I give you my word, that will be as strong a bond to me, as if I had laid my hand on the Bible. I don't require that to bind me" (*MF* 445). She has no respect for "the external shell of form and ceremony"— Maine's term for early Roman practices that applies equally well to the Tullivers' use of the Bible. For Maggie, the "conditions of mind" are the essential component of a promise. She explains this idea in responding to Stephen's claim that he is "breaking no positive engagement. . . . If you are not absolutely pledged to Philip, we are neither of us bound" (*MF* 570). Maggie counters that "the real tie lies in the feelings and expectations we have raised in other minds. Else all pledges might be broken, when there was no outward penalty. There would be no such thing as faithfulness" (*MF* 570). These ties are invisible and do not depend for enforcement upon the threat of damages in a breach of promise suit. Maggie refuses the lawyers to whom Bathsheba would have recourse, dismissing Stephen's distinction between tacit and positive promises as legalistic hair-splitting. Fellow-feeling motivates promises, obligates promisers, and explains Maggie's conclusion: "I consider myself engaged to [Philip]—I don't mean to marry any one else" (*MF* 569). Although she desires Stephen no less than he does her, she refuses to contravene the internal and implicit promise made to her cousin and childhood lover. Whatever she may have consciously intended concerning Philip, she is bound by the expectations and hopes raised in him by her behavior.

Even as it reflects the verdicts of Victorian courts and the House of Commons, *The Mill on the Floss* complicates the terms of the debate. Eliot does not merely substitute a moral norm for a legal one. Maggie rejects any felicific calculus, even that employed by Vernon Whitford. Her quasi-engagements to two men demonstrate that promissory principles and practices are seldom as unambiguous as promisers or society in general might hope. Like the words (or even the kisses) with which they are made, promises "mean several things," and their performative bonus is more often a burden than a boon. The strain between the principle and practice of betrothal is particularly problematic because of its indeterminate status. Maggie is not quite engaged to and not quite free of either man—and is so within a social space that is itself intermediary. She is neither single nor married, neither free to marry nor bound by wedlock. For her part, Eliot neither doubts that promises should be fulfilled nor underestimates the hazards of navigating the "neither" world of betrothal.

In attempting to traverse the Rubicon, Maggie Tulliver drowns in the Floss. Her experience affords a spectral glimpse into the invisible conditions transforming ordinary streams into treacherous rivers. The next chapter approaches the dangerous currents of betrothal from the opposite shore, that is, from the perspective of broken rather than of "faithful" promises—with apologies to Henry Tilney for the supererogatory adjective.

CHAPTER 3

Legal Fictions: Narrating Breach of Promise

Just as the phrase "faithful promise" is in Henry Tilney's mind a redundancy, the term "breach of promise" is in the estimation of many Victorians a virtual contradiction in terms. The pervasiveness and potency of the norm of promise-keeping leave little room for consideration of what to do with people who do not keep their word, especially in affairs of the heart. When internal means of control fail—as they do not with Maggie Tulliver—or when the individual's fear of not being "trusted any more if he refuse to perform what he promis'd" dissipates, what means of enforcement can be brought to bear upon delinquent promisers? Laboring under the unresolved antitheses between two forms of commerce and two conceptions of marriage, Victorians find themselves in a quandary concerning those who break engagements, whether recidivists in the mold of Don Juan or innocents of a Pickwickian kind, whether schemers like Lizzie Eustace or pranksters like Bathsheba Everdene.

This chapter focuses on the only option open to a society imprisoned by its sense of promissory progress. Having evolved beyond primitive justice and abandoned the barbarity of trial by combat, the Victorians possess no alternative to trial by jury to resolve questions of honor. Progress of this sort, however, seems to many a mixed blessing. While the fate of the Troglodytes may not be imminent, breach of promise laws are taken as both a sign and an example of ominous devolutionary developments. Charles MacColla caustically observes in his 1879 study of breach of promise law: "the poetry of love is now wedded to the trammels of the law. The offspring of this union is the action of breach of promise of marriage."[1] Even defenders of the law must admit that this fractious child of ill-suited parents is itself proof of some kind of failure, whether responsibility for it lies with individuals, institutions, or someplace else entirely.

Trollope's Lady Fawn is one register of this decline. She expresses more than nostalgia in lamenting the changeable, and seemingly interchangeable, alliances of her son, Lizzie Eustace, and Frank Greystock: "When she was told that under the new order of things promises from gentlemen were not to be looked upon as binding, . . . she was very unhappy. She could not disbelieve it all, and throw herself back upon her faith in virtue, constancy, and honesty. She rather thought that things had changed for the worse since she was young, and that promises were not now as binding as they used to be."[2] Lady Fawn articulates what seems to be a widespread sense that civilization has reached a sorry state when a gentleman's word is good only when constrained by law—and an even worse state when a lady turns to the law to keep him honest. Breach of promise laws affront Victorian standards of privacy and gender, offend middle-class norms of propriety, and challenge the sentimental ideology of promise-keeping.[3] An 1874 essay in the *Pall Mall Gazette* refers to Trollope's *The Small House at Allington* to support the view that a jilted woman who would seek legal redress falls entirely outside the boundaries of respectability: "To a lady of delicacy, and one whose feelings have been deeply wounded, it would simply be an insult to talk of pecuniary compensation. Imagine, for instance, Lily Dale bringing an action of this nature against Adolphus Crosbie."[4] The temporal distance from Catherine Moreland's supposed solecism and Lily Dale's passive acceptance of her broken engagement to the narratives of unfaithful promises echoing from courtrooms and amplified by the press may be insignificant, but the social distance between them is prodigious.

The litigation of romance seems so offensive that some are inclined to look wistfully upon the passing of the age of dueling. One MP during the 1879 debate begrudgingly admits that breach of promise laws play a socially necessary role but regrets that "there was not more wholesome dread of the 'big brother,' who was restrained by law from inflicting chastisement, and duels were practically abolished. The only remedy left was to bring an action in order to expose the conduct of the man, and vindicate the character of the woman."[5] In *The Eustace Diamonds*, when Lizzie lets it be known that she will not allow herself to become notorious for being "the woman that Lord Fawn had jilted," her protector and admirer, Frank Greystock, who happens to be an attorney, replies, "I will not fight him,—that is, with pistols; nor will I attempt to thrash him. It would be useless to argue whether public opinion is right or wrong; but public opinion is now so much opposed to that kind of thing, that it is out of the question"—sentiments echoed by his adversary, Lord Fawn (*ED* 1:216, 245).[6] A comic example of the place of dueling in the Victorian imagination occurs in *Diana of the Crossways* (1885). The novel opens with the threat of a duel over an alleged insult on the dance floor. For Meredith, however, setting the "jilting" in a ballroom and not at the altar indicates that the scene is purely comic. It has none of the dark tones of *The Tragic Comedians* (1880), which culminates with a pointless—and fatal—duel. Consistent with the comedy of the episode, Sullivan Smith's threats contain more sound than substance, and the scene is readily defused by the common-sensical hero, Thomas Redworth, who subsequently provides the ultimate protection of the lady in question by marrying her. This lady, the eponymous protagonist, jokes that Smith, who could always be counted on to assume the role of "big brother" to an unprotected woman, has been rendered obsolete by a distinctly class-conscious mechanism for enforcing codes of honor:

> Society is a big engine enough to protect itself. I incline with British juries to do rough justice to the victims. She has neither father nor brother. I have had no confidences: but it wears the look of a cowardly business. With two words in his ear, I could arm an Irishman to do some work of chastisement:—he would select the rascal's necktie for a cause of quarrel: and lords have to stand their ground as well as commoners. They measure the same number of feet when stretched their length.[7] (*DCW* 207)

Death may be a democrat, but in an enlightened society, death sentences are no longer imposed for breach of promise. As the site of contested feminine honor shifts from outdoors to indoors, bullets give way to verbal volleys, big brothers are replaced by well-armed attorneys, and fraternal chivalry is supplanted by paternalistic jurisprudence.

While few seriously desire a return to the age of dueling, it is no less true that few are satisfied with the modern mechanism of policing promising. No one, however, seems content, in the words of the Solicitor General, simply to "leave a real injury practically without remedy at all."[8] The remedy and its ills, therefore, remain sources of controversy, the nature and scope of which become more clear from an examination of two narratives of contested promises, Trollope's *An Old Man's Love* (*OML*, 1882) and Dickens's *The Pickwick Papers* (1836–37), and from a comparison of these novels with breach of promise trials arising from similar situations and dealing with related issues. The "legal fictions" of my chapter title thus refers not only to novels in which legal, quasi-legal, or potentially legal stories are depicted, but also to the stories of broken promises told in Victorian courtrooms. Comparing jurisgenerative and jurispathic narratives leads to a third meaning of the phrase "legal fiction": the technical definition of "an assumption or supposition that something which is or may be false is true, or that a state of facts exists which has never really taken place."[9] However different published novels and publicized trials might be in language, form, and objective, this third sense of legal fiction suggests a common link between them. This link anticipates and enables the turn to the "nonlegal" fictions of Brontë, Eliot, Meredith, Trollope, and James in later chapters.

AN OLD MAN'S LOVE

In the post-pugilistic period, the only alternatives open to jilted women seem to be either the passivity of Lily Dale (the path taken by Mary Lawrie in *An Old Man's Love*) or the scandal of Lizzie Eustace (the choice of Mrs. Bardell in *The Pickwick Papers*). Mary's example provides a double perspective on promising—one looking back to the pious rhetoric of the early Victorians, the other anticipating the legal action of the late Victorians and Edwardians. In this novel, Trollope focuses on the extent to which potentially litigable distinctions have entered the consciousness of those who would nonetheless resolutely shun the prospect of a breach of promise trial. Mary Lawrie confronts legalistic differentiations when she reluctantly agrees to marry her much older guardian, Mr. Whittlestaff, even though she still loves John Gordon, from whom she has not heard in three years. Like Wellington, Gordon is rejected by his lover's family because of poverty and leaves England. Having made a fortune in the diamond fields of South Africa, he returns to propose but arrives a few hours after Mary's betrothal to another. Questions such as: "Should or can Mary break her engagement?"; "Should Mr. Whittlestaff release her from her promise?"; and "Should John Gordon ask either to do so?" turn upon two factors: the brevity of the existing engagement between Mary and Mr. Whittlestaff and the absence of a "positive" engagement between Mary and John.

Mary Lawrie's situation reflects several of those already discussed: like Fleetwood, she instantly regrets her promise; like Wellington, she is willing to marry without love; like Maggie, she is unwilling to marry the man she does love. She staunchly defends the position of Adam Smith, even though in doing so she, in effect, agrees to "sacrifice herself to her promise."[10] She upholds the principle that a "promise is a promise, though it be but an hour old" (*OML* 85). The model informing her thinking on engagement and motivating her version of "duty before desire" is that of the commercial contract. She may not quite think of herself as a "bale of . . . ," but she does hold that her husband-to-be "had, as it were, taken complete possession of her, by right of the deed of gift which she had made of herself. . . . [W]as she not his property, to do as he pleased with her?" (*OML* 56, 169–70). The kiss that he requests and is allowed formally seals their compact: she "would not begrudge him kisses if he cared for them. They were his by all the rights of contract" (*OML* 43). Having given her word, she feels bound by it, even though she thinks of many reasons for not becoming Mrs. Whittlestaff. She must remind herself that promises are not made in the subjunctive mood; the timing—and even the fact—of John's return is irrelevant, at least from the legalistic perspective. Her calculation of the right and wrong of the thing is, in the last analysis, not quantitative—and certainly not hedonistic: "She did love John Gordon . . . but still she would marry Mr. Whittlestaff, and do her duty in that state of life to which it had pleased God to call her. There would be a sacrifice—a sacrifice of two—but still it was justice" (*OML* 149).

Mr. Whittlestaff initially takes the same strictly moralistic perspective upon promising, which is understandable since ethics and self-interest concur in his case. Described as the "sort of dog whom you cannot easily persuade to give up a bone" (*OML* 100), he cannot see why he should release the bride-to-be from her pledge: "Was it natural that a man should give up his intended wife, simply because he was asked?" (*OML* 106). He reinforces the suspect logic of self-interest by turning to a utilitarian calculation of the prospective happiness of the two hypothetical marriages, reversing Mary's computation and concluding that she will be much more secure, therefore, more happy with him than with a man whose fortune depends upon speculation in diamonds (*OML* 78). Support for his insistence that Mary keep her promise comes from the fact she is not and was never engaged to Gordon. He knows that "not a word had passed her lips that could be taken as a promise [to Gordon]. There had not been even a hint of a promise" (*OML* 39, 65). Gordon also admits that there has been no "absolute promise. . . . It is true. I am left without an inch of ground on which to found a complaint. There was no word; no promise" (*OML* 71, 74). This admission provides bitter comfort to Mr. Whittlestaff, for it means that he is technically entitled to marry a person who does not love him. It gives him a reason for holding Mary to her promise but confirms a more basic reason for not doing so.

Neither Mary Lawrie nor Mr. Whittlestaff finally believes that the principle both defend so vigorously should be applied to their situation. While uttering no public rebuttal or even doubt of the philosophy that "a promise is a promise," Mary inwardly accedes to John's argument, which reprises Stephen Guest's: "There had been no promise,—no word of promise. But he felt that there had been that between them which should have been stronger than any promise" (*OML* 75). She questions the honor of Mr. Whittlestaff, who it seems "had made up his mind without any effort, and was determined to abide by it. He had thought it well to marry her; and having asked her, and having obtained her consent, he intended to take advantage of her promise" (*OML* 153). Her thoughts, however, do little justice to his private torment—a point that Trollope brings home to readers by exploiting the ironies of Mr. Whittlestaff's first words in the novel. When he learns that Mary's mother has died, leaving her alone and him in line to assume parental responsibility, he exclaims: "I'll be whipped if I will have anything to do with her" (*OML* 1). But he does, reluctantly becoming her guardian and fear-fully—yet happily—her fiancé. His sensitive nature and conscience, however, are sorely lashed during the agonizing processes of making and then retracting his proposal of marriage. For like Mr. Western, Mr. Whittlestaff has already been jilted, and he now fears that it will happen again: "To have attempted twice, and twice to have failed so disastrously! He was a man to whom to have failed once in such a matter was almost death. How should he bear it twice and still live?" (*OML* 154). In this novel, Trollope is less interested in the social perception and psychological impact of jilting, to which both Western and Whittlestaff are so sensitive, than in the legalistic distinctions affecting the existence and force of an engagement. Mr. Whittlestaff has every right "to take advantage of her promise" but knows that he would be wrong to do so.

While both believe that the engagement should be broken, neither is willing to make the first move. Whittlestaff thinks: "But now if she would tell him that she wished to be relieved from him, and to give herself to this stranger, she should be allowed to go. But he told himself also that he would carry his generosity no further. He was not called upon to offer to surrender himself. The man's coming had been a misfortune; but let him go, and in process of time he would be forgotten" (*OML* 92). That Mary will forget Gordon is wishful thinking—as the past three years prove. He reluctantly admits that love is "stronger than any promise" and frees Mary from her "fatal promise" (*OML* 235). It is Whittlestaff, then, not Mary, who is to be sacrificed and for whom the promise is fatal. The marriage for which he steps aside will make two rather than one happy and render one rather than two miserable—and in both calculations Mr. Whittlestaff is the odd man out.

BEACHEY V. BROWN

The lover's triangle in *An Old Man's Love* leads to a very different conclusion from that of *Beachey* v. *Brown* (1860), a case of breach of promise decided unanimously in favor of the plaintiff. Elizabeth Beachey is already betrothed to Charles Yeales when she enters a second engagement to Henry Langford Brown. Upon learning of the prior betrothal, Brown breaks the engagement—and is sued for doing so. His defense is based upon the claims, first, that a prior engagement abrogates any subsequent to it and, second, that the plaintiff's silences about her romantic past and present situation are certainly deceptive, if not fraudulent, and constitute proof of bad character. In the eyes of the law, however, it doesn't and they don't. The nonplussed defendant must wonder why the first plea fails to provide technical justification of the breach (preexisting contract) and why both factors do not raise sufficient doubt about his fiancée's character to vindicate his action. The legalistic fine points that preoccupy all three characters in the novel are swept aside by the court as moral niceties having no relevance to the case.

The fact of Elizabeth Beachey's engagement to Charles Yeales is disregarded: a previous engagement has no legal effect upon a second betrothal. To Henry Langford Brown, this detail is anything but immaterial, since he maintains that he would never have promised to marry the plaintiff had he known of her betrothal. In summarily dismissing his argument, the court falls back on the logic of Adam Smith: any exception to law necessarily weakens it. In the words of one of the judges:

> Such a defence as this seems to be very dangerous. I do not know where we could stop. We might come to cases . . . where a party refuses to perform his contract because he had less fortune now than when he made the contract; or he might complain of defects in the plaintiff's person; he might say, had I known of such and such circumstances I should not have liked to make the engagement. The plea really comes to no more. He might complain that what he took to be a beautiful head of hair turned out to be a wig.[11]

Distinctions—and proceedings—of this kind would surely mortify Mr. Whittlestaff, yet it is exactly such distinctions upon which he pins his faint hope of making Mary his wife. He ultimately rejects legalistic thinking so as not to punish Mary by marrying her, but the court employs it to punish Brown for not marrying Beachey.

The decision in *Beachey* v. *Brown* rests upon a problematic legal distinction. It is held that the plaintiff's prior engagement is a "pre-contract" and not, therefore, "an impediment to a marriage with another party."[12] Beachey is free to marry Brown (therefore, he is obligated to marry her) because "the plaintiff has made not a previous contract of marriage, but a promise to make such a contract."[13] By this logic, engagements have little, if any, legal significance. They are simply a means to an end; a precontract, like a prefix, has meaning only in conjunction with the "contract," or word, following upon it. This differentiation, however, seems no more helpful than the suggestion in the *Examiner* that engagement is a "pause." If betrothal is a kind of nebulous pre-promise (a promise to make a promise) and only marriage is a promise proper, then what can be the meaning of promises to marry? Distinguishing between promises (betrothal) and contracts (marriage) is of limited use in resolving this quandary, because it leaves the legal status of the former entirely unclear.[14] Nor does this distinction explain why Beachey need not keep her promise to Yeales, but Brown is legally liable for breaking his promise to Beachey. (One wonders, for instance, what the outcome might have been had Yeales sued Beachey for breach of her contract with him.[15]) There is an obvious inconsistency in all of this because what seems to be a (nonbinding) precontract for the plaintiff is a (binding) contract for the defendant.

An interesting hypothetical narrative accompanies the claim that the defendant is obligated to keep his promise. The plaintiff's attorney intimates that the defendant is doubly guilty, being in effect responsible for two jiltings—one by, the other of, Beachey. In rebutting the implication that his client's romantic history speaks poorly of her character, Mr. Jones asks: "How does it appear but that the defendant might treat the breach of the existing contract as a mark of regard to himself?"[16] He insinuates that Brown is a Don Juan who has seduced his client away from her lover and heartlessly abandoned her. This possibility seems to have resonated with Justice Hill, whose opinion is accompanied by the suggestion that the "defendant might be the very person who induced the plaintiff to break that contract, by winning her from her first love: it would be hard that he should be allowed to set that up as a reason for not performing his contract or paying damages for the breach of it."[17] A slight and indirect insinuation from the plaintiff's attorney is developed into a fuller and—one imagines—a formulaic story, whose ending features poetic justice rendered by a big brother wearing black robes and wielding a mighty gavel.

The defendant's second plea—that he has been kept in the dark—is also rejected, specifically because the plaintiff does not overtly lie about her past; she merely fails fully to disclose it. Justice Crompton implies that fraud requires a sin of commission rather than omission: "Concealment may be active or passive. A man may attempt to conceal a flaw in a ship's side by fastening something over it; or he may say nothing about it. Here is nothing active."[18] What he merely suggests is expressly stated by the Chief Justice, Sir Alexander Cockburn:

> There are a great many things a man might desire to have communicated to him, and yet the non-disclosure of such circumstances—such as debts owing, excitability of temper, and other things, which a man might well desire to be made acquainted with—would not form a ground for the non-completion of the contract. It may be *morally right* that such things should be communicated to him, but he cannot excuse himself for a non-completion of the contract on such grounds.[19] (my emphasis)

As with the hypothetical hair that turns out to be a wig, the Chief Justice offers exaggerated or nebulous possibilities ("excitability of temper" or "other things") in order to dismiss ordinary and concrete actualities. The court refuses to consider the middle ground, which is precisely where the Whittlestaffs and Lawries—and probably the Beacheys and Browns—reside. Recourse to legal objectivism leads to the inevitable conclusion: "the non-disclosure of a fact, which is material in the mind of the defendant, is not enough" to justify breaking a contract.[20] As a consequence, lovers are well advised to deal with one another "at arm's length." The attorney for the plaintiff says as much when he asserts that it is "the *business* of the defendant to inquire before he makes the contract. . . . He was bound to decide for himself whether he knew enough of the circumstances to make it advisable for him to enter into the contract" (my emphasis).[21] This position amounts to little more than *caveat emptor*. Moral right might provide some consolation to the defendant, but he still must pay for a business deal gone bad.

A comparison of the novel and the trial reveals that for the characters of *An Old Man's Love* moral right outweighs legal right. Mr. Whittlestaff invokes the technicalities of the case—the time of the engagement, the absence of a prior engagement—but finally decides that for reasons of the heart a promise to marry should not be unconditional and that Mary should be released from her engagement. For her part, Mary is much more forthcoming about a much less significant detail than is Elizabeth Beachey. She errs on the side of candor, and, while she might think of herself as part of a commercial contract, her business ethics are quite different from the plaintiff's. Elizabeth Beachey relies upon the technicalities of her case (the precontractual status of betrothal, the definition of fraud in terms of active misrepresentation) to enforce her engagement without considering her fiancé's affections—whatever the state of her own might be. For Trollope, legal considerations are not unimportant, but they inform rather than decide courses of action. The trials of love should be conducted by the principals, not their proxies (whether these surrogates take the form of big brothers or bewigged barristers), and they should be conducted in private, not in public (whether these venues are clandestine, such as a field in France, or widely advertised, such as a courtroom in London).

BARDELL V. PICKWICK

It is into just such a courtroom that Mr. Pickwick is hauled on Valentine's Day, a "reg'lar good day for a breach o' promise trial" (*PP* 508). Readers have readily, but mistakenly, concluded that the guilty verdict and £750 fine are a miscarriage of justice.[22] In the popular imagination, Mrs. Bardell personifies the exploitation of breach of promise laws by the very people they are intended to protect. The view that Mr. Pickwick is traduced by Mrs. Bardell and her rapacious lawyers, however, does not do full justice to the complexities of the situation. In showing that the plaintiff does indeed have a case, Dickens exposes the liabilities: first, of construing marital promises no differently from standard commercial contracts; second, of applying unequivocal rules to ambiguous circumstances; and, third, of assuming that the conventions of legal narrative are consonant with those of ordinary stories. *The Pickwick Papers* interrogates the very stereotypes that it invokes, complicating and qualifying the satire of the legal system.

The popular narrative of breach of promise actions features Pickwicks at various stages of life ruined by the machinations of litigious and unprincipled women—usually either "young and attractive but sophisticated women" or "hungry spinsters and designing widows of the Bardell type."[23] Replacing the chivalric narrative of feminine innocence and weakness is one of female sensuality and cunning. In this version of things, every successful breach of promise action entails two seductions, that of the hapless male defendant followed by that of the helpless male jury. In *Diana of the Crossways*, Meredith suggests that one way in which men disguise their fear of female sexual power is to overwrite the tale of seduction with one of rescue. Diana Merion ridicules the jury and the justice system by imagining the impanelling of "the mysterious enshrouded Twelve" who will determine the litigants' fate. All jurors answer

> to their names of trades and crafts after the manner of Titania's elves, and were questioned as to their fitness, by education, habits, enlightenment, to pronounce decisively upon the case in dispute, the case being plainly stated. They replied, that the long habit of dealing with scales enabled them to weigh the value of evidence the most delicate. Moreover, they were Englishmen, and anything short of downright bullet facts went to favour the woman. For thus we right the balance of legal injustice toward the sex: we conveniently wink, ma'am. A rough, old-fashioned way for us! Is it a Breach of Promise?—She may reckon on her damages: we have daughters of our own.[24] (*DCW* 130)

While the unsophisticated juror broadly winks at the attractive plaintiff, the more refined among Diana's upper-class acquaintances indulge in private innuendo. Perry Wilkinson, for instance, hints that during the criminal conversation trial against Lord Dannisburgh, Diana's alleged lover, "a miniature of the incriminated lady was cleverly smuggled over to the jury, and juries sitting upon these cases, ever since their bedazzlement by Phryne, as you know . . . " (6). His insinuating ellipsis is an example of what is subsequently called "the dot language, crudely masculine" (*DCW* 390), and it suggests that the dismissal of the husband's suit proves only the power of his wife's beauty; it does not, nor could it, vindicate her character. Whether expressed in the language of winks or of ellipses, the judgments of male juries invariably redound to the discredit of female litigants. Women are susceptible to a kind of triple jeopardy involving the personal scandal of having been jilted (or accused of immoral behavior); the public dishonor of having sought legal redress (or having been named in a legal action); and the inescapable invocation of the "Phrynean complex," the belief that domestic trials, both in origin and resolution, are evidence of nothing so much as of a woman's insidious sexual power.[25]

To the gauntlet of sexual biases confronting female plaintiffs in breach of promise actions must be added the further obstacle of class prejudice. Even supporters of the action for breach of promise readily admit that no woman of the upper classes would ever consider a lawsuit. The condescension in the argument of one Member of Parliament makes this aristocratic prejudice more than clear: "It was an action little used amongst the upper classes, but in the middle and lower middle class it was most valuable."[26] Evidently women below a certain rank do not have reputations to lose. Plaintiffs are not merely assumed to be of the lower classes; they are presumed to be mercenary opportunists. The cultural narrative of innocent women ruined by false promisers is recast as a tale of wealthy men seduced by goldbricking sirens, or of hard working men of modest means preyed upon by foraging females. Well-intended laws have become a source of ill-gotten gain. In the opinion of Robert C. Brown, breach of promise actions are initiated almost exclusively by "the adventuress and the woman of shady character, who has no reputation to be lost, and whose actual needs (or better, wants) can be supplied by the coin of the realm."[27] The commingling of gender and class biases confirms the fact that, regardless of the ostensible verdict, female plaintiffs are guilty. The infamous case of *Finney* v. *Garmoyle* (1884), in which a well-known actress sues a lord, fulfills all of the stereotypes of class and gender according to which plaintiffs are judged. In the words of one editorialist commenting on the case: "when a woman brings an action of this sort she places herself beyond the pale of delicacy and sympathy. . . . It is just as if one were to interfere between a woman and a ruffian who was beating her and then find the lady suddenly putting one aside, squaring up in scientific style, and inflicting severe punishment on her injurer."[28] The pugilistic simile invokes shades of the now superfluous big brother—and expresses the writer's latent fear of gender equity. The lady in the case inflicts punishment upon her injurer to the tune of £10,000, but in the process sustains a fatal blow to her reputation. The class difference between Mrs. Bardell and her lodger is not as great as that between an actress and an aristocrat; nonetheless, Dickens's voice is easily added to the swell of opposition to breach of promise actions.

The Pickwick Papers, however, should not be read simply as erecting a maternal icon to accompany the sexual one of which Miss Finney is an avatar. The courtroom histrionics of Dodson and Fogg's "much-injured and most oppressed client" (*PP* 559) do suggest that Mrs. Bardell is an accomplished actress. No Phryne, the plaintiff can rely upon neither youth nor beauty to sway the hearts of male jurors, but she takes advantage of a mother's tears for her fatherless child "to awaken the full commiseration and sympathy of both judge and jury" (*PP* 556). Although Dickens's comic widow symbolizes in legal and popular discussion the abuses of breach of promise laws, she is not quite the consummate actress and hardened cheat featured in popular narratives. Even in the midst of litigation, for instance, Mrs. Bardell refuses to exaggerate Mr. Pickwick's faults, confessing to Sam Weller: "Whatever has happened . . . I always have said, and always will say, that in every respect but one, Mr Pickwick has always behaved himself like a perfect gentleman" (*PP* 444). Her remarks further suggest that she had no intention of entrapping her lodger: "It's a terrible thing to be dragged before the public, . . . but *I see now* that it's the only thing that I ought to do" (*PP* 446, my emphasis). The implication is that she has been persuaded to adopt her present course—perhaps by friends like Mrs. Cluppins, who says, "there *is* law for us women, mis-rable creeturs as they'd make us, if they could" (*PP* 445), and certainly by lawyers. Mrs. Bardell claims "that this business was, from the very first, fomented, and encouraged, and brought about, by these men, Dodson and Fogg" (*PP* 754). Thus some of the criticism aimed at Mrs. Bardell is deflected onto the second of the popularly conceived villains in the public debate over breach of promise laws: lawyers.

The legal profession provides a popular target for public ire and literary satire. At the close of Mary Elizabeth Braddon's *Lady Audley's Secret*, for instance, the indolent protagonist, a nonpracticing barrister, changes his irresolute ways, but, in some respects, not for the better: "Mr. Audley is a rising man upon the home circuit by this time, and has distinguished himself in the great breach of promise case of Hobbs *v*. Nobbs, and has convulsed the court by his deliciously comic rendering of the faithless Nobb's [sic] amatory correspondence."[29] Braddon's ironic sketch confirms the low regard in which breach of promise cases are held, and it emphasizes the role of the skillful lawyer in manipulating language and constructing narratives to serve self-interested ends. If Dickens softens the stereotype of women, he does nothing to mitigate the popular image of the legal profession. Mr. Pickwick recognizes the "base conspiracy between these two grasping attorneys, Dodson and Fogg" (*PP* 326), but is unable to elude their clutches. As Sam Weller says: "Battledore and shuttlecock's a wery good game, vhen you an't the shut-

tlecock and two lawyers the battledores, in which case it gets too excitin'
to be pleasant" (*PP* 351). The benefits of *Bardell* v. *Pickwick* accrue
only to lawyers, illustrating the general belief that in the legal system
"writs are issued, judgments signed, declarations filed, and numerous
other ingenious machines put in motion for the torture and torment of
His Majesty's liege subjects, and the comfort and emolument of the
practitioners of the law" (*PP* 504). When Serjeant Buzfuz transmogrifies
a case of mistaken intention into one of "revolting heartlessness and . . .
systematic villainy" (*PP* 561), and when Dodson and Fogg turn against
their own client, the heartlessness and villainy appear to reside entirely
on one side—that of the legal profession itself.[30]

Despite Dickens's indulgence in comic stereotypes of women and
lawyers, his portrayal of breach of promise is both more subtle and more
complex than the popularized interpretation of *Bardell* v. *Pickwick* indicates. The scene of the alleged promise is ambiguous and inconclusive,
illustrating both the uncertainty that may attend the "*certain form of
words*" with which promises are made and the importance of context in
determining the meaning, and even the existence, of a promise. What
begins as a comedy of errors becomes a penal tragedy for Mr. Pickwick
and a legal farce for readers. In the disputed scene, Mr. Pickwick ner-
vously and evasively broaches the subject of hiring a manservant; Mrs.
Bardell eagerly interprets his circumspect remarks as referring to marrying her. Thinking that she is recommending herself as a prospective wife,
she unwittingly encourages his plan. Neither understands—nor could be
expected to understand on the basis of what is said—the other's intentions. If anything, the nonverbal communication of the scene supports
her reading of his mysterious and unprecedented behavior. Looking
"very hard at Mrs Bardell," Mr. Pickwick says: "the person I have in my
eye . . . I think possesses these qualities" (*PP* 231). She has no way of
knowing that "eye" refers to "mind's eye" and "person" to Sam Weller.
Her observation of "a species of matrimonial twinkle in the eyes of her
lodger" (*PP* 230) is not unjustified, since Mr. Pickwick's words are given
this meaning by his body language, that is, by his looking into Mrs.
Bardell's eyes at the same time that he says, "the person I have in my
eye." Henry Sidgwick considers circumstances of precisely this kind in
The Methods of Ethics (1874). He defines promises so as to "include not
words only, but all signs and even tacit understandings not expressly signified in any way, if such clearly form a part of the engagement," and
he further notes that "obscurity and misapprehension sometimes occur;
and in the case of the tacit understandings with which promises are often
complicated, a lack of definite agreement is not improbable."[31]

This understated "lack of definite agreement" is comically overstated by Dickens. In fact, all of Pickwick's comments are consistent

with Bardell's mistaken belief that he is "going to propose" (*PP* 231).
Given the context, an eligible bachelor speaking with comely widow,
hers may be the more likely explanation. His inquiry about the cost of
keeping two rather than one and his comment upon her little boy's now
having a companion "who'll teach him . . . more tricks in a week than
he would ever learn in a year" (*PP* 232) readily support an interpretation to which "her wildest and most extravagant hopes had never dared
to aspire" (*PP* 231). However unscrupulous her subsequent behavior,
Mrs. Bardell has good reason to believe that Mr. Pickwick has proposed
marriage.

While a legal case can certainly be made for the engagement, it
would be difficult to make an ethical one, since Mr. Pickwick has never
entertained even the slightest notion of marriage to his landlady. The
scene would appear to produce an embarrassing misunderstanding, not
a contract of marriage. Sidgwick's intentional theory of promising—
employed by Maggie Tulliver in pondering the dilemma of how she
becomes "promised" to two men when she is betrothed to neither—
offers an exemption from promise-keeping that many rely upon to
exonerate Mr. Pickwick (and Maggie). The issue is

> whether, when a promise has been understood in a sense not intended
> by the promiser, he is bound to satisfy expectations which he did not
> voluntarily create. It is, I think, clear to Common Sense that he is so
> bound in some cases, if the expectation was natural and such as most
> men would form under the circumstances. . . . The normal effect of lan-
> guage is to convey the speaker's meaning to the person addressed (here
> the promiser's to the promisee), and we always suppose this to have
> taken place when we speak of a promise. If through any accident this
> normal effect is missed, we may say that there is no promise, or not a
> perfect promise.[32]

Mr. Pickwick does not intentionally raise Mrs. Bardell's expectations,
and common sense would seem to clear him of wrongdoing. Even after
taking intentions and expectations into account, however, it is unclear
that "not a perfect promise" is not a promise. Is Mrs. Bardell's "expectation . . . natural and such as most [wo]men would form under the circumstances"? If so—and it is far from out of the question that it might
be—then adjudicating the conflict between Pickwick's intention and
Bardell's expectation becomes more difficult than the jury's verdict for
the plaintiff and the public's for the defendant would indicate. While
there is no guarantee that admitting "the conditions of mind" (in
Maine's formulation) or the "question of sentiment" (in Willes's) into
its deliberations would have changed the jury's verdict, it certainly
would have made the process of reaching it more adequate to the complexity of the situation.

The radical separation of the law from its human contexts is satirized in other Dickens novels, notably *Bleak House*. Guppy proposes to Esther Summerson only after assuring himself that his offer of marriage is "without prejudice," that is, will have no legal consequences: "Would you be so kind as to allow me (as I may say) to file a declaration—to make an offer!"[33] In the context of betrothal, such legalism seems absurdly out of place, but Guppy's efforts are not all that removed from those of the Member of Parliament who urges his colleagues in 1879 to consider breach of the marriage promise "simply as a legal question. A contract was entered into between two parties, and the breach of that contract was fraught with serious injury to one party, if the other broke it heartlessly."[34] This recommendation does, in fact, describe the position generally taken by the judicial system throughout the nineteenth century, with one important qualification—heartlessness. Even the "revolting heartlessness" of which Pickwick is accused is not necessarily a relevant consideration. Justice Willes's opinion in *Hall* v. *Wright* is reconfirmed in 1893, when it is wryly observed from the bench that "love is not a necessary element in a breach of promise case."[35] Factors complicating the application of rules to circumstances, such as intentions and emotions, are dealt with by legislators and judges in the same way that Mr. Jaggers handles the client who enters his office on the verge of tears: "Now, look here my man. . . . Get out of this office. I'll have no feelings here."[36] This radical separation is an object of satire in *Great Expectations* (where it is comically replicated by Mr. Wemmick), as it is in *The Pickwick Papers*; however, if the legal system is guilty in *Bardell* v. *Pickwick*, it is not of a miscarriage of justice but of inflexible formalism. In summing up the case for the jury, Justice Stareleigh follows the "old-established and most approved form" (*PP 575*). His summation—"[if] Mrs Bardell were right, it was perfectly clear that Mr Pickwick was wrong" (*PP 575*)—is proof, not that he is an incompetent judge, but that he would make a terrible novelist.

Dickens's novel is dedicated to the propositions, first, that it is not perfectly clear that if the plaintiff is right, the defendant is wrong, and, second, that love *is* a necessary element in a breach of promise case. The fact that this is not so in legal contexts owes a good deal to a precedent-setting case heard not long before the publication of the *The Pickwick Papers*. In *Honyman* v. *Campbell* (1831), a trial that also hinges on the evidence of letters in the absence of an unambiguous promise, the Lord Chancellor resolutely dismisses any consideration of intention (or of love) in betrothal: "the only question is as to the existence of the promise. . . . There must be a promise, and the promise must be mutual and binding on both parties; for *the law attaches on the promise and not on the intention*" (my emphasis).[37] Dickens comically documents the consequences of such thinking when Sam Weller sends a valentine to his beloved—not, however, without taking legalistic precautions worthy of Mr. Guppy.[38] He makes sure that Mary, unlike Boldwood, will not discover the identity of the sender, telling his father: "Never sign a walentine with your own name" (PP 543). To do so is to become liable to "being 'wictimized'" (PP 544) in the manner of Mr. Pickwick. Sam, therefore, signs the letter, "your love-sick Pickwick," allegedly because the name is easy to spell and to rhyme, but possibly because he wants Mary to know, but not to be able to prove, the identity of the sender. The irony, of course, is that the false signature makes his employer the potential "wictim" of another breach of promise trial—one that, if Honyman v. Campbell is any indication, would easily cost Pickwick another £750 or so.

PROMISSORY BIGAMY

Legal history reveals one consistent exception to the narrative of broken promises exemplified by Honyman v. Campbell and satirized by Bardell v. Pickwick. It occurs in cases of "bigamous promises." When defendants make multiple promises, their incompatible contracts are almost invariably taken as proof of deceitful intention. This exception to the rule of excluding intent reveals that adjudicative rules are contextually bound and selectively invoked; in effect, they are themselves a part of a narrative of breach of promise. This variance in rule application confirms Stanley Fish's claim that in both "law and literature it is ways of reading, inseparable from the fact of the institution itself, and not rules or special kinds of texts that validate and justify the process of rational interpretation."[39] The "ways of reading" promissory bigamy point to an ascendant social narrative that is more significant in breach of promise trials than either expectations or intentions.

The betrothals of men either already engaged or married are such a blatant affront to Victorian values that courts readily admit intent into their deliberations. Defendants in these cases are invariably treated in the "rough, old-fashioned way" described in Diana of the Crossways. An example of such a case is Short v. Stone (1846), in which the defendant disregards his betrothal to Mary Short and marries another woman. Not surprisingly, opinions are united in favor of the plaintiff; what is surprising, however, is this comment by Chief Justice Lord Denman: "We must look at this case with a view to the feelings and intentions of the parties at the time of entering into such a contract. . . . It is unnecessary to inquire what cases, among those which have been mentioned, are analogous to this, because here the intent must be considered."[40] Particularly offensive to the court seems to have been the line of reasoning put forth by Mr. Butt on behalf of the defendant. He argues that, technically speaking, it is still possible for Stone to keep his promise to the plaintiff. His claim rests upon the conventional legal interpretation of the promise of marriage, which is that engagement implies marriage *within a reasonable time*. This deliberately ambiguous phrase is reinterpreted by Butt to mean "at a possible time"; that is, if the aggrieved plaintiff will simply wait for either divorce or death to bring about the reasonable time, the defendant will surely fulfill his promise to her. The judges concur that, even were the present Mrs. Stone to die, making it possible for the defendant to keep his promise to Mary Short, the breach occurs at the moment of his marrying another. *Short v. Stone* demonstrates that a system generally willing to take into account only the fact, and not the circumstances, of a promise does occasionally break with custom to consider "the feelings and intentions of the parties." The explanation for Lord Denman's view becomes clearer when *Short v. Stone* is seen in relation to cases in which the behavior of the defendant appears to have been even more egregious.

Men like Stone, who find themselves in the circumstance of being both betrothed and married, have little chance of avoiding a judgment for damages. In *Wild v. Harris* (1849), the defendant is already married when he becomes engaged to the plaintiff. His attorney asserts that his client cannot be liable for a promise whose fulfillment would mean violating laws against bigamy: "Here, the promise, being to do an illegal thing, is absolutely void."[41] This line of thinking seems to have impressed the court only by its outrageousness. Justice Wilde expresses "the general feelings of mankind" when he rules that "[i]t would be strange, indeed, to allow the defendant to rely upon his own wrong, to set up his fraudulent concealment of his marriage, in order to discharge himself from his promise."[42] Amazingly, this opinion does not discourage the defense attorney in *Millward v. Littlewood* (1850) from attempting the same argument. Serjeant Jones tries to circumvent the issue of "a reasonable time" by arguing that his case differs from *Wild v. Harris* in "that there the promise alleged was to marry within a reasonable time, here it is to marry generally."[43] This argument is buttressed by a familiar claim: his client's betrothal cannot be enforced because a preexisting marriage renders "a contract of this kind *contra bonos mores*, and against public policy. . . . Besides at the time of the promise, the defendant could not perform it, and, therefore, the promise is void."[44] Neither argument is accepted: in the words of Justice Parke: "The promise by the defendant to marry the plaintiff implies, on his part, that he is then capable of marrying, and he has broken that promise at the time of making it."[45] The contract cannot be literally enforced, but the defendant can be made to pay for its breach.

A comment of Chief Baron Pollock in *Millward* v. *Littlewood* indicates the strength of the court's objections to arguments like those of Butt and Jones. Pollock actually hazards a comment upon the "question of sentiment": "I think it is inconsistent with that affection which ought to subsist between married persons, that a man should, while his wife is alive, promise to marry another woman after his wife's death."[46] It should be noted, however, that there is little enthusiasm for following Pollock's lead into the realm of the affections. The other justices concur with his opinion, but neither feels it desirable to "express any opinion, whether a promise by a married man to marry a woman after his wife's death, is valid or not."[47] Such reticence notwithstanding, these cases involving men who fail sufficiently to honor the sanctity of marriage are suggestive because they so directly contravene the otherwise unvarying stance of the courts on the matter of intention. Evidently, when plaintiffs bring their stories into alignment with the cultural and ideological narratives that underwrite breach of promise laws, rules and principles are adapted accordingly. Such judicial license could not be risked when the plaintiff's story is opposed to popular narratives of married life, as they are, for example, in *Hall* v. *Wright* and *Beachey* v. *Brown*. But when men are so brazen as to disregard engagements and verbally violate their wedding vows, judges feel safe to go well beyond the forms of the law and to comment directly upon the issue of intent.

A number of general conclusions follow from this discussion of *An Old Man's Love*, *The Pickwick Papers*, and the court cases related to them. The most obvious point, perhaps, is that, with the single exception of promissory bigamy, popular and legal stories about the conduct and the contracts of courtship are incompatible. Popular narratives are about "jiltings" rather than anything so formal as "breach of the promise to marry"—about broken hearts and lost reputations more than broken contracts and lost livelihoods. Correlatively, in the popular mind, plaintiffs in breach of promise actions are shameless exploiters of the law; in the legal mind, they are innocent women who turn to surrogate family members to protect them from vile seducers. Whereas public opinion is apt to consider intentions and affections when assessing imperfect promises, legal opinion examines primarily the formal and external aspects of betrothal. As a result, the general public opposes breach of promise laws, arguing that the only people to suffer from their elimination would be "eloquent junior counsel, needy and speculative attorneys, and proprietors of newspapers"; the legal community defends them, maintaining that any weakening of the law would leave innocent women without "compensation for a bruised or broken heart, as well as any actual pecuniary loss she might have sustained."[48] Neither narrative entirely drowns out the other. The popular story has the much wider audience, but the legal narrative the more influential one, which explains why the action for breach of the promise to marry is retained long after popular sentiment turns beguiling women and conniving lawyers into icons of legalized greed.

A second point is that the interaction of popular and legal stories is pragmatically more complicated than these neat conceptual antitheses appear to suggest. A comparison of the fictional case, *Bardell* v. *Pickwick*, to the actual trial, *Bessela* v. *Stern* (1877), reveals that the popular narrative derived from (and simplifying) the novel does have significant consequences outside of the context of literature. *The Pickwick Papers* contributes to changing the procedures by which breach of promise trials are conducted, especially with regard to more stringent evidentiary standards.[49] Yet even were the revised procedures in effect at the time of *Bardell* v. *Pickwick*, it is far from certain that the result would have been different. Although "material evidence" of betrothal is required after 1869, given the interpretation of this phrase, even the testimony of "the unimpeachable female" (*PP 559*), Mrs. Cluppins, would have been sufficient to convict Mr. Pickwick. In *Bessela* v. *Stern*, the only "proof" of the engagement comes from the plaintiff's sister, who testifies to having once heard and once overheard the defendant profess his willingness to marry. Though it is difficult to see this testimony as material evidence, it is held to be conclusive by the court, despite this warning from one judge: "I see the danger of holding there was evidence in support of the promise. It is not too much to suppose that a woman under similar circumstances does sometimes fancy that a promise has been made to her."[50] In light of this case, the verdict against Mr. Pickwick is not merely unsurprising; it seems a foregone conclusion. Thus while *The Pickwick Papers* contributes to procedural reforms in Victorian courtrooms, it does little to affect the character or the outcome of breach of promise cases. Changes are enacted, but their impact is muted by judicial conservatism. The revised procedures tend to confirm rather than change legal practice. *The Pickwick Papers*, therefore, implies critique but accomplishes complicity. Popular and legal narratives may be surficially incompatible, but insofar as they bear upon how promises to marry are handled by the legal system, they gravitate toward a single closed narrative.

A third conclusion partially explains the second. The confluence of popular and legal narratives may be due to the subtending narrative of protecting the fair sex. When the stories told in court are of male promissory profligacy (*Short* v. *Stone*, *Wild* v. *Harris*, and *Millward* v. *Littlewood*), the refuge of formalism is unnecessary. Assured of the consonance of legal and popular narratives, the court feels free to discuss intentions and affections. This conclusion is consistent with Robert

Cover's account of the "language" out of which legal narratives emerge. He explains that legal traditions include "not only a corpus juris, but also a language and a mythos—narratives in which the corpus juris is located by those whose wills act upon it. These myths establish the paradigms for behavior. They build relations between the normative and the material universe."[51] This language and mythos, which is what Tanner refers to in describing Maggie's return to the language of St. Oggs, have their origin in the extralegal discourse of promising. In those instances in which the human story brought into the courtroom coincides with the mythos underwriting the system of law, justices are at liberty to invoke intention and affection. When the human story is at odds with the chivalric language and mythos, courts fall back upon principle and form. The apparent exception to principles of jurisprudence, therefore, is actually the confirmation and continuation of a traditional practice—that encoded in longstanding and deep-seated cultural stories.

My final conclusion concerns the general circumstance of realistic fiction to which *The Pickwick Papers* constitutes an exception. While judges are reluctant to admit questions of the heart into the law, it is also the case that writers are equally hesitant to introduce the law into matters of the heart. Dickens's satire concerns a legal action that seldom finds its way into the pages of a realistic novel. The general exclusion of breach of promise trials from fiction, however, is parallel in effect to the admission of intent into the courtroom: it tends to confirm an underlying cultural narrative. By removing potentially litigable courtship practices from the courtroom and returning them to the drawing room, novelists may simply be reinscribing the view that romance and engagement are private affairs; therefore, they may simply be retelling a conservative social narrative about romantic love. This is not to say, however, that depictions of betrothal in fiction are invariably conservative—quite the contrary. Freed from the pragmatic objectives and legal constraints, novelistic representations of promising can be more innovative and more "true" than their nonfictional counterparts.

THE TRUTH OF LEGAL FICTIONS

Before turning to such novels, I would like to take up the question, not of the differences between legal and extralegal narratives, but of what they have in common. Whether authorized by license of the bar or generated by poetic license, what characteristics do successful narratives share? To begin this inquiry, I will return briefly to the scene of Mr. Pickwick's introduction to the convention of "legal fictions." On his way to court, Mr. Pickwick encounters "three or four men of shabby-genteel appearance" and wonders "to what branch of the profession these dingy-looking loungers could possibly belong" (*PP* 656). His attorney, Mr. Perker, explains to his incredulous client that their presence can be accounted for by the legal fiction of sham bail:

> "Yes, my dear sir—half a dozen of 'em here. Bail you to any amount, and only charge half-a-crown. Curious trade isn't it?" said Perker, regaling himself with a pinch of snuff.
>
> "What! Am I to understand that these men earn a livelihood by waiting about here, to perjure themselves before the judges of the land, at the rate of half-a-crown a crime!" exclaimed Mr Pickwick, quite aghast at the disclosure.
>
> "Why, I don't exactly know about perjury, my dear sir," replied the little gentleman. "Harsh word, my dear sir, very harsh word indeed. It's a legal fiction, my dear sir, nothing more." (*PP* 657–58)

This legal fiction legitimizes and incarnates what would otherwise be a form of illegal fiction, perjury. In exchange for a small sum, "a slim and rather lame man in rusty black, and a white neckerchief" (*PP* 656), completely unknown to Mr. Pickwick, is prepared to vouch for his character, while the court willingly suspends its disbelief. Mr. Perker is right: it is a "curious trade"—and a "trade" in the sense not only of profession but also of the sale of truth for cash and convenience. The difference between legal and illegal fictions, between acceptable and unacceptable lies, entails more than simply harsh words. By calling attention to something that the legal community would describe as a fiction but that the general public might more aptly call a lie, this scene invites examination of the meaning and status of fictions both within and outside of the law.

Sir Henry Sumner Maine views fictions as one of several means of legal evolution—a position also advanced by Sheldon Amos, who writes in *The Science of Law* (1872) that legal fictions are the means by which "the imaginative reverence for old symbols and formalities is deferred to while more or less perceptible change is introduced into the substance of the law."[52] For Jeremy Bentham, however, a legal fiction is nothing more than an officially sanctioned fraud: a "vile lie" of use to nobody "but the inventors and utterers of it, and their confederates."[53] The principle of utility dictates that truth-telling is always preferable to lying; therefore, even if the fiction were perpetuated for beneficial reasons—as Maine and Amos contend—why not simply enact the changes necessary to accomplish the particular goal without the fiction and its attendant deception? Bentham caustically observes that there can be only two reasons for legal fictions: "either that of doing in a roundabout way what they [judges] might do in a direct way, or that of doing in a roundabout way what they had no right to do in any way at all."[54] His animus rivals Pickwick's incredulity, and the source of his censure goes beyond an objection to the self-serving mystifications of legal jargon to encompass the misuse of all language.

Everyday discourse does require, in Bentham's view, the use of "fictions"—words and expressions necessary for communication but that do not refer to actual things. We talk, for instance, as if there were something like the "mind," but we should not assume that the word refers to a known entity: "To language, then—to language alone—it is that fictitious entities owe their existence; their impossible, yet indispensable existence."[55] Fictitious terms facilitate the business of daily living, thinking, and talking, but they compound the inherent tendency to verbal confusion lamented by scholars from Locke to Mill. Lest unwary speakers fall into the careless error of accepting words for things, fictions should be avoided whenever possible and identified when not. While linguistic fictions may be necessary, even beneficial, legal fictions are neither. Even when not employed in questionable ways, legal fictions are detrimental because they consciously condone deviations from "the truth, the whole truth, and nothing but the truth."

Bentham's view of the legal system and its fictions is not far removed from Dickens's portrayal of the Circumlocution Office or, for that matter, from Carroll's depiction of the trial of the Knave of Hearts (another case hinging upon indeterminate written evidence). Although Alice prides herself on legal knowledge gleaned from newspapers, she could not possibly make sense of proceedings in which rules are invented on the spot, evidence lacks "an atom of meaning," and sentences precede verdicts.[56] The King of Hearts, in his capacity as judge, cannot quite decide whether Alice's testimony is one thing or its opposite: "important—unimportant—unimportant—important"(AW 93), and his pun—"Then the words don't *fit* you" (AW 96)—is especially fitting since fitting words to circumstances is exactly what it at issue in trials—and in the legal fiction of sham bail. Presented with this fiction, Mr. Pickwick might well wonder: "appearance—nonappearance—nonappearance—appearance," since the process of securing bail obliterates the distinction between them. Bentham explains how it works:

> The defendant pays an attorney, who pays an officer of the court for making in one of the books of the court an entry, importing that on such a day two persons bound themselves to stand as sureties for the defendant; undertaking, in the event of his losing his cause, and being ordered to comply with the plaintiff's pecuniary demand, either to pay the money for the defendant or to render his body up to prison. No such engagement has been taken by anybody.—The persons spoken of as having taken it, are not real persons but imaginary persons; a pair of names always the same, John Doe and Richard Roe.[57]

By means of this sleight of hand, a defendant is able to be "constantly present in a place where he never set his foot."[58] The profit from this magic act goes to courts and lawyers, who charge fees for the feat of prestidigitation, and to the bondsmen themselves, who stand to earn "half-a-crown" if employed by the likes of Mr. Pickwick—and, of course, to defendants who need not wait in prison for their trial and who might wish to stage a disappearing act of their own.

Sham bail provides an apt introduction to the larger issue of (extra) legal narratives because it foregrounds the key issue of language and narrative in relation to things and experience. The legal fiction intended to secure appearance in fact accomplishes nonappearance, deliberately confusing the antonymic meanings of "appearance" in everyday usage.[59] Narrators of any tale necessarily engage this contradictory logic of (non)appearance (as do promisers) and necessarily allow words "to work by their own force." To do so, whether addressing a jury of peers or simply peers, tellers employ conventions common to all forms of narrative—conventions that obscure the distinction between real and fictitious entities, or, in other words, that function in the same manner as the legal fiction of sham bail.

The role of the narrative in law has been a subject of increasing interest among scholars, whose attention turns to the degree to which all levels of the legal system, from written laws and unwritten practices to courtrooms and legislative chambers, are imbued with aspects of storytelling. A legal action, for example, typically begins with a client's tale, which is then recast by lawyers and contested in court, and it concludes with yet another retelling in the form of a jury's verdict or a judge's opinion. James Boyd White thus describes law as a "literary and rhetorical system" that

> is a way of telling a story about what has happened in the world and claiming a meaning for it by writing an ending to it. . . . The process is at heart a narrative one because there cannot be a legal case without a real story about real people actually located in time and space and culture. . . . The story will in the first instance be told in the language of its actors. That is where the law begins; in a sense this is also where it ends, for its object is to provide an ending to that story that will work in the world.[60]

A process of translation is at work here, from and back into "the language of its actors." The more successful legal narratives are those inflicting the least violence upon this language—those establishing the closest fit, as the Red King might say, between the stories told at the outset and the conclusion of the proceedings. Put in these terms, although their language differs, the work of the lawyer is not so different from that of the novelist. The attorney must craft a story or an interpretation that will be persuasive with juries and judges. Toward that end, a grasp of the requirements of storytelling is as important as a firm command of the facts in the case.

The narrative or rhetorical aspects of an account, whether legal, historical, or literary, are crucial to its suasiveness. The long-established recognition that realism in literature is a matter of stylistic and generic conventions is equally relevant to the various "narratives of law," from the sworn statements of John Doe, Richard Roe, and the "three or four men of shabby-genteel appearance" awaiting employment outside of Sergeant's Inn; to the passionate narrative of Serjeant Buzfuz before the Court of Common Pleas; and no less to the encompassing sociocultural narratives underwriting the judicial process overseen by the "two queer little eyes" (*PP* 554) of Justice Stareleigh. The statements made during trials by lawyers and witnesses are persuasive to the degree that they adhere to the conventions that have come to signify a truthful or a probable story in a given place and time. As Bernard S. Jackson puts it in *Law, Fact, and Narrative Coherence*: "Truth is a function not of discourse, but of the enunciation of discourse. If we cannot judge whether the semantic content of stories ('factual' or 'fictional') is true, we can at least judge who we think is *telling the truth*, in the sense of most adequately persuading us that s/he is fulfilling the sincerity conditions of the act of making a truth-claim."[61] This statement succinctly formulates "the law of narratives," which asserts that our sense of reality owes less to the facts of a case than to the way in which they are narrated. If this is so, then it may be more accurate to say that stories themselves, rather than individuals, are on trial in the courtroom.

Narrative probability is a significant factor in determining legal outcomes. Another way, therefore, to formulate the "law of narratives" is to amend Aristotle's famous dictum to read: "With respect to the requirements of art *and of law*, a probable impossibility is to be preferred to a thing improbable and yet possible."[62] Probability depends to a great extent upon two narrative categories, correspondence and coherence, and Serjeant Buzfuz fully understands the significance of both. He shapes Mrs. Bardell's story to correspond with the encompassing cultural narrative upon which breach of promise laws are based and with the narrative forms prescribed by those laws. In doing so, he conjoins justice, as demanded by law, and poetic justice, as defined by his own melodramatic narrative. He also constructs a completely coherent plot, one in which no fact is left unexplained and all factors point to a single conclusion. In doing so, he attains jurispathic success. When the trial is over, his is the only story left standing.

Buzfuz's tale, however, is embedded within the narrator's legal fiction, which reverses the judgment against the defendant. The reversal of the verdict is unanimous because the narrator succeeds on three distinct levels of narrative correspondence: extratextual, intertextual, and intratextual. Extratextual correspondence refers to the common views, first, that true stories are those that reflect common experience and, second, that reality can be passively and neutrally conveyed in language. These assumptions, for instance, explain Mr. Pickwick's unusual pretrial visit to Serjeant Snubbin. Susceptible to Lucius Mason's bias that "all lawyers are liars," Pickwick fears that his attorney will resort to trickery rather than appeal to truth: "You know from your experience of juries . . . how much depends upon *effect*: and you are apt to attribute to others, a desire to use, for purposes of deception and self-interest, the very instruments which you, in pure honesty and honour of purpose, and with a laudable desire to do your utmost for your client, know the temper and worth of so well, from constantly employing them yourselves" (*PP* 518). Mr. Pickwick wants "the truth and nothing but the truth"; however, what he dismisses as mere "*effect*" constitutes a significant part of the narratives of both law and fiction. The attorneys for the plaintiff are the masters of such effects, as is demonstrated by Mrs. Bardell's histrionic entrance into the courtroom—a performance that impresses even Pickwick's attorney: "Capital fellows those Dodson and Fogg; excellent ideas of effect, my dear sir, excellent" (*PP* 556). Pickwick is abashed by his solicitor's approval of the meretricious production. The bare facts are obscured by showy performances. Fictions outside of a trial (such as sham bail) are bad enough, but fictions during the proceedings are an outrage.

Mr. Pickwick subscribes to a long-standing suspicion of rhetoric. In his mind, the truth stands apart from the telling of the truth. This view is expressed by another Dickens hero who runs afoul of the law, George Rouncewell:

> "I have stated to the magistrates, 'Gentlemen, I am as innocent of this charge as yourselves; what has been stated against me in the way of facts, is perfectly true; I know no more about it.' I intend to continue stating that, sir. What more can I do? It's the truth."
> "But the mere truth won't do," rejoined my guardian. (*BH* 620)

Dickens implies that legal theatrics have become so sophisticated that "truth" must now be modified by "mere." Mr. Jarndyce's skepticism is famously echoed by Mrs. Bagnet: "It won't do to have truth and justice on his side; he must have law and lawyers" (*BH* 656). Like Rouncewell, Pickwick admits facts unfavorable to himself; for example, he will not allow Serjeant Snubbin to cross-examine Mrs. Cluppins because "her account was in substance correct" (*PP* 565). This dedication to moral principle and integrity of character may be admirable, but insisting upon narratives untainted by rhetoric is hazardous. Left to their own resources, these two innocent victims of the "dreadful conjunction of appearances" (*PP* 326) face bleak consequences.

Eliot's trope of the novelist as sworn witness, for instance, is a Pickwickian attempt to minimize the impact of the teller upon the tale and to diminish readers' suspicion of rhetoric. Her narrator shuns the role of "clever novelist" and is "content to tell my simple story, without trying to make things seem better than they were; dreading nothing, indeed, but falsity" (*AB* 222). Pickwick would have Snubbin play the same role, with the result of further criticizing a system in which "the mere truth" leads to a false verdict. Dickens adopts the identical stance; he is a truthful and an authoritative witness. In correcting the false stories of Buzfuz and others, he exonerates Mr. Pickwick, strikes a blow for "the mere truth," and reaffirms the principle of extratextual correspondence.

Although the narrator's tale is persuasive because it corresponds with what actually happened (i.e., with the "fictional reality" of the novel), the success of *The Pickwick Papers* with the reading public reveals the extent to which Dickens is also the master of intertextual correspondence—the matching of courtroom stories to ideological narratives. Recent empirical studies of juried trials confirm that "people carry around with them a stock of socially constructed narratives, acquired through the whole range of their social experience (including education). A significant factor affecting the plausibility of a newly-communicated story is the degree to which it fits a narrative which already exists within this stock of social knowledge."[63] Juries are charged to decide the facts of a case, but they will do so by comparing those facts with the ideological narratives according to which they make sense of themselves and their world. Dickens's story clearly suits popular Victorian stereotypes of lawyers, plaintiffs, and their carefully staged performances—a point confirmed by cases like *Short* v. *Stone*, *Wild* v. *Harris*, and *Millward* v. *Littlewood*. Verdicts for female plaintiffs are most certain, and judicial comments most pointed, when narratives are intertextually correspondent. Defense attorneys like Butt, Jones, and Snubbin have little chance when the plaintiff's tale is closely linked to prevailing narratives of gender and chivalry. Serjeant Buzfuz directly appeals to the mythos of female virtue wronged, and his story is doubly effective because it involves a second sacred myth, that of the child. The appearance of the distressed mother and her fatherless child has an immediate impact: "the judge was visibly affected, and several of the beholders tried to cough down their emotions" (*PP* 556). The guilty verdict is assured from the moment that Buzfuz's masterful tale reinforces the stories that the jurors have doubtlessly heard and told throughout their lives.

The third level of narrative correspondence entails the translation of a litigant's story "in his own words" into the appropriate legal genre. Intratextual correspondence is not a matter of convincing a jury that a story is probable but of insuring that a plaintiff's or defendant's story conforms to the forms of the law—as, for example, the defendant fails to do in *Hall* v. *Wright*. Irrespective of extra- or intertextual correspondence, stories fail if not couched in terms that suit the generic criteria for legal narratives. This point is also supported by empirical study. Litigants who speak for themselves and not through legal counsel "often lack any understanding that the law imposes highly specific requirements on narratives. In presenting accounts in court, witnesses rely on the conventions of everyday narratives about trouble and their informal cultural assumptions about justice. From the law's perspective, such accounts often have disabling shortcomings."[64] Failing to match personal narrative with the appropriate legal form, individuals are likely to feel that they have been victimized by the law. Such surely is the case with Mr. Pickwick, whose imprisonment bespeaks a system obsessed with technicality, obscured by jargon, driven by fulsome rhetoric, and typified by specious theatricals. The coalescence of intra- and intertextual narratives and the suppression of the extratextual narrative (defendants are not allowed to testify in breach of promise actions) leave no possibility within the law for hearing the story of an innocent man.

THE SEXUAL NARRATIVE: HYMEN(E)AL BREACHES

Outside the law, of course, Mr. Pickwick is acquitted, and his narrative is rewritten as the tale of an ordinary citizen and plain speaker defeated, but not corrupted, by crafty lawyers and a self-serving system of justice. The defendant's acquittal in the popular imagination, however, is no less an "*effect*" of narrative than is his conviction in the courtroom. Dickens's orchestration of the trial exemplifies this point. By presenting Pickwick's instructions to Snubbin and by eliding most of Snubbin's and Phunky's part in the trial, Dickens keeps the hero in quarantine, isolated from association with and contamination by the law and lawyers. Dickens himself remains detached from the infection of law by presenting evidence of Pickwick's case from the extra- and antilegal perspective of the narrator. More significant than this legal prophylaxis, however, is Pickwick's sexual innocence. Dickens is able to overturn the jury's verdict by keeping Pickwick free from the taint, not of law, but of sexuality. Were Pickwick more like Don Juan than Don Quixote, his conviction with the public would be assured, but, as it is, even a narrativist much less skilled than Dickens would prevail in the court of public opinion.

That sexual narratives underwrite the story of breach of promise is clear from the history of trials in which male defendants fare better than Pickwick. If, for example, neither Beachey's engagement nor Wright's tuberculosis is sufficient grounds, when might a man break an engagement without legal liability? As surely as Stone, Harris, and Littlewood must pay, defendants are exonerated if they can establish the plaintiff's licentiousness. Initially, English common law accepts a number of reasons for unilaterally ending a betrothal, but the allowable defenses are narrowed drastically by the 1850s. At the beginning of the century, for instance, bad character alone is a sufficient reason for breaking one's promise of marriage. In *Foulkes* v. *Selway* (1801), the verdict for the defendant is based solely on the plaintiff's bad reputation among her neighbors: "Character here was the only point in issue. That was public opinion, founded on the conduct of the party, and was fair subject of enquiry; he therefore thought, that what that public thought, was evidence on the issue as it then stood."[65] At this relatively early stage, judges are also willing to consider the prospects for happiness in marriage and to exonerate defendants when evidence suggests that promises, if kept, would contribute only to the unhappiness of both parties. Thus Lord Ellenborough sums up *Leeds* v. *Cook & Wife* (1803) in this way: "if the Plaintiff had conducted himself in a brutal or violent manner, and threatened to use her ill, a woman, under such circumstances, had a right to say she would not commit her happiness to such keeping; and she might set up such defence, and it would be legal."[66] Although Mrs. Cook's plea does not go this far, Ellenborough's opinion indicates a leniency toward promise breakers that diminishes from this point on. The issue of bad character is still a legitimate defense in 1816, but evidentiary standards are higher than in *Foulkes* v. *Selway*. In *Baddeley* v. *Mortlock and Wife*, Chief Justice Gibbs rules: "If a woman improvidently promise to marry a man, who turns out upon inquiry to be of bad character, she is not bound to perform her promise. But she must shew that the plaintiff is a man of bad character. The accusation is not enough."[67] Ultimately, however, bad character carries no more weight with judges than does bad hair, as *Beachey* v. *Brown* documents.

As the issue of character becomes less important, so too does the definition of character become more narrow. In time, it comes to mean only one thing: sexual behavior. In *Irving* v. *Greenwood* (1824), for instance, the plaintiff has a child after her engagement but before her marriage. In summing up the case for the jury, the judge outlines the decisive issue: "If you think that the defendant was not the father of the child, he is entitled to your verdict; for if any man, who has made a promise of marriage, discovers that the person he has so promised to marry is with child by another man, he is justified in breaking such promise."[68] "Loose and immodest" behavior by plaintiffs becomes and remains the one sure defense against breach of the promise actions. Two cases of 1844 further illustrate the narrowed definition of bad character. In *Harbert* v. *Edgington*, the defendant's plea is based upon his learning (after becoming engaged) that his fiancée is not "a person of sober and temperate habits"; in fact, she is "in the habit of getting drunk with wine and spirituous liquors."[69] In *Bench* v. *Merrick*, the defendant argues that his breach is justified because he does not learn until after his betrothal that his future wife is "a woman of unchaste and immodest behaviour, and of incorrect habits and conduct, and bad character and reputation"—which is to say that she had an illegitimate child some ten years earlier.[70] The defense based on drunkenness is rejected; that alleging sexual misconduct, although based entirely on a single incident a decade earlier, is accepted.

Bench v. *Merrick* presents a unified inter- and intratextual narrative of women's sexual impurity subsequently challenged by *Tess of the d'Urbervilles*. The "great campaign" of Hardy's heroine begins "after an event in her experience which has usually been treated as fatal to her part of protagonist"—and, it must be added, of wife.[71] The cases are remarkably similar. Both the plaintiff in the trial and the protagonist of the novel are condemned by their lovers and rejected by society for having been seduced by economic superiors; both give birth to children who do not survive infancy; considerably after the deaths of their children, both become engaged to men who are themselves guilty of prior sexual misconduct.[72] Bench, like Tess, tries but fails to tell her fiancé of her sexual history: "she had written three of four letters to explain her situation herself, but had not courage to send them."[73] Neither man, on the contrary, reveals his past nor feels it important that he do so, and neither appears to suffer serious social repercussions from his behavior and silence. For both women, sexual pasts have dramatic consequences. Sorrow, Tess's illegitimate child, condemns her in Angel's eyes as surely as Bench is condemned in Merrick's—and her society's.

Hardy might have had reason to hope that Tess would be exonerated by a jury of her peers, had he known of the presiding officer's summation for the jury in *Bench* v. *Merrick*. Serjeant Atcherley considerably tempers the representation of the plaintiff as an unchaste and immodest woman: "There is no imputation whatever on the character of the plaintiff except the transaction of 1831. If the defendant, in your opinion, has not established his defence, there will then be the question of damages; and in that case, in consequence of the misfortune (calling it by no harsher name) in 1831, the plaintiff cannot be said to be entitled to so large a compensation as one on whose reputation no imputation had ever rested."[74] "Transaction" and "misfortune" are far from the judgmental terms that one expects, and they suggest that Atcherley hopes that the plaintiff would prevail. Hardy provides even more explicit instructions to his "jury," not only in the subtitle, "A Pure Woman Faithfully Presented," but also in repeated narrative comments to the effect that Tess's misfortune derives from "nothing more tangible than a sense of condemnation under an arbitrary law of society which had no foundation in Nature" (*TD* 353). Despite these judicial/authorial instructions, the protagonists are condemned for their "transactions," revealing that sexual attitudes change very little between 1844 and 1891. Merrick is vindicated, Angel is rewarded with Liza Lu (coincidentally, Bench's child is fathered by her sister's husband), and Hardy, whose novels seem never to suit the intertextual narratives of his day, soon abandons novel writing altogether.

The social principle by which Tess stands convicted is well established in law by mid-century. The verdicts in *Harbert* v. *Edgington* and *Bench* v. *Merrick* are indirectly confirmed in *Beachey* v. *Brown* (1860). The plaintiff's prior engagement is immaterial; only the sexual question is relevant. In rejecting Brown's plea, Chief Justice Cockburn adverts to the one accepted defense against the charge of breach of promise: "Where it turns out that a woman is of unchaste conduct, which goes to the very root of the contract of marriage, . . . the man is released from his contract."[75] Once freedom of contract is firmly established as the dominant principle of English jurisprudence, previously accepted defenses are summarily rejected. For instance, while "bodily infirmity arising after the contract is a good reason for either party to break it off" in 1796, the loss of health is clearly not a good defense after *Hall* v. *Wright* in 1859.[76] The 1868 edition of Joseph Chitty's *A Treatise on the Law of Contracts and upon Defences to Actions Thereon* confirms that "no infirmity, bodily or mental which may supervene or be discovered after the making of the contract to marry—*unless it be incapacity on the part of the man or want of chastity on the part of the woman*—can be relied upon by either, as a ground for refusing to perform such contract" (my emphasis).[77] The allowable defenses (male impotence, female chastity) clearly establish betrothal as a promise of sexual exclusivity, in addition to reinscribing a sexual double standard (Chitty is as silent as Merrick and Clare on the subject of male chastity).

When Tess asks herself, "Was once lost always lost really true of chastity?" (*TD* 150), it is clear that Hardy's answer is different from his society's. The history of the pleas in breach of promise cases indicates that social laws become, if anything, more draconian during the half-century preceding the publication of the novel. An essay on the same subject published in 1946 further suggests that sexual attitudes do not change all that much in the fifty years or so after its publication. W. J.

Brockelbank, a staunch opponent of the action for breach of promise to marry, offers this sarcastic observation: "Be it noted that our courts seem to demand only that the plaintiff be *virgo intacta*. All is a question of the condition of the flesh. The mind may be poisoned with filth, and the character hardened by ugly habits; in short, the spiritual hymen may have suffered many a breach, but if the physical one is intact, the defendant will have no better alternative than to marry her or pay damages."[78] Hardy, of course, poses the converse situation—physical breach and spiritual integrity—but a similar conclusion can be drawn: breach of promise actions, to say nothing of public definitions of morality, hinge upon a trivial, albeit an often objectively verifiable, criterion.

This criterion explains a previously undiscussed aspect of *Hall* v. *Wright*. One of the judges in the case addresses the role of sexuality in betrothal and marriage in an unusually frank way—frank, that is, by Victorian standards. The issue of sexual relations arises because the defendant's plea does not clearly conform to intratextual narratives of allowable pleas. Uncertain of what Wright means by the averment that he is "incapable of marriage without great danger to his life," the justices try to imagine just what it is about marriage that might be life-threatening. Is the danger posed by the marriage ceremony itself, the consummation of the marriage, or the general duties of the married state? The layman's response might well be an exasperated, "What's the difference?", but in light of the allowable defenses cited by Chitty, the second contingency is of particular relevance. If the defendant is physically incapable of fulfilling the sexual contract, then it can be argued that a valid marriage is impossible, since only marriages that have been consummated are legally recognized. In the words of one of the justices, if Wright cannot consummate the marriage, although he can "go through the ceremony of marriage; . . . he cannot marry: the ceremony would not be binding: . . . and the contract to marry is broken by the calamity of his becoming impotent."[79] This line of argument, however, places the court in the unusual situation of enforcing a contract that cannot be performed. This anomaly, accepted in cases of defendants' promissory bigamy, is more troubling in *Hall* v. *Wright* because the breach owes more to an act of God than to male misconduct.

To some extent, *Hall* v. *Wright* hinges upon the lawyers' failure in the courtroom rather than the defendant's hypothetical failure in the bedroom. Lord Campbell opines that Wright's story would have been more forceful had he provided "evidence that, at the time when he ought to have married the plaintiff, he had become unfit for the procreation of children without danger to his life."[80] Since impotence is not the issue in his opinion, Campbell decides for the plaintiff. Justice Bramwell, by contrast, sees the sexual issue as central to the case and reframes the argument in terms of sexual satisfaction rather than of reproductive duty. He so fully realizes his "desire to speak with all reserve," however, that modern audiences might find it difficult to recognize the melodramatic tale of sexual passion embedded in his hypothetical narrative of the litigants' married life:

> to possess the lawful means of gratifying a powerful passion with the alternative of abstaining or perilling life is indeed to incur a risk of "intense misery instead of mutual comfort:" and it does seem to me, with great respect, a great mistake to lose sight of these considerations, and suppose happiness can be found in such a marriage by the gratification of an innocent desire to enjoy the *consortium vitæ* with the man, obtain rank and station as his wife, and be dowable of his lands. Moreover, this is to think only of the woman and not of the man, who might object that her wishes, however innocent, were very unreasonable towards him in wishing him to put himself in the temptation of perilling his life; and he might even doubt the innocence of such a desire.[81]

Bramwell's comparative frankness produces a story that—in its most innocent version—entails irresistible sexual urges and ensuing marital discord and that—at its most melodramatic—involves material acquisitiveness and murder by means of carnal intercourse. It is a startlingly dark and sexually charged hymeneal tale. Modesty and legalese notwithstanding, the judge provides a dramatic demonstration of the pivotal role of narrative in law.

Such sensational tales (and from such sources) are rare, even in morally suspect genres like the novel. Of the works considered in the succeeding chapters, only *The Wings of the Dove* includes a sexual compact of the sort seen in *Finlay* v. *Chirney* (1888), a case in which the plaintiff is seduced "under a promise of marriage, a child being born in August, 1884." Finlay loses her suit for several reasons, including the fact that her arrangement with the defendant is held to be "contrary to public policy, morality and decency."[82] The same might well be said of Kate Croy's acquiescence to Merton Densher's sexual agreement in *The Wings of the Dove*, a novel that generally exhibits Justice Bramwell's reserve as well as his melodramatic vision. James is uninterested in the legal ramifications of his characters' promises, which include a secret engagement, seduction, a redefined betrothal, and its apparent abandonment. He explores their emotional consequences and, like Hardy, challenges restrictive sociolegal formulae, whether hymenal or hymeneal. Irrespective of concerns about extratextual correspondence, Hardy and James, like novelists generally, enjoy latitude not granted their legal colleagues. They are, therefore, typically concerned less with correspondence than with coherence—the issue to which I now turn.

THE FICTION OF LEGAL TRUTHS

The issue of coherence arises in the scene of Mr. Pickwick's introduction to sham bail. Not understanding the situation and "not wishing to hurt the man's feelings by refusing" (*PP* 657), Pickwick accepts a card and nods to the man proffering it—actions tantamount to a promise of employment. When observed by Mr. Perker, the man is quickly dismissed:

> "I beg your pardon, sir," said the lame man. "The gentleman took my card. I hope you will employ me, sir. The gentleman nodded to me. I'll be judged by the gentleman himself. You nodded to me, sir?"
>
> "Pooh, pooh, nonsense. You didn't nod to any body, Pickwick? A mistake, a mistake," said Perker.
>
> "The gentleman handed me his card," replied Mr Pickwick, producing it from his waistcoat-pocket. "I accepted it, as the gentleman seemed to wish it—in fact I had some curiosity to look at it when I should be at leisure. I—"
>
> The little attorney burst into a loud laugh, and returning the card to the lame man, informing him it was all a mistake, whispered to Mr Pickwick as the man turned away in dudgeon, that he was only a bail. (*PP* 657)

In displaying the manners of a gentleman, Mr. Pickwick unwittingly invokes the conventions of an entirely different language. The prospective bail construes Pickwick's actions according to the practices of his "branch of the profession," understandably thinking that his services have been engaged. The mistake is easily rectified by Perker; however, it emphasizes the propensity of even quite simple incidents to generate ambiguities. The trivial exchange between Pickwick and the bail is open to two coherent, but entirely incompatible, narratives.

The incident at Sergeant's Inn provides an apt analogue to that leading to Pickwick's arrest in the first place. Both instances are characterized by ambiguous actions and mistaken engagements. The exchange between Pickwick and Mrs. Bardell lends itself with equal justification to drastically different interpretations depending upon one's initial assumption. Both stories of engagement—that is, of Sam and to Martha—are compelling not only because they correlate with the "facts" but also because they are internally consistent. The exchange between Pickwick and the sham bail may be read with equal facility in different languages, that of the gentleman (or the Benthamite philosopher), who despises any untruth, and that of the court system, which depends for its smooth operation upon any number of legal fictions. Thus with no awareness of having made either of them, Mr. Pickwick breaks two engagements: one to Mrs. Bardell and the other to the sham bail.

One reason that Mrs. Bardell is not as easily dismissed as a semireputable member of the legal underclass is that her story is placed in the hands of a skilled narrator, who transforms it into a remarkably coherent narrative. Serjeant Buzfuz weaves a tale that consistently meets the criteria of good melodrama. There is a virtuous heroine, "the lonely and desolate widow"; a rank villain in an exotic setting, "the ruthless destroyer of this domestic oasis in the desert of Goswell Street"; and a suspenseful plot: "[t]he serpent was on the watch, the train was laid, the mine was preparing, the sapper and miner was at work" (*PP* 60–63). Buzfuz offers comedy (although his attempt at humor is quickly followed by a "relapse into the dismals" [*PP* 563]), romance, and a happy ending—so long as the jury will cooperate in the final chapter. In *The Melodramatic Imagination*, Peter Brooks observes that recognizing the forces of evil in melodrama often "requires a full-fledged trial, the public hearing and judgment of right against wrong, where virtue's advocates deploy all arms to win the victory of truth over appearance and to explain the deep meaning of enigmatic and misleading signs. This clarification of signs . . . is the necessary precondition for the reestablishment of the heroine."[83] In decoding the cryptic letters, explaining the ambiguous proposal, and vindicating the "desolate widow," Serjeant Buzfuz authors a perfect melodramatic plot. His "story in the trial," therefore, is fully the equal of Dickens's ironic "story of the trial," which presents an entirely different explanation for Mrs. Bardell's desolation.[84]

The "clarification of signs" is the salient feature of Buzfuz's narrative of evil insinuating itself into the garden on Goswell Street. A uniform reading of base betrayal is placed upon all of the mundane details of Mr. Pickwick's dealings with his landlady, including his seemingly innocuous correspondence. Two brief notes—the first reading: "Chops and Tomata sauce"; the second: "I shall not be at home till to-morrow. Slow coach. Don't trouble yourself about the warming pan" (*PP* 562–63)—suddenly become "enigmatic and misleading." According to the plaintiff's attorney, they "are covert, sly, underhanded communications, but, fortunately, far more conclusive than if couched in the most glowing language and the most poetic imagery" (*PP* 562). In his construction, the warming pan is significant by virtue of its very insignificance:

> Why is Mrs Bardell so earnestly entreated not to agitate herself about this warming pan, unless (as is no doubt the case) it is a mere cover for hidden fire—a mere substitute for some endearing word or promise, agreeably to a preconcerted system of correspondence, artfully contrived by Pickwick with a view to his contemplated desertion, and which I am not in a condition to explain? (*PP* 563)

Apart from the characteristics of Buzfuzian rhetoric—the reliance upon rhetorical question, the argument *from* metaphor (a warming pan can be expected to cover a fire) and *by* metaphor (the letter itself must be a figurative warming pan)—this argument is of interest as an instance of the hermeneutic logic in evidence throughout the tale. His thinking resembles that of the King of Hearts, who, in response to the Knave's claims that he did not write the unsigned letter and that it cannot be proven that he did, says: "If you didn't sign it . . . that only makes the matter worse. You *must* have meant some mischief, or else you'd have signed your name like an honest man" (*AW* 94). In both cases, obvious meanings are discarded in favor of concealed significances, and the inferred secret meaning is then confirmed by a contradictory return to the norm of ordinary behavior. Common sense dictates, for instance, that honest men sign letters and virtuous bachelors do not concern themselves with domestic details. Hence Buzfuz asks the jury, "[W]ho *does* trouble himself about a warming-pan? When was the peace of mind of man or woman broken or disturbed by a warming-pan, which is in itself a harmless, a useful, and I will add, gentlemen, a comforting article of domestic furniture?" (*PP* 563). In agreeing that warming pans are harmless, useful, and perhaps even comforting, the jury finds itself agreeing that this particular warming pan must contain simmering passions. A trivial domestic note, therefore, becomes evidence for a double sexual plot, the first, between the lovers themselves and, the second, by one of them against the other.

Dickens might be suspected of exaggerating in *Bardell* v. *Pickwick*, but at least one contemporary judge, Lord Fitzgerald, feels that Buzfuz's methods are, if anything, unnecessarily moderate and circumspect. Referring to the first letter, for example, he maintains that "Buzfuz lost a good point here, as he might have dwelt on the mystic meaning of tomato which is the 'love apple,' that here was the 'secret correspondence,' the real 'cover for hidden fire.'"[85] Nor would Buzfuz's argument seem far-fetched to those following the criminal conversation suit filed against the prime minister, Lord Melbourne, by George Norton in 1836. Sir William Follett, attorney for the plaintiff, argues that Lord Melbourne's letters, if nothing else (and there appears to have been very little else), prove an adulterous relationship with Lady Caroline Norton. Buzfuz's tactics owe a good deal to Follett, who explains letters between the accused in this way:

> These three notes, which have since been found, relate only to his [Lord Melbourne's] hours of calling on Mrs. Norton, nothing more; but there is something in the style even of these trivial notes to lead at least to something like suspicion. Here is one of them: "I will call about ½ past 4 or 5 o'clock. Yours, Melbourne." There is no regular beginning of

the letters; they don't commence with "My dear Mrs. Norton," or anything of that sort, as is usual in this country when a gentleman writes
to a lady. Here is another . . . "How are you?" Again there is not beginning, as you see. . . . They seem to import much more than the words
convey. They are written cautiously, I admit—there is no profession of
love in them, they are not love-letters, but they are not written in the
ordinary style of correspondence usually adopted . . . between intimate
friends.[86]

The absence of intimacy is offered as confirmation of it. Follett's argument by innuendo and suggestion is readily dismissed by the court; Buzfuz, however, has corroborating evidence for his reading of Pickwick's
notes—evidence provided by Pickwick's own inept counsel.

Proof of Pickwick's shady character inadvertently emerges as a
result of Phunky's incompetent cross-examination of Winkle. The testimony concerning Pickwick's "being found in a lady's sleeping apartment at midnight" (*PP* 570) is especially damning since it comes from
one of the defendant's friends, and the incident leads to "the breaking
off of the projected marriage of the lady in question, and had led . . . to
the whole party being forcibly carried before George Nupkins, Esq.,
magistrate and justice of the peace, for the borough of Ipswich" (*PP*
570). The implication of sexual misconduct is not rebutted, and the tale
of "a romantic Adventure with a middle-aged Lady in Yellow Curl
Papers" (*PP* 378) adds credibility to the suspicion that Pickwick is at it
again. Other evidence is provided by Susannah Sanders, who corrobo-
rates the claim that Pickwick "distinctly and in terms" (*PP* 562) proposes marriage to Mrs. Bardell. Her interpretation of finding the plaintiff in the defendant's arms exhibits the now familiar logic of rejecting
mundane explanations for more exotic alternatives: "Mrs Bardell
fainted away on the morning in July, because Pickwick asked her to
name the day; knew that she (witness) fainted away stone dead when Mr
Sanders asked *her* to name the day, and believed that everybody as
called herself a lady would do the same, under similar circumstances"
(*PP* 571). The code of "a lady," invoked by Mrs. Sanders, along with
the tale of the rake, suggested by the history of Miss Witherfield, confirms Serjeant Buzfuz's interpretation of the notes and seals the villain's
fate.

It is not unusual, of course, for letters to play a significant role in
breach of promise trials, as Braddon's satiric reference to "Nobbs's
amatory correspondence" indicates. The precedent-setting case, *Honyman* v. *Campbell*, establishes that direct evidence of betrothal is not
necessary, provided that a promise might reasonably be inferred, for
example, from letters. There is, however, a marked difference between
Sir R. B. J. Honyman's letters and Pickwick's notes. The former con-

tain distinct declarations of affection, which the Lord Chancellor quotes as evidence of a promise of marriage.[87] Follett's strained effort to build upon this precedent might seem ill-conceived, and Dickens's parody of it exaggerated, were it not for subsequent cases like *Vineall* v. *Veness* (1865). In this instance, the defendant's letters are much closer in romantic pitch to Melbourne's than to Honyman's. While longer and more intimate than Pickwick's to his landlady, these letters contain no indication of an engagement and no stronger endearment than "my dear Elizabeth." Justice Bramwell sums up the case for the jury by saying that there is "little, if any, evidence of a distinct binding bargain."[88] Despite these instructions, the decision is for the plaintiff. Here, as in *Bessela* v. *Stern*, lenient evidentiary standards elicit sympathy for arguments like that of Robert C. Brown: "good would undoubtedly be done by restricting the power of unscrupulous women to bring this suit on faked evidence, but if the defendant has been unwise enough to write any letters, and if the broad rules of implication laid down in the fictional (but hardly exaggerated) case of *Bardell* v. *Pickwick* are to be applied, this will not furnish any great protection to the unfortunate defendant."[89] Although Follett fails in 1836, it is clear that his line of argumentation is a viable one in the second half of the nineteenth century, and for a good while after that—Brown is writing in 1929.

Follett's argument "for something like suspicion" in Lord Melbourne's correspondence anticipates a legal maneuver that Mrs. Norton encounters in her next courtroom confrontation with her husband. The "license of the Bar" resembles a legal fiction in that it gives attorneys the freedom to generate suppositional narratives without assuming the burden of proving them. In this legal version of poetic license, a barrister fabricates completely coherent but entirely hypothetical counternarratives. The sole purpose of these purely theoretical fictions is to cast doubt upon the testimony and interpretations of witnesses for the other side—as successfully occurs, for instance, in *Beachey* v. *Brown*. In attacking this form of legalized lying, Caroline Norton offers the example of a "barrister having to defend a man for burglariously entering a house by night, [who] suggested in behalf of his burglar, that he might perhaps have had a love-appointment with the lady of the house! The extraordinary insult being complained of the barrister pleaded 'license of the Bar.'"[90] Buzfuz perhaps takes fewer liberties than this imaginative lawyer, but he, too, admits that he cannot explain the "preconcerted system of correspondence" alleged to exist between Mr. Pickwick and Mrs. Bardell.

Mr. Skimpin's examination of Nathaniel Winkle provides another example of raising doubt as a legal strategy—and of constructing narratives as the means of doing so. In response to "edifying browbeating" and "excessive badgering" (*PP* 569, 571), Winkle reports having heard Mr. Pickwick

> "call Mrs Bardell a good creature, and I heard him ask her to compose herself, for what a situation it was, if any body should come, or words to that effect."
>
> "Now, Mr Winkle, I have only one more question to ask you. . . . Will you undertake to swear that Pickwick, the defendant, did not say on the occasion in question, 'My dear Mrs Bardell, you're a good creature; compose yourself to this situation, for to this situation you must come,' or words to *that* effect?"
>
> "I—I didn't understand him so, certainly," said Mr Winkle, astounded at this ingenious dove-tailing of the few words he had heard. . . .
>
> ". . . but you will not swear that Pickwick did not make use of the expression I have quoted? . . ."
>
> "No, I will not," replied Mr Winkle. (*PP* 568–69)

Skimpin's "ingenious dove-tailing" takes full advantage of the license of the Bar, not only suggesting an alternative interpretation of the scene but also placing entirely different words in the witness's mouth. This narrative is effective, not because it is true, but because it cannot be proven false. The witness cannot swear to the exact words, whatever his initial interpretation of them, and the examiner can suggest any number of credible versions of them. Skimpin shares his superior's hermeneutic strategy, but only insofar as his narrative contravenes the more obvious and likely one provided by Winkle. Otherwise, his tack is quite different. Buzfuz crafts a single coherent narrative that moves remorselessly to the only possible conclusion. Skimpin, on the contrary, suggests that any number of coherent but contradictory explanations are possible, therefore, that the defendant's version cannot be conclusively accepted as the one true story. Together, these strategies lead inexorably to the melodramatic conclusion ghost-written by Buzfuz himself: a verdict of guilt.

DICKENS V. BUZFUZ

The license of the bar is a jurisgenerative stratagem. It appears to frustrate the jurispathic objective of a trial but, in fact, serves this end in a deliberately subversive way. When successful, the license of the bar leads to a verdict that is imposed, not because one story is credited at the expense of another, but because all stories are subject to more or less equal doubt. In literary narratives, a single text yields any number of competing or qualifying interpretations, but ambiguity or indeterminacy is not arbitrarily resolved by fiat. Fiction often resists closure and undermines the coherence upon which it depends. There are, however, limits to literature's jurisgenerative impulse, and it would appear that *The Pickwick Papers* approaches them insofar as the judgment against the defendant is definitively reversed by readers. Thus, while there is no doubt of Mr. Pickwick's innocence, readers do become aware of the role of narrative in constructing their verdict. We see that Dickens is no less a melodramatist than Buzfuz and no less free with poetic license than Skimpin is with the license of the bar. The similarities between novelists and lawyers generate paradoxical and destabilizing effects. On the one hand, they seem further to discredit lawyers by suggesting that they are different from novelists only in that they do not admit their fictions; on the other hand, they discredit authors by implicating them in the rhetorical methods that are parodied by attribution to lawyers. The net effect may be skepticism of all legal fictions, whether authored by lawyers or novelists, but it is also consciousness of the extent to which all levels of reality are imbued with storytelling.

Dickens engages the dialectic of legal/fictional similarity and difference in several ways but always toward the single end of raising narrative consciousness. One method of making readers aware (and wary) of narrative is to sow the seeds of skepticism of his own story. For example, in the guise of Eliot's sworn witness, the narrator presents an accurate and authoritative account of events, including the ambiguous proposal scene. Readers become privileged witnesses; they know, for example, as jurors do not, both what Mr. Pickwick intends to discuss before Mrs. Bardell faints and what he says to her afterwards. They have no doubt that his words are more to the effect originally reported by Winkle than subsequently suggested by Skimpin (*PP* 232). Superior knowledge thus enables them to discredit the spurious story concocted by Mrs. Bardell's attorneys. But this certainty is undercut by the realization that their own strategies of reading are no different from the interpretive methods of the discredited lawyers. Readers, for instance, may sense that they merely reinscribe—because they do no more than reverse—the melodramatic categories of good and evil featuring so prominently in Buzfuz's narrative. They may also feel that their hermeneutic circularity is no different from Follett's or Buzfuz's—or worse, that Follett's and Buzfuz's is no different from Sidgwick's (and their own) appeal to the rule of "Common Sense" in cases of imperfect promising. An appeal to the criterion of what "most men would [do] under the circumstances," on the one hand, can be no more than an appeal to another story, and, on the other hand, is likely to result in a proliferation of contradictory accounts of reasonable behavior.[91] The

"truth" devolves to a question of which common sense is more persuasive: is a warming pan just a warming pan or might it be a "cover for
hidden fire"? The answer may never be seriously in doubt, but readers
must recognize nonetheless that their interpretation—the "true" story of
the letters—is still only a story.

Involvement in the interpretive strategies employed by the discredited attorneys is the primary means by which Dickens leads readers to
wonder if their own jurispathic narrative is entirely reliable. The layered
narratives in *The Pickwick Papers* mean that the same scrutiny brought
to bear upon Buzfuz by the narrator might also be applied to the narrator by readers. When narrative ("the story in the trial" authored by Buzfuz) and counternarrative ("the story of the trial" authored by the narrator) are compared, both may be questioned. For example, another
instance of layered narratives is found in Mrs. Bardell's "for rent" sign.
By reading Mrs. Bardell's life according to a norm that is largely of his
own interested construction, Buzfuz—reminding us of Hans Meyrick—
reaches the conclusion that has defined the particulars in the first place.
This is his version of how the defendant comes to Goswell Street:

> I intreat the attention of the jury to the wording of this document.
> "Apartments furnished for a single gentleman"! Mrs Bardell's opinions
> of the opposite sex, gentlemen, were derived from a long contempla-
> tion of the inestimable qualities of her lost husband. . . . Mr Bardell
> was once a single gentleman himself; *to* single gentlemen I look for pro-
> tection, for assistance, for comfort, and for consolation; *in* single gen-
> tlemen I shall perpetually see something to remind me of what Mr
> Bardell was, when he first won my young and untried affections; to a
> single gentleman, then, shall my lodgings be let. (*PP* 560)

In this scheme of things, Mrs. Bardell's sign, with the key word, "single," speaks less to her desire for a husband than to her good-natured
trust of unmarried men. Jurors hear much more on this subject from
Buzfuz than they ever do from Snubbin, whose silence surely enhances
this interpretation. The narrator, however, provides readers with evidence to which neither Buzfuz nor the jury is privy. We alone learn, for
instance, that Mrs. Bardell "had long worshipped Mr Pickwick at a distance" (*PP* 231). Furthermore, having seen the very slender grounds
upon which she is "all at once, raised to a pinnacle to which her wildest
and most extravagant hopes had never dared to aspire" (*PP* 231), readers may be inclined to construe "single" as meaning "eligible" and as
signifying nothing so much as her desire for a second Mr. Bardell. Failing to become Mrs. Pickwick, she changes the sign to "conversable single gentlemen" (*PP* 897). The added adjective is necessary to ward off
single gentlemen who might be intent upon remaining so. Thus the nar-

rator encourages readers (and critics) to indulge in logic similar to that transforming "tomata sauce" into "love apple": "conversable" can only mean "eligible *and* interested."

This point/counterpoint between Buzfuz and the narrator occurs at other moments in the novel, and again only readers receive what is purportedly the whole story. The most dramatic instance is the synopsis of Pickwick's behavior presented to the jury at the onset of the proceedings by Buzfuz. This story is discredited by a higher authority, who originally and authoritatively tells readers and readers alone what happens that day in July. The figurative and literal heavyweight, Mr. Serjeant Buzfuz, therefore, is easily defeated on appeal by the disembodied voice to which he cannot respond.

Unnamed, the narrator stands outside common law (even if he cannot entirely escape the "law of narratives"). He also stands outside of the author's onomastic humor at the expense of the legal system. Dickens plays upon names in several ways. First, he satirically suggests the court system's inability to render justice to individuals by its inability to get names right: Phunky becomes Monkey; Cluppins becomes successively Tuppins, Jupkins, and Muffins; and Nathaniel becomes Daniel. The nominal drift is compounded by names that are sufficiently similar to be confused. Is Skimpin or Snubbin for the plaintiff? Second, he chooses names that are laughably improbable but ironically apt. The seriousness of Buzfuz's story is discredited by his name. Onomatapoetically, the tale and the teller are nonsensical drones—the story is mere buzzing, the lawyer an industrious insect. Poetically, tale and teller are fuzzy—the tale in the double sense of obscuring facts and confusing witnesses and members of the jury, the teller in the double sense of being fuzzy-headed, that is, of having a muddled sense of justice and of wearing a wig. Third, the buzz of silly names is transformed into the figure of Echo, or of Babel, by the narrator's nominal absence. In remaining nameless, the narrator hopes to dissociate himself from the comic confusion of this kangaroo court.

The implicatory structure of the novel, the mutually reflecting but competing layers of narrative and metanarrative, militates against this attempt to remain unnamed. The narrator must at least accept the title, Counsel for the Defense, when he analyzes the methods of the attorneys for the plaintiff and actively rebuts their story. For example, when Mr. Buzfuz opens his remarks with a compliment to the intelligence and impartiality of the jury, the narrator says: "Counsel usually begin in this way, because it puts the jury on the very best terms with themselves, and makes them think what sharp fellows they must be" (*PP* 559). When Buzfuz describes the late Mr. Bardell as having "glided almost imperceptibly from the world, to seek elsewhere for that repose and peace which a custom-house can never afford," the narrator translates: "Mr Bardell . . . had been knocked on the head with a quart-pot in a public-house cellar" (PP 559). In this manner, the narrator further becomes a privileged witness for the defense, one not subject to cross-examination in the manner of the hapless Winkle.

The narrator also weighs in on the side of Snubbin and Phunky by effacing them. Readers are promised "*a full and faithful Report*" (PP 552) of the proceedings but receive very little information concerning the defense offered by Pickwick's attorneys. For example, of "a very long and a very emphatic" closing statement by Snubbin, we are told only that he "bestowed the highest possible eulogiums on the conduct and character of Mr Pickwick; but inasmuch as our readers are far better able to form a correct estimate of that gentleman's merits and deserts, than Serjeant Snubbin could possibly be, we do not feel called upon to enter at any length into the learned gentleman's observations" (PP 575). This direct address to readers resembles Serjeant Buzfuz's opening flattery of jurors, and readers may be tempted to think of themselves as "sharp fellows." But if they have learned anything from the example of the gullible green-grocers and chemists who make up the jury, readers at the very least should be aware of "how much depends upon *effect*" and to recognize this manipulation of their sentiments. The narrator is less a witness than a judge in this instance, ruling with unimpeachable authority upon a tale of his own telling. He is also the consummate rhetorician, despite appearing to the contrary, and he skillfully aligns readers with himself as the privileged and final court of appeal. Not only Dodson and Fogg, therefore, are to be numbered "among the sharpest of the sharp" (PP 897).

If Buzfuz wins the first trial, it is clear that Dickens wins the second. This verdict, however, is itself subject to appeal, and the grounds for appeal are sown by the narrator's own mastery of "*effect*." Another way of putting this is to say that jurisgenerative fictions tend to breach the "promise of narrative," especially insofar as it involves the expectation of closure. In the words of Shoshana Felman: "literature is precisely the *impossibility of choice*: the impossibility of keeping the promise of meaning, of consciousness; the impossibility of not continuing to make this promise and to believe in it."[92] In the case of *Dickens* v. *Buzfuz*, the correct verdict is a nonverdict. The jury is not out; it's hung.

The Pickwick Papers complicates the simplified and idealized formula of poetic justice definitive of melodrama (both plaintiff and defendant end up in jail) and satirizes various forms of "poetic license" freely practiced by the legal system (lying lawyers go unpunished and enriched). The principal objective of Dickens's legal fiction is to foster an awareness of the role of narrative in the law. The point for readers is less a matter of choosing between Buzfuz's melodramatic "The Ruthless Destroyer" and the narrator's comic "A Dreadful Conjunction of Appearances" than of recognizing the narrative foundations of both. When the stories are considered jointly, and not as mutually exclusive alternatives, attention is diverted from the issue of the truth of one tale or the other and directed toward the verbal strategies and narrative logic common to both. The "narrative of law" in this case is intended to produce understanding of the "law of narrative."

Having suggested how Dickens's story of a breach of promise action is more complicated than a mere verdict for or against the defendant would indicate, I would like to turn to the rendering of breach of promise in extralegal contexts. The following chapters focus on narrative strategies less in terms of the legal than the linguistic and social aspects of promising. Mrs. Bardell's mistaken impression that her lodger has proposed may be humorous; Mr. Pickwick's prosecution for breach of that promise may be lamentable; but the scene in which he tries to tell his landlady of his intention to hire a servant reveals that promises are embedded in ambiguous circumstances and emerge—often none too clearly—from a dialogical process. Most promises remain embrangled in these confusing contexts, and few promisers become litigants. Promising, like storytelling, may be defined legally and understood socially, but it is practiced individually. As a result, it is necessarily relative, endlessly variable, and invariably problematic, as writers from Brontë to James promise to demonstrate.

CHAPTER 4

Engaging Lies in Jane Eyre

On the night before her wedding is to take place, Jane Eyre is troubled by a sense of foreboding, as she later explains to Rochester:

> On sleeping, I continued in dreams the idea of a dark and gusty night. I continued also the wish to be with you, and experienced a strange, regretful consciousness of some barrier dividing us. . . . I thought, sir, that you were on the road a long way before me; and I strained every nerve to overtake you, and made effort on effort to utter your name and entreat you to stop—but my movements were fettered, and my voice still died away inarticulate.[1]

Jane, of course, does not know that this oneiric barrier takes the corporeal form of a Mrs. Rochester currently residing at Thornfield. Mr. Rochester believes that his marriage to Bertha is nothing more than "an obstacle of custom—a mere conventional impediment" (*JE* 247). Were this claim presented in a court of law, he would assuredly meet the fate of real-life defendants like Harris and Littlewood. Brontë, however, has no interest in hypothetical breach of promise actions; indeed, the power of law and custom pales when confronted with the protagonists' passion. *Eyre* v. *Rochester* might make a very good case for the plaintiff, but it would be an indifferent—or at the least a different—novel.

Jane's nightmare of inarticulate desire suggests that more is at stake than common law, as Rochester seems to believe, or even ethical norms, such as she grapples with after learning his uxorial secret. Brontë's skeptical fiction questions not only the practice of promising but also the very language with which betrothals are made. On the one hand, the fetters that restrict Jane's movement signify an eroticized version of the promissory paradox. The lovers' desire depends upon the distance (or pause) imposed by betrothal but threatened by marriage. To cross the marital Rubicon thus may be to dilute the passions of embarkation. On the other hand, Jane's dying voice is not simply the result of premarital jitters. She and Rochester confront an even more basic problem than the paradox of promising and that is the (mis)uses of language itself. He habitually speaks in misleading ways. She speaks more honestly, nonetheless fears that her voice will fail when she most needs it. The liabilities of language extend beyond Jane and Rochester to encompass all speakers in the novel, who have good reason for concern about the medium they employ.

The skepticism about language expressed in the novel is both more varied and more radical than that voiced by Locke, Tooke, Coleridge, or Mill. Fears about language use take two quite different forms, depending upon whether it is believed that words are too weak to serve human needs or that human needs are too frail to survive verbal expression. The former attitude varies from the conviction that language is inherently unequal to the demands placed upon it (ontological fear), to the belief that words are readily misused by mendacious speakers and that such duplicity is virtually undetectable (pragmatic fear), to the concern that telling one's story inevitably invokes the irreconcilable claims of truth and plausibility (narrative fear). The ontological fear of language raises the possibility that experience and articulation are incompatible by nature. Words may fail speakers at any time, not only at moments of emotional intensity such as those depicted in Jane's nightmare. A less severe attitude is that love and language are at odds in practice rather than in principle. The "honeyed terms" (*JE* 302) of romance are particularly susceptible to calculated abuse, as the flattering epithets of Céline and Rochester (*JE* 172–75) and the metaphoric contests of Blanche and Rochester (*JE* 207–9) demonstrate. The tales with which courtships are conducted, besides revealing the deceit accompanying promises of love, serve readers as an embedded figure of the tale of romance told to them. Hence suspicions about the uses of autobiographical narrative, which originate with Jane's learning how to make her story plausible to Miss Temple and are reinforced by Rochester's selective and misleading accounts of his past, may spread to encompass *Jane Eyre* itself.[2]

If such are the trepidations deriving from the belief that language falsifies reality, quite different fears affect those who hold that words possess an explosive power to reveal rather than to distort or simply to conceal the truth. Underlying this belief is the conviction that words can turn actions into lies and men into liars (*JE* 343), hence exactly reversing the supposition of the first type of logophobia (according to which actions are the proofs of true or false speaking). Language now assumes a power seemingly disproportionate to its size, since it takes but "one careless word" (*JE* 245), as Rochester says, or "[o]ne drear word" (*JE* 342), as Jane says, to destroy happiness. Mrs. Reed will not tolerate even "one syllable" (*JE* 60) from Jane. The silence imposed upon her niece, lest she utter "some fatal word" (*JE* 342), places Jane in double jeopardy. Not only does the loss of voice threaten the integrity of self, but also the inability to make herself heard, combined with her force of character, leaves no alternative for expression but the kind of passionate utterance that—when it does erupt—carries the speaker beyond the formulations of conventional society and into the inarticulateness that a logophobic society is quick both to associate with insanity and to use as further justification for enforced silence. Rhetorical oppressors also face a dual danger. Not only do they typically have the most to lose from revelatory utterances, but they themselves may also be susceptible to the incoherent excess heard, for example, in Rochester's "frantic strain" (*JE* 345) when his bigamous plot is foiled.

A primary consequence of logophobia is recourse to alternative, and it is hoped more reliable, languages. Afflicted with fears of either variety, characters seek new forms of expression and communication. Logophobic lovers of the first type are apt to turn to the "natural" language of the body as an alternative to voices that either "die away inarticulate" or "draw you into a snare deliberately laid" (*JE* 327). Suspecting that all spoken words are either definitionally or intentionally equivocal, the skeptical lover relies upon "words almost visible" (*JE* 182), the language of looks that is reputedly more trustworthy than its audible counterpart. A suitor's promises of love and marriage can be trusted only when corroborated by the eyes, "the faithful interpreter" (*JE* 344) of the soul. Apprehensive lovers may even find themselves in the paradoxical situation of accepting silence as the only reliable expression of erotic desire. According to this logic, if a glib tongue signals a shallow heart, then Jane's voiceless nightmare is an eloquent statement of love.

Logophobic lovers of the second type, fearing language's potential for plain-speaking rather than for tergiversation, turn neither to the body nor to silence. They adopt one of two stratagems: either they seek refuge in the very forms of social confabulation mistrusted by those experiencing the first kind of language fear, or they invoke a higher "supernatural" discourse. In the first instance, the "conventionally vague and polite" (*JE* 162) language of social interchange is used to conceal awkward or isolating silences. Flirtation in the "key of sweet subdued vivacity" (197) mutes objectionable voices and avoids the double-edged violence accompanying unbridled expressions of passion. The stultifying effect of these safe but nonexpressive modes induces Rochester and Jane to develop an alternative method of courtship. Their love talk is typified by a counterpoint of witty "answers" that he calls "ready and round" (*JE* 341) and that she calls "impetuous [and] republican" (*JE* 308). Erotic desire, however, remains unvoiced in this unconventional courtship discourse. Thus when Jane can no longer suppress her love, she appeals to a "supernatural" language, claiming to speak not "through the medium of custom, conventionalities, nor even of mortal flesh" (*JE* 281). Similarly, when Rochester seems on the brink of losing her, he appeals to her "spirit . . . not [her] brittle frame" (*JE* 345).

In so doing, the lovers attempt to circumvent the body's unreliable inter-preters by means of an unmediated appeal from and to the soul.

In practice, both alternative languages—"natural" and "supernatu-ral"—prove to be as problematic as that to which they are a reaction, and their failures leave speakers in an even deeper quandary. No mode of discourse reliably reveals the speaker's spirit; none affords the certi-tude of a transcendental signified. Speakers, therefore, find themselves driven back upon the very communicative forms from which they sought to escape. Rochester, fearing that the "natural" language of his face will belie his asseverations of good character, has no choice but to ask Jane to "take my word for it." In the same way, his "supernatural" appeal to her spirit gives way to an attempted carnal embrace of her "brittle frame," therein merely reenacting previous failed courtship pat-terns. Language and counterlanguage prove liable to the same abuses. Furthermore, Brontë's resorting to a *logos ex machina* to bring her lovers together at the end of the novel is unlikely to restore readers' con-fidence in linguistic efficacy. There seems to be no escaping the Babel of equally flawed, equally feared, discursive modes.

Logically, the two forms of logophobia would seem to be mutually exclusive. The beliefs that language does not work and works only too well, that love is best expressed by silence and by oratorical ferocity, are obviously incompatible. Dialogically, however, such is not the case. Logophobic lovers are lost in a linguistic labyrinth rife with competing, contradictory, and ultimately unreliable signs. No communicative mode in *Jane Eyre*, irrespective of individual fears or beliefs, escapes the pos-sibility of equivocal and potentially destructive use. No language stands outside the confines of the labyrinth or of the narrative itself. This unre-liability, therefore, ultimately expands to encompass the narrator and even the author, giving readers themselves ample reason for logopho-bia.[3]

The logic of the first type of language fear leaves speakers in an irre-solvable dilemma. As Jane's nightmare suggests, if deep feeling is anti-thetical to articulation, then by necessity and not simply by choice the subject of talk must be limited to the comparatively superficial experi-ences amenable to linguistic formulation and convention. It is not sim-ply that words are insufficiently vivid or precise to be trusted—not merely a matter of finding the right locution to suit the occasion. At issue rather is the efficacy of linguistic expression itself, especially since powerful feelings seem to render the individual incapable of speech. Jane is aware that she suffers from this situational aphasia: "It is one of my faults, that though my tongue is sometimes prompt enough at answer, there are times when it sadly fails me in framing an excuse; and always the lapse occurs at some crisis, when a facile word or plausible pretext is specially wanted to get me out of painful embarrassment" (*JE* 277–78). Facile words and plausible pretexts are the currency of social exchange. Jane is occasionally conversant in this language, admitting, for instance, that she lies to Georgiana Reed (*JE* 262). Nevertheless, she cannot express heartfelt emotions as readily as she makes social excuses. Hence her dialogues with Rochester are perforated by silences when she either loses her voice or cannot trust herself to speak.

One defense against this vocal failure is simply to redefine inarticulateness as a form of romantic expressiveness. Silence is held to be more articulate than language ever could be. A "sad" failure in words bespeaks a praiseworthy capacity to feel. Speech on certain occasions signifies only the superficiality of the spoken. If Jane could speak love, she could not be in love. *Jane Eyre* thus poses the romantic notion that silence is a particularly credible erotic statement. Speechlessness may have "nothing to say," but its ostensive dimension—the here and now, the *visible* aspect of being unable to speak—says it all.

A less extreme and more typical form of the same type of language fear is primarily, and comfortably, a matter of social convention. Language, it is feared, cannot in its ordinary usage adequately describe experience; reality stands always beyond the reaches of articulation and expression. Since individual circumstance will necessarily be compromised by the generalized locutions of a convention-bound medium, discourse functions chiefly as a means of social expedience or entertainment. The effect of this belief is not paralytic silence but complacent chatter and seemingly untroubled acknowledgment of verbal failure, exemplified by such remarks as, "I loved him . . . more than words had power to express" (*JE* 292), and, "I hold myself supremely blest—blest beyond what language can express" (*JE* 475). The formulaic nature of speech is taken for granted, and protests against the limits of expressiveness are conventional and clichéd. The social—and sociable—nature of this attitude fosters a sense of indolence about ordinary language that insulates speakers from logophobia. There is, for example, no sense of urgency attending the failure of words when Jane experiences shame (*JE* 99), foreboding (*JE* 307), sorrow (*JE* 324) and other unnamable emotions (*JE* 378). While she is unable to depict her feelings, she is also unconcerned about such lapses in expressive or narrative power. Convention thus functions to attenuate the very fear it instigates.

Courtship itself becomes largely a matter of convention, especially among the upper classes, for whom the language of performance and the language of love are inseparable. For Rochester and his friends romantic conquests are achieved by various kinds of theatrics, whether literal, like the Corsair song of Donna Bianca and Signor Eduardo, or figurative, like the artificial rhetorical contests accompanying their song. In either case, the actions are imitative, and the words reiterative. While Blanche "repeat[s] sounding phrases from books" (*JE* 215), Rochester "chooses a style of courtship which . . . was . . . in its very carelessness, captivating" (*JE* 214). In such dramatic performances, style counts more than substance, and love counts for very little at all. Success depends less on what individuals say than on whom they impersonate (the voice heard most frequently in drawing room at Thornfield is Byron's).[4]

Acting of this kind is but a specific instance of the general conversational and erotic norm among this class, which is "(what is vernacularly termed) *trailing*" (*JE* 202). To trail is to elicit unwarranted belief for the purpose of humiliation or seduction. In the vernacular sense as well as in common practice, trailing is actually leading—or more accurately misleading—a gullible lover either into or out of marriage. Brontë, however, fully exploits the ambiguity of trailing both in this sense and in its more typical usage as "following." For instance, Rochester hopes to trail Jane into becoming his mistress (since she cannot legally be his wife), but it is by trailing Céline in the second sense that he himself is led out of marriage. In the theatrics at Thornfield, the picture becomes even more complicated: Blanche thinks that she is trailing Rochester in the first sense. In actuality he is trailing her in both senses—in the first, by concealing his lack of interest in marrying her and the legal proscriptions against doing so, and, in the second, by exposing her exclusively commercial motivation for marriage.

The prototype of these seductive performances in *Jane Eyre* is an occasion of an apparently different nature: Adèle's introduction to her governess. Since adult courtship might be described as a specialized and extended form of introduction, this scene presents, along with Rochester's ward, the defining characteristics of romantic discourse. Equally prominent in Adèle's recitation and in lovers' conversations is performance. To introduce herself to the new governess, Adèle selects a song and a poem from an apparently extensive, slightly risqué repertoire. The former concerns "a forsaken lady" (*JE* 184) and the disguise by which she plans to gain revenge on her lover. The latter, a fable by La Fontaine, illustrates Adèle's "attention to punctuation and emphasis, . . . flexibility of voice, and . . . appropriateness of gesture" (*JE* 134). These aspects of style, exactly those deictic and ostensive references lost in novelistic transcription, are more important to the meaning of the performance than the words Adèle mouths. Style is what counts in this society, and on this occasion style identifies the speaker as Céline more than it is Adèle. In effect, this scene introduces the mother, speaking ventriloquially through her daughter. Jane meets, then, not only a little girl, whom Rochester subsequently calls the "miniature of Céline Varens" (*JE* 170), but also her mother—the ghostly presence that explains Rochester's distaste for his ward's "prattle" (*JE* 161). The mother's voice, as articulated by her daughter, blends with Bertha's laugh in a Furies' chorus from which Rochester cannot escape and to which Jane is very nearly deaf (*JE* 298).

Unlike Maisie Farange, whose situation resembles Adèle's in several important ways, Adèle can only quote; she cannot analyze.[5] In impersonating Céline, therefore, her own voice is largely eclipsed. Yet her unself-conscious style, "the lisp of childhood" (*JE* 134), is audible and essential to understanding the performance. In the contrast between the vocative strains of mother and daughter, Jane detects past performances and intuits a good deal about Céline: "The subject seemed strangely chosen for an infant singer; but I suppose the point of the exhibition lay in hearing the notes of love and jealousy warbled with the lisp of childhood" (*JE* 134). Because the song and recitation are double-voiced, Jane is able to infer the mother's "bad taste" (*JE* 134) in trailing her daughter for her friends' amusement.

A greater challenge to Jane's acuity and sensitivity to the double-voiced quality of performance is posed by the courtship of Blanche and Rochester. During the game of charades, for example, Blanche and Rochester mime both a wedding ceremony and the ventriloquial courtship of Rebecca by Isaac through Eliezer. The subject, Bridewell, is replete with ironic echoes concerning marrying well, the imprisoning effects of not doing so, and the potentially criminal consequences of ignoring conjugal law. ("Bridewell" is also an echo from the earlier wordplay when it is agreed that Rochester resembles Bothwell, unscrupulous third husband of Mary Queen of Scots. "Both-well" extends the meaning of "bride-well" to the situation of the would-be bigamist.) Even more telling than these thematic ironies, however, is the structural function of the scene, especially as it pertains to the issues of language and performance.

The game of charades is both an embedded figure and a specific instance of the typical practice of conversation and courtship. In the game, words are announced as playthings; in lovers' talk generally, they are treated as such but are disguised as something quite serious. Under the aegis of play, unannounced attitudes toward the language of love are given free reign. The artificial boundaries of the game allow words to be severed from one context and applied with impunity to another. The severance is of a distinctive nature: conceptual context and significance (yielding in this instance two distinct words, "bride" and "well") produce a literal and arbitrary text ("Bridewell"). Although guessing this name is the object of play, the term has no semantic connection with either the processes of play or the words that produce it. The visual and referential logic that makes "bride" and "well" correct choices has nothing to do with the literal and additive reasoning that produces the correct answer, "Bridewell." Successful language is language that sounds right, irrespective of reference. Signifieds are eclipsed; signifiers refer only to other signifiers.

This situation obtains outside the game whenever courtship is conducted by impersonation and quotation rather than by statement. Words then refer to other words; texts and contexts are severed and arbitrarily juxtaposed, as is obviously the case in Rochester's gipsy disguise and less obviously so in his wooing of Blanche. The aristocrats' game further recalls Adèle's performance in that both entail dramatic impersonation and both feature "notes of love and jealousy." While the child's performance is innocent, her guardian's transformation of courtship into a figurative game of charades (in part by using the literal game) is not. The deceitful ventriloquism of the dramatic performance is compounded by Rochester's self-conscious manipulation of texts and dramatis personae. In the second of the tableaux, for example, Eliezer (played by Rochester) speaks ventriloquially for Isaac, who courts Rebecca (played by Blanche). Presumably, Eliezer is also Rochester's emissary to Blanche—at least, no one in the room seems hesitant to apply the action of the game (the biblical text) to the lives of the players (the social context). This connection is consistent with the structural procedure of charades but reverses its semiotic logic; that is, the audience restores the missing signifieds by going outside the boundaries of the game. Rochester plays upon this maneuver in joking with Blanche: "Well, whatever I am, remember you are my wife; we were married an hour since, in the presence of all these witnesses" (*JE* 214). The joke is both on Blanche, who will never become the bride in life that she was in the pantomime, and on the "witnesses," who are similarly deceived by Rochester's dramaturgy. Encouraged by the freedom of play, the audience conflates text and context. No one interprets the scene correctly because all rely on the shared, though unannounced, rules of amorous pursuit that Rochester exploits.

Jane, who knows little about either the rituals of drawing room courtship or the rules of parlor games (*JE* 211), also misconstrues the many-voiced performance. "Jealousy" rather than "Bridewell" is the more accurate guess of the game's meaning, since Eliezer is really Rochester's emissary to Jane. The significance of the charade is not conceptual but performative: it can be enacted but not encapsulated in language. Rochester's objective is perlocutionary: he wants Jane to feel jealousy, therefore, to be amenable to his illicit plans. In terms of the dynamics of introduction and seduction, he is both Céline and Adèle, that is, both jaded director indulging his poor taste and earnest actor confidently courting the audience's favor. That the two voices go undetected is testimony to his ventriloquial skill (although the ultimate ventriloquist is perhaps St. John Rivers, who in courting claims to speak not only for Jane's mute heart [*JE* 427] but also for God [*JE* 431]). Jane is, in fact, jealous but does not discern Rochester's attraction to her.

An additional aspect of this drawing room game returns us to the question of visual language as an alternative to the distorting echoes of love talk. Charades emphasizes the visual over the verbal. Although words are the object of the game, its procedures are pantomimic. Its interest and challenge lie in the skills of scenic presentation and interpretation. Charades, therefore, is the appropriate choice of a logophobic society whose very commitment to rhetorical performances occasions a mistrust of them. Outside the game, the fear of language and the concomitant appeal to the visual are manifest in an endemic tendency to read faces rather than to trust words.[6] Language too often provides either a veneer of social ease hiding potentially disruptive feelings or a facade of romantic feeling concealing devious intentions. Countenances, many believe, provide direct and reliable expressions of feeling. Especially in matters of the heart, individuals are inclined to trust what they see, not what they hear.

When Jane struggles to understand her feelings for Rochester, for example, she concludes that she must love him, because she "understand[s] the language of his countenance and movements" (*JE* 204). When he proposes to her, she consults his visage to alleviate the fear that he "play[s] at farce" (*JE* 283). Only after reading his looks does she place any credence in his words. In this instance, the two languages are mutually reinforcing, but such is not always the case. In the furor surrounding Bertha's attack upon her brother, for example, Rochester utters nothing but words of encouragement and succor. His face, on the contrary, expresses what this "plausible pretext" attempts to conceal. Jane intuits something of his actual feelings by reading his visage: "a singularly marked expression of disgust, horror, hatred, warped his countenance almost to distortion, but he only said—" (*JE* 242). While accurately interpreting this expression, she pays insufficient attention to the drastic difference between Rochester's bilingual messages. Blinded by love, she monologizes the scene and suppresses its incongruous notes.

Rochester, too, places great value on the unspoken language of faces. He is confident of his ability to read others' visages and early on tells Jane: "beware, by the by, what you express with that organ [the eye]; I am quick at interpreting its language" (*JE* 167). Although this claim is tarnished by his subsequent mistake about her eye color (*JE* 287), he repeatedly relies upon the language of looks, suspecting that talk is often no more than so much conventional nonsense and so many polite lies. As he retells it, his engagement to Jane is the direct result of a "speechless colloquy" (*JE* 296) of which she can have known nothing. When Jane asks if he is not rather capricious in his treatment of women, he replies that he can be trusted with women of "clear eye and eloquent tongue" (*JE* 289). Rochester perhaps refines his society's standard of truthfulness by crediting only those statements made in both languages; nevertheless, even when verbal and visual messages are in accord, deception is possible, as his own discursive practice suggests. Rochester's equivocal use of the language of looks is obvious when he pretends to be a gipsy fortune-teller and construes Jane's character from "the face: on the forehead, about the eyes, and in the eyes themselves, in the lines of the mouth" (*JE* 226–27). That his own face is blackened and shaded by a hat provides an outward sign of his duplicity. But even without the disguise, Rochester seems to take a perverse pride in his puzzling countenance: "it [is] scarcely more legible than a crumpled, scratched page" (*JE* 283). He exploits this illegibility to keep interlocutors in disadvantaged positions. Visual expressions are used in the same way as words are, that is, to confuse rather than to clarify.[7] "[O]ne of his queer looks" (*JE* 274) easily frustrates Mrs. Fairfax, but "his strange and equivocal demonstrations" (*JE* 251) are equally confusing to so skilled a reader as Jane.

Because eyes can be as misleading as tongues, no medium of communication can alleviate the fear of deception. When Rochester feels that neither his "clear eye" nor his "eloquent tongue" will elicit credibility, he appeals to the feared entity itself, language. Indeed, if no communicative means can be trusted, what alternative is there but to "take one's word for it"? On several occasions, therefore, he asks Jane simply to trust him and to accept his word. He wants her, for example, to believe in his inherent goodness: "Nature meant me to be, on the whole, a good man, Miss Eyre; one of the better kind, and you see I am not so. . . . Then take my word for it—I am not a villain" (*JE* 166–67). It is hard to know what ethical standard Rochester appeals to in making this assertion, but the rhetorical norm is obvious: it is the operative principle of charades further monologized. Rochester assumes the roles of both sides in the game, not only staging the scene but also supplying its meaning. His text—his word—bears no relation to the context of silence and suppression it reputedly addresses. Giving his word, therefore, is merely another deceptive performance. For Jane, who once again stands outside the boundaries of the game, taking his "word for it" means accepting his silences and suppressions as truthful, that is, as containing nothing villainous. After their espousal, she in effect asks if his word can be trusted: "You will not exclude me from your confidence if you admit me to your heart?" Rochester's answer is ominous: "You are welcome to all my confidence that is worth having" (*JE* 290). The qualification makes all the difference. His silence is a lie, and it makes his promises lies as well.

Rochester's promises often take the form of a pseudopromise consistent with the courtship discourse of his society. They are intended as a proof of love but reveal only the unreliability of such proofs. For instance, Rochester clearly manipulates the conventions of promising when he agrees to Jane's request that she and Adèle "be both safe out of the house before your bride enters it" (*JE* 254). In the context of this conversation, both understand "your bride" to be Blanche Ingram, as she was in the charades. Rochester's promise may not be entirely false, since he knows Blanche will never enter Thornfield Hall as Mrs. Rochester; nevertheless, it is doubly misleading: first, because it sustains the cruel pretense that he will marry Blanche, and, second, because his bride, Bertha, is already in the house.

Rochester's promises, rather than entailing an obligation to the promisee, are unilateral statements of desire, uttered without regard for the promisee's wishes—indeed, sometimes without a promisee at all. Having resolved upon pursuing his own happiness irrespective of social or moral restraint, he tells Jane: "I will keep my word: I will break obstacles to happiness, to goodness—yes, goodness. I wish to be a better man than I have been, than I am" (*JE* 174). He can keep this promise to himself only by breaking his word to others, for example Bertha. His promises are not to be believed; in fact, they are not promises but threats, warnings of what he will do *to* others rather than promises of what he will do *for* them.[8] The communicational impasse to which the fear of language leads, therefore, is fortified by Rochester's appeals to his word. Whether in the form of polite lies or of impolite promises, words and their users are untrustworthy. And this is an obstacle that Rochester cannot break, even after the barriers to happiness figured in Jane's dream have been removed.

All performances and languages contain the discordant notes that should alert audiences to their unreliability. This inherent dissonance is emblematized by the one line of Adèle's recitation that is cited by Jane: "*Qu'avez-vous donc? lui dit un de ces rats; parlez!*" (*JE* 134).[9] The peremptory command, "*parlez*," which is characteristic of Rochester's discursive method (*JE* 164, 290, 458), conveys the impatient, even aggressive, tone of many of the novel's "parleys" (*JE* 50, 219). It also echoes Jane's introduction to readers: "What does Bessie say I have done?" (*JE* 39), therein continuing at Thornfield the atmosphere of fear and guilt and the themes of accusation and punishment that define Jane's experience of Gateshead as well as Lowood. Nevertheless, the line seems strangely chosen if it is intended to function as a conventional introduction. The question *"Qu'avez-vous donc?"* self-reflexively asks what is wrong with this scene. It is not, for instance, a question of the kind that defines introductions ("Who are you?"), and it is not spoken by the expected person (should not Jane question Adèle?). Furthermore, it is not a question at all, but a quotation that inappropriately introduces a former mistress onto a stage already crowded by the presence of a wife and a fiancée.

The discordant notes echoing throughout Adèle's performance radiate beyond it to envelop the narrator and her readers. The choice of this line from all those repeated by Adèle testifies to the narrator's control and skill. But how are readers to respond when the narrator indulges in precisely the amusement that Céline apparently found in her daughter and that Jane feels is in poor taste? The suspicion of the uses to which language may be put inevitably spreads from characters to narrator and author. For example, our reaction to the childish euphemism that describes the mother's running off to Italy with a musician as going "to the Holy Virgin" (*JE* 133, 176) is presumably no different from Céline's enjoyment at "hearing notes of love and jealousy warbled with the lisp of childhood." In effect, the scene manifests the kind of dialogical exploitation that it appears to reject. Readers, caught up in a tale of trailing, have reason to suspect the narrator's intentions with regard to them.

The burlesque depictions of Georgiana and Eliza Reed, as well as of the Dowager and Miss Ingram, are further examples. Readers are apt to enjoy the lampoon of Rev. Brocklehurst, especially when the sight of curly hair sends him into a fit of fundamentalist zeal: "Why, in defiance of every precept and principle of this house, does she conform to the world so openly—here in an evangelical, charitable establishment—as to wear her hair one mass of curls?" (*JE* 96). That his own daughters boast "a profusion of light tresses, elaborately curled" (*JE* 97) heightens the satire of the scene and contempt for Brocklehurst. But the narrator, who ridicules this hypocrisy, indulges in it when presenting characters for whom she maintains a degree of animus. The very "top-knots" ordered guillotined by Brocklehurst are taken by Jane to be a sign of worldliness and superficiality and are used by the narrator to convey disapprobation. Georgiana Reed has "hair elaborately ringleted" (*JE* 60, 257) and interweaves "her curls with artificial flowers" (*JE* 62); Adèle flaunts "a redundancy of hair falling in curls to her waist" (*JE* 132, 199); Blanche, whose hair is a "jetty mass of curls" (*JE* 189), is seldom mentioned without reference to these "[c]raven ringlets" (*JE* 191); and Rosamund Oliver, too, displays "the ornament of rich, plenteous curls" (*JE* 389). If with Miss Temple we laugh at Brocklehurst (appropriately her silent mockery is described as "the involuntary smile that *curled*" her lips [*JE* 96, my emphasis]), must we then not include the narrator in our critical amusement?[10]

Even more problematic, however, is the novel's presenting an interpretive norm that is inaccessible to its readers. Adèle's introduction implicitly establishes a hermeneutics of performance that can be applied to dramatized discourse in general and especially to recitational courtship. To hear only a speaker's voice and to ignore the voice of quotation is necessarily to misconstrue the scene. Audiences and auditors must be sensitive to at least three factors: utterance, text, and context. Readers, however, cannot hear speakers' words. Writing occludes the ostensive reference essential to interpretation. In this sense, writing functions as do Rochester's promises: they merely confirm what has been previously expressed in another and a now inaccessible medium. The novel posits a hermeneutic ideal that can never be applied to novels themselves. Thus, while readers may be insulated to some extent from the trailing by characters, we are left in the uncomfortable position of having to take the narrator's "word for it."

The second form of logophobia may explain why *Jane Eyre*, unlike conventional autobiographies, does not begin with an account of the protagonist's birth or earliest memory. The novel opens with the reserved heroine's discovery of "quite a new way of talking" (*JE* 71) and her first experience of the power of her own voice. Jane's initial words, like Adèle's recitation of *La Ligue des Rats*, sound the note that something is wrong. When John Reed physically attacks her for "impudence in answering mamma" (*JE* 42), Jane responds verbally by likening him to wicked Roman emperors, a comparison drawn "in silence, which I never thought thus to have declared aloud" (*JE* 43). For her uncharacteristic and seditious outburst, this "infantine Guy Fawkes" (*JE* 58) is imprisoned in the Red Room. She will not be silenced, however, and subsequent verbal rebellions are even more explosive. First, in a "strange and audacious declaration" (*JE* 59), she renews and expands her attack upon the Reed children. Next, refusing to be banished to the nursery—a place of enforced childhood, as well as of solitary confinement—she disruptively intrudes upon the adult world of discourse, routing her aunt from the breakfast-room. In this scene, Mrs. Reed begins speaking "in a tone which a person might address an opponent of adult age than such as is ordinarily used to a child," but she is quickly reduced to murmuring "*sotto voce*" (*JE* 68). The force of Jane's tirade is such that her aunt still suffers from it on her deathbed: "I feel it quite impossible to understand: how for nine years you could be patient and quiescent under any treatment, and in the tenth break out all fire and violence" (*JE* 267).

The pattern of Jane's childhood—nine years of quietude followed by "fire and violence"—is repeated in adulthood. She herself recognizes that she can remain silent only so long: "I know no medium: I never in my life have known any medium in my dealings with positive, hard characters, antagonistic to my own, between absolute submission and determined revolt. I have always faithfully observed the one, up to the very moment of bursting, sometimes with volcanic vehemence, into the other" (*JE* 426). In certain circumstances and after a certain time, her voice is irrepressible. First with her guardian, then with her employer, and finally with her cousin, Jane cannot refrain from speaking:

> [I]t seemed as if my tongue pronounced words without my will consenting to their utterance: something spoke out of me over which I had no control. (*JE* 60)

> *Speak* I must: (*JE* 68)

> An impulse held me fast—a force turned me round. I said—or something in me said for me, and in spite of me—(*JE* 273)

> I said this almost involuntarily. . . . The vehemence of emotion, stirred by grief and love within me, was claiming mastery, and struggling for full sway, and asserting a right to predominate, to overcome, to live, rise, and reign at last: yes—and to speak. (*JE* 279–81)

Echoes of the lessons of silence and conventional speech are heard in the narrator's effort to detach herself from her own outspokenness. In making it seem as if someone else were responsible for these outbursts, Jane gives free and forceful expression to otherwise repressed feelings yet retains the values of modesty and passivity. The demure governess remains distinct from the now adult Guy Fawkes, who speaks out to resist the domineering efforts of her employer, when he suggests sending her to Ireland, and of her cousin, when he proposes taking her to India. Perhaps recalling her aunt's experience, Jane says of her cousin: "he had not forgotten the words; and as long as he and I lived he never would forget them" (*JE* 436). Jane does not often assert herself, but she leaves an indelible impression when she does. She refuses St. John's proposal precisely because she knows that marrying him would entail an intolerable suppression: "But as his wife . . . forced to keep the fire of my nature continually low, to compel it to burn inwardly and never utter a cry, though the imprisoned flame consumed vital after vital—*this* would be unendurable" (*JE* 433). The fiery disruptiveness of passionate expression is the only means of protesting the inevitable cost of repression: self-immolation. Jane refuses to be "hurried away in a suttee" (*JE* 301) for either Rivers or Rochester.

A calmer, though no less rebellious, assertion of self is heard in each of Jane's two betrothals. She subverts the protocol of proposals on both occasions: at Thornfield, Rochester says, with some justification: "by the by, it was you who made me the offer" (*JE* 291), and again at Ferndean Jane herself admits that she has "[p]erhaps too rashly overleaped conventionalities" (*JE* 460) in proposing marriage. As in the scenes of Adèle's introduction and Rochester's fortune-telling, the unexpected person asks the questions. In these instances—to reverse the earlier formulation—it might be said that if Jane does not speak love, she cannot be in love.

The fear of linguistic expression, whether passional or merely unconventional, leads to two defensive maneuvers. Safest is abstinence; however, complete silence is seldom either possible or practical. At Thornfield, for example, despite Rochester's commanding Adèle (*JE* 160), enjoining Jane (*JE* 181, 238), and threatening Mason (*JE* 238, 242) to be silent, his secret is eventually revealed. An alternative prophylactic measure is polite small talk of the sort mistrusted by logophobes of the first kind. The happy hum of insignificant social banter muffles potentially threatening words, like Mason's, or voices, like Bertha's. The courtship discourse of Rochester and Jane represents a variation of this second protective strategy. Their stylized combative dialogue is hardly polite, but it does keep threatening erotic forces at bay. Courtship rhetoric in this instance functions by safeguarding against the very emotions that it is the means of expressing.

The greatest security against the disruptive force of language is, of course, silence. Hence Mrs. Reed, who dislikes "cavillers or questioners" (*JE* 39), commands silence from Jane "until [she] can speak pleasantly" (*JE* 39) and will release her from the Red Room "only on condition of perfect submission and stillness" (*JE* 49). When Jane proves unable to manage even conventional civility, she is restricted "to the silent and solitary nursery" (*JE* 60) until her exile to Lowood. Mrs. Reed accuses Jane of deceit, not because she lies, but because she speaks. Rev. Brocklehurst reinforces this judgment, promising that all liars will meet the awful end of little Martha G—(*JE* 67). His warning of the "lake which burneth with fire and brimstone" (*JE* 66) is repeated by Rev. Rivers when Jane resists his will (*JE* 442). Both men rely on the Word to invalidate the voices of those who question their positions. Such insecurity also explains why Jane's first day at Lowood is repeatedly punctuated by commands of "Silence!" (*JE* 77–78) and why Brocklehurst specifically orders that she be excluded from the girls' conversation (*JE* 98–99). Even Helen Burns, presumably without Mrs. Reed's reason to fear them, feels that Jane asks "rather too many questions" (*JE* 83). Helen's passive acceptance of persecution is taken as a sign of Christian heroism—ironically expressed in terms of being "silent as an Indian" (*JE* 100). By contrast, Helen compares Jane's resistance to injustice to the practices of "[h]eathens and savage tribes" (*JE* 90). St. John Rivers would surely agree, especially when she refuses to become his wife in order to serve as a missionary to the heathens of India. Although she endures the oppression of two ministers in silence, at least for a time, she finally cannot accede to the chauvinism of either man.

For most of the time—nine years out of ten—Jane accepts the example of her fellow student and the lesson of Lowood. She seems, if anything, to have learned the advantage of conventional expression. By restraining her sense of injustice, for example, she is able to frame the story of her past in language "most moderate—most correct" (*JE* 102–3), thus to win Miss Temple's help in rebutting the accusation that she is a liar. The narrator's elision of all but a few months of her eight years at Lowood is evidence of her tranquil life there. Just before leaving the school, Jane assesses her character in terms reminiscent of Helen: "I was quiet" (*JE* 116). Although she is more restive than restful, as her departure from Lowood proves, the lesson of silence is never lost upon her. At Thornfield, she stifles her curiosity with Mrs. Fairfax, recalling Helen's etiquette: "it was not polite to ask too many questions" (*JE* 128). When commanded by Mr. Rochester to "Speak," she refuses, thinking to herself but not saying to him: "If he expects me to talk for the mere sake of talking and showing off, he will find he has addressed himself to the wrong person" (*JE* 164). Her temperamental reserve produces this compliment from her employer, "You are no talking fool" (*JE* 181). And when she leaves Thornfield, she resolves, in words that Rev. Brocklehurst surely would have condoned, "to wait His will in silence" (*JE* 361). Although she does not quite live up to this resolve, she is sufficiently quiet to hear "His will," if such it is, which calls her to Ferndean.

The second defensive stratagem is illustrated when guests arrive at Thornfield. The "[l]aughing and talking . . . jests and gaiety" (*JE* 233) drown out the lunatic laughter emanating from the third floor. Rochester, of all conversationalists in the novel, is the most in command of the medium of polite social exchange. Even at times of emotional crisis, such as Mason's arrival and subsequent stabbing, he is never at a loss for a "facile word." Immediately following both occasions, he can be heard speaking "cheerfully" (*JE* 234, 248) with his guests. The most frequently heard example of this social "noise" is the elaborate, playfully antagonistic courtship language evolved by Rochester and Jane.

The "blunt sentence[s]" (*JE* 68) that shocked Mrs. Reed are their ordinary form of social intercourse. The relatively safe but also superficial language of romance frustrates Rochester to the point of impetuously remarking, "Confound these civilities!" (*JE* 161). He asks Jane to "dispense with a great many conventional forms and phrases" (*JE* 165) because they stifle spontaneity and frustrate naturalness (*JE* 170). And he is impressed that when questioned she "rap[s] out a round rejoinder, which, if not blunt, is at least brusque" (*JE* 162). Jane is able to talk with him in the first place because his "roughness . . . set me at my ease" (*JE* 145); his "harsh caprice laid me under no obligation" (*JE* 152). Ultimately her disregard for discursive amenities rivals his: "The sarcasm that had repelled, the harshness that had startled me once, were only like keen condiments in a choice dish: their presence was pungent, but their absence would be felt as comparatively insipid" (*JE* 217). The sarcasm and harshness are more than matters of style. The medium becomes the message when Jane credits the sincerity of his marriage proposal precisely because of its "incivility" (*JE* 283). Nonconventional and even rude language becomes for her the sign of truthfulness and the means of intimacy (and she misreads this language just as she had the language of looks).[11] The courtship of Jane and Rochester confirms the hermeneutic principle that she first applied to Adèle's recital, but it reverses conventional meaning: sarcasm is now a basic component of the language of love.

Rochester's courtship of Jane may be more intense, because more serious, than that of Blanche, but it is as seriously flawed. It resembles the "charivari" (206) played by Blanche on her governess; indeed, Rochester's introduction to his governess is accomplished by means of a "rude noise" (*JE* 143). His conversation on this and subsequent occasions is manipulative and misleading. Even on the very night of his proposal, he persists in the cruel illusion that he is engaged to Blanche and concocts a parodic story about sending his lovesick employee off to Bitternutt Lodge, which is chock full of O'Gall girls in need of a governess. The witticism can be amusing only to him—and perhaps to readers who are again implicated in a joke whose good taste Jane might question. She directly but mildly rebels against such "trailing" when Rochester disguises himself as a gipsy fortune-teller: "I believe you have been trying to draw me out—or in; you have been talking nonsense to make me talk nonsense. It is scarcely fair, sir" (*JE* 231). Since their first encounter, Rochester has consistently claimed an unfair dialogical advantage. Jane's prenuptial nightmare of vocal failure, in fact, alludes to their first meeting. At that time, she is unable to "utter [his] name" because she does not know who he is, and as in the dream he leaves her behind on the road. Rochester plays any number of such games at Jane's expense, including, as he admits, spying and feigning disinterest (*JE* 341). Thus, although the style may be slightly different, he is no less disingenuous with Jane than he is with Blanche.

Both courtships—the pretended and the intended—are character-ized by deceit. With Blanche the method is imitative, a courtship by quo-tation. With Jane the method is inventive; their love talk is characterized by imaginative conceits in which she typically figures as a fairy and he as an Oriental emir. In the most extended of these metaphors, Rochester spins a fairy tale of life on the moon, with pink clouds for clothing and manna for sustenance.[12] Jane tells Adèle "not to mind his badinage" (*JE* 296), but she herself would do well to borrow from her pupil's "fund of genuine French skepticism" (*JE* 296). Rochester, in Adèle's estimation, "has not kept his word" (*JE* 134) because, although he did bring her to England, he has not remained there with her (an allegation that could be made with even greater justice by Bertha). His wish to leave the "com-mon world" (*JE* 296) behind expresses a desire to ignore common cus-toms and laws—a desire that makes him, in more ways than Adèle understands, "*un vrai menteur*" (*JE* 296).

His style of courtship produces lively dialogue but also casts the speakers into the roles of rhetorical antagonists. Jane's and Rochester's engagement often resembles slapstick comedy more than comic romance: for smiles they substitute grimaces; "for a pressure of the hand, a pinch on the arm; for a kiss on the cheek, a severe tweak of the ear" (*JE* 302). The objective of this physical and verbal fencing is to maintain distance rather than to establish common ground.[13] Jane delib-erately frustrates any show of love: "Soft scene, daring demonstration, I would not have; and I stood in peril of both; a weapon of defence must be prepared—I whetted my tongue" (*JE* 301). It is no wonder, then, that Rochester complains that "under the pretence . . . of stroking and sooth-ing me into placidity, you stick a sly penknife under my ear!" (*JE* 162, also see 306). She admits employing a "needle of repartee" (*JE* 301) not merely for defensive purposes but also for the charm of rhetorical con-trol. She relishes the "pleasure" and, one might add, the power "of vex-ing and soothing him by turns" (*JE* 187).[14] "A true Janian reply" (*JE* 272), therefore, is anything but true, if by "true" is meant serious or direct. The effect of this courtship of sharpened tongues and pointed conversations is to make distance and detachment the indices of love. Their love talk is hardly the "kindly conversation" (*JE* 333) that Rochester claims to have missed with Bertha and that we never see with Blanche. It is, rather, another instance of manipulation, concealment, and eroticized antagonism.

Neither silence nor small talk nor verbal sparring can assuage lan-guage fear because none reliably accomplishes the objective of repress-ing secrets and all preclude meaningful communication. The selective silences of Mrs. Reed and Mr. Rochester, for example, prove that fail-ing or refusing to speak can be as duplicitous as and even more dangerous than speaking. Mrs. Reed, who demands silence from her ward, spitefully practices it to deprive Jane of her family and inheritance—and painfully pays for it on her death bed (*JE* 267). In seeking a second wife, Rochester apparently forgets the lesson of his first marriage, when a conspiracy of silence about "family secrets" (*JE* 320) ensnares an unsuspecting spouse (*JE* 332). Even less obviously self-interested silences can be dangerous. Jane's secrecy with the Riverses, for example, very nearly has the same effect of her aunt's with her, that is, of depriving her of both family and financial independence. While refusing to become an English Céline Varens (*JE* 298, also see 288, 308), she too readily becomes Jane Elliot, therein symbolically denying her identity. The "name casually written on a slip of paper" (*JE* 416) that enables St. John to identify his cousin is yet another, albeit a quiet, assertion of self despite Jane's conscious wishes.

Even direct and passionate speech, which is taken to be a "supernatural" alternative to imposed silences or stylized methods of courtship, is proven to be flawed.[15] The passionate protestations that punctuate Jane's and Rochester's romantic rodomontade are no more "true" or effective than the imposed silences and the manipulative conversations that seem invariably to backfire. John Kucich points out that "passionate displays are calculated both to conceal rather than to reveal the true nature of desire, and to assail the strategic reserve of others."[16] But even were direct and passionate speech less studied, therefore less deceitful, than other discursive modes, it can be voiced only with significant risk to the speaker. It leads to social ostracism at the least and to physical and emotional isolation at the worst. The speaker need not have the book thrown at her, as Jane literally does, to know that "criminal conversation" exacts a social penalty. The psychological effects of unlicensed expression are even more traumatic: "A child cannot . . . give its furious feelings uncontrolled play, as I had given mine—without experiencing afterwards the pang of remorse and the chill of reaction" (*JE* 69). After venting her anger to Mrs. Reed, Jane feels "poisoned" and is unable to find pleasure, either in her books or in nature. Her victory is an "aromatic wine it seemed, on swallowing, warm and racy; its afterflavour, metallic and corroding" (*JE* 70).

This metaphor is also used to describe Jane's adult experience, for example, when she confesses her love to a man she knows is married. Although she does not tell Rochester that she has forgiven him (*JE* 326), she cannot allow him to deny her love: "I ought probably to have done or said nothing; but I was so tortured by a sense of remorse at thus hurting his feelings, I could not control the wish to drop balm where I had wounded. 'I *do* love you'" (*JE* 331). This "balm" is very nearly as intoxicating as aromatic wine. Speaking her love very nearly carries Jane into acting on it. She does resist, however, despite Rochester's argument that running off to his "whitewashed villa on the shores of the mediter-ranean" (*JE* 331)—if not a form of going to the Holy Virgin—at least violates no divine law. To become his mistress, he argues (anticipating the arguments of Stephen Guest), will be to "transgress a mere human law, no man being injured by the breach" (*JE* 343). She escapes by recalling the time "when I was sane, and not mad—as I am now . . . I am insane—quite insane, with my veins running fire" (*JE* 344). The fig-ure of speech that Jane uses after speaking out to Mrs. Reed also describes her state of mind on this occasion. Of the earlier scene she says: "A ridge of lighted heath, alive, glancing, devouring, would have been a great emblem of my mind . . . ; the same ridge, black and blasted after the flames are dead, would have represented as meetly my subse-quent condition, when half an hour's silence and reflection had shown me the madness of my conduct" (*JE* 69–70). Later, when her hopes of marriage are dashed, and again after a period of reflection, she returns to images of madness and destruction—frost accomplishing what flames had before:

> A Christmas frost had come at midsummer; a white December storm had whirled over June; ice glazed the ripe apples, drifts crushed the blowing roses; on hayfield and cornfield lay a frozen shroud: lanes which last night blushed full of flowers, to-day were pathless with untrodden snow; and the woods, which twelve hours since waved leafy and fragrant as groves between the tropics, now spread, waste, wild, and white as pine-forests in wintry Norway. (*JE* 323)

Whether black or white, the landscape of the soul after such passionate explosions is cold and barren—as cold as England must seem to some-one from the West Indies, as barren as "old thorn trees" (*JE* 131) must appear to a woman accustomed to tropical groves.

Bertha, of course, is the extreme example of the madness of uncon-trolled passion and expression.[17] It is significant that in a novel rife with fears about language, the greatest danger is to have no human voice at all. While Jane can be "a mad cat" (*JE* 44) and has, by her own admis-sion, brief moments of insanity (*JE* 44, 344), Bertha seems a "wild ani-mal" (*JE* 321), having only "lucid intervals of days—sometimes weeks" (*JE* 336).[18] "[O]ral oddities" (*JE* 141–42)—shrieks (*JE* 235), gibberish (*JE* 242), yells (*JE* 322), curses (*JE* 334), foul vocabulary (*JE* 335)—con-stitute her primary language. Bertha's and even Jane's insanity may be the result of victimization, but the victimizer is also implicated in the costs of suppression. Thus, Grace Poole's description of Bertha seems generally appropriate to her husband, who is consistently "rather snap-pish, but not 'ragious'" (*JE* 321). He, too, has periodic outcries that rival

Jane's and Bertha's in intensity and violence. After the public revelation of his secret thwarts the plan to take a second wife, he becomes crazed: "His voice was hoarse; his look that of a man who is just about to burst an insufferable bond and plunge headlong into wild licence" (*JE* 330). Rochester's "flaming glance" is like the "draught and glow of a furnace" (*JE* 344) and poses as great a threat as Bertha's pyromania. Jane fears that he may go mad as a result of her disappearance (*JE* 454), and if the possibly hyperbolic innkeeper is to be believed, Rochester does become "savage—quite savage on his disappointment: he never was a mild man, but he got dangerous, after he lost her" (*JE* 452). Danger may be a condition of life itself, but in *Jane Eyre*, expressing love seems to be especially perilous, producing either trailing and duplicity, on the one hand, or railing and insanity, on the other.

The only expression of love open to Jane at Thornfield is indistinguishable from its opposite; that is, she must leave. In one sense, her departure seems the logical conclusion of a courtship in which rhetorical antagonism is the sign of love. The paradoxical expression of one sentiment by its opposite raises the issue of whether any expression stands outside the pervasive mistrust of language use. It further invites the possibility that the logophobia endemic in the novel is potentially epidemic outside of it. The attitudes of the central character and narrator can be discerned in the author, and their skepticism may easily infect readers. The nascent vocal power of the protagonist coincides with the initial appearance of the autobiographer, Jane Eyre, and of the novelist, Currer Bell. The fledgling author's tentative assertions of self closely resemble those of the protagonist. When Brontë refers to Currer Bell as "an obscure aspirant" and a "struggling stranger" (*JE* 35), one thinks of Jane, who is surely both of these things as a young orphan, when the novel opens, and as a novice author, when it closes. Her autobiography, written after ten years of married life, might be seen as the latest incident in the pattern of "break[ing] out all fire and violence" in ten-year intervals. A habitually quiet demeanor, combined with unexpectedly vehement language, contributes to the Reed household's feeling that Jane is duplicitous. Given the "fire and violence" of the novel itself, readers may harbor similar suspicions not only about Jane Eyre but also about Currer Bell and ultimately about Charlotte Brontë herself.

Despite their prejudice, the Reeds are justified in suspecting, if not duplicity, then at least dissimulation, from Jane. Abigail Abbott expresses the general sentiment when she says, "I never saw a girl of her age with so much cover" (*JE* 44). For instance, as Jane awaits John Reed's blow, she entertains herself by "mus[ing] on the disgusting and ugly appearance of him who would presently deal it" (*JE* 42). The silent mockery of the master, never heard by him, is, however, plainly heard in the narrator's tone: "Habitually obedient to John, I came up to his chair: he spent some three minutes in thrusting out his tongue at me as far as he could without damaging the roots" (*JE* 42).[19] The incipient but silent wit of the ten-year-old child receives expression in the hyperbole and caricature of the thirty-year-old narrator, who settles the girl's debt against her persecutors. The description of a tongue thrust out to the point of damage is the product of the sharp tongue of a sardonic adult, indeed, the very "whetted tongue" that Jane applies playfully to Rochester and unmercifully to characters like the Reeds. *Jane Eyre* may well be the fulfillment of the niece's threat to her aunt: "I will tell anybody who asks me questions this exact tale. People think you a good woman, but you are bad, hard hearted. *You* are deceitful" (*JE* 69).

Further indication that the adult narrator is capable of the "dangerous duplicity" (*JE* 50) suspected in the child is her occasional inconsistency. For example, Jane tells the story of the wronged but generously penitent stepchild returning to her aunt's deathbed: "Forgive me. . . . If you could be persuaded to think no more of it, aunt, and to regard me with kindness and forgiveness . . . *you have my full and free forgiveness*" (*JE* 267–68, my emphasis). She claims, some ten years after the fact, that the "gaping wound of my wrongs was now . . . quite healed" (*JE* 296).[20] Yet even twenty years later, Jane can neither overlook nor forgive Mrs. Reed's cruelties. So importunate is her resentment that she actually addresses the dead woman in her story: "Yes, Mrs Reed, to you I owe some fearful pangs of mental suffering. But I ought to forgive you" (*JE* 52). Her "ought" clearly indicates that she has not yet done so, whatever impression she wishes to convey by dramatizing their last conversations. Similarly, her claim not to judge those who mistreat her as she wanders from Whitcross to Marsh End reveals as much about Jane's social outrage as their lack of charity. She says: "I blamed none of those who repulsed me. I felt it was what was to be expected, and what could not be helped: an ordinary beggar is frequently an object of suspicion; a well-dressed beggar inevitably so. To be sure, what I begged was employment; but whose business was it to provide me with employment?" (*JE* 355). She may expect indifference to her suffering, but the ironic tone is also bitter reproof of it.

In the course of her autobiography, Jane claims to be "merely telling the truth" (*JE* 140), and she jokes with this idea when offering a mock apology "to the romantic reader . . . for telling the plain truth" (*JE* 141). Such jokes, as Rochester discovers, have a way of redounding upon the teller. Readers are likely to suspect that the tale is far from plain, especially since the narrator treats them much as characters do each other. For instance, the "illustration" (*JE* 449) of how Jane felt upon seeing the ruins of Thornfield has precisely the effect of Rochester's explanations:

it confuses rather than clarifies, encouraging readers to the mistaken impression that he is dead. In addition, Jane's is a horror story-within-a horror story that recalls her youthful enthusiasm for fantastic tales. The narrative of Thornfield in ruins features crows circling a burned-out mansion and references to "the silence of death" and "the solitude of a lonesome wild" (*JE* 450). The scene is straight out of Bewick and provides a frame for a story of tragic love and loss, whose central scene reveals a lover bent over "a vision of beauty—warm, and blooming" (*JE* 449) thought to be asleep but actually dead. The tale would be appropriate were Rochester to have died in the fire, but of all lovers and would-be lovers in Jane's tale only Bertha—that "foul German spectre— the vampire" (*JE* 311) dies. The joke would appear to be on readers, who have already been implicated in forms of humor shown to be in poor taste and to be used manipulatively. Ultimately, however, the joke is on the narrator, who, by reinforcing the logophobia rampant on the level of acting and speaking, becomes subject to it herself.

The novel provides several other examples of disingenuous narration. When Jane, for instance, tells herself "a plain, unvarnished tale" (*JE* 190) concerning an "indigent and insignificant plebeian" (*JE* 191) in order to destroy her romantic illusions about Rochester, readers are made aware of the ulterior motives that narration can serve. Jane uses her drawings in a similar way, as Annette Tromly has shown: "Jane creates the portraits [of Rochester, Blanche, Rosamund, and herself] to contain and control her feelings (her own and others') rather than to represent her subjects."[21] No one is taken in by this self-conscious manipulation, at least not for long, nor should readers be fooled when a similar tale is told by the narrator. Jane, for instance, adopts the pose of humility and self-effacement when she apologizes for writing the autobiography of an "insignificant existence" (*JE* 115). But this stance is belied by the autobiography itself, the writing of which entails no small act of egoism. Jane may state that the life she narrates is "insignificant," but this explanation of her method suggests otherwise: "I am only bound to invoke memory where I know her responses will possess some degree of interest" (*JE* 115). Writing her own story is the conscious and natural culmination of the signature that unconsciously announces her identity to St. John; it is the adult version of the edited tale told to Miss Temple to defend against the charge of deceit. Her narrative, readers may suspect, is less autobiography than apologia.

As we have seen, Currer Bell also maintains the pose of insignificance, deprecatingly describing her novel as "a plain tale with few pretensions" (*JE* 35). Perhaps we are intended to respond to this pretense with impatience, as Rochester does when Jane is formally introduced to him: "Oh, don't fall back on over-modesty" (*JE* 153). But readers of the "unknown and unrecommended Author" (*JE* 35) will quickly suspect the unimposing persona presented by Currer Bell (the pseudonym itself is a kind of "cover"), especially when the expression of gratitude to Public, Press, and Publishers, which seemingly augments her facade of docile self-effacement, is immediately followed by an acerbic attack upon the "timorous or carping few" (*JE* 35) who find the novel to be an affront to religion and morality. After Currer Bell's identity is revealed, Charlotte Brontë continues the rhetorical strategy of her editorial persona. With sarcastic understatement, she describes her response to a critic as "a quiet little chat," but her words are clearly not "framed to tickle delicate ears" (*JE* 36). Readers, therefore, are justified in concluding that what Rochester has described as "a sly penknife" is but another name for the author's sly pen.[22]

Presented with a tale of sensational incident and strong feeling, readers are placed in a position resembling the protagonist's when she watches the arrival of Rochester and his guests at Thornfield. Exposed to a fascinating, foreign, but forbidden world, Jane experiences "an acute pleasure in looking—a precious yet poignant pleasure; pure gold, with a steely point of agony: a pleasure like what the thirst-perishing man might feel who knows the well to which he has crept is poisoned, yet stoops and drinks divine draughts nevertheless" (*JE* 203).[23] *Jane Eyre* offers readers their own "divine draughts." Like St. John Rivers, we indulge ourselves in a tale of "love rising like a freshly opened fountain" (*JE* 399), although, unlike him, we are likely to drink fully, not limiting ourselves to a scanty fifteen minutes' indulgence. Thoughts of Rosamund Oliver are to him like a "sweet inundation" of pastoral fields "assiduously sown with the seed of good intentions, of self-denying plans. And now it is deluged with a nectarous flood—the young germs swamped—delicious poison cankering them" (*JE* 399). With the help of a prophylactic pocket watch, this "cold, hard man" (*JE* 400) survives the seductions of art—both Jane's drawing of "the Peri" (*JE* 389) and her accompanying narrative of conjugal contentment. Readers, however, may be less resolute, for the narrator toys with us as impishly and as mercilessly as Jane does with St. John, enticing us with divine draughts of fiction, sweeping us away upon a flood of nectarous words.

The emblem of Jane's and Rochester's passion is the "lightning-struck chestnut-tree" (*JE* 469). From its "strong roots . . . unsundered below" (*JE* 304) a fruitful conjugal union emerges—after, of course, providential punishment by fire. The emblem of St. John's ascetic desire is the "overshadowing tree, Philanthropy" (*JE* 401). From this "wild stringy root of human nature" (*JE* 401), a mighty missionary develops. He "hews down like a giant the prejudices of creed and caste" (*JE* 477)—at least after his own "pruning and training" (*JE* 401). Perhaps unnoticed after the gods of orthodoxy have completed the gardener's task, however, is the poetic "upas tree" (*JE* 328), the emblem of the reader's aesthetic experience. Its "delicious poison" is language itself. As great as our fears about words and their uses may be as a result of Charlotte Brontë's art, it is precisely because of that art that we have "surfeited [ourselves] on sweet lies, and swallowed poison as if it were nectar" (*JE* 190).

Jane herself experiences the pleasure of devouring books when she is at Marsh End (*JE* 376), but this gratification does not explain why she chooses to write one. The personal incentives for self-assertion would seem to have been removed when she acquires wealth and relations through inheritance, followed by status and family through marriage.[24] Furthermore, one would expect Jane, whose "treacherous slate" (*JE* 97) has previously exposed her to opprobrium, to avoid taking up a stylus again. In the first thirty years of her life, she pens little more than a newspaper advertisement and several letters with explicitly practical purposes. She does not keep a diary or journal, unlike Richardson's Pamela, whose situation so closely resembles hers in other ways.[25] Her only expressive outlet is painting, a pursuit stimulated by the little childhood reading that she has done. Even after eight years at Lowood, she must admit to having read "[o]nly such books as came in my way; and they have not been numerous, or very learned" (*JE* 155). How, then, are we to account for the emergence of the autobiographer from a character neither a writer nor a reader?

Neither the texts of Jane's childhood reading nor the many embedded narratives within *Jane Eyre* itself offer encouragement to the prospective autobiographer. The former are largely escapist fantasies, at least they become so to a child hungry for adventure. The latter are motivated—and usually marred—by self-interest. Intratextual personal narratives tend to function as negative exemplars of the two dominant modes and motives for telling one's story: ecstasy and interrogation. Ecstatic narrative originates within the self and leads to a kind of ejaculatory expression; interrogated narrative is coerced by another and results in an equally one-sided but much more constrained and controlled story. Both forms are displayed during Adèle's introduction to Jane. The motive for her uninvited performance is ecstatic; its childhood exuberance takes her out of herself, and her mother appears in miniature on the stage. The dramatic tale that she recites, whose tone is signified by the rat's command, "*Parlez*," is inquisitional and ominous.

Although these modes are in many ways opposite, they have in common one important factor: a lack of narrative distance. When Jane observes that the "eagerness of a listener quickens the tongue of a narrator" (*JE* 278), she explains one reason for this loss of detachment. In ecstatic narrative, the interlocutors' roles are collapsed within the self, as tellers lead themselves on solipsized narrative excursions. Helen's "daydreams" (*JE* 89) and Jane's solitary and unspoken "bright visions" (*JE* 141) exemplify the monological and escapist nature of these internal narrative rhapsodies. Helen returns to the "visionary brook" (*JE* 89) of her childhood, and Jane opens an "inward ear to a tale that was never ended—a tale my imagination created, and narrated continuously; quickened with all of incident, life, fire, feeling, that I desired and had not in my actual existence" (*JE* 141). Even when an audience is present and the words are articulated, the ecstatic teller does not speak to others. In the midst of a conversation with Jane, for example, Rochester addresses a "bonny wanderer" (*JE* 168) and a "hag" (*JE* 170) known only to himself. During the fortune-telling episode, Jane and Rochester become virtually oblivious to each other's presence. Jane is "wrapped . . . in a kind of dream" (*JE* 228), and he "rave[s] in a kind of exquisite delirium" (*JE* 230). The coalescence of dialogical roles within the teller in these tales of unsatisfied desire means that the speakers lose themselves in verbal worlds having little to do with practical exigencies. While there is no evidence that this delirium visits Jane in the process of writing, readers are at least made aware of the possibility that her final narrative, the novel itself, is also a tale of wish-fulfillment. Readers should also be sensitive to the effects of what Ricoeur calls the "double eclipse of the reader and writer" in narrative.[26] That is, given the absence of the reader from the act of writing (and conversely of the writer from reading), dialogical roles are necessarily collapsed in a manner analogous to that of ecstatic narrative. Jane's "dear readers" exist only in her imagination, but, more to the point, actual readers, dear or otherwise, are apt to find themselves repeating her experience during the fortune-telling: "One unexpected sentence came from her lips after another, till I got involved in a web of mystification" (*JE* 228).[27]

Interrogatory, no less than ecstatic, tales are typified by a lack of narrative distance. In the latter, this lack is typically but not invariably occasioned by the absence of the auditor; in the former, it is the direct result of the threatening and invasive presence of the auditor. The imaginative license that typifies ecstatic narrative, however, is absent altogether from the tales resulting from Brocklehurst's (*JE* 64–65), Rochester's (*JE* 152–56), and Rivers's (*JE* 363, 372–73) inquisitions of Jane. And while ecstatic narrative produces a visionary tale, interrogated narrative results in a secretive and often misleading story. The coercion of these narratives eliminates distance by denying the teller control of her story, and the response to this intimidation is likely to be partial rather than full disclosure. Jane openly censors her story to the Riverses (*JE* 363, 373) and secretly edits it for Rochester (*JE* 464–65, 472). Diana Rivers defends the right to secrecy (*JE* 373), but Jane's uses of this tactic, as well as Rochester's blatant abuses of it, may incline readers to wonder what has been left out of the tale presented to them, apart from eight boring years at Lowood and details concerning her wanderings after leaving Thornfield, of which she exasperatedly writes, "Let me condense now. I am sick of the subject" (*JE* 355).

In recognizing the possibilities for deception in Jane's internal narratives, readers may become distanced from the teller. Her autobiography, therefore, may also engender the dialogical distance precluded by ejaculatory and interrogatory narrative. In this regard, Jane's story can be seen as an extension of her courtship discourse with Rochester. Throughout their courtship, she attempts to sequester herself from Rochester. She avoids him on the evening that he proposes (*JE* 276), resists setting the wedding date (*JE* 287), dreads its arrival once it has been set (*JE* 303), and wishes that time would stop on the night before she is to be married (*JE* 307). The success of distancing as an erotic strategy suggests that Jane may well have adopted this tack in her fiction. Her relation with the oft-invoked Reader is certainly as thorny as that with her employer.[28] With both, Jane employs a rhetorical method calculated to maintain the distance that motivates loving in the one case and reading in the other.

To understand the erotics of distance we might turn to Julia Kristeva's analysis of the Song of Songs.[29] Although allusions to this book are not among Brontë's many references to the Old Testament, it offers a number of parallels with *Jane Eyre*, many of which can be described in terms of the barriers and distances figured in Jane's prenuptial dream. For instance, in both texts an economic gap exists between a woman without social status and a privileged man. The rhetorical structures of the works are oppositional: in both, love is expressed in a counterpoint of voices establishing a powerful and powerfully erotic poetic dialogue. Another barrier is theological and juridical: the Song of Songs and *Jane Eyre* address the anarchic threat of the erotic to the structures of religion and law.

Kristeva focuses on the elusive and inaccessible nature of the lovers' relationship in the Song of Songs and concludes that "the absolute tension of love for the Other" (*TL* 90) is centrally important: "Supreme authority, be it royal or divine, can be loved as flesh while remaining essentially inaccessible; the intensity of love comes precisely from that combination of received jouissance and taboo, from a basic separation that nevertheless unites" (*TL* 90). The "separation that unites" has consistently defined Jane and Rochester's situation. Apart from differences in age and experience, a social proscription divides employer and "paid subordinate" (*JE* 165). When that gap is overcome by betrothal, Jane reimposes the economic obstacle and implements various rhetorical strategies to "keep [him] in reasonable check" (*JE* 302). At the very moment she admits that Rochester has become an idol eclipsing her view of God, she resolves to "maintain that distance between you and myself most conducive to our real mutual advantage" (*JE* 301). And just when that advantage is about to be compromised by marriage, the lovers are separated by Rochester's preexistent marriage—a legal hiatus made literal by Jane's flight from Thornfield. Marriage threatens the tension that generates erotic intensity. If the condition that spawned their passion is to be sustained, fulfillment must remain in the future. Thus Jane may be speaking presciently when she tells Rochester that the tales of fashionable society "generally run on the same theme—courtship; and promise to end in the same catastrophe—marriage" (*JE* 227–28).

An appropriate figure of Jane and Rochester's love, therefore, is the promise—not the lying promises of his duplicitous courtship but the linguistic act itself. The very premise of the promise is incompletion; its cathetic force inheres in the tension between desire for and distance from the promised act. When Rochester asks Jane to "[p]romise me one thing," she replies, "I'll promise you anything, sir, that I think I am likely to perform" (*JE* 254). In saying this, and in previously withholding a promise because she "might be obliged to break it" (*JE* 252), Jane alludes to the predictive rather than the obligational dimension of promising. Emphasis shifts to the element of futurity that is predicated by promises and that sustains their significance. Promises in *Jane Eyre* tend to be not so much descriptive of the emotions that give rise to them as they are constitutive of the anticipatory anxiety upon which those emotions depend. They speak not of the present, and even less of a fixed point in the future, but of a dynamic indeterminacy defined by these points. There is no better example of this than betrothal, which by its very nature enacts a separation—in time as well as between intention and action—whose premise is unity. The promise to marry both negotiates and sustains the contradictions between now and then, between the erotic and the social, between jouissance and taboo. As Kristeva puts it:

> Love in the Song of Songs appears to be simultaneously in the framework of conjugality and of a fulfillment always set in the future. . . . One is thus faced with a true dialectical synthesis of amorous experi-

ence, including its universally disturbing, pathetic, enthusiastic, or melancholy aspect on the one hand, and its singularly Judaic feature on the other—legislating, unifying, subsuming burning sensuousness toward the One. (*TL* 98)

Promising in these terms is less a synthesis than a dialectical suspension. The marriage promise places Jane and Rochester in an erotically charged, but essentially ambiguous relation. Their cohabitation is neither concubinal nor conjugal. Amorous experience is indulged by deferment and circumscribed by language. Conversing itself becomes an erotic activity. Jane, for instance, delights in "vexing and soothing him by turns." Such talk, however, implicates promissory love in the logophobia to which all utterance is subject.

Throughout the novel the rhetoric of promising is consistent with that of trailing. Perhaps the best proof of this is Rochester's giving a new meaning to the "promise of narrative." On the one hand, he has no intention of keeping "the promise of narrative" when it comes to his past. That tale can have neither proper beginning nor accurate ending and key episodes must be excluded, if it is to further the plan to marry Jane. Even when Rochester promises to speak plainly, he elides more than he includes, making his narratives at best partial and at worst fabricated. On the other hand, he gives a new meaning to the phrase, "the promise of narrative." That is to say, he continually promises stories that he has no intention of delivering. He tells Jane that he will explain more fully "some day" (*JE* 170,171), and then uses a formula that might be construed to mean "never": "when we have been married a year and a day, I will tell you; but not now" (*JE* 313).

Other promises given to Jane are typically misleading, not because they will not be kept, but because they do not purport to be acts of courting at all. For example, both Rochester and Rivers elicit or make promises concerning Jane's future employment. Maintaining the pretense that he will marry Blanche and that Jane must leave Thornfield, Rochester asks that she promise to "trust this quest of a situation to me" (254). Rivers responds in similar fashion to her wish for honest employment: "If such is your spirit, I promise to aid you, in my own time and way" (*JE* 375). Both promise help; each intends marriage. Thus their promises can be fulfilled only ironically. Jane's suitors reverse the strategy of Don Juan, who promises *to* marry in order *not* to do so. In effect, Rochester and Rivers promise *not* to marry in order *to* do so. The opposite strategies, however, yield identical results: suspicion of lovers' language.

By having Mrs. Rochester write the story of her life, Brontë reasserts the distance and futurity encoded in promises and threatened by marriage. Jane's autobiographical voice resists the legitimizing and monolo-gizing force of married life. She professes complete happiness, observing, for example, that she and her husband "talk, I believe, all day long" (*JE* 476). Readers who recall that "*tete-à-tete*" conversation" (*JE* 299) has previously served as a kind of hand-to-hand combat will not be sur-prised by this garrulity, but they may well question Jane's profession of "perfect concord" (*JE* 476). Given the teasing in- and misdirections with which she tells Rochester of her life after leaving Thornfield (all with the aim of eliciting "his old impetuosity" [*JE* 470]), readers have every rea-son to suspect that Jane's voice is once again used to establish the eroti-cized distance that typifies betrothal. Furthermore, the biblical metaphor applied to this marital unity is double-edged. Jane says that she has become "bone of his bone and flesh of his flesh" (*JE* 476; Gen. 2:23). Frances Power Cobbe, writing in 1868, says that this "noble Ori-ental metaphor" unwittingly reveals the threat posed to women by mar-riage, which resembles nothing so much as the mating of tarantulas after which one partner is literally consumed by the other.[30] Although she has the genders reversed (the male tarantula is eaten), Cobbe's interpretation aptly describes women's legal position after marriage. Fearing if not legal then psychological consumption, Jane unconsciously asserts her distance from a domineering partner and her need for, if nothing else, "at least a new servitude" (*JE* 117). In invoking Genesis to describe her marriage, she also ingeminates the tension between the sacred and the profane heard previously in Rochester's supernatural discourse and rein-forced by his telling Jane that she, not the "beneficent God" to whom he appeals for her return, is "the alpha and omega of my heart's wishes" (*JE* 471). These dissonant strains suggest a counterpoint to the happy hum of conjugal conversation. To write her story is to bring it into ques-tion, for she can escape neither logophobia, which the internal tales of love dramatize, nor the dialectic of distance and desire, to which all such tales are subject.

As Jane's summary allusion to Genesis suggests, Eve stands behind this wifely narrative, in addition to both the Shulamite maiden and Delilah. When Rochester fears Jane's questions, he both pleads and threatens: "for God's sake, don't desire a useless burden! Don't long for poison—don't turn out a downright Eve on my hands!" (*JE* 290). His upright wife does prove to be a "downright Eve," however, and in ways that he cannot envision. The "apple of his eye" (*JE* 476) offers readers a seductive narrative fruit that threatens the complacency and univocal power of authority. Brontë's Eve, like the heroine of the Song of Songs, "by an adventure that conjugates a submission to legality and the vio-lence of passion" (*TL* 99–100), leaves readers with the ambivalent knowledge that her narrative may be as unreliable as it is nectarous.

From the rhetorical and erotic violence of *Jane Eyre*, we turn to a pastoral world of labor and natural piety in *Adam Bede*. Eliot's Eve is more madonna than temptress, and language more likely a source of curiosity than of deception. The *logos ex machina* that brings Adam and Dinah together has a very human explanation and conveys the reverential rather than the passional nature of seemingly "slight words" (*AB* 465). The radical linguistic fears emerging from the gothic setting and fiery passions of *Jane Eyre* have a quiet antidote in the bucolic world and the enduring loves of *Adam Bede*.

CHAPTER 5

Right Speaking in Adam Bede

Readers of *Adam Bede* are introduced to Hayslope through the eyes (and ears) of an outsider who is passing through the village. In a "treble and wheezy voice, with a slightly mincing accent," the landlord of the Donnithorne Arms informs this stranger: "They're cur'ous talkers i' this country, sir; the gentry's hard work to hunderstand 'em" (*AB* 26). Mr. Casson's remark, of course, reveals its own curiosities, and his interlocutor might well empathize with the more celebrated traveler whose entry into unfamiliar territory prompts the exclamation: "'Curiouser and curiouser!' cried Alice (she was so much surprised, that for the moment she quite forgot how to speak good English)" (*AW* 145). While Loamshire bears slight resemblance to Wonderland, uninitiated auditors are likely to find not only its dialect but also its conversational habits to be a source of curiosity and "hard work." For example, someone expecting speakers to address one another face-to-face and at a reasonable proximity will be surprised to learn that the "true rustic turns his back on his interlocutor, throwing a question over his shoulder as if he meant to run away from the answer, and walking a step or two farther off when the interest of the dialogue culminates" (*AB* 30).[1] In "The Natural History of German Life," Eliot observes that among the peasantry each province has its own "style; namely, its dialect, its phraseology, its proverbs and its songs, which belong alike to the entire body of the people."[2] *Adam Bede* offers a veritable dialectical mapping of rural England at the beginning of the century. It includes not only the "style" of the Loamshire *Bauernthum* and the sociolects of the upper classes, but also the mixed or multiple dialects of those who by experience, like Casson, or by education, like Adam, find themselves somewhere between the peasantry and the nobility. In order to depict bygone times and diverse dialects, even the narrator resorts to what is by contemporary standards "a strange mode of speaking" (*AB* 197). With diachronic change added to synchronic variation, readers must feel that curious language is pandemic and that "good English" is in jeopardy.

Mr. Casson, himself considered to be a "hodd talker" (*AB* 327) by the villagers, debates the issue of proper speech with Bartle Massey. As a result of fifteen years' service to the Donnithornes, this butler turned barkeeper arrogates to himself an expertise in "dilecks" (*AB* 26) and "right language" that is ridiculed by the village schoolmaster: "You're as about as near the right language as a pig's squeaking is like a tune played on a key-bugle. . . . You talk the right language for *you*. When Mike Holdsworth's goat says ba-a-a, it's all right—it 'ud be unnatural for it to make any other noise" (*AB* 327). Bartle's caustic wit may impress the Saturday evening crowd at the Donnithorne Arms, but it does little to illuminate one of the central preoccupations of the novel: the question of right speaking. The relativism implied by Bartle's quali-fication, "for *you*," should not obscure his belief in proper speech, which is, in fact, the basis of the criticism. Massey is an exacting teacher, one who—if his standards of penmanship provide any indication—demands precise speech from his pupils: Adam "knew by heart every arabesque flourish in the framed specimen of Bartle Massey's handwrit-ing which hung over the schoolmaster's head, by way of keeping a lofty ideal before the minds of his pupils" (*AB* 226).

The schoolmaster has more than a little in common with that "trea-sury of correct language," Susan Garth (M 402). Mrs. Garth instructs her children in grammar (as her husband does Fred Vincy in penman-ship) "and in a general wreck of society would have tried to hold her 'Lindley Murray' above the waves" (*M* 276). In *Middlemarch*, a deluge of slang, or perhaps merely the rising tide of middle-class respectability, prompts a similar debate about right speaking. Fred, while reserving the right to ridicule slang of "the wrong sort," nevertheless asserts that "all choice of words is slang . . . correct English is the slang of prigs who write history and essays" (*M* 126).[3] Bartle's account of right language and Fred's of slang reveal a curious contradiction: on the one hand, both acerbically assert that language use is relative and imply that notions of propriety based on nature, class, or culture are arbitrary; on the other hand, each assumes an underlying standard of proper speech—one that allows the misanthropic schoolteacher to criticize the social pretensions of an innkeeper and the disaffected university student to scoff at the pre-tentious rhetoric of shopkeepers (*M* 126). If these two views are repre-sentative, it would seem that a distinct distaste for affected speech and an indistinct notion of standard English are widely shared among the liberally minded—or at least the well-educated—of Eliot's provincial world.

This curious contradiction is also exhibited by the narrator, who imitates "substandard" dialects when verisimilitude demands it but mocks peculiar speaking when it results from affectation, as in the case of Mr. Craig. Mrs. Poyser compares him to "a cock as thinks the sun's rose o' purpose to hear him crow" (*AB* 201); the narrator describes him as "a superior man . . . [who] was never aware that his conversation and advances were received coldly, for to shift one's point of view beyond certain limits is impossible to the most liberal and expansive mind; we are none of us aware of the impression we produce on Brazilian monkeys of feeble understanding—it is possible they see hardly anything in us" (*AB* 200). If his speech is any indication, however, Mr. Craig may be more like a Brazilian monkey than he would care to admit. Readers are told that, apart from the slightly "stronger burr in his accent, his speech differed little from that of the Loamshire people about him" (*AB* 201). In short, there is more resemblance than difference between the gardener and those whom he looks down upon as if they were a lesser species.

As with Fred and Bartle, the narrator exhibits a veneer of tolerance that belies an attitude of linguistic *hauteur*. By his pretentious behavior, Mr. Craig may invite the narrator's sarcasms, but how is the condescending tone toward Bartle's ponderous students to be explained? The narrator remarks: "It was touching to see these three big men, with the marks of their hard labour about them, anxiously bending over the worn books. . . . [I]t was almost as if three rough animals were making humble efforts to learn how they might become human" (*AB* 229). Just as these "full-grown children . . . touched the tenderest fibre in Bartle Massey's nature" (*AB* 229), the narrator claims an empathic connection to primitive speakers, admitting occasional yet "quite enthusiastic movements of admiration towards old gentlemen who spoke the worst English" (*AB* 182). But this confession, which might be taken as evidence of liberality, is attended by the same absence of self-consciousness typifying Casson's and Craig's linguistic superiority. The "worst English" can only be measured against a standard dialect, and the narrator's intermittent admiration indicates only a priggish disapproval of dialectical deviance. Eliot herself manifests this attitude when she remarks that "the slow gaze . . . the slow utterance, and the heavy slouching walk [of the English peasant] remind one rather of that melancholy animal the camel."[4] If language is our Rubicon, as Müller maintains, then clearly the peasantry—variously likened to English goats, Brazilian monkeys, and African camels—has yet to cross.

Adam Bede, completed in 1859, anticipates a decade that according to Dennis Taylor "inaugurated in England a widespread historical consciousness of language. Simultaneously, the decade marked a most ferocious debate over correct speech and was a sort of climax of the prescriptive tradition."[5] The linguistic climate in which the novel is written, however, is quite different from the one it depicts. The disagreement between Casson and Massey is but a faint harbinger of the 1860s. Hayslope in 1799 is largely untouched by such grammatical debates; its dialect retains the oddities that Eliot associates with a bygone time and a way of life increasingly threatened by social and technological upheaval: "The peculiarity of the peasant's language consists chiefly in his retention of historical peculiarities, which gradually disappear under the friction of cultivated circles."[6] In novels like *Adam Bede*, Eliot in effect answers Coleridge's call for a "natural history" of language. In so doing, she also points to the loss of expressiveness that accompanies increasingly standardized speech. What, Eliot asks, would be the effect of a perfect philosophical language about which Locke and Mill speculate:

> Suppose, then, that the effort which has been again and again made to construct a universal language on a rational basis has at length succeeded, and that you have a language which has no uncertainty, no whims of idiom, no cumbrous forms, no fitful shimmer of many-hued significance, no hoary archaisms "familar with forgotten years"—a patent deodorized and nonresonant language, which effects the purpose of communication as perfectly and rapidly as algebraic signs. Your language may be a perfect medium of expression to science, but will never express *life*, which is a great deal more than science. With the anomalies and inconveniences of historical language, you will have parted with its music and its passion, with its vital qualities as an expression of individual character, with its subtle capabilities of wit, *with everything that gives it power over the imagination.*[7] (The latter emphasis is added.)

Eliot's defense of "the anomalies and inconveniences of historical language" owes something to Wordsworth's "Preface" to *Lyrical Ballads* (a book coincidentally dismissed by Arthur Donnithorne as "twaddling stuff" [*AB* 73]) and also to Tooke's *Winged Words*.[8] Tooke, in refuting eighteenth-century theories of artificial language, calls attention to the spoken language of "artless men; who did not sit down like philosophers to invent '*de petits mots pour être mis avant les noms.*'"[9] By dramatizing the colors, smells, and sounds of such artless men, the "hodd talkers" of sixty years before, Eliot both reaffirms the expressive power of "natural language" and questions the prescriptive attitudes that she herself exhibits.

In alluding to "the power [of language] over the imagination," Eliot sounds a theme familiar to readers of *Winged Words*. She further suggests that the power of words may in part be due to their historical presence, that is, to the very fact that they have become "familiar with forgotten years." Eliot expresses an opinion that might be taken as a motto both for the etymological study of language of her day and for mid-Victorian realistic fiction: "The sensory and motor nerves that run in the same sheath, are scarcely bound together by a more necessary and delicate union than that which binds men's affections, imagination, wit, and humour, with the subtle ramifications of historical language."[10] Unlike Tooke, who warns against the syntactic confusions of grammarians, Eliot recognizes the expressive possibilities of both synaptic connections and historical practices. Unlike Wordsworth, who is troubled by the "faulty expressions" occasioned by the "arbitrary connections of feelings and ideas with particular words and phrases,"[11] Eliot celebrates the "fitful shimmer of many-hued significance" of language.

Adam Bede investigates this significance in three discursive "settings" or modes: sermons, courtship, and agrarian symposia. Each of these modes—homiletic speech (whether literal or figurative), courtship discourse, and occasional oratory—reveals a dynamic interplay of curious and correct language. If curiosity is the salient characteristic of rustic speaking, then uncertainty may well be its chief consequence. The provincials of Loamshire are unrepentant linguistic skeptics. "Where's the use o' talkin'" is an often sounded refrain, one that expresses the general sense that words are powerless to affect the timeless realities of death, weather, and human obstancy. Beyond this sense of resignation to the human condition, however, Eliot suggests that the contradictions of speaking and the complexities of language are more profound than these passive provincials might suspect.[12] By posing the problem of speakers whose "national language may be instinct with poetry unfelt by the lips that use it" (*AB* 275), Eliot complicates the Romantic notion of *Volkstimme*. She implies—like Trench, but without his overt Christian interpretation—that speakers say more than they know.[13] This verbal "bonus" is readily apparent in the practice of promising and the process of betrothal, which is shown to be Adamic in a secular rather than a biblical sense.

The scene that prompts Mr. Casson's remark about "cur'ous talkers" introduces a form of communication that cuts across class lines and dialects: homiletic speech.[14] This discursive mode is widely practiced and occurs in two forms: figurative sermons, to which readers are introduced by Adam's "sarmunt" (*AB* 2) in the workshop, and literal sermons, of which the first example is Dinah's "a-praying and a-groaning" (*AB* 21) on the Green. The latter offers an instance of homiletic discourse especially marked by curiosity: it is unorthodox in both doctrine and delivery. The Evangelical message comes from a woman, on a weekday, and—strangest of all—it arouses the interest of virtually everyone in Hayslope. Even the stranger, Colonel Townley, finds that his "curiosity to see the young female preacher proved too much for his anxiety to get to the end of his journey" (*AB* 38). Like all of Hayslope, he is intrigued by the novelty of the situation. With the possible exception of the "knot of Methodists" on the Green (*AB* 28), all of the onlookers—both the men, who are "chiefly gathered in the neighbourhood of the black-smith's shop," and the women, whose "stronger curiosity" (*AB* 31) brings them to the edge of the Green—are drawn to the scene by other than pious motives.

This singular scene provides a prime example of the peculiarities to which literal homiletic speaking is susceptible. The prayer with which Dinah begins announces the tripartite structure of what will follow: "Lord, open their ears to my message, bring their sins to their minds, and make them thirst for that salvation which Thou art ready to give" (*AB* 34).[15] Perhaps knowing her audience, Dinah first concentrates on opening the ears of the merely curious. She aligns herself with the Christian paradigm as reenacted by Wesley: difference and distance (which establish the authority to speak) appealing to similarity and propinquity (which establish the credibility necessary to be heard). She offers herself as an example of one inspired by the gospel, brought to her by "a good man preach[ing] out of doors, just as we are here" (*AB* 35, 36). Wesley, she recalls, seemed to have "come down from the sky to preach" (*AB* 35)—as did Christ, and as Dinah might as well have since she "comes out o' Stonyshire, pretty nigh thirty mile off" (*AB* 27). Indeed, both Adam and his mother mistake her for a celestial being.[16] Yet just as Christ "spoke words such as we speak to each other" (*AB* 37), Dinah addresses the people not as an outsider but as a comrade: "I am poor, like you: I have to get my living with my hands" (*AB* 42). In order to gain the ears of her audience, she appears as an angel and speaks as a laborer.

Having succeeded in winning a hearing—"the traveller had been chained to the spot against his will . . . [t]he villagers had pressed nearer to her" (*AB* 37, 39)—Dinah enters the second stage of her sermon, a lurid portrayal of Christ's suffering and of human guilt. No longer content with a sense of communalism, she addresses her audience individually, "beseeching them with tears to turn to God while there was still time" (*AB* 38). The result is a general sense of discomfort and several instances of discomfiture giving way to distress. Sandy Jim, for instance, is left with a "confused intention of being a better fellow . . . and cleaning himself more regularly of a Sunday" (*AB* 39). The confounding of an unsullied soul and a clean body questions the value of Dinah's attempts at spiritual antisepsis. Bessy Cranage, who "belonged unquestionably to that unsoaped lazy class of feminine characters" (*AB* 39), tears off the earrings that symbolize her "slackness in the minor morals" (*AB* 39). Her subsequent reversion to jewelry and "such small finery as she could muster" (*AB* 266) comically deflates the significance of Dinah's achievement.[17] Even Dinah's modest estimate of her accomplishment is exaggerated: "I saw no signs of any great work upon them, except in a young girl named Bessy Cranage" (*AB* 98). Dinah may win an audience, but she does not entice anyone into the fold.

The final movement of the sermon depicts "the joys that were in store for the penitent" (41). This good news seems emotionally and rhetorically anticlimactic, however, and the hour-long sermon winds down to the singing of hymns.[18] Colonel Townley, who has been more taken with the "inward drama of the speaker's emotions" (*AB* 42) than with her message, rides off to the accompaniment of "that strange blending of exultation and sadness which belongs to the cadence of a hymn" (42). This mixed note concludes Dinah's curious performance, which has itself been a "strange blending" of rhetorical modes and tones. Her delivery features a dramatic "variety of modulation," from "plaintive appeal" to "pleading reproach" (*AB* 37, 38, 40). The net effect of her words is concomitantly mixed. On the one hand, she "thoroughly arrested her hearers" (*AB* 37–38). Even Wiry Ben, despite "almost wishing he had not come to hear Dinah . . . couldn't help liking to look at her and listen to her" (*AB* 39). On the other hand, the narrator comments that "the village mind does not easily take fire, and a little smouldering vague anxiety that might easily die out again was the utmost effect Dinah's preaching had wrought in them at present" (*AB* 39). Her words are at once a masterpiece of "sincere unpremeditated eloquence" (*AB* 42) and a proof of the failure of language, even at its most earnest and ingenuous, to accomplish its objective.

Mr. Irwine suggests that Dinah's successes, however slight, may owe less to her oratorical zeal than to her attractive face. She, on the contrary, envisions herself as an invisible conduit of the Lord's "good news" (*AB* 35), claiming to resemble the burning bush: "Moses never took any heed what sort of bush it was—he only saw the brightness of the Lord" (*AB* 97). Yet the narrator's botanical metaphor for Dinah's appearance as she mounts the cart to preach on the green suggests a blooming rather than a burning bush: her face makes "one think of white flowers with light touches of colour on their pure petals" (*AB* 34).[19] Wiry Ben's joke further emphasizes that she is far from a disembodied spiritual voice: "I'll stick up for the pretty women preachin': I know they'd persuade me over a deal sooner nor th' ugly men" (*AB* 32).[20] Similarly, Bessy Cranage is more preoccupied with questions such as "whether it was better to have such a sort of pale face as that, or fat red cheeks and round black eyes like her own" (*AB* 39) than she is interested in Dinah's message. Many in the audience possess a "curious sacrilegious eye" (*AB* 132) rather than a pious religious heart.

This impressive, yet largely ineffectual, sermon extends Eliot's investigation of right speaking from a matter of dialect or even of rhetorical mode to language itself. The consequences of literal homiletic discourse have little to do with the words actually spoken. Whatever the circumstances or text, whoever the speaker, sermons seem to have a limited impact on their audiences. Successful preaching is always qualified and sometimes contradictory, as Adam's defense of Mr. Irwine's comfortable and even complacent Christianity suggests. On the one hand, Adam asserts that "nobody has ever heard me say Mr. Irwine was much of a preacher" (AB 180). On the other hand, he claims that the rector "said nothing but what was good and what you'd be the wiser for remembering" (AB 181).[21] A heterodox conclusion might be drawn from Adam's observation: being a good preacher has little to do with saying "what was good." At the very least, Adam implies that Mr. Irwine is heard, to the extent that he is, only because his goals are modest. The minister addresses neither profound emotions nor complex religious questions, sensing, perhaps, that neither he nor the congregation is equal to such subjects.

Mr. Irwine is nevertheless much more popular than his successor, Mr. Ryde. Whereas Mr. Irwine's sermons are like "looking at a full crop o' wheat, or a pasture with a fine dairy o' cows in it; it makes you think the world's comfortable-like" (AB 100), Mr. Ryde's are "a dose o' physic, he gripped you and worreted you, and after all he left you much the same" (AB 180).[22] The reasons for Mrs. Poyser's views are to be found less in what the ministers actually say on Sunday than in their "way of preaching in the weekdays" (AB 179–80), that is, their manner of daily living. Ryde's failure as a resident of Loamshire accounts for his failure as a minister of God. He is niggardly and proud, and "his preaching wouldn't go down well with that sauce" (AB 179). Irwine, on the contrary, knows the interests as well as the activities of his rustic parishioners, and acts with open friendliness toward them. According to Adam, the rector "preached short moral sermons, and that was all. But then he acted pretty much up to what he said" (AB 180). His successes as a preacher, however qualified they might be, have more to do with his actions than with his words.

Similarly, Dinah's eventual popularity in Loamshire has virtually nothing to do with her public speaking. Her "maggot o' preaching" (AB 459), as Mrs. Poyser puts it, is appreciated only by Seth, and only he regrets her decision to give it up. Attempts at conversion—of Hayslope in general or of Hetty in particular—produce little more than temporary tears (AB 41, 160). But Dinah's quiet ways and "words of comfort" (AB 314) are welcome everywhere. Her good works are a language generally "understood far better than the Bible or the hymn-book" (AB 459). In this regard, she resembles Mr. Irwine. For both, successful preaching has nothing to do with sermonizing; it is a matter of secular practice rather than of religious principle. And in this regard, Dinah's "silencing" at the end of the novel is perhaps less significant than some critics would make it, since she continues the only form of preaching that has heretofore been shown to be efficacious, that is, "talking to the people a bit in their houses" (*AB* 506).

Beyond questioning the word of God's ministers, Eliot seems to question the efficacy of the word of God. Biblical language commands neither the attention nor the acquiescence of the Loamshire faithful. Everyone has a different "translation" or interpretation of sacred texts, and the meaning of the Scriptures curiously proliferates and metamorphoses in human mouths. Lisbeth tells Seth that "thee allays makes a peck o' thy own words out o' a pint o' the Bible's," and she continues: "An' when the Bible's such a big book, an' thee canst read all thro't, an' ha' the pick o' the texes, I canna think why thee dostna pick better words as donna mean so much more nor they say" (*AB* 55). Lisbeth's complaint has the virtue and the force of simplicity. Adam shares his mother's views of "texes"; he disapproves of his brother's "argumentative spiritualism" and prefers a biblical passage that "wants no candle to show't" (*AB* 59, 58). Perhaps for that very reason, he is both as likely to turn to Benjamin Franklin as to St. Paul for guidance in everyday life (*AB* 55) and as eager to read the Bible for "history, biography, and poetry" (*AB* 470) as for theology. He is especially hostile to the arcane doctrinal matters that play so large a role in sectarian theological disputation. He recounts the time in the past when he "began to see as all this weighing and sifting what this text means and that text means . . . was no part o' real religion at all. . . . I found it better for my soul to be humble before the mysteries o' God's dealings, and not be making a clatter about what I could never understand" (*AB* 181). Theological debate usually has more to do with self-interest than with religion. Indeed, one factor affecting all homiletic discourse, from the most learned to the most enthusiastic, is a general suspicion that it is motivated by the concerns of speakers rather than the needs of auditors.

A comic instance of this false pride is the running feud between Joshua Rann and Will Maskery. Joshua may recognize that he should not use the "words of the Bible . . . to say my own say wi'" (68), but he is no less contentious for this understanding. Labeled "a blind Pharisee" by Will, he responds by calling his antagonist "the rampageousest Methodis as can be," and accuses him of "a-usin' the Bible i' that way to find nick'names for folks as are his elders an' betters!" (*AB* 67). Joshua's depiction of the misuses of the Bible is as apt of him as it is of Will, and as appropriate to the congregation as it is to the clergy. In this instance, as well as in common practice, "nick'names" like Arminian or Calvinist (*AB* 180) are missiles hurled by religious antagonists.

Another use of the Bible proposed by evangelical Christians seems calculated to minimize both doctrinal disputes and the imprint of self-interest upon religious practice. Seeking "Divine guidance by opening the Bible at hazard" and "having a literal way of interpreting the Scriptures" (*AB* 47–48) should circumvent the possibility of God's Word being used "to say [your] own say wi'." But Dinah's arbitrary selection of biblical passages to resolve personal dilemmas conveniently coincides with her own inclinations and confirms the sense that the Bible is generally used for self-interested objectives. On two separate occasions, she not surprisingly turns to the Acts of the Apostles to reconfirm her resolve to preach (*AB* 43–44, 158–59). Dinah may claim that the word of God passes directly through her, but a distinctly human "dileck" is clearly discernible.

Neither sermons nor their biblical sources, therefore, are unequivocal. Since the word of God must pass through human translators, sacred language invariably expresses at the least the intonations of speakers and quite often their interests as well. Whether as rigorous as Dinah's or as relaxed as Irwine's, homilies are defined by a curious double-voicedness that justifies a congregation's benign indifference, or even active skepticism. Furthermore, in a novel in which sermonizing plays such an important role, homilies are surprisingly ineffective. The preaching of the two central figures, Rev. Irwine and Dinah Morris, testifies to the weakness of words. Only when literal homilies take the form of actions, that is, only when words are translated into "preaching in the weekdays," can they be effective.

Figurative preachers do not meet with a much warmer reception than their literal counterparts. The first of the many examples of secular sermonizing in *Adam Bede* occurs in the first chapter when Adam delivers a homily on work. The first words actually uttered in the book are from a hymn that he sings: "Let all thy converse be sincere, / Thy conscience as the noonday clear" (*AB* 18). Sincerity, however, is no guarantee of effectiveness, as is demonstrated by Adam's addresses to his coworkers on the evils of slack work habits and to his brother on the dangers of "being oversperitial" (*AB* 21). For one "impatient of devout words" (*AB* 374), Adam is remarkably prone to uttering them. The impact upon the audience is quite similar to that of Dinah's preaching: Seth is meek and pious, while the mechanicals remain largely unrepentant. Sandy Jim ironically congratulates Adam on "the best sarmunt I've heared this long while" (*AB* 22), and Wiry Ben exclaims, "Bodderation, Adam! . . . lave a chap aloon, will'ee? Ye war afinding aut wi' preachers a while agoo—y' are fond enough o' preachin' yoursen" (*AB* 23). Having evoked more comedy than seriousness among his coworkers, Adam gives literal meaning to the phrase "muscular Christianity." He pins Ben against a wall with an "iron grasp" and threatens to "shake the soul out o' [his] body" (*AB* 19). The irony of his unholy threat exposes the futility of either sermons or shakings with the reprobates in the workshop—or in Loamshire generally.

Other noted secular sermonizers are Mrs. Poyser and Bartle Massey. While both are respected, their shrill tones and sharp tongues are as likely to alienate an audience as to win a hearing. In many ways their rivalry echoes that of Joshua Rann and Will Maskery, and their attitude toward one another is fairly indicative of the seriousness with which their words are taken by others. Bartle, an "impatient loquacious man" (*AB* 235), does not perceive the grating sound of his own misogynistic voice when he describes "the sound of women's voices [as] always either a-buzz or a-squeak. Mrs. Poyser keeps at the top o' the talk like a fife" (*AB* 233). Even his prize pupil, Adam, says that Bartle has "a tongue like a sharp blade . . . it never touches anything but it cuts" (*AB* 167). Mrs. Poyser, who also possesses a tongue "like a new-set razor" (*AB* 336), compares Bartle to those whose "tongues are like the clocks as run on strikin', not to tell you the time o' the day, but because there's summat wrong i' their own inside" (*AB* 495). She seems unaware that this epithet is further proof—as if more were needed—of her own "cutting eloquence" (*AB* 81), a habit of speech that leads Mr. Irwine to joke that she has both given her husband "many a good sermon" (*AB* 454) and "stock[ed] a country with proverbs" (*AB* 336).

Neither these proverbs nor Bartle's barbs, however, seem particularly effective. His specialty is the "rather heated exhortation," delivered without discrimination to recalcitrant and successful students alike, with little impact upon the former group (*AB* 229–30) and repressed laughter from the latter (*AB* 238). Mrs. Poyser's preferred genre is the "setdown" (*AB* 188), administered, for example, to Molly and Dinah but most famously to Squire Donnithorne. Her ranting has no effect at all in the first two cases and produces only amusement at the Squire's expense in the last. The most probable consequence of Mrs. Poyser's having "her say out," expulsion from Hall Farm, is prevented only by the Squire's death. A fair amount of energy is thus expended on discourses of limited impact, whose motivation seems to come more from the speakers' having "summat wrong i' their own inside" than from having any hope of making something right on the outside. Bartle, Mrs. Poyser, and Adam are unrepentant sermonizers, and one must wonder why, since so little seems to be accomplished as a result of their efforts.

Given the general curiosities of the homiletic mode, it is perhaps not surprising that things become "curiouser and curiouser" when sermonizers become suitors. Courtship—the second of the novel's primary discursive modes—bears a marked similarity to religious discourse. The strangest effect of Dinah's spiritual rhetoric, for example, is the offer of marriage that follows immediately upon the conclusion of her sermon. Seth Bede's proposal has obviously been prompted by more than this one event; nevertheless, it seems to have been inspired by and taken the form of her sermon. In an effort to gain Dinah's ear, Seth couches his offer of love in religious terms, delivering a homily on the biblical injunction to marry. One of the passages that he cites directly echoes Dinah, who began with an allusion to Christ's conversion of a Samaritan woman at Jacob's well (John 4:17). Dinah rejects Seth's offer, explaining that she "is not free to marry. . . . God has called me to minister to others. . . . He has called me to speak his word" (*AB* 45). Disregarding the implications of Dinah's New Testament allusion, Seth turns to another meeting at the very same well in an effort to persuade Dinah to become Rachel to his Jacob (Gen. 29).[23] The secular homily has little impact, however, and like Dinah's sermon it winds down to a hymn from the Methodist collection. Seth's song, however, idolatrously replaces the references to God with the name of his earthly love—faintly echoing the erotic strain of Song of Songs. He may not be confounding the spiritual with the physical, as Jim does, but he surely conflates their rhetorical modes. The narrator's remark that "[l]ove of this sort is hardly distinguishable from religious feeling" (*AB* 47) is small consolation for Seth.[24] Although he accepts Dinah's decision, the passionate kiss and betrothal of Jacob and Rachel loom behind this scene and suggest that eroticism and piety may not always be so easily reconciled.

Seth's pious love is appropriate for a novel with the premise that "[n]either are picturesque lazzaroni or romantic criminals half so frequent as your common labourer" (*AB* 178). Readers should not expect Byronic rhetoric and Brontëan embraces, and, indeed, the narrator refers disparagingly to "heroes riding fiery horses, themselves ridden by still more fiery passions" (*AB* 48), of whom in *Adam Bede* Arthur Donnithorne is the closest, albeit a pallid, representative. Although Adam assumes that Hetty has fallen prey to "that way o' talking gentlefolks have" (*AB* 311), we are privy to very few of Arthur's "soft" or "fond" words (*AB* 141, 203). His seductive language is summarized rather than quoted, perhaps because very little linguistic effort is needed to overcome so willing a victim.[25] Hetty's beauty is, in fact, a more eloquent and forceful erotic medium than Arthur's words. The expression of her face deafens him to the lower class accents of her speech: "While Arthur gazed into Hetty's dark beseeching eyes, it made no difference to him what sort of English she spoke" (*AB* 134). The narrator's irony underscores a now familiar theme: language seems oddly beside the point. Words are either inefficacious or bothersome to ardent lovers.

Although more attention is given to the courtship of "common labourers" than of "romantic criminals," the conclusion reached concerning the efficacy of language is substantially similar. Words of love, if Adam's example is any indication, are merely a formality. Like Seth, Adam's courtship is derived from the example of Jacob and evidenced by a willingness to work and to wait for the right to marry. As Jacob labored fourteen years for the privilege of marrying Rachel, Adam is resolved to work "hard for years for the right to kiss" Hetty (*AB* 289). The multiple ironies of Lydia Donnithorne's needlework, which depicts the kiss of Jacob and Rachel (*AB* 237), thus encompass Adam as well as Seth. A kiss of this nature is far from Dinah's mind when Seth cites this biblical episode (they part with a handshake), and Hetty is preoccupied with Arthur when she kisses Adam. Given the association of love with labor, it is ironic that the embroidery becomes the basis of the dispute between Adam and the Squire over the value of work. Having earned the Squire's disfavor, Adam must wait even longer—as did Jacob after "earning" Leah—before he will be in the financial position to marry. For him, courtship is in several senses a labor of love.

Adam's principles of work and marriage have a negative corollary. Love, which depends upon labor, is also a threat to it. In "The Workshop," Seth is good-naturedly ridiculed when his romantic preoccupations interfere with the attention given to the door on which he is working. In "Adam on a Working Day," the tables are turned, and Adam must laugh at himself for planning his life with Hetty on his way to a job: "A pretty building I'm making, without either bricks or timber. I'm up i' the garret a'ready, and haven't so much as dug the foundation" (*AB* 205–6). Words may be an ineffectual or an inappropriate expression of love, but labor, the more eloquent language, may be endangered by that which it is intended to further.

In effect, Adam shares the belief present in *Jane Eyre* that courtship should be mute—an attitude that is reinforced by temperament: "the big, outspoken, fearless man was very shy and diffident as to his lovemaking" (*AB* 252). He possesses "no fine words" (*AB* 339) with which to woo his beloved. His mute method would appear to have much to recommend it, since he wins the hands of two women, and in the process defeats two formidable rivals: Arthur for Hetty (granted, by default) and God for Dinah. Adam does eventually speak openly of love, but it is to confirm, not to elicit, the beloved's feeling. Thus only after he is sure of the other's love will he speak his own (*AB* 219).

When he does finally speak to Hetty, his words seem calculated more toward winning a business partner or converting a "dratchell" (*AB* 211) than to gaining a wife. In the first of two courtship scenes with Hetty, he says nothing of his love, speaking initially of Arthur's "handsome" words concerning his business prospects (*AB* 217) and then lecturing Hetty about her "love of finery" (*AB* 218). Predictably, this effort at conversion fails—or succeeds ironically as evidenced by Hetty's donning Dinah's clothes in jest (*AB* 218). Despite tempering his true feelings, Adam speaks with enough zeal that he fears having actually conveyed "all the thoughts he had only half-expressed" (*AB* 219). His didactic courtship resembles his brother's; the Bedes are prone to apply homiletic means toward erotic ends. In the second courtship scene, Adam again begins with the subject of his commercial prospects—this time Jonathan Burge's offer of "a share in his business" (*AB* 342). Hetty is spared another sermon, however, when he misreads her blush as a sign of love and rushes into the proposal long delayed by practical concerns. "Rush" would seem somewhat exaggerated, since the proposal, when it is finally made, takes the form of the promise of material comfort that Adam takes to be the highest expression of love: "I could afford to be married now, Hetty—I could make a wife comfortable" (*AB* 343).

Adam is more direct about his feelings with Dinah, whom he first wooed on behalf of his brother (*AB* 456, 465). Yet not until Adam has an indication of Dinah's love does he speak his own—not until then does he even realize that he is in love. In effect, all of Adam's words and actions have been a kind of unintended courtship discourse. He wins Dinah's heart without having addressed it. In that regard, his labor of love has something in common with her "weekday preaching." When he is finally propelled to propose by his mother's revelation of the state of Dinah's affections, his words are earnest and direct. He stresses that Dinah need not forsake the word of God by marrying him, sounding—yet again—like his brother Seth.

After Adam follows Dinah to Snowfield, he unintentionally engages in a form of the ventriloquial courtship previously practiced on his brother's behalf. Dinah—for all intents and purposes wedded to the Word—is apparently addressed by a spiritual presence. In a reversal of earlier episodes in which the heavenly is confounded with the earthly, Dinah mistakes the terrestrial for the divine. She hears a celestial voice before seeing the human speaker: "She started without looking round, as if she connected the sound with no place. 'Dinah!' Adam said again. He knew quite well what was in her mind. She was so accustomed to think of impressions as purely spiritual monitions that she looked for no material visible accompaniment of the voice" (*AB* 501). The double-voiced quality of the scene alludes to the earlier episode of Seth's proposal but with a clearer sense that physical love may have a spiritual component. Despite the carnal implications of Dinah's numerous blushes in Adam's presence, she is ultimately won over by a "spiritual monition."[26] Adam's call is not quite the *logos ex machina* that brings *Jane Eyre* to its happy resolution, but it has a similar effect. In both novels, a felicitous congruence of piety and passion is brought about by a supra- if not supernatural voice. The kiss of "deep joy" (*AB* 501) that seals their promise to marry does not threaten the pious tone of the scene. Dinah says that her acceptance of Adam is "Divine Will" (*AB* 501), and the narrator provides the conjugal homily: "What greater thing is there for two human souls than to feel that they are joined for life—to strengthen each other in all labour, to rest on each other in all sorrow, to minister to each other in all pain, to be one with each other in silent unspeakable memories at the moment of last parting" (*AB* 501). This memento mori is reminiscent of the valedictory paragraphs of *Jane Eyre*, which focus on St. John Rivers. Even the allusion to "silent unspeakable memories" suggests that in the end Eliot shares some of Brontë's skepticism about language.

The airy ideal represented by Adam and Dinah is beyond the reach of most characters in the novel, who are entirely comfortable at the kind of "village wedding" previously described by the narrator: "an awkward bridegroom opens the dance with a high-shouldered, broad-faced bride, while elderly and middle-aged friends look on, with very irregular noses and lips, and probably with quart-pots in their hands" (*AB* 176). Scenes of this sort provide the setting for the last and the most inclusive mode of speaking in *Adam Bede*: occasional oratory. Rustic venues also lead to rhetoric tinged with didacticism, but it is more festive than either homiletic or romantic discourse, as we see during Arthur's birthday celebration and the harvest dinner. The oratory of these agrarian symposia concerns neither spiritual nor erotic love but the social bonds uniting the community. While carefully evoking the manners and mores of this turn-of-the-century agricultural community, these episodes provide further commentary on the mixed nature and limited effectiveness of human speech.

The feudal social order of Loamshire survives betrayal by the man whose majority is celebrated at the first of these symposia, but in the midst of the panegyrics to "the young squire" (*AB* 69), an anarchic theme is sounded—one more substantial than "the noise of the toasts" (*AB* 262) that frightens the fragile upper-class spinsters, Miss Donnithorne and the Misses Irwine. The bacchanalian note of this occasion invites comparison with the drinking and speech making of Plato's *Symposium*. The topic of Eliot's dialogue is not eros but "'unloving love' . . . of a masculine kind" (*AB* 250). This oxymoron, used by Mr. Irwine to describe the "curious contradiction" (*AB* 249) in the character of Arthur's grandfather, applies to much of the verbal action of this surficially tranquil scene. The comic debate on who will sit where (the motivation being social rather than erotic as in Plato), the festive occasion (a birthday rather than a dramatic prize), the relatively formal eulogies, and the entirely informal bibulousness—all characterize Eliot's as well as Plato's dialogue and establish a carnivalesque, if not an outright Dionysian, atmosphere.[27]

The first speaker of the day is Mr. Poyser, who has been previously described as an "antithetic mixture" (*AB* 144). His encomium of Arthur Donnithorne is indeed mixed, so much so that at its conclusion his wife decides that her husband and men generally exist on the wrong side of the Rubicon: "men are mostly so tongue-tied—you're forced partly to guess what they mean, as you do wi' the dumb creatures" (*AB* 262). Mrs. Poyser is closer to the truth than Mr. Poyser, who believes that he has been unequivocally clear: "That's what I mean, an' that's what we all mean; and when a man's said what he means, he'd better stop" (*AB* 256). Although he professes enthusiasm about Arthur's prospective ascendancy, this endorsement owes more to hatred of the grandfather than to admiration of the heir. Mr. Poyser's praise is at best qualified; for example, he does not say that Arthur is honorable, merely that he has not proven himself to be dishonorable. And although he cannot know it, the few words of direct compliment—"You speak fair an' y'act fair" (*AB* 256)—are blatantly false in light of Arthur's treatment of Hetty. Another indication of the equivocal nature of the speech is Mr. Poyser's barely suppressed keenness to dispute Luke Britton's agricultural practices, an eagerness standing in marked contrast to the reluctant obligation accompanying his remarks about Arthur. His address demonstrates, therefore, that "unloving love of a masculine kind" is limited neither to the aristocratic families (the Squire and his grandson) nor to landlords and tenants (the Squire and the Poysers); it also describes the relations between the tenants themselves (Poyser and Britton).

Mr. Poyser's double-edged speech sets the tone for all that follow. The young squire is greeted with "rapping . . . jingling . . . clattering . . . and shouting" (*AB* 257). This cacophony is nevertheless "a strain of sublimest music" (*AB* 257) to Arthur, whose "light-hearted" and glib acknowledgment is in marked contrast to his predecessor's "slow speech" (*AB* 257). Insofar as it concerns Adam's promotion, Arthur's speech is ingenuous but empty. Only much later, for instance, will Mr. Poyser realize: "a fine friend he's been t' Adam, making speeches an' talking so fine" (*AB* 394). Insofar as it concerns his grandfather, Arthur's address is disingenuous but polite. He tactfully tricks the crowd into drinking the health of one whose "name's no better than a brimstone match in everybody's nose" (*AB* 333). The toast is not refused and is, to that extent, a success. But a counterpoint of disaffected grumbling is clearly audible. The narrator tells us, "the bucolic mind does not readily apprehend the refinements of good taste" (*AB* 258), nor does it recognize that the speaker has inherited his ancestor's capacity for "smooth-tongued palaver" (*AB* 329). One might expect Mrs. Poyser to discern the connection, since not long after hearing the grandson say, "I delight in your kitchen," and, "I think yours is the prettiest farm on the estate" (*AB* 87), she is told by the grandfather: "What a fine kitchen this is," and, "I like these premises, do you know, beyond any on the estate" (*AB* 328). But she is deaf to these echoes and only later comes to the kinesthetic association of the sound of Arthur's name with the smell of a brimstone match.

Mr. Irwine follows Arthur. His "well-brushed but well-worn black" contrasts with the young Squire's "new fashioned clothes" (*AB* 259), and his words are simple and substantial rather than glib and ostentatious. The rector echoes Mr. Poyser's optimism about Arthur (albeit in much more refined terms) and Arthur's praise of Adam. But even Mr. Irwine's good humor and unaffected words cannot overcome the community's unloving love. The resentment of Adam's superiority, evident in "The Workshop," now ripples through a higher social class. Mr. Irwine's toast to Adam is greeted with "a goodwill [only] apparently unanimous" (*AB* 260). Jonathan Burge, who owns the workshop, must try his "best to look contented" (*AB* 260) at Adam's elevation to a rank that rivals his own. When Adam rises to speak, the effects are even more mixed, since he lacks the polish of the previous two speakers and addresses the crowd with blunt and almost gruff directness. Unlike Mr. Poyser, he feels "no shyness about speaking, not being troubled with small vanity or lack of words" (*AB* 260)—especially on the subject of work. Whereas the women feel that Adam is too proud, the men are "of the opinion that nobody could speak more straightfor'ard" (*AB* 261)— though we must assume that Mr. Casson, who has always felt that Adam is "lifted up an' peppery-like" (*AB* 28), and Mr. Burge do not share this opinion. If Arthur has thought too much of the effect of his words upon his audience, Adam has thought too little of it, and his speech does not promote social harmony.

The symposium is at most a qualified success, temporarily and uneasily uniting its participants. When goodwill is unanimous (toward Arthur), it is misplaced; when half-hearted (toward Adam), it only barely conceals undercurrents of animosity and jealousy. The speeches in tone as well as reception, therefore, demonstrate that occasional oratory, no less than religious addresses and romantic discourse, is part of a paradoxical verbal world. This conclusion is reinforced by a second symposium, a harvest dinner marking the end of the agricultural season and featuring many of the characters kept on the margins of the coming-of-age celebration. The narrative focus on this occasion is shifted downward socially, and the Poysers now play the role of bemused social superiors previously enacted by the Donnithornes and Irwines. This banquet is a feast of mechanicals. The early stages of the supper are a relatively sober affair, since the "lyricism of the evening was in the cellar at present, and was not to be drawn from that retreat just yet" (*AB* 491). With the singing of the harvest song, accompanied by the mandatory consumption of ale, the tenor of the celebration progresses from the lyrical to the bacchanalian.[28]

This symposium illustrates what Bakhtin describes as the operative principle of the Socratic dialogue in general: "Socratic laughter . . . and Socratic degradations . . . bring the world closer and familiarize it in order to investigate it fearlessly and freely."[29] The narrator seems bent on reversing the announced intention of remaining distant from scenes and characters that are too painfully rustic: "The jocose talk of haymakers is best at a distance; like those clumsy bells round the cows' necks, it has rather a coarse sound when it comes close, and may even grate on the ears painfully; but heard from far off, it mingles very prettily with the other joyous sounds of nature" (*AB* 204).[30] It is only from a distance, for example, that Adam experiences the echoing cry of "Harvest Home!" as "a sacred song" (*AB* 485). If experienced too intimately, discordant voices and rude behavior belie the idealizations of the pastoral poetry and popular taste: "When Tityrus and Meliboeus happen to be on the same farm, they are not sentimentally polite to each other. . . . The bucolic character at Hayslope, you perceive, was not of that entirely genial, merry, broad-grinning sort, apparently observed in most districts visited by artists" (*AB* 488–89)—a point already intimated by the rivalry of Martin Poyser and Luke Britton. The harvest dinner emphasizes the clownish ways of the farmhands, not always kindly exposing their limited expressiveness: "there was seldom any gradation between bovine gravity and a laugh" (*AB* 489, also see 30). Alick the shepherd, who "never relaxed into the frivolity of unnecessary speech" (*AB* 491), exemplifies this cowlike taciturnity. His conversations with Kester Bale are "confined to an occasional snarl" (*AB* 488), and with Ben Tholoway to casting a "suspicious eye, for ever upon" (*AB* 489) his mistrusted coworker. These inarticulate disputes gainsay the celebratory spirit and establish contestation rather than cooperation as a keynote of pastoral society. Even upon a convivial occasion like the harvest celebration, the laborers remain a tight-lipped group, and perhaps luckily so, since they, too, are bound by an "unloving love."

The exception to the general taciturnity that rules until the harvest keg has been tapped and tasted is "half-witted Tom Tholer . . . a great favourite on the farm, where he played the part of the old jester, and made up for his practical deficiencies by his success in repartee. His hits, I imagine, were those of the flail, which falls quite at random, but nevertheless smashes an insect now and then" (*AB* 486–87). The narrator, however, refrains from recording his jests "lest Tom's wit should prove to be like that of many other bygone jesters eminent in their day—rather of a temporary nature, not dealing with the deeper and more lasting relations of things" (*AB* 487). The principle of aesthetic distance is thus reasserted, and garrulity is associated with being half-witted. Tom, like Bartle Massey's students, is depicted as subhuman.

When tongues are finally loosed—despite Mrs. Poyser's attentive monitoring of the ale—the result is a contest of dueling voices that dispels any misconceptions about the simple harmony of rustic songs. A "*sotto voce* performance of 'My love's a rose without a thorn,' . . . gradually assume[s] a rather deafening and complex character" (*AB* 495). When a rival singer, "capable of a copious crescendo," launches into a version of the "Three Merry Mowers," a jarring contest of flower and scythe is the result. The dissonant battle is brought to an end when Kester "set up a quavering treble—as if he had been a alarum" (*AB* 496) and the party is brought to a cacophonous conclusion.

The conversation of the social superiors on this occasion (those who had been seated upstairs at Arthur's birthday dinner) is different from that of the mechanicals, but it has a predictably similar effect. The "good-natured amusement" (*AB* 487) that they take at the expense of the farm workers is likely to be experienced by readers with regard to them—no more so than when the talk turns to politics and the war with France. Neither Mr. Poyser nor Mr. Craig seems much in favor of peace, the former because of the beneficial effect of war on agricultural prices, the latter because he feels that the British government poses a greater threat to individual well-being than the French army does. The debate on the abilities of the French would seem to be won by Craig with a "triumphant specimen of Socratic argument" (*AB* 493). But when Adam contradicts him, the others are left "puzzled by this opposition of authorities" (*AB* 493). The last word among these political pundits is Mrs. Poyser's: "Ah, it's fine talking. . . . It's hard work to tell which is Old Harry when everybody's got boots on" (*AB* 492)—and, it might be added, his tongue wagging. The operative mode in this scene is Socratic dialogue, not Socratic argument, but there is little "fine talking" in evidence.

When the topic turns from the French to women (the issue of cleverness being the connection), the disputants are Bartle Massey and Mrs. Poyser. The resulting contest of wit provides considerable entertainment, if little common sense. According to him, a woman thinks "two and two 'll come to make five, if she cries and bothers enough about it" (*AB* 494). According to her, men "are mostly so slow, their thoughts overrun 'em, an' they can only catch 'em by the tail. I can count a stocking-top while a man's getting's tongue ready an' when he outs wi' his speech at last, there's little broth to be made on't" (AB 494)—views familiar from her assessment of her husband's performance at the coming-of-age celebration. Arguments are not resolved, and opinions are unchanged; the net effect of the argument seems merely to augment the pandemonium of the annual event.

The narrator provides a gloss on the entire scene when discussing the lyrics of the harvest song itself. After speculating about its origin, which is uncertain, the narrator comments: "Some will perhaps think that they detect in the first quatrain an indication of a lost line, which later rhapsodists, failing in imaginative vigour, have supplied by the feeble device of iteration. Others, however, may rather maintain that this very iteration is an original felicity, to which none but the most prosaic minds can be insensible"[31] (AB 490). In addition to providing an example of a loss of linguistic color in modern times, the song serves as a figure of language in general. However it is interpreted, there can be neither certitude about its origin nor consensus about its meaning. In fact, "meaning" is strangely irrelevant to usage, since the song functions primarily as an excuse for bibulousness. Its toast of health to master and mistress are parodic echoes of the earlier toast to Squire Donnithorne. The harvest song defines a rural tradition that endures largely unaffected by the language in which it is celebrated.

Given these pervasive problems with language, it is not surprising that the residents of Hayslope have a fairly well-developed set of expressions to characterize the limitations of speaking. Even the compulsively talkative must often admit that there is no use for further conversation. Mrs. Poyser repeatedly laments, "Where's the use o' talkin'," for instance, when confronted with Dinah's intransigence on the point of returning to Snowfield (AB 85). Another of the novel's celebrated talkers, Bartle Massey, raises this question with regard to women in general (AB 240). Dinah hears this rhetorical query not only from her aunt but also from Lisbeth Bede, who refuses words of consolation after Thias's death: "But where's the use o' talkin' to me a-that'n? Ye canna make the smart less wi' talkin'" (AB 114). Less surprisingly, even one not inclined to "speak at random" (AB 237), Adam Bede, uses this expression to point to a situation in which words have a limited effect (AB 167). Another favorite phrase, "It's fine talkin'," applies to circumstances or suggestions that seem fit for nothing better than idle banter and that should not be confused with the serious business of daily life. One may talk, for instance, about having supper when there's work to be done (AB 50), or of a previous employer when the current one must be satisfied (AB 82, 449), or of dancing when the family is in mourning (*AB* 271), but such talk is fruitless.

The frequency and relative fixity of such expressions suggest that the residents of Hayslope do not have a great deal of faith in the spoken word and are inclined to be a rather resigned lot. Even Mr. Irwine echoes this pessimism, though it seems a strange sentiment for a preacher. Recognizing that Dinah's Methodism is an expression of her nature, he sees no reason to root out the heretic: "He must be a miserable prig who would act the pedagogue here: one might as well go and lecture the trees for growing in their own shape" (*AB* 97). His analogy echoes that used by Mrs. Poyser to express the futility of speaking to Dinah: "I know it 'ud be just the same if I was to talk to you for hours. You'd make me the same answer, at th' end. I might as well talk to the running brook and tell it to stan' still" (*AB* 86)—or try to move a rooted tree (*AB* 448). Whatever their comparisons may indicate about Dinah, they also reveal the common belief that nature is a preexistent and unalterable force, one that is unaffected by human desires and deaf to human words.

If Reverend Irwine's pessimism seems incongruous, it is nothing compared to the narrator's, whose skepticism about expressive limitations applies even to himself. Readers may sense admirable candor and lack of pretense when he admits that "it is a very hard thing to say the exact truth, even about your own immediate feelings—much harder than to say something fine about them which is *not* the exact truth" (*AB* 176). Or perhaps remembering the lyrics of Adam's opening hymn, they may reluctantly admit the wisdom of the narrator's acknowledgment that "[h]uman converse . . . is not rigidly sincere" (*AB* 182). But what can their attitude be toward a novel whose narrator suggests that at a fundamental level of experience and feeling, words are superfluous: "our firmest convictions are often dependent on subtle impressions for which words are quite too coarse a medium" (*AB* 341)? When this "hard thing" becomes impossible, we may well begin to question both teller and tale:

> *It is of little use* for me to tell you that Hetty's cheek was like a rosepetal . . . ; *it is of little use* for me to say how lovely was the contour of her pink-and-white neckerchief . . .—*of little use*, unless you have seen a woman who affected you as Hetty affected her beholders. . . . I might mention all the divine charms of a bright spring day, but if you had never in your life utterly forgotten yourself in straining your eyes after the mounting lark, or in wandering through the still lanes when the fresh-opened blossoms fill them with a sacred silent beauty like that of fretted aisles, *where would be the use* of my descriptive catalogue? I could never make you know what I meant by a bright spring day. (*AB* 90–91, my emphasis)

The narrator implies that words are ancillary to and entirely dependent upon experience. His narrative can be fully understood only by those for whom it is to some degree supererogatory, that is, for those already familiar with it. Stories can convey neither thought nor experience to those not previously possessing them. Language, therefore, when not superfluous is inadequate, and in either case it is likely to be misleading. Readers may with some justification ask of the narrator, "Where's the use of talking?" and of themselves, "What's the use of reading?"

Many characters echo the sentiment that words are "too coarse a medium," but while their skepticism is perhaps less radical it may also be more ingenuous than the narrator's. The general consensus is that the deepest and most important feelings are the least capable of expression. Their fears are largely pragmatic rather than ontological (to return to the terms applied to *Jane Eyre*), but no less consequential for that fact. Dinah, for instance, has little confidence in ordinary human discourse, telling Mr. Irwine that she often has thoughts "that I could give no account of, for I could neither make a beginning nor ending of them in words" (*AB* 96). This is Adam's view as well, though, if anything, he is even more skeptical. When discussing "deep speritual things in religion," he claims that "[y]ou can't make much out wi' talking about it, but you feel it" (*AB* 180). He goes even further in suggesting that language itself can be a barrier to understanding feelings, for in "finding names for your feelings, . . . you can talk of 'em when you've never known 'em, just as a man may talk o' tools when he knows their names, though he's never so much as seen 'em, still less handled 'em" (*AB* 180). For Adam, names, far from revealing reality, may actually blind people to it. He thus establishes a corollary to the first principle of language among the people of Loamshire. If the basic assumption about language is that words refer to and take meaning from, but do not affect, the natural order, then the corollary is that words are empty and even dangerous when not anchored in nature and experience.

Mrs. Poyser's homey epithet expresses the general feeling that the value of words does not extend beyond their referential function: "Some cheeses are made o' skimmed milk and some o' new milk, and it's no matter what you call 'em, you may tell which is which by the look and the smell" (*AB* 100). Readers who expect comfort from this commonsense wisdom will be dismayed to learn that the language of nature itself is confusing and virtually impossible to interpret. Were Mrs. Irwine correct in saying that "Nature never makes a ferret in the shape of a mastiff" (*AB* 72), there would be no difficulty in reading natural signs. But the narrator suggests that, even if nature's language were reliable, human interpreters are not: "Nature has her language, and she is not unveracious; but we don't know all the intricacies of her syntax yet, and in a hasty reading we may happen to extract the very opposite of her real meaning" (*AB* 154). This difficulty would not seem to be insurmountable, since with time individuals may learn to read their world, just as Bartle's students learn to decipher the intricacies of orthography: "The letters," one of his pupils complains, are so "'uncommon alike, there was no tellin' 'em one from another,' the sawyer's business not being concerned with minute differences such as exist between a letter with its tail turned up and a letter with its tail turned down" (*AB* 227). In nature, however, the turn of a tail does not possess singular and unchanging significance.

As in *Jane Eyre*, a look at nature's most frequently consulted text, the human face, suggests that nature's syntax may be indecipherable.[32] While it is said of Mr. Irwine that "there was a certain virtue in that benignant yet keen countenance, as there is in all human faces from which a generous soul beams out" (*AB* 194), this correspondence between spirit and body is not apparent in all cases.[33] The face of beauty with its "dear deceit" (*AB* 156) poses a serious problem for readers of nature's texts. Hetty's attractiveness certainly takes in Adam, who under the influence of love thinks himself "a great physiognomist" and "an adept in the language [of Nature]" (*AB* 153). According to the narrator, his interpretive failure is part of a general masculine weakness: it is "impossible not to expect some depth of soul behind a deep grey eye with a long dark eyelash, in spite of an experience which has shown . . . that they may go along with deceit, peculation, and stupidity" (*AB* 154). Natural signs are susceptible to misreading because overlaid with conventional meaning; they cannot be known or expressed except through fallible human interpretation and language. Thus Adam mistakes Hetty's blush as a sign of love for him (*AB* 215) and entirely overlooks the significance of Dinah's blushes (*AB* 120, 464). As the narrator of *Daniel Deronda* (*DD*) observes: "A blush is no language: only a dubious flag-signal which may mean either of two contradictories" (*DD* 474). Whatever a face may express of the soul, the lover of that face will read only the text that he inscribes upon it.

Having corrected the lover's myopia with a sober dose of inductive reasoning, thereby having seemingly detached physical appearance from moral character, the narrator goes on to rejoin them, if only in a humorous way: "One begins to suspect at length that there is no direct correlation between eyelashes and morals; or else, that the eyelashes express the disposition of the fair one's grandmother, which is on the whole less important to us" (*AB* 154). The possibility that Hetty's face expresses an ancestor's character would seem to be a joke were it not for the fact that the narrator returns to the subject of Hetty's phylogenetic brows. Just as Adam misreads her appearance and gestures at Hall Farm, he does so at the Chase, leading the narrator to comment:

Hetty's face had a language that transcended her feelings. There are faces which nature charges with a meaning and pathos not belonging to the single human soul that flutters beneath them, but speaking the joys and sorrows of foregone generations—eyes that tell of deep love which doubtless has been and is somewhere but not paired with these eyes—perhaps paired with pale eyes that can say nothing; just as a national language may be instinct with poetry unfelt by the lips that use it. (AB 275)

If so, then claims for nature's veracity are empty, since it is virtually impossible to decipher natural language.[34] It speaks, but of what or whom we cannot know. Even were human readers invariably percipient, they are presented with texts whose meaning is encoded by an undeterminable hereditary process. That this is especially true of the human visage is reaffirmed in *The Mill on the Floss*, when "Maggie's phiz" is described as seeming to have been

moulded and coloured with the most decided intention. But that same Nature has the deep cunning which hides itself under the appearance of openness, so that simple people think they can see through her quite well, and all the while she is secretly preparing a refutation of their confident prophecies. . . . [T]he dark-eyed, demonstrative, rebellious girl may after all turn out to be a passive being. (MF 84–85)

Like Maggie, Hetty possesses the dark eyes signifying a passionate nature that she does not possess; her body language expresses a national characteristic that she personally lacks. Therefore, what is true of human communication, specifically that "national languages may be instinct with poetry unfelt by the lips that use it," is equally true of the language of nature.

Natural and human languages are equally susceptible to misinterpretation, so much so that the conventional distinctions between the natural and the human inevitably break down. We have already heard human speakers compared to cows and camels in particular and to "rough animals" and "dumb creatures" in general. References to the limited expressive powers of dogs further establish a pattern of similarity rather than of difference between dumb creatures and loquacious humankind.[35] The narrator comically introduces this theme by describing Adam's dog in these terms: "Poor fellow, he had not a great range of expression" (AB 24). This understated personification takes on a more serious tone when Dinah also finds in Gyp an image of the human situation: "I've a strange feeling about the dumb things as if they wanted to speak, and it was a trouble to 'em because they couldn't. I can't help being sorry for the dogs always, though perhaps there's no need. But they may well have more in them than they know how to make us understand, for we can't say half what we feel, with all our words" (*AB* 122). The theme of canine communication is taken up by Mr. Irwine in a somewhat different context: "The commonest man, who has his ounce of sense and feeling, is conscious of the difference between a lovely, delicate woman and a coarse one. Even a dog feels a difference in their presence. The man may be no better able than the dog to explain the influence the more refined beauty has on him, but he feels it" (*AB* 265). Whatever the implication about the common man, Irwine seems to reaffirm his mother's views concerning "the shape of a mastiff" and to add to them a superstitious belief in the ability of dogs to read nature's language.

The anthropocentric view of nature voiced by these two ministers of God yields a comparison unflattering to humans, who are lowered more than animals are raised. These observations have a common implication: language is not a glorious ability distinguishing humankind from the rest of creation. Eliot resists the comfort taken by many Victorians in the sentiments expressed by Max Müller: "Where, then, is the difference between brute and man? What is it that man can do, and of which we find no signs, no rudiments, in the whole brute world? I answer without hesitation: the one great barrier between the brute and man is *Language*. Man speaks, and no brute has ever uttered a word."[36] Perhaps, but according to Eliot, the brutes have little reason to do so. Humans—whether in canine, caprine, simian, bovine, or cameline form—have very little to crow about.

Given the entrenched sense of what language cannot do and the pervasive doubt about the reliability of what it can do, the possibility of right speaking would seem to be very limited indeed. As we have seen, doubts about the efficacy of language lead characters to a narrowly utilitarian attitude toward conversation. The answer to the question "Where's the use?" might well be, "Where there is use."[37] When Adam distinguishes the names of tools from the knowledge of their use, his warning might be taken as an implicit recognition that words are rightly used when used as tools, that is, as means to specific and realizable ends. These pragmatic sentiments minimize but can neither escape nor ultimately allay the pervasive doubt of language, because, as the examples of Rev. Irwine and Dinah suggest, the most effective speeches are not a matter of words alone. This point is reinforced by Adam during the health-drinking when he says, "There's no occasion for me to say any more about what I feel towards him [Arthur]: I hope to show it through the rest o' my life in my actions" (*AB* 261). This is the closing line of the speech, and it expresses the communal sense that words without action are of little value and that words about the future are of no value whatsoever. In using the occasion to say that there is "no occasion" for speaking further, Adam suggests that there are very few occasions upon which words can be of much use.

Adam is, however, capable of varying his language in ways that increase its effectiveness. For example, he adapts words to specific audiences and purposes: "whenever he wished to be especially kind to his mother, he fell into his strongest native accent and dialect, with which at other times his speech was less deeply tinged" (AB 52). Although he may never use other than "simple strong words" (AB 416), he has learned to use them in different ways. His diglossia, in fact, is a significant development in Eliot's "natural history of English life." It signals the end of the peasant "style" and challenges the geographically isolated and socially static nature of provincial life. Defined in these terms, right speaking is not a matter of an essential personal or national language, as in Bartle Massey's "right for *you*"; nor it is a matter of avoiding slang and following the prescriptions of a standard dialect; rather, it is a question of adapting speech to circumstance. The debate between Casson and Massey is pointless. Adam prospers, as does Dinah, in part because he learns that correct speech is an adaptive strategy, not a normative dialect.

Like the logophobes of *Jane Eyre*, Adam seeks an alternative to ineffectual forms of speaking. He places hope neither in the natural nor supernatural languages attractive to Jane and Rochester, but in the symbolic order of numbers—his version of the "universal language on a rational basis" that Eliot sees as a thankfully unobtainable ideal. Numerical calculation promises clarity and force in many of the situations that reduce speakers to asking, "What's the use o' talkin'?" The language of numbers not only transforms timber into cottages and barns, but also holds the promise of imposing order on the more tangled constructions of human feeling and action. After his father dies, for instance, Adam thinks to himself: "the natur o' things doesn't change, though it seems as if one's own life was nothing but change. The square o' four is sixteen, and you must lengthen your lever in proportion to your weight, is as true when a man's miserable as when he's happy" (AB 119). Thus it is not simply, as Sally Shuttleworth explains, that Adam's thinking "is founded on a mathesis: in accordance with the principles of mathematical addition, the whole equals the sum of its parts. In *Adam Bede*, Adam's progress towards economic differentiation is constantly presented in terms of a mathematical calculus."[38] Beyond economics, morality itself is a matter of calculation for Adam, who repeatedly sees in the laws of mathematics the principles according to which human life might be organized. On another occasion, for example, he couches worldy wisdom in precisely these terms: "It's well we should feel as life's a reckoning we can't make twice over; there's no real making amends in this world, any more nor you can mend a wrong subtraction by doing your addition right" (*AB* 198).

"Mensuration," in Adam's terms, is attractive because it replaces ordinary (and unreliable) language and promises both precision and predictability—in his formulation it even pushes religion to the margins of daily life. His ethics of labor is expressed in simple mathematical terms: "if a man . . . makes two potatoes grow istead o' one, he's doing more good, and he's just as near to God as if he was running after some preacher" (*AB* 53–54). But when quantitative principles are applied to human experience, Adam finds that life is not so neatly measured and understood. Bartle Massey sardonically makes this point—also by referring to an exemplary vegetable—in a way that eludes his practically minded pupil:

> But where's the use of all the time I've spent in teaching you writing and mapping and mensuration, if you're not to get for'ard in the world and show folks there's some advantage in having a head on your shoulders, instead of a turnip? . . . Leave that to fools that never got beyond a sum in simple addition. Simple addition enough! Add one fool to another fool, and in six years' time six fools more—they're all of the same denomination, big and little's nothing to do with the sum!
> (*AB* 238)

Adam should have learned this lesson when he tries to leave his family at age eighteen. The "mensuration book" (*AB* 58) that he carries to guide his escape provides no reliable measure of the guilt that quickly drives him back to Loamshire. He is subsequently able to articulate the connection between numbers and experience, but he only gradually realizes that adapting formulae or principles to circumstances is fraught with difficulty: "It's the same with the notions in religion as it is with math'matics—a man may be able to work problems straight off in's head as he sits by the fire and smokes his pipe, but if he has to make a machine or a building, he must have a will and a resolution and love something else better than his own ease" (*AB* 179). Adam's moral meaning here is essentially the same as that which Rev. Irwine unsuccessfully suggests to Arthur: "When I've made up my mind that I can't afford to buy a tempting dog, I take no notice of him, because if he took a strong fancy to me, and looked lovingly at me, the struggle between arithmetic and inclination might become unpleasantly severe" (*AB* 147). The parable is lost upon the young squire whose social arithmetic is no match for sexual inclination. Mensuration may be essential in business and finance, but it offers no reliable solution to the ethical quandaries of daily living.

This limitation is especially clear with Adam, for whom the relation between social arithmetic and sexual inclination is the reverse of what it is for Arthur. Lisbeth, for instance, consistently reads affairs of the heart more clearly than her son. Seeing his infatuation with Hetty and judging her character with greater insight, Lisbeth laments: "An' he so wise at bookin' and figurin', an' not to know no better nor that!" (*AB* 54). Despite or perhaps because of his "head-piece for mathematics" (*AB* 397), Adam is slow to learn its limits. When he and his mother discuss the likelihood of Seth's marrying Dinah, Lisbeth says,

> "Where's th' use o' talkin' a-that'n? She caresna for Seth. . . . Thy figurin' books might ha' tould thee better nor that, I should think, else thee mightst as well read the commin print, as Seth allays does."
> "Nay, Mother," said Adam laughing, "the figures tell us a fine deal, and we couldn't go far without 'em, but they don't tell us about folks's feelings. It's a nicer job to calculate *them*." (*AB* 141–42)

Adam expresses what he cannot practice. The geometry of love is not to be so easily calculated, and Adam is more than a little obtuse when it comes to matters of the heart. Lisbeth, who is her son's conversational opposite, sees far more clearly than he does—both in this scene and later when she turns to the subject of Dinah's heart. Mr. Ryde may be "as ignorant as a woman" of "math'matics and the natur o' things" (*AB* 179), as Adam maintains, but he himself is doubly ignorant of women, for he both misunderstands and miscalculates them. Bartle's irony directed at the woman who thinks "two and two 'll come to make five" applies to Adam as much as to his misogynistic teacher.

Mathesis, which promises to provide a pragmatic alternative to the contradictions of language use, ultimately complicates them, therein ironically reinforcing the general skepticism to which it is purportedly a corrective. But mathesis also accentuates the pragmatic dimension of language. Speech in Hayslope is less referential than functional. Language does not point; it exists; and verbal structures possess a nearly physical reality rivaling the solidity of Adam's sturdily constructed buildings. His sentiment in this regard is widely held in Hayslope, "When I've said a thing, if it's only to myself, it's hard for me to go back" (*AB* 166). Applied to promising, this attitude virtually invests the promise with a material presence; promises are tantamount to the thing promised. For instance, upon returning home to find that his father has not completed a job, Adam complains: "It's fine talking about having supper when here's a coffin promised to be ready at Brox'on by seven o'clock tomorrow morning, and ought to ha' been there now, and not a nail struck yet. . . . Isn't the coffin promised? Can they bury the man without a coffin? I'd work my right hand off sooner than deceive people with lies i' that way" (*AB* 50). His view that a broken promise is a lie seems both harsh and inexact—motivated by anger with his father rather than directed at the nature of promises. But Adam speaks more truthfully than it might seem, especially in a society that holds language to be a form of action. Promising a coffin is not building it, any more than saying a cheese is fresh will make it so, but promises do seem to carry more retrospective than prospective significance. Such promises speak of states of being, not of mind, hence Adam's incredulity at so anomalous an entity as a promised but unbuilt coffin.

The promise of marriage is no different in this regard. It confirms the past more than it constructs the future. Adam, for instance, cannot be hurried into "any premature words" (*AB* 341), and his courtship seems desultory only because it is virtually coterminous with and indistinguishable from his daily working and speaking life. His proposals of marriage articulate what has been done, not what remains to be done or what it is hoped will be done. The distinction made by Hume between interested and disinterested commerce has no place in Hayslope. A promise, whether to build a coffin or to take a wife, might with some justification be described as a foregone conclusion. Such conclusions are not infallible, but neither are they lies.

Promises of this kind are the opposite of what promises are for Mr. Tulliver and his son—a verbal barrier, erected on the Bible, to constrain future behavior. The promise of marriage between Adam and Dinah speaks less *to* the future than *of* the past. It testifies both to his mute (and unconscious) labor of love and to her "weekday preaching." Their betrothal is, in a sense, based upon the Bible, but not literally so as with the Tullivers. Just as Maggie says that she does not need the family Bible to make a promise, Dinah significantly does not open her Bible "for direction" (*AB* 43) in deciding whether to accept Adam's proposal. Heretofore she has not trusted the unassisted voice of her conscience. For instance, in deciding whether to speak to Hetty before returning to Stoniton, she is "not satisfied without a more unmistakable guidance than those inward voices. There was light enough for her, if she opened her Bible, to discern the text sufficiently to know what it would say to her" (*AB* 158–59). But when considering Adam's proposal, she is content to listen "faithfully for the ultimate guiding voice from within" (*AB* 497). She realizes that married life in Loamshire may be consistent with and not opposed to a Christian life, and she accepts the imprint of human voices upon sacred words. In a sense, her literal reading becomes figurative, enabling her to recognize a metonymic contiguity between divine and human love. Her acceptance is expressed in overtly religious terms: "My soul is so knit to yours that it is but a divided life I live without you. . . . I have a fulness of strength to bear and do our heavenly

Father's Will that I had lost before" (*AB* 501). Ironically, Seth's homily on marriage has finally won a convert.

The role of religion in courtship invites comparison of *Adam Bede* to *Jane Eyre*. Valentine Cunningham has written that "Methodism . . . provided for the Brontës a rhetoric of passion. . . . But by appropriating the rhetoric of Methodism's love of God, exploiting the language of Divine love for earthly love, they deceived the world."[39] I fully agree but want to suggest that the nature of the deception concerns less "the authoresses' profound sexual innocence," as Cunningham maintains, than their assertion of the compatibility of conventionally opposed realms: the carnal and the spiritual. The promise of marriage between Rochester and Jane, as we have seen, is a mechanism of eroticized postponement and distancing. Brontë sustains those energizing tensions by appropriating the language of divine love for earthly passion in a way that accentuates the latter. Jane's application of the phrase, "bone of his bone and flesh of his flesh," to her marriage reinscribes the carnal within the framework of Christian marriage. For Adam and Dinah, religious rhetoric is a means of overcoming rather than enacting "a separation that unites." When Dinah is converted to humanism (as St. John Rivers is not), *Adam Bede* becomes more pious and less passionate than *Jane Eyre*. While both novels adapt sacred rhetoric to profane ends, the engagement of Adam and Dinah harmonizes the discordant strains of sacred and profane love at a register closer to the former than the latter, therein reversing Brontë's emphasis.

The promise of marriage between Adam and Dinah brings together, as closely as is humanly possible, the human and the spiritual—words and the Word. Their betrothal exemplifies the halting and modest power of language to confirm powerful emotions that two otherwise exemplary individuals do their best to ignore or to suppress. The means "by which two human souls approach each other" may be simple, but it is not trivial, as the narrator remarks: "Those slight words and looks and touches are part of the soul's language; and the finest language, I believe, is chiefly made up of unimposing words, such as 'light,' 'sound,' 'stars,' 'music'—words really not worth looking at, or hearing, in themselves, any more than 'chips' or 'sawdust:' it is only that they happen to be the signs of something unspeakably great and beautiful" (*AB* 465–66). It is another indication of the curiosity of words that they may become the spoken sign of the unspeakable. Eliot's prosaic examples—chips, sawdust—return us to Adam's workshop and to the silent labor of love and love of labor. To the extent that it does so, language acquires meaning through social and personal experience and is necessarily limited to and by such experience. Words cannot transcend these limitations, but they can at least quietly put to rest some of the doubts to which they are subject. Romantic love, according to the narrator, is an example of "*impersonal* expression"; it is, he explains, more than "a woman's love that moves us in woman's eyes—it seems to be a far-off mighty love that has come near to us, and made speech for itself there" (*AB* 339). Whatever their failings, unimposing words, such as those for simple natural phenomena and plain hard work, intimate whatever connection language can have to *logos*. Slight words stand to the unspeakable as do promises to the thing promised. By words of love, the unspeakable is intimated; by promises of love, a spiritual union is confirmed—and by any standard and in any dialect, this felicitous connection constitutes right speaking.

Meredith, no less than Eliot, is interested in "characters . . . and their speech" (*E* 1:1). In *The Egoist*, however, attention shifts not only from the laboring classes to "the drawing-room of civilized men and women, where we have no dust of the struggling outer world" (*E* 1:1), but also from dialect to figurative language and from the prosaic to the poetic. Despite the prohibition of (saw)dust, Meredith's vision is strikingly similar to Eliot's in that the language of promising, so often thought of as strictly referential and constative, is reconsidered in expressly pragmatic terms.

CHAPTER 6

Promising Marriage in The Egoist

George Eliot warns readers of *Middlemarch* that "all of us," no less than Mr. Casaubon, "get our thought entangled in metaphors and act fatally on the strength of them" (*M* 111). An example of such a tangle is Mr. Stelling's description of Tom Tulliver's mind as "peculiarly in need of being ploughed and harrowed by these patent implements [etymology and demonstration]: it was his favourite metaphor, that the classics and geometry constituted that culture of the mind which prepared it for the reception of any subsequent crop" (*MF* 208). The narrator implies that Mr. Stelling's mental culture might itself be somewhat barren by offering an alternative trope: Tom's mind resembles a stomach, and feeding him Latin is like giving someone "cheese in order to remedy a gastric weakness which prevented him from digesting it" (*MF* 308). As painful as giving dairy foods to someone with lactose intolerance might prove to be, the application of the wrong metaphor can have even more drastic consequences. In this instance, the choice of tropes determines the course of Tom's education and shapes his future life, prompting from the narrator a general observation about the dangers of metaphorical thinking:

> It is astonishing what a different result one gets by changing the metaphor! . . . O Aristotle! if you had had the advantage of being "the freshest modern" instead of the greatest ancient, would you not have mingled your praise of metaphorical speech as a sign of high intelligence, with a lamentation that intelligence so rarely shows itself in speech without metaphor,—that we can so seldom declare what a thing is except by saying it is something else? (*MF* 208–9)

In expressing such fears, or at least in posing such a question, Eliot articulates suspicions held by many concerning metaphorical speech. She also observes that literal and figurative are virtually inseparable and anticipates the poststructural insight that language moves laterally along a chain of signification without ever narrowing the gap between itself and "what a thing is."

Were Eliot herself "the freshest modern," she may well have answered this only apparently rhetorical question with an emphatic—but inherently unstable—reversal of the hierarchy of literal and figurative, and greeted the resulting linguistic free play with ludic delight rather than lamentation. Victorians, however, are generally less eager than postmoderns to pursue the ramifications of glimpses into the force and the danger of figurative speaking. Thus it remains for twentieth-century critics to apply such insights to novels like George Meredith's *The Egoist*, of which it is not surprisingly claimed that the language deconstructs itself, therein questioning the adequacy of figurative speech and challenging the possibility of stable meaning. Daniel Smirlock, among others, devotes particular attention to the concept of synecdoche:

> Meredith's novel proposes the reliability of traditional psychological synecdoche, just as it does linguistic synecdoche, but ultimately undermines the principle by putting forth a contrary model, and emphasizing that the part does not always represent the whole, that centers of linguistic and psychic meaning shift constantly, and with them the representational validity of their supposedly synecdochic parts.[1]

Severed from its referent, the figure can and must be endlessly and variously refigured—a circumstance perhaps confirmed by the length, complexity, and intricacy of *The Egoist* itself.

Meredith himself playfully acknowledges the frustrations engendered by his recondite style. He ironically subtitles the prelude, "A CHAPTER OF WHICH THE LAST PAGE ONLY IS OF ANY IMPORTANCE" (*E* 1:1) and later apologizes for his "full mouthed language" (*E* 1:267). Yet he indulges his taste for elaborate and extended figurative language to such an extent that readers may find themselves comparing Meredith's description of the Book of Egoism to his own book about an egoist: "Inordinate unvaried length, sheer longinquity, staggers the heart, ages the very heart of us at a view" (*E* 1:2). His remarkable prolixity and poetic style constitute a puzzling and paradoxical response to the possibility that a metaphor may create rather than merely reflect reality or that a part bears no necessary representational relation to the whole. While many of Eliot's and Meredith's contemporaries may have admitted—some reluctantly—that the Adamic power of direct naming represents little more than theocentric nostalgia, few would have denied that figurative language—saying "what a thing is . . . by saying it is something else"—provides a serviceable, even if indirect and somewhat unreliable, alternative. Meredith, however, goes further, following Aristotle in recognizing the power of figurative language and defending it as a civilizing force. The narrator of *Diana of the Crossways*, for instance, comments that the "banished of Eden had to put on metaphors, and the common use of them has helped largely to civilize us. The sluggish in intellect detest them, but our civilization is not much indebted to that major faction" (*DCW 275*). "Metaphor" here is itself a synecdoche for all figurative language, and Meredith's fiction "puts on metaphors" with such impunity that the sluggish may never get started and the agile must wonder if they are not sluggish.

Diana of the Crossways self-reflexively considers the contradiction between suspicion of figurative language and Meredith's periphrastic style. The novel's eponymous heroine directly mirrors Meredith's own position at the crossroads of tropophilia/phobia. Diana Merion is a writer of formidable verbal powers—as celebrated for the style of her fiction as the brilliance of conversation. She shares her creator's propensity for tropes whose difficulty borders on the catachrestic, as well as for epithets whose brevity verges on the cryptic. Meredith draws from his own experience in molding Diana and her critics, one of whom, "actuated by the public taste of the period for our 'vigourous homely Saxon' in one and two syllable words, had complained of a 'tendency to polysyllabic phraseology'"(*DCW* 245). While dismissing objections to her difficult style, Meredith does criticize Diana's tendency to use learning and wit, whether in a *roman à clef* or in postprandial reparteé, to avoid confronting personal difficulties. She does not, as a novelist, "'chameleon' her pen from the colour of her audience" (*DCW* 13), but she does, as a woman, use language as a form of protective coloration. Her verbal power, therefore, is not a step out of "flint and arrowhead caverns to intercommunicative daylight" (*DCW* 20) but a flight from the recesses of her own unconsciousness. She stands as an example, therefore, that even the most sophisticated tools may serve primitive ends.

Diana eventually recognizes that writing serves as an "escape out of the personal net" (*DCW* 203), and she abandons her career to marry Thomas Redworth. "Metaphors were her refuge" (*DCW* 275), and marriage replaces them; the woman's wedding is the writer's funeral. Diana's marriage challenges the value and the place of figurative language. She, like Dinah Morris, resists marrying and does not easily renounce her public voice. In marrying Adam, Dinah exchanges the Word for words; in marrying Redworth, Diana gives up the figurative for the literal. He seems to embody the value of direct speaking, and Diana approvingly describes her husband as one who "does not supply me with similes; he points to the source of them" (*DCW* 435).[2] A man whose "bluntness killed flying metaphors" (*DCW* 418), Redworth both inhibits others' poetic predispositions and deflects any such language directed at himself, as Diana says: "similes applied to him will strike you as incongruous" (*DCW* 475). Her sentiments suggest a rejection of "winged words" in favor of that in which they are grounded, solid English soil. That this is generally, but not entirely, so is suggested by Redworth's leaving the practical world of business for occasional flights into the discursive realm of his wife. Although her "tongue . . . always outflew him" (*DCW* 485), under her influence he at least hazards a figure of speech or two. In general, however, one imagines that Diana abandons the crossways—where opposed values like public/private and figurative/literal exist in active tension—for the distinctly unpoetic refuge of marriage.

Meredith avoids the problem of reconciling marriage and metaphor in *The Egoist* by focusing exclusively on engagement. Diana's roles are here divided and diminished. That of writer is taken by Laetitia Dale, whose early attempt at being a poet is widely assumed to be the cause of her poor health. That of the witty conversationalist is taken by Clara Middleton, whose "ready tongue" serves a "natural wit, crystal wit" that is often misunderstood because the "corrupted hearing of people required a collision of sounds" (*E* 1:47). Although her verbal play is more muted, less dazzling than Diana's, Clara nonetheless finds that when she ventures into the realm of the poetic, her similes are interpreted as evasion and occasionally equated with prevarication. The suspicion of figurative language confronting Clara as well as Diana is perhaps best understood in terms of Jonathan Culler's distinction between two ways of thinking about the relation of the figurative to the literal. The first, the *via philosophica*, "locates metaphor in the gap between sense and reference, in the process of thinking of an object, event, or whatever *as* something. . . . Metaphor thus becomes an instance of general cognitive processes at their most creative or speculative."[3] This is Coleridge's view of the constitutive power of the figural, and it is evident in Eliot's astonishment at the "different result one gets by changing the metaphor." The second perspective, the *via rhetorica*, "locates metaphor not in the gap between sense and reference but in the space between what is meant and what is said: between a literal or proper verbal expression and a periphrastic substitute."[4] This view of the rhetorical power of metaphor returns us to Locke's warning about "all the artificial and figurative application of Words Eloquence hath invented" (III.x.43). It explains the suspicion that is applied *a fortiori* to witty women, like Clara Middleton, and also prepares us for Meredith's anatomy of the English gentleman as "a lively dialoguer, one for witty bouts, with something in him . . . beyond mere wit" (*E* 1:196).

The relation between the proper and the periphrastic is exemplified by Willoughby Patterne and Horace De Craye. While most characters have some capacity in each conversational mode, De Craye masters both: "he had it [his Irish tongue] fully under control, so that he could talk good sense and airy nonsense at discretion" (*E* 1:273). He is entirely capable of indulging in nonsense purely for the sake of amusement and delights in the resources of wit and language. But his calculated obfuscation can also have ulterior motives, such as the desire to prevent

Willoughby from finding Clara after she flees Patterne Hall. Correctly sensing that his friend's verbal play is mere temporizing, Willoughby exasperatedly says,

> "Upon my word, you talk at times most unintelligible stuff, to be frank with you, Horace. Give it in English."
> "'Tis not suited, perhaps, to the genius of the language, for I thought I talked English."
> "Oh, there's English gibberish as well as Irish, we know!" (*E* 2:16)

Willoughby's Anglo-Saxon pride and impatience with metaphorical speaking are evident in his stereotypical view of Ireland as the land of blarney. As an Irishman in England, Colonel De Craye is marked by metaphor, an ethnic bias that has a gendered correlative: his banter is primarily appropriate for women, who are readily seduced by "an Irish tongue and gentlemanly manner" (*E* 1:207). As the exchange with Willoughby suggests, De Craye is both a victim and an exploiter of British stereotypes of the Irish.

De Craye's experience demonstrates one of the possible relations between speaking figuratively and promising. For him, these are not merely analogous but complicitous activities. When he swears, it is not upon the Bible but "upon [his] eloquence" (*E* 1:205), as if a poetic tongue were in and of itself a guarantee of honest intent. In fact, the opposite is true, for his glibness is dedicated to "do[ing] mischief to women and avoid[ing] the vengeance of the sex" (*E* 1:259). It is not without some justification, therefore, that he is described as a "voluble beast . . . created to ensnare women" (*E* 2:163). He exploits the promise of meaning as readily as that of marriage in order to suit his seductive intentions. In the figure of De Craye, the contagion of figuration spreads to promising to marry.

Since the entire plot of *The Egoist* revolves around Clara's attempt to break a promise to marry, it is natural that logophobia takes two interrelated forms: suspicion of metaphor and of promises. When Clara tries to end her betrothal to Willoughby Patterne, her "word," that is, her promise, is dismissed for being, like a metaphor, fanciful but not true. When she turns to metaphor in order to convey the truth of her emotions, she hears from Mrs. Mountstuart Jenkinson an interdict, "Defer the simile" (*E* 2:141), and from Laetitia Dale a plea, "this is too serious for imagery" (E 2:310). These reactions signal not only tropophobic disapproval of the witty woman but also social censure of the jilt. A contextual look at these passages explains these fears, suggests the extent to which they are unjustified, and demonstrates that Meredith's attitude toward language is more complex than that of his untrusting characters.

Three distinct modes of discourse emerge from an analysis of these scenes. Against the limitations of constative speaking, typified by Willoughby Patterne's psychological egoism, and of performative speaking, exemplified by Mrs. Mountstuart's verbal egoism, Meredith opposes the possibilities of what Clara Middleton calls "real talk," which is associated with the third of her suitors, Vernon Whitford. Such speaking is dialogical: it is creative, not merely reflective, and interactive, not simply active. The test of this discursive mode is promising, specifically, promising marriage. By redefining the conventional understanding of this act, Meredith suggests both the power and the limits of language itself.

In any number of instances throughout *The Egoist*, garrulity is held to be a moral failing—hence the varied vocabulary of pejorative terms for talking, such as gabbling, rattling, chattering, babbling, jabbering, and buzzing—if that is the sound of angry bees. Women and the Irish are portrayed as being the primary violators of the masculine English code of civilized reserve, which polices talkativeness by associating it with the subhuman—in Willoughby's phrase, with "bleating and barking and bellowing" (*E* 1:60). This code is particularly damning of figurative language, which has no place in a world that asks that words be "taken for the very meaning of the words" (*E* 1:126). The code of literalism does allow two exceptions, although this marginalization is itself an effective form of regulation. The first is courtship, in which a man, as Clara notes, "is allowed a softer dialect" (*E* 1:61). But even when capable of "the lady's tongue" (*E* 1:147), men are likely to dismiss the result as "lamentable cooing stuff" (*E* 2:66). Willoughby, fully capable of "womaniz[ing] his language" (*E* 1:40), is also blind to the effect of his doing so. Clara, for instance, recognizes that "he talked excellently to men, at least in the tone of the things he meant to say; but that his manner of talking to women went to an excess in the artificial tongue—the tutored tongue of sentimental deference of the towering male" (*E* 2:89).[5] The second figurative ghetto is literature. Willoughby tells Clara, "I detest artifice. Poetry is a profession" (*E* 1:77). Metaphors may be sold, but the commercial taint precludes their admittance into the conversation of gentlemen. Their proscription is not merely a class bias, however; the more encompassing accusation against metaphors is that they are nonserious, and Willoughby is "a more than commonly candid English gentleman in his avowed dislike of the poet's nonsense, verbiage, verse" (*E* 1:202).

This distrust of poetic nonsense seems not to be exclusively male, for on parallel occasions Mrs. Mountstuart and Laetitia Dale criticize

Clara Middleton's tendency to figurative speech. The scenes are linked by a number of similarities: both are duologues in which Clara's interlocutor is more inquisitor than equal discussant. Each suspects her of elusiveness and, worse, of a lack of candor concerning her relationship with Colonel De Craye. In both cases, Clara is enlightened about something of which she was unaware before the dialogue began, although her knowledge results less from anything said by her interlocutors than from her own sensitivity to the dialogical process itself. With Mrs. Mountstuart, she acknowledges her love for Vernon Whitford; with Laetitia Dale, she learns of Vernon's love for her. Readers may find her ignorance of these things, her selective blindness as Laetitia describes it (*E* 2:309–10), to be scarcely credible or entirely culpable, yet it partially explains the appearance to her interlocutors of equivocation. Furthermore, their suspicions are not entirely unjustified, since Clara has demonstrated that she is fully capable of "fibs, evasions, the serene battalions of white lies parallel on the march with dainty rogue falsehoods" (*E* 2:1). On the occasion of these two duologues, however, talking proves to be a process that discovers, rather than obscures, truth, and figurative speech is shown to be an instance of "language's intrinsic capacity to surpass its own (putative) limits."[6]

When Clara appeals to Mrs. Mountstuart for help, she is cross-examined with the rigor of a defense attorney approached by a recidivist. Clara must say "in six words" why she has changed her mind about marrying Willoughby Patterne:

> "I found I could not give him the admiration he has, I daresay, a right to expect. I turned—it surprised me: it surprises me now. But so completely! So that to think of marrying him is. . . . "
>
> "Defer the simile," Mrs. Mountstuart interposed. "If you hit on a clever one, you will never get the better of it. Now, by just as much as you have outstripped my limitation of words to you, you show me you are dishonest."
>
> "I could make a vow."
>
> "You would forswear yourself." (*E* 2:141–42)

Unsatisfied, Mrs. Mountstuart agrees to help only if Clara "can reply to a catechism" (*E* 2:142) concerning the disposition of her heart. The result, apparently, is not catechistic but confessional, for Clara admits: "There is one . . . " (*E* 2:143). In saying this, she does not simply acknowledge an accomplished fact; rather, she discovers a heretofore unarticulated emotion. But because Clara says no more, Mrs. Mountstuart concludes the examination essentially as she began it, confused about the reason for the rejection of Willoughby. Clara, then, may well have "succeeded in telling me nothing" (*E* 2:144), as Mrs. Mountstuart claims, but the more significant point is what she learns by speaking "out more than she had ever spoken to herself. . . . [I]n doing so she had cast herself a step beyond the line she dared to contemplate" (*E* 2:144). This "line" is personal and romantic; that is, Clara admits for the first time the possibility of loving another rather than simply of not loving Willoughby. It is also interpersonal and linguistic. Clara leaves the discursive territory known as Patterne Hall, where language is held to be purely referential, reflecting an objective, prelinguistic realm. She similarly crosses out of the territory of social discourse, where talk is exclusively an entertaining and self-contained diversion. In the verbal world she now enters, conversation is an active process, one in which saying can make it so.

Several additional points can be made about this exchange. First, it must be pointed out that Clara does not utter the simile to which Mrs. Mountstuart objects. The ellipses in the passage are Meredith's; hence Mrs. Mountstuart anticipates and, one suspects, projects her own rhetorical proclivities onto Clara. The younger woman's dialogical identity is inferred as much from the older woman's nature as from anything Clara herself has actually said. Mrs. Mountstuart is a verbal egoist, and nothing pleases her more than to have her witticisms echoing across the county (*E* 1:11). Her typical objective in speaking is at once self-referential and ironically self-effacing: the former in that she uses language to redound upon herself as the leading aphorist of the neighborhood, the latter in that she exists primarily in words; that is, she has little substance apart from the echoes of her own voice. In her practice of social discourse, rhetorical effect takes precedence over accuracy; therefore, she "detest[s] analysis" of her epithets, which possess "an outline for vagueness" and are "flung out to be apprehended, not dissected" (*E* 1:51).[7] What Mrs. Mountstuart objects to is not figurative language; she is, after all, its master. Rather she fears that she will be victimized by her own discursive practice. Clara may or may not have been on the verge of simile; Mrs. Mountstuart's suspicion, however, is that wit and fluency will dazzle rather than enlighten. She implicitly accuses Clara of her own weakness: "Mrs. Mountstuart was a lady certain to say the remembered, if not the right, thing" (*E* 1:10).

A second point concerns Mrs. Mountstuart's implied assertion that to talk, or perhaps to talk on, is to lie. Verbosity is equated with prevarication. According to this logic, since Clara does not confine herself to the six-word limit, she must be lying, and the more she talks the more she lies. This principle is more than either a reflection of Mrs. Mountstuart's preference for the aphoristic mode or a deduction from her experience of conversative society. It also expresses her predisposition to think of Clara, not as a liar, but as a skilled manipulator of men and a master of the language of amorous deceit. Mrs. Mountstuart's predisposition is exploited by Willoughby in the conversation occurring immediately before this one. He speaks of Clara's supposed jealousy of the "fatal" (*E* 2:120) bond between Laetitia and himself. While Mrs. Mountstuart dissects "his sentimental tone" (*E* 2:121) and claims to recognize "a design" (*E* 2:123) in what he says, she overestimates her own perspicacity. She fails to see "the skill with which he had sown and prepared Mrs. Mountstuart's understanding to meet the girl" (*E* 2:124–25). Hence she cultivates this carefully planted seed into a fully blossomed script in which Clara, because jealous of Laetitia, flirts with De Craye in order to evoke Willoughby's jealousy and bring him into submission. Mrs. Mountstuart's modesty in praising Clara—"Ah! my fair Middleton, am I pretending to teach you? You have read him a lesson" (*E* 2:133)—is doubly false. On the one hand, she praises her own inventiveness rather than Clara's accomplishment, and, on the other hand, she credits her own imagination for an idea actually sown by Willoughby. Because her reading is flawed, her lesson about words and their use will of necessity be similarly mistaken.

Readers expect greater sensitivity from Laetitia Dale. But while her discursive identity is radically different from Mrs. Mountstuart's, she too suspects Clara's similes—no more so than when confronted with the improbable tales, first, of the Egoist's suitability to become Laetitia's husband and, second, of Vernon's disinclination to become Clara's. Knowing the state of Vernon's affections, Laetitia interrogates Clara about her feelings, relentlessly repeating the question: "If he had spoken?" (*E* 2:309–11). When evasiveness is interpreted as a rejection of Vernon, Clara tries to correct the impression:

> "Dearest, if I may convey to you what I was, in a simile for comparison: I think I was like a fisherman's float on the water, perfectly still, and ready to go down at any instance, or up. So much for my behaviour."
>
> "Similes have the merit of satisfying the finder of them, and cheating the hearer," said Laetitia. "You admit that your feelings would have been painful."
>
> "I was a fisherman's float: please, admire my simile: any way you like, this way or that, or so quiet as to tempt the eyes to go to sleep. And suddenly I might have disappeared in the depths, or flown in the air. But no fish bit."
>
> "Well, then, to follow you, supposing the fish or the fisherman, for I don't know which is which. . . . Oh! no, no: this is too serious for imagery." (*E* 2:310)

Because Clara attempts a simile, rather than simply allowing Laetitia's reading to stand uncorrected, and because the "simile chafed her wits with a suspicion of meaning" (*E* 2:310), Laetitia presses the point, intuits Clara's love, and reveals Vernon's.

When she talks to Laetitia at this point, Clara is ostensibly no longer in need of help, having been effectively released from her engagement earlier that day. But this exchange proves that she still profits from the dialogical process. She hears from Laetitia an implausible "tale of an antiquary [Vernon] prizing a battered relic of the battle-field [Clara herself]" (*E* 2:312), which, simile notwithstanding, is true. More important than what Clara hears, however, is what happens to her during the colloquy. Specifically, she apprehends the effect of her loose talk with De Craye upon others and upon her own character. As before, therefore, this dialogue takes her "beyond a line," and once again the trespassed line is both erotic and verbal. Previously, she learned that she could love another; now she discovers that "[t]o be loved . . . is to feel our littleness" (*E* 2:312). Although she rejects Willoughby's notion of purity in marital affairs when it is applied to Vernon (*E* 2:295), she has inculcated this norm concerning herself. Thus she confesses "shame" (*E* 2:312) at the prospect of Vernon's proposal to a "battered relic." Yet she now realizes that she can be both blameworthy and beloved. Her fishing float simile, then, is apt. It recalls both Vernon's synecdochic description of the world as a river alternately clear and muddy, troubled and at rest, and her own recollection of the "mulier formosa" (*E* 2:86), the fish/woman whose mixed being is a figure of human nature itself.[8] The linguistic border that she crosses opens into a similarly mixed world. Previously, she learned the power of language to create, not merely to reflect. Not only is that lesson reinforced, but she also discovers the dangers and responsibilities of this linguistic power.

The conversation with Laetitia amplifies the observations made of Clara's earlier talk with Mrs. Mountstuart, placing additional emphasis on the issue of speech and gender.[9] First, although Clara utters the simile not spoken previously, Laetitia's response is nevertheless a projection, an expression of her own tropophobia. Her fear of imagery has an emotional and a physiological basis: she is convinced that the "silly verses" (*E* 2:197) of her youth shamed her character and that the attempted career of poet ruined her health. Furthermore, like Willoughby's maidenly aunts, she believes that "the gift of humorous fancy is in women fenced round with forbidding placards; they have to choke it" (*E* 1:92). Women must be conversationally "cloistral" (*E* 1:131). Even after freeing herself from Willoughby's imaginative domination, Laetitia can neither abandon a "habit of wholly subservient sweetness, which was her ideal of the feminine," nor recover from "the unhealed wound she had sustained and the cramp of a bondage of such old date as to seem iron" (*E* 2:96). Mrs. Mountstuart has said that "[e]loquence is a terrible thing, in women" (*E* 2:133), and Laetitia, who denies possessing it (*E* 2:176), agrees. She continues to fear, therefore, "the dreadful power" of Clara's voice, both because it is unfeminine and because, having been "strangely swayed" (*E* 1:191) by it, she recognizes a potential threat to her submissive reclusion.

Second, this fear of vocal power, which echoes one of the forms of logophobia in *Jane Eyre*, accounts for the prejudice of Patterne Hall that, specifically for women, to speak is to lie. Clara herself tells Laetitia that "very few women are able to be straightforwardly sincere in their speech" (*E* 1:190), an observation accepted by Laetitia and explained by differences in the education of men and women. The narrator reinforces this view, explaining that women "have to practice much simulation" (*E* 1:131), because to use "plain speech is to be guilty of effrontery and forfeit the waxen polish of purity, and therewith their commanding place in the market" (*E* 2:2; also see *E* 1:145). An alternate view leading to the same conclusion is that women are inherently and naturally duplicitous. For example, Willoughby says that they possess a "power of putting on a face" lacking in men, who must "learn the arts which come to women by nature" (*E* 2:116). His ideal of the "waxwork sex" is that "their tongues are curbed by rosy pudency" (*E* 2:126). The dilemma is obvious: to speak plainly is to be immodest, but to speak modestly is to be duplicitous. Thus Laetitia's fear of eloquence, even of language itself, is not simply personal and idiosyncratic; it expresses a societal and conventional suspicion of articulateness in women. If male power is to be assured, the metaphoric knife that the Patternes have wielded socially and economically to build their estate must also be used verbally, that is, to silence Clara's Irish tongue.

Masculine sexual (as well as social) domination is directly threatened by women's seductive language: after all, "a clever tongue will gain . . . a leg" (*E* 1:192). Laetitia, like Mrs. Mountstuart, has accepted the seed planted by Willoughby concerning Clara's "little feminine ailment," but she diagnoses an even more serious affliction. Unlike Mrs. Mountstuart, Laetitia does not facilely attribute Clara's blamable intimacy (*E* 2:75) with De Craye to jealousy, nor does she read the conquest as testimony to Clara's proficiency in the language of love. Rather, she interprets this flirtation as an indictment of women in general:

> Laetitia's bosom swelled upon a mute exclamation, equivalent to: "Woman! woman! snared ever by the sparkling and frivolous! undiscerning of the faithful, the modest and beneficent!"
> In the secret musings of moralists this dramatic rhetoric survives. . . . [S]he was jealous on behalf of her sex: her sex's reputation seemed at stake, and the purity of it was menaced by Clara's idle preference of the shallower man. (*E* 2:97)

Thus, while Mrs. Mountstuart reads lessons in the art of love, Laetitia moralizes on proper feminine behavior; while Mrs. Mountstuart criticizes from the point of view of a woman's investment in a linguistic mode of existence, Laetitia judges from a different perspective, that of women's contamination by talk. Ironically, the two women reach the same conclusion. And, ironically, the guilty verdict is accepted by the conversational criminal. Her transgression, Clara feels, has been to have "gone clamouring about more immodestly than women will bear to hear of, and she herself to think of" (*E* 2:312)—a conclusion seemingly worthy of the moralist's "dramatic rhetoric" in service of a masculine god. Yet she recognizes that her fault has been more than a matter of merely offending male definitions of social propriety. She has also unqualifiedly accepted the social use of language, placing too much confidence in words, using them—and misusing them—to seduce De Craye. Having accepted the language of love and rationalized its use, she becomes its victim and can hear nothing else, especially Vernon's silence: "I wanted his voice; but silence, I think did tell me more: if a nature like mine could only have had faith without hearing the rattle of a tongue" (*E* 2:313).

The significance of these two comparatively brief scenes may be confirmed by a return to *Diana of the Crossways*, which, like *The Egoist*, invokes a suspicion of figuration at the same time that its sometimes ponderous tropes suggest that Meredith himself has difficulty "distinguish[ing] between the simple metaphor and the superobese" (*DCW* 45).[10] The opening chapter, "Of Diaries and Diarists Touching the Heroine," contains no small number of these hefty tropes since it includes both Diana Merion's witticisms and the meta-witticisms of the diarists who cite and comment on them. Later chapters offer several scenes replete with overstuffed dinner-table conversations of a complexity and figurative excess that surely would have overawed the provincial Mrs. Mountstuart Jenkinson but that essentially reflect her tropological method and performative objective.[11] These symposia are perhaps a sign of sophistication and high culture, but they are also no more than an intermediary stage in what Meredith imagines as the evolution of civilization:

> When a nation has acknowledged that it is as yet but in the fisticuff stage of the art of condensing our purest sense to golden sentences, a readier appreciation will be extended to the gift: which is to strike not the dazzled eyes, the unanticipating nose, the ribs, the sides, and stun us, twirl us, hoodwink, mystify, tickle and twitch, by dexterities of lingual sparring and shuffling, but to strike roots in the mind, the Hesperides of good things. (*DCW* 2)

Within the discursive confines of dining and drawing rooms such "lingual sparring and shuffling" are relatively harmless. In "the war of the sexes" (*DCW* 10) generally and in marriage particularly, however, "quips of metaphor" (*DCW* 121) and "vocabulary in irony a quiverful" (*DCW* 49) may inflict serious wounds. When Diana directs "'sallies'" at her husband, for example, the injury is compounded by his thin skin and thick mind: "it was the worse for him when he did not perceive their drift" (*DCW* 156). The unintended consequence of her witticisms is an accusation of criminal conversation. Bested in a verbal duel with his wife, Augustus Warwick chooses a new weapon—"lawyers' lingo" (*DCW* 143)—with which to carry on the spousal warfare. The reason for his legal action against Lord Dannisburgh is not his wife's adultery. Diana may have been untactful, but she has not been unfaithful. She is a conversational criminal of an entirely different kind: "English women and men feel toward the quick-witted of their species as to aliens, having the demerits of aliens—wordiness, vanity, obscurity, shallowness, an empty glitter, the sin of posturing. A quick-witted woman exerting her wit is both a foreigner and potentially a criminal" (*DCW* 122).[12] While innocent of the formal legal charge, she has violated the general social injunction against wit in women. There are those, like Lady Wathin, who will always indict her merely for speaking, but her culpability stems not from the fact that she speaks, but from the way that she speaks—as she herself admits. Her "relish for ridicule" (*DCW* 69) is more than a social protest against Victorian censorship of women; it exemplifies the "fisticuff stage" of human social relations, ontogenetically and phylogenetically. Diana says that she "shot her epigrams at the helpless despot, and was at times—yes, vixenish; a nature driven to it, but that was the word" (*DCW* 162). Riddled with epigrams—and also riddled by them—her husband responds to these attacks in a modern, but no less primitive, way—he files a lawsuit.

While fears of figuration in *Diana of the Crossways* are consistently linked with patriarchy, they are also generalized to encompass even the narrator, who has occasion to question his own tropes. Describing a distant view of London, for instance, he alludes to "a murky web, not without colour: the ever-flying banner of the metropolis, the smoke of the city's chimneys, if you prefer plain language" (*DCW* 44).[13] The reversion to plain language is a concession to literal-minded readers that is reaffirmed when the narrator compares his own language to that of a "grandiloquent man of advertizing letters"—an unflattering likeness prompting him to retract the phrase "'banner of the metropolis.' That plush of speech haunts all efforts to swell and illuminate citizen prose to a princely poetic" (*DCW* 45). To the stolid Englishman, the "plush of speech" is everywhere to be mistrusted, whether because commercial and meretricious, as in this instance; or gendered and "unnatural," as with women; or national and fatuous, as with the Irish.[14]

In *The Egoist*, tropopohobia is especially associated with the first of three distinct discursive modes, each of which manifests a varying degree of sensitivity, expressiveness, and creativity. The first mode reveals a "constative" bias; that is, words are held to have fixed meaning, and sentences are judged true or false according to a referential criterion. Mrs. Mountstuart and Laetitia, for example, want "the facts" and expect Clara's replies to convey knowledge about her feelings without the distractions or misrepresentations of figuration. The most consistently constative speaker is Willoughby himself, whose discourse typifies what Meredith calls "primeval chattering" (*E* 1:2). Such language is a direct gesture; words are transparent references to the things needed to sustain the self. This naive discourse is a "symbolic alphabet of striking arms and running legs, our early language" (*E* 2:182). Conversation of this kind, however, is as common on the estates of the aristocracy as in the caves of "our o'er-hoary ancestry" (*E* 1:2). In practice there is little linguistic difference between "an unleavened society," where speech is "a low as of the udderful cow past milking hour" (*E* 1:4), and "ultra-refined" drawing rooms, where words are often no more than "shrieks of the lamentable letter 'I'" (*E* 1:131). The similarity between the primitive and the civilized is accentuated by the correspondence of Willoughby's ejaculatory "I" to his body language: "he straighten[ed] his whole figure to the erectness of the letter I" (*E* 1:19).[15] Meredith makes literal that which in *Daniel Deronda* is a simple comparison: "Suitors must often be judged as words are, by the standing and the figure they make in polite society" (*DD* 358). For primitive speakers, the only figure of speech is, in effect, the body itself—a point reinforced by an example of speech of the second kind, Mrs. Mountstuart's figurative apothegm, "*he has a leg*" (*E* 1:11).

The second mode of discourse reveals a "performative" bias toward language. Words are valued for what they do, and typically what they do is entertain the members of "leavened" society. Hence, when Mrs. Mountstuart describes Willoughby as having a leg, she is concerned primarily with rhetorical effect and only secondarily with representational accuracy. To the "artist in phrases" (*E* 2:77), words and their use are ends in themselves. Language is self-referential rather than referential; its alphabet is literal rather than symbolic. Among those whose existence is dedicated to witty talk, the only figures are figures of speech. The corporeal, for example, is doubly obscured by Mrs. Mountstuart's synecdoche, which, first, accentuates Willoughby's social, as opposed to his physical, presence and, second, diverts attention from the comely aristocrat to his witty guest. Her polished epithet represents "the triumph of the spiritual, and where it passes for coin of value, the society has reached a high refinement" (*E* 1:12). The triumph is a Pyrrhic one, and its currency is of dubious value. The oxymoronic juxtaposition of the spiritual and the monetary registers Meredith's awareness of the unacceptable cost of such verbal investment. Performative discourse is not invariably a sign of progress.

Ethical norms are lost in a conversational world governed exclusively by rhetorical principles. For example, Mrs. Mountstuart disapproves of sarcasm on grounds of oratorical pragmatism not humane concern (*E* 2:130). The arbiters of correct speech and judges of verbal disputes are academics like Professor Crooklyn and Dr. Middleton, who can be relied on to awake "for the judicial allocution in a trice" (*E* 2:150).[16] Seldom agreeing among themselves, these pedants conduct erudite debates in abstract discourse, typically concerning the technicalities of language itself. They appear, therefore, to be the verbal opposites of the primitives insofar as their alphabet is arbitrary and literal, not symbolic, and their language is intransitive, not referential. But like the social primitives, the academic egoists are concerned with nothing outside of their own petty interests, endlessly picking at a "little inexactitude of phrases" like domestic fowl (*E* 2:110). There is no clearer instance of this learned but primitive pettiness than Dr. Middleton's interpreting Clara's articulation of "the vowels I and A" as a "vulgarization of our tongue" (*E* 1:215). Her words on this occasion are broken and hesitant because of her emotional distress, but he is oblivious to the sounds of his daughter's unhappiness, hearing only a clumsy recitation by the student into whose head he had "beaten some small stock of Latin . . . and a note of Greek. . . . I had hoped once . . . but she is a girl" (*E* 1:232, the final ellipsis is Meredith's). The system of rhetorical norms and discursive justice shared by this society and adjudicated by its scholars establishes language as an end in itself and restricts women's voices to ornamental accompaniment or to silence.

Among these speakers, "criminal conversation" could be only a literal, not a euphemistic, term. Marriage means being "interlinguistic" (*E* 1:207) with only one person, and women, married or not, are encouraged to believe that talking to men is improper. After Clara has confided in Vernon, for instance, she accuses herself of "dire misconduct" (*E* 1:182). Laetitia also thinks it incredible that "a young lady should speak on the subject of the inner holies to a man, though he were Vernon Whitford" (*E* 1:282). Even Vernon, who can make an exception for Clara's speaking to him, cannot extend this "leniency to the young lady's character when there was question of her doing the same with a second gentleman" (*E* 2:24). Despite this bias, Vernon seems generally ill at ease among those whose verbal brilliance is exercised at significant human cost. Only professional wits, like Colonel De Craye and Mrs. Mountstuart, and academics, like Dr. Middleton and Professor Crooklyn, are fully at home in this isolated linguistic world. Someone like Lady Busshe, "a woman barren of wit, stripped of style" (E 2:161), is denied entry despite her commitment to gossip. Others, like Vernon and Clara, may visit Patterne Hall but are more comfortable in a less arid universe of discourse.

Presumably, this new logosphere lies outside of marriage, as Willoughby Patterne defines it, and outside of society, as Patterne Hall represents it. This alternative mode of speaking is implied by the phrase "real talk" in Clara's description of Vernon: "he could scarcely be said to shine in a drawing-room, unless when seated beside a person ready for real talk" (E 1:86). Her conversations with Mrs. Mountstuart and Laetitia do not begin as examples of this mode, but they evolve into the creative interchange that distinguishes this from other kinds of talk. Both constative and performative speech in *The Egoist* are essentially monological: the former is a unilateral assertion, the latter a verbal contest whose objective is having the last word. Each is typified by self-reference: the first, in the sense that all words refer to the needs of the individual, the second, in the sense that all words refer to themselves. Both, therefore, are the languages of egoism, depending upon either the social or the rhetorical domination of the other. "Real talk" borrows from both modes but is qualitatively different from them. It represents what speech should be and can do but seldom is or does. Like the primitive speaker, the "realist" invokes the referential dimension of language, although refining it in at least two ways. First, words are freed from purely egocentric reference and use, and, second, language is not seen as a direct gesture, a transparent allusion to something outside of itself. Words themselves are acknowledged as objects of reference, a point implicit in Meredith's assertion that the Comic Spirit focuses exclusively upon characters "and their speech" (E 1:1). "Real talk" also resembles academic and salon discourse in acknowledging the performative function of language, but again with two complicating factors. First, words do more than merely entertain the leisure and academic classes, and, second, the act of speaking itself is implicated in what words do; hence language can do more than it appears to say.

In "real talk" a transactive connection links words, speaking, and experience. Referentiality and truth, therefore, are not reified; they are contextualized. And while this context is never exclusively verbal, neither does it exclude the verbal. The significance of speech entails both the speaker and the interlocutor as the links between words and the world. As such, human and rhetorical figures are unified rather than opposed. This is, in effect, the import of the luncheon-table discussion of "rough truth."[17] Dr. Middleton defines what subsequent speakers demonstrate: a "rough truth" imparts "a powerful impregnation of the roughness of the teller" (*E* 2:150). His circular definition shifts the emphasis from the nature of roughness to that of truth. Any act of speaking will be more or less "true" insofar as it reveals the speaker in relation to the interlocutor(s). This is especially the case with figurative language, which calls attention to words and how they are used, making visible and self-conscious what is often merely implicit and tacit. Recognizing this, the "realist" need be neither tropophobic nor logophobic. Clara, for instance, discovers the power of conversation, as opposed to the "dreadful power" of eloquence, in her dialogues with Mrs. Mountstuart and Laetitia Dale. By self-consciously scrutinizing her role in these conversations and by understanding the connection between words and feelings, she learns that "real talk" is a creative process. Because speaking acts inwardly as well as outwardly and because it always functions as a two-way mirror but never simply as a mirror, words must be used with care and responsibility. Thus, while her duologues advance Meredith's comic plot by removing some of the obstacles to the lovers, they more importantly develop Clara's understanding of language itself. Ironically, therefore, they prepare for the repetition of the act that has gotten her into so much trouble, that is, promising marriage.

No verbal act would seem to be "rougher" than promising in that it self-consciously and necessarily refers to the speaker; it is performed in the first person singular. In the two scenes just discussed, for example, neither interlocutor trusts Clara's promises. In the first, Clara wants to prove her sincerity to Mrs. Mountstuart by taking a vow. This offer, however, calls into suspicion the very nature of promising because her oath would abrogate a prior promise to Willoughby. Mrs. Mountstuart's apparently justified reply is that in this instance to swear would be to forswear. Her skepticism concerning Clara's word perhaps explains why she resorts to a "catechism." The religious connotation suggests the sacredness of the proceedings to the discursive reprobate, and its rigid format of question and answer, with a limitation upon the length of replies, restricts what Mrs. Mountstuart suspects is an inclination to fulsome language and empty promises. Laetitia shares the doubt but not the method. When Clara metonymically promises her heart, Laetitia synecdochically replies: "Present me with a part—but for good! . . . I mean no unkindness; but is not the heart you allude to an alarmingly searching one?" (*E* 2:94). Laetitia's skepticism is expressed in an appeal to the very thing that is doubted: Clara's word. Her plea is more successful than Mrs. Mountstuart's precisely because it acknowledges, rather than circumvents, the "unkindness" that all women face. Clara's request to break her engagement reinforces the stereotype of female inconstancy—an image of which both women are acutely conscious.[18] In this scene and later when she accepts Willoughby's proposal, Laetitia learns that promises might be "for good" but that they are not forever. A promise may be a promise, but the promise kept is seldom the promise made. Searching hearts are a human, not a female, characteristic. Promising cannot guarantee that searches will be successful, but it may—as here between Laetitia and Clara—establish the trust that makes them possible.

The nature and significance of promising become clearer in light of men's promissory behavior. Colonel De Craye, for instance, places little importance on the care and responsibility with which he uses language, often "uttering nonsense that amusement may come of it" (E 2:73). On a basic level, therefore, he consciously and repeatedly breaks the promise of language itself, that is, to mean something and to mean what he says. Exemplary of this conversational carelessness are the occasions on which he enlists his considerable wit in the service of Clara Middleton, all the while hoping to become the groom rather than the best man at her wedding. In a novel of pitched conversational battles (E 1:181), "great-gunnery talk" (E 2:56), and frequently discharged verbal volleys (E 2:101), De Craye is a skilled and generally successful rhetorical strategist. The suddenness with which he becomes "interlinguistic" with Clara, for example, signals to many at Patterne Hall that he will follow in the steps of Captain Oxford by "wresting the prize from a rival" (E 1:260). Despite envisioning himself in the role of Paris to Willoughby's Menelaus and Clara's Helen (E 1:258), De Craye is himself finally carried off by a formidable general of dinner-table battlefields (E 2:72), Mrs. Mountstuart.[19]

One of the Colonel's many staged performances suggests why he is able to seduce Mrs. Mountstuart but not Clara. The county's leading lady of wit flirtatiously tells the dialogically dashing De Craye, "Really, were I fifteen years younger. I am not so certain . . . I might try to make you harmless" (E 2:149).[20] The feat, rather defeat, would be considerable, since the Colonel is "a veteran handsome man of society numbering six and thirty years . . . [with] nearly as many conquests" (E 1:259). An accomplished Don Juan, De Craye indirectly alludes to his prototype when he proposes to Clara that the company act a play, The Irishman in Spain, in which the impoverished Patrick O'Neill visits a Spanish nobleman whose engaged daughter is carefully guarded by a duenna. Both the Spanish setting and the dramatic situation invoke the model of Don Juan, with De Craye cast as the amorous hero and Clara as his victim. According to the script, Patrick loses the letter of introduction to Don Beltran d'Arragon and finds himself alone and hungry in a foreign country: "It's all through dropping a letter I'm here in Iberia instead of Hibernia, worse luck to the spelling!" (*E* 1:220). The purely verbal humor prompts Clara to explain that an Irishman would aspirate the "H," making it less likely that "Iberia" and "Hibernia" could be confused. Furthermore, when asked to play the role of Dona Serafina, Clara resists, claiming not to have the violet eyes that Patrick/Horace sees in Serafina/Clara. By appealing to reality, she frustrates the continuation of the play and diverts the Colonel's performance into harmless banter. No matter how the script might end in his imagination, the "human play" (*E* 1:257), insofar as it involves Clara, is destined to be a source of frustration to the Irishman in England.

Because Mrs. Mountstuart, unlike Clara, is committed to a primarily verbal existence, it is appropriate that she and De Craye drive off together as the curtain falls. Their literary styles are different—she is given to compression, he to expatiation—yet both are dedicated to saying the remembered rather than the right thing. He, even more than she, is invested in verbal play for its own sake. His amusement is not merely verbal but erotic as well, since language for him is "a field of enjoyment, not of knowledge."[21] In addition to serving as the means to amorous ends, words are a source of erotic pleasure in and of themselves. De Craye exhibits an attitude to discourse that Shoshana Felman argues is typical of Don Juan:

> The desire of a Don Juan is thus at once desire for desire and desire for language; a desire that desires *itself* and that desires its own language. Speech is the true realm of eroticism, and not simply a means of access to this realm. To seduce is to produce language that enjoys, language that takes pleasure in having "no more to say." To seduce is thus to prolong, within desiring speech, the pleasure-taking performance of the very production of the speech.[22]

Such language is self-referential; it can have nothing to say to Clara's appeals to Irish dialects or eye color. De Craye, as we have seen, is largely unconcerned with the truth of what he says, readily admitting to speaking nonsense (*E* 1:204) in order to win Clara's affection. Although the strategy results in a setback in "the game of love" (*E* 2:331), De Craye recovers his tongue in less than five minutes after learning of Clara's preference for Vernon. His love is more on his tongue than in his heart, and he leaves the stage as he entered it, talking. The final sounds of the novel are those of his words "enchanting Mrs. Mountstuart" (*E* 2:331).

Perhaps Don Juan's most successful rhetorical strategy is promising marriage. The promise of marriage, in fact, might be said to be the central preoccupation of *The Egoist*. Because Meredith is less concerned with seduction than engagement, less interested in sexual/erotic affairs than in social/conventional ones, De Craye's thirty-odd conquests receive virtually no attention, while the second of Willoughby's three betrothals occupies most of the novel. Apart from a willingness to marry Clara, the two suitors are as dramatically different as John Bull and Don Juan. Willoughby is unflatteringly compared to De Craye as a rhetorician (*E* 2:112). He is intimidated by witty and learned speech, although his pride prevents retreat in the face of superior oratory. In the course of verbal skirmishes, therefore, he commits solecisms (*E* 1:169, 227), misses the point (*E* 1:231), and, in direct violation of the discursive rules of polite society, vents his resentment of superior rhetoric, whether it be the Colonel's obtuse humor (*E* 2:65–67) or the Doctor's abstruse erudition (*E* 2:83). When he senses defeat in the war of words or is unable to carry the day with "phrases of perfect choiceness" (*E* 1:15–16), he reverts to a primitive strategy: "the pugilistic form . . . administered directly on the salient features" (*E* 2:66), what Dr. Middleton describes as "a phrase of assault . . . ostentatiously battery" (*E* 2:67). Willoughby bears little resemblance to De Craye, but they share a common fate: neither succeeds with Clara.

The difference between the two friends is most apparent in their approaches to the language of love. Both in content and manner De Craye's tales of romance—of courtings, honeymoons, and weddings—contrast sharply with Willoughby's "lectures on the aesthetics of love" (*E* 1:256). Willoughby ridicules the "womanized" language of courtship with its "lamentable cooing stuff" (*E* 1:40, 2:66). His love talk, accurately but ironically described by himself as "ta-ta-ta-ta ad infinitum" (*E* 2:122–23), alienates rather than entrances:

> Sir Willoughby was a social Egoist, fiercely imaginative in whatsoever concerned him. He had discovered a greater realm than that of the sensual appetites, and he rushed across and around it in his conquering period with an Alexander's pride. On these wind-like journeys he had carried Constantia, subsequently Clara; and however it may have been in the case of Miss Durham, in that of Miss Middleton it is almost certain she caught her glimpse of his interior from sheer fatigue in hearing him discourse of it. (*E* 2:183)

Clara too late perceives the "contrast of his recent language and his fine figure" (*E* 1:60). Willoughby would surely have fared better had he let his famous leg do all the talking: "Such a leg . . . will walk straight into the hearts of women. Nothing so fatal to them" (*E* 1:13). When he begins speaking, subjecting Clara to "love's catechism" (*E* 1:43–44) and insisting that "plighted faith, the affiancing of two lovers, is a piece of religion" (*E* 1:174), she is driven out of his arms and very nearly into a railway carriage with De Craye. The latter's "Irish tongue" (*E* 1:203, 207) is more than equal to the former's "fine figure."

Despite the significant differences between Willoughby and De Craye, the social Egoist resembles Don Juan in repeatedly promising marriage. Each, therefore, is in the contradictory situation of offering or appearing to offer that which reiterated acts of promising contradict. On the one hand, they promise the stability of meaning. Willoughby, for example, insists, "my word stands for me," and believes that a "broken pledge [is] a form of suicide" (*E* 2:207). De Craye only pretends that his promises correspond to his intentions. On the other hand, they offer the stability of a permanent social institution—a permanence that, in Willoughby's view, endures even "beyond death" (*E* 1:57). By repeating promises, Willoughby Patterne (unconsciously) and Don Juan (consciously) deny the conventional significance of betrothal. The logic of social discourse—that to talk on is to lie—ironically undercuts their own discourse, for the more often they promise, the less likely they will be trusted. Willoughby Patterne employs promises constatively to create a secure and self-reflecting linguistic world. Don Juan uses them performatively, just as De Craye relies upon anecdotes and nonsense. Whereas Willoughby elicits such promises in order to enslave, Don Juan gives promises in order to seduce. Nevertheless, the consequences of their promissory behavior are identical: neither's promises are credible; each belies the words he utters by the very act of uttering them.

Don Juan, of course, does not believe his own promises. As Felman points out, he plays "with the *illusion* of constancy inherent in the promise, an illusion in which he scarcely believes himself. This is why he is, mythically speaking, the figure of Inconstancy, of Unfaithfulness. . . . Unbelieving, the mythical seducer refuses to be seduced by his own myth, refuses for his part to be seduced by language, to believe in the promise of meaning."[23] Willoughby Patterne, on the contrary, is entirely seduced by his own promises. Fully believing in the power of language to convey and to fix meaning, he takes espousal to be tantamount to marriage and impervious to time and change. The word once uttered, whether to banish Flitch (*E* 1:205–6) or to engage Clara, cannot be retracted. Saying, he wants to believe, makes it so, yet his linguistic and psychological egotism contravenes this faith. His pledges of constancy to Laetitia (chapters thirty-one and forty), his midnight proposal to her followed the next morning by his insistence that Clara keep her promise to marry him, even his calculated rhetoric on a "breach of faith" (*E* 2:211) belie his words. Dependent upon the adulation of others, therefore subject to vicissitudes outside of his control, the Egoist struggles for constancy through words. But because he uses language to stop the dialogical process in which words can be creative and not merely reflective, his promises establish only the impossibility of promising as it is conventionally understood. Clearly, Willoughby cannot fix and control experience within a linguistic world. Nor can he expect his promises to be credible when they are repeated and repeatedly broken.

Since both Willoughby and Clara break the promise to marry, *The Egoist* would seem to question the significance of any promise and to raise the possibility that language itself is unreliable, leaving silence as the only alternative to inaccuracy or deception. If we are, as Vernon says, "at the mercy [of] our natures" (*E* 1:14), then no promise can be trusted, and the hedonistic calculus represented by "four happy instead of two miserable" becomes the only operative principle of social behavior. Indeed, Willoughby's machinations at the end of the novel seem to verify such calculation, since of the two imminent marriages one will be happy and neither miserable. The fortuitous confluence of Willoughby's plans with Clara's searching heart suggests that nature and happenstance may be more important in shaping human behavior than individual promises. If so, what reason is there to assume that the unarticulated promise between Clara and Vernon at the end of the novel will be more promising than Willoughby's garrulous pledges?

That we do not actually hear Vernon propose to Clara seems appropriate since they are brought together as much by silence as by speech. It is Vernon's refusal to speak his love that serves both as its profession and its proof (*E* 2:311–13). His rhetorical strategy, or nonstrategy, succeeds where Willoughby's lectures and De Craye's anecdotes fail, perhaps because in a world given over to social wit, silence is more trustworthy than speech. Silence, however, is neither more nor less reliable than talking. Only in combination can either have meaning, and in the conversative society of Patterne Hall, the expected figure/ground relation of speech and silence is inverted: talking constitutes the background against which silence can be heard.[24] In the noise of gabbling, rattling, chattering, babbling, jabbering, and buzzing, silence becomes communicative; it is voiced.

Vernon's habitual silence both establishes and accentuates the significance of what he does say. He is clearly different from either of Clara's suitors. Not a "complacent talking man" (*E* 1:65), he seems most comfortable ensconced in the library; lacking "the persuasive tongue" (*E* 2:75), or what he himself calls the "lady's tongue" (*E* 2:35), he prefers isolated Alpine walking tours to social confabulation. Although capable of wit and erudition, he is "not a man who played on words" (*E* 1:209); therefore, he is unequal to Willoughby's sermons or De Craye's doublespeak. His discursive limitations, for example, are readily apparent when he attempts to notify Clara of the result of his talk with Willoughby (about her desire to leave Patterne Hall), without revealing this information to her father. Unaware of his "clumsy double meaning," he asks Dr. Middleton about a poetic line that will indirectly communicate his message to Clara: "Will this pass, do you think?—'In Asination's tongue he asinates:' signifying, that he excels any man of us at donkey-dialect" (*E* 1:293). Vernon indirectly refers to Willoughby's stubbornness in holding Clara to her promise, but he also unwittingly describes his own asinine performance. He can get the line "to apply" with neither interlocutor. Clara is incensed at these academic "absurdities" (*E* 1:294), and Dr. Middleton, perhaps finding the line itself to be an example of the "donkey-dialect," replies: "This might do:—'In Assignation's name he assignats:' signifying, that he pre- eminently flourishes hypothetical promises to pay by appointment" (*E* 1:294). The further neologistic nonsense drives Clara from the room, presumably to prepare for an assignation of her own with Lucy Darleton, while Vernon retreats from the contest he himself began into a meditation on the subject of common sense. Dr. Middleton, of course, unknowingly refers to a central issue in the novel, the nature of that enigmatic promise to promise, betrothal. His poetic line, like Vernon's, describes both Willoughby, whose promises of marriage tend to be hypothetical, that is, occurring in name only, and to Vernon himself, whose character promises meaning but who seems to break that promise in this instance.

While talking need not produce nonsense and promises need not always be unfulfilled, Meredith appears to reinforce such fears. He seems both to valorize silence by flatteringly describing the tight-lipped Vernon Whitford and to break the implicit authorial promise to present readers with all the important dramatic action. He omits such key episodes as the two duologues in which Vernon is informed of Willoughby's proposals for his marital settlement.[25] In both, one person (first Clara, then Willoughby himself) proposes to Vernon that he marry a third person (first Laetitia, then Clara). The proxy proposals are instigated by Willoughby as extensions of his own wedding plans with Clara and Laetitia, successively (though for awhile it seems simultaneously). Subsequent references to these conversations reveal that in both Vernon politely rejects the proposals made on his behalf but without his consultation. When Clara broaches the subject of marrying Laetitia, he declines "the idea of marriage" itself and responds to the "two fiery minutes of broken language" with which she condemns "the prospect of the yoke." He does so, however, with what she feels is "logical coolness . . . excessive coolness" (*E* 1:181–82). When Willoughby approaches him with the plan to marry Clara, Vernon dismisses the idea as "impossible, out of the question, but thanked Willoughby for the best of intentions, thanked him warmly" (*E* 2:278). The difference in "temperature" between the scenes is an accurate measure of the state of his

affections; the similarity in response testifies to the absurdity of the proposals. Only the supreme egoist would assume that his word stands for
himself and for everyone else too. With the malign humor of the Comic
Spirit itself, Vernon ridicules Willoughby's presumption and inconstancy by raising this issue with Dr. Middleton (who has just argued that
"when faith is broken by one, the engagement ceases" [E 2:247]): "Sup-
posing he had succeeded [that is, Willoughby succeeded in eliciting from
Laetitia a promise to marry Vernon] . . . should I have been bound to
marry?" (E 2:249–50). The ensuing discussion is interrupted by
Willoughby's objection "to insufferable nonsense" and terminated by
Mrs. Mountstuart's arrival. The point, however, is obvious. Whatever
their significance, promises have meaning only for those making them.
Willoughby's ventriloquism is itself a false promise. Furthermore, the
proposal is particularly comic in this instance, because Willoughby
attempts to elicit a promise to marry someone else (Vernon) from the
woman (Laetitia) to whom he himself has just proposed.

Textual silence also surrounds Clara and Vernon when they meet,
ostensibly to discuss Willoughby's intention that they marry. Readers
are not given the scene but subsequently learn that Vernon will not rise
to the bait, conversing instead about Alpine hiking, classical literature,
and political economy (E 2:309). The silence increases exponentially
when, in later speaking to Laetitia, Clara elliptically refers only to Vernon's "avoidance . . . " (E 2:309). She misreads his silence as mere kindness to her and a polite disapproval of Willoughby's plan (just as her
own evasiveness has previously been misconstrued by Laetitia). Vernon
does, of course, disapprove of the plan: such brokering of marriages is
repellant, but he also loves Clara, who has now been released from her
engagement. Their love, however, is silenced by the plan itself, since
anything that they might say will appear to be cribbed from
Willoughby's master plan. Clara imposes a silence upon Vernon as he is
about to propose: "not in this house!" (E 2:315). The residual echoes of
the Egoist's broken promises taint words of love uttered in Patterne
Hall.

Although no promise of marriage is actually heard, a tacit understanding has clearly been reached. Their unarticulated "promise" syn-
thesizes two discursive modes into an instance of "real talk." The first
promise between them occurs in "the symbolic alphabet of . . . arms
and . . . legs." Their "union of hands" (E 2:317) signifies to Laetitia and
to readers that Clara now willingly gives what Willoughby has repeatedly asked for, her hand in marriage. Though Willoughby is often
shown forcibly grasping her hand as a sign of possessing her heart, only
with Vernon is this figure of speech made literal—and meaningful. The
second expression of engagement occurs in the style of the performative

speaker. The "spirit of Dr. Middleton . . . [having] blown into Vernon" (*E* 2:315), he indirectly reveals his feeling for Clara through the metaphor of mountain climbing—a topic and a trope dear to both. Their dialogue may hardly seem like "forthright outspeaking" (*E* 2:315), yet both know that a proposal is forthcoming on their Alpine tour, a setting that will once again make figurative speech literal. Thus not only constative and performative discourse but also figures (hands) and figures of speech (mountains) are united in a "real," albeit a silent, promise.

Vernon's unnarrated duologues are opposite in nature but equal in importance to Clara's conversations with Mrs. Mountstuart and Laetitia. They reveal that narrative silence may be as expressive as narrated tropes. These are communicative silences, implicating readers in an ongoing and creative dialogical process, one much like those experienced by Clara and her interlocutors. Readers must give voice to these scenes, and in speaking them come to discover their meaning. In this manner, fictional discourse itself can be an instance of "real talk." Meredith reverses the strategy of Don Juan, playing on readers' expectations, not to seduce them, but to engage them in the "living and frank exchange" (*E* 1:65) that is Clara's ideal of marital, and Meredith's of textual, relations.

The two focal points of this chapter are brought together when it is recognized that "real" promises function as a form of figurative speech. Contemporary critics have argued that Meredith's synecdoches prove only that "the part bears no necessary representative relation to the whole"—prove, in effect, that Meredith's figures figure only the impossibility of figuration.[26] While my reading qualifies such radical linguistic skepticism, this thinking can be analogously applied to the uncertain and unpredictable "representative relation" between intentions and actions in promising. Thus, just as Meredith's synecdoches and Clara's similes cannot be read literally, pledges of love and promises of marriage cannot be taken literally, in part because there can be no guarantee that the promised action will be carried out. But this restriction upon how lovers' discourse can be interpreted implies only that promising marriage cannot mean what betrothal conventionally has signified, not that it is an empty act. The force of such promises is figurative, referring to the nature and intensity of the speaker's feeling. They are a categorical example of "rough talk," although one easily transposed into the "smooth talk" of Don Juan. While Meredith's reconsideration of promising seemingly poses a loss of security for promiser and promisee alike, what *The Egoist* demonstrates about language in general and promises in particular is that even in the instances of deliberate misuse of speech, such as Mrs. Mountstuart's gnomic or De Craye's and Willoughby's romantic utterances, only those who seek the security of closed universes of meaning or who immerse themselves exclusively in worlds of words need fear the dynamic processes of discourse.

Meredith recognizes that the practice of promising and the institution of marriage are linked in their dependence on the idea of the constative. He anticipates the insight of Shoshana Felman, who writes: "If every marriage is, of course, a promise, every promise is to a certain extent a promise of marriage—to the extent that every promise promises *constancy* above all, that is, promises consistency, continuity in time between the act of commitment and the future action."[27] By ending the novel in the mountains of Switzerland above the Lake of Constance, Meredith ironically and subtly reminds readers that process, as well as stasis, characterizes all human communication. It is not, therefore, "Constance-y"—either lacustrine or linguistic—that is promised. Laetitia's marriage proves the opposite of what it might appear to: she is far from the "ideal of constancy" (*E* 2:246) everyone sees in her. Nor can Vernon's and Clara's implicit promise of marriage be assumed to reinstate the promise of constancy that so much of the novel has undercut. The promise of marriage simply cannot have unequivocal cognitive or performative significance. The tacit promise that concludes the novel indicates that feeling and speaking are dynamic processes qualitatively different from the formulaic speech of the appropriately named Patterne Hall. Because the lovers' promise refers to the relations between feeling, speaking, and each other, it speaks *of* the present more than *to* the future. Yet in making the promise, in speaking their love, Vernon and Clara help to create that which they promise, therefore, to bridge that gap between intention and action. For those responsive to the figurative action of promising, saying can make it so. To that extent, like figures of speech, promises are meaningful and become creative rather than merely reflective. And, to that extent, Vernon and Clara will have a promising marriage.

Although Clara Middleton finds it virtually impossible to become a "jilt," Alice Vavasor in *Can You Forgive Her?* does so with a facility that Clara could only envy and with a frequency that questions the appropriateness of the phrase "noble jilt." Her multiple betrothals shift the emphasis from language more squarely to promising itself. Trollope's interest in figuration, especially as it characterizes the seductive languages of politics and romance, is secondary to the social consequences of making and breaking promises to marry. Nevertheless, for all their differences in style and emphasis, Trollope's views about betrothal are remarkably similar to Meredith's. In both *The Egoist* and *Can You Forgive Her?* drastically different attitudes toward promising obscure the fundamental similarities in attitude between John Bull and Don Juan. This unexpected resemblance speaks less to character of the promisers than to the meaning of promises themselves, and it reveals a need to rethink the nature of betrothal. With Eliot and Meredith, then, Trollope believes that the value of promises inheres in their pragmatic rather than their contractual force.

CHAPTER 7

Questioning Rhetoric in
Can You Forgive Her?

In *Leviathan*, Thomas Hobbes warns of the nonsense that results when "men make a name of two names whose significations are contradictory, and inconsistent," and he offers as an example "'incorporeall body' . . . [which is] as absurd and insignificant as a 'round quadrangle.'"[1] This impossible figure does seem, however, to describe Alice Vavasor's circuitous path to matrimony in *Can You Forgive Her?* In the words of her father: "I do call it square. It has come round to the proper thing."[2] The geometric illogicality implied by his figures of speech—a round route resulting in a square figure—is more vividly expressed by Mr. Grimes, the aptly named political operative who protests that he is "as round as your hat, and as square as your elbow" (*CYFH* 1:130).[3] Grimes's avowal of integrity is subverted by the figurative paradox with which it is expressed. Indeed, the misshapen publican contorts himself to fit the political mold—round or square—of whichever party—Conservative or Liberal—will "come down with the stumpy" (*CYFH* 2:317), that is, supply the ready cash. While Alice does not share this mercenary bent, her marital plans are at least as changeable as his political allegiances. The "noblest jilt that ever yet halted between two minds" (*CYFH* 2:355) is alternately engaged to two men a total of four times.[4] Because the novel ends basically where it begins, this circumambulation seems simply to return Alice to square one. Her reengagement to John Grey may justify the assessment that things have come round to be square, but another "name of two names whose significations are contradictory" is needed to describe her character: "noble jilt."

Trollope is, of course, better known for a comfortable relation to readers and to his craft than for an interest in rhetorical paradox and linguistic complexity. No writer seems less likely to elicit what Thomas Love Peacock's Mr. Flosky describes as "the vulgar error of the *reading public* to whom an unusual collocation of words, involving a juxtaposition of antiperistatical ideas, immediately suggests the notion of hyperoxysophistical paradoxology."[5] Such collocations, juxtapositions, and notions would seem to be entirely foreign to a style that, in Trollope's words, strives to be "as ready and as efficient a conductor of the mind of the writer to the mind of the reader as is the electric spark which passes from one battery to another battery" (*A* 235). The commonplace view of his style as "uniformly easy, flowing, clear, plain, unlaboured, unaffected, unmannered, and above all businesslike" indicates that he has largely achieved his goal.[6] C. P. Snow, among many others, has observed that Trollope is not "much given to rhetoric."[7] Nevertheless, his fiction exhibits an abiding concern with the languages of courtship and seduction, both of voters and of lovers. These recurring interests virtually, but paradoxically, insure that his novels will be concerned with precisely the inflated style and elaborate rhetoric that he holds to be inappropriate in fiction.

The seeming contradiction of Trollope's shunning in style precisely that to which he is attracted in subject is readily seen in the treatment of political rhetoric in *Can You Forgive Her?* Politics no less than romance generates linguistic contradictions, such as "advanced . . . conservative Liberal" (*A* 291)—the exponentially oxymoronic phrase, evocative of Grimes, but actually used by Trollope to define his own philosophy. Although the illogical nomenclature might suggest otherwise, one of Trollope's primary criticisms of government is its tendency toward self-serving verbal obfuscation. The Palliser novels illustrate this point but complicate the satire by juxtaposing the dynamics of political action with the vagaries of marital choice. Laura Standish's "semi-social and semi-political" evenings (*PF* 1:355) exemplify the confluence of the seemingly disparate pursuits of a spouse and a career. On such occasions, political discussion is often enlisted to advance romantic interests, and flirtatious conversation is employed to enhance political prospects. In addition to limning the erratic interconnections of personal and professional desire, Trollope's dual focus in these novels functions, if not to de-emphasize elements of plot (such as the suspense of erotic or political congress), then at least to accentuate the rhetorical structure and linguistic medium common to both.

The role of rhetoric in politics is perhaps self-evident, yet Trollope's direct and self-effacing style tends to obscure his subtle insinuation of questions of rhetoric into the conduct of romance. When Glencora Palliser says, "Romance and poetry are for the most part lies. . . . I have seen something of them in my time, and I much prefer downright honest figures" (*PR* 2:327), she unknowingly echoes her creator's view of fictional discourse and unwittingly articulates his criticism of courtship and betrothal. Trollope complicates this opinion, however, by showing that Alice's lovers, despite their diametrically opposed characterizations as Don Juan and John Bull, possess a single rhetorical identity. This contradiction reveals that the perplexities of linguistic practice are analogous to and complicated by the entanglements of love—a point for which the phrase "noble jilt" is itself evidence. Mr. Flosky might relish this term simply for its "juxtaposition of antiperistatical ideas," but then Mr. Flosky is one for whom "nothing is but what is not" (*NA* 10) and who might assume that the phrase "incorporeall body" refers to the "genuine untangible ghosts" among whom he claims to live (*NA* 121). Trollope, on the contrary, goes to great pains to make his characters corporeal and tangible. In the figure of Alice Vavasor, he reveals how the complexities of experience give substance and meaning to irrational and seemingly impossible rhetorical figures.

Trollope uses two tropes, and the speech acts associated with them, to explore the circuitous routes taken even by language intended to function "like electric sparks" in a battery. The first, oxymoron, is associated with naming and is illustrated by the title originally considered for the novel, *The Noble Jilt*; the second, rhetorical question, is connected with promising, and is exemplified by that ultimately chosen, *Can You Forgive Her?* Together these titles imbricate eros and erotesis, suggesting that while Trollope himself may have preferred "downright honest figures," he is not so naive as to believe that they preclude paradoxical expressions and equivocal meanings. He may never be accused of the "hyperoxysophistical paradoxology" with which Peacock satirizes Coleridge, but he is more than a little interested in the "collocations of words" with which courtships are conducted.

Oxymoron is a particularly appropriate figure for one of Trollope's favorite novelistic situations, that of wavering between two suitors.[8] Both the trope and the topos entail duality but assume unity. The process by which semantic vis-à-vis romantic unions are achieved, however, is quite different. Speakers possess a flexibility denied to lovers by the conventions of courtship and the canons of marriage. Only in words can mutually exclusive possibilities be happily wedded. In love, rivals are not so neatly managed; harmony can be achieved only hegemonically. Hence Alice's two minds become one only when one of them has been suppressed and the corresponding lover banished. As Jeannette explains to Mrs. Greenow, who cannot decide whether Captain Bellfield or Mr. Cheesacre is to be made the happiest man alive: "There's some things as you can cry halves about, but there's no crying halves about this" (*CYFH* 2:67). While oxymoron is a kind of "crying halves," it has little in common with courtship, after which the wrong choice of a spouse may well produce a crying (in the sense of tearful) half. As Solomon surely understood, this commonsensical and seemingly just norm proves to be neither. Its additive logic is inconsistent with synthetic language and circumstances; its communal ethos is inappropriate to exclusive institutions like marriage. "Crying halves" provides little assistance to lovers trying to accommodate contradictory utterances to monolithic cultural institutions or to reconcile supple rhetoric with unyielding social circumstances.

Oxymoron focuses attention on the appellative function of words, the power of naming in social and political contexts. Within the regimented structure of Victorian courtship and marriage, Trollope singles out pejorative social labels, such as "jilt" or "flirt," in order to suggest that such labels may accomplish more than merely identifying criminal conversationalists. If the jilt, as a breaker of promises, threatens social conventions and systems, then the "noble jilt" falls entirely outside social boundaries, which depend upon a principle of exclusion foreign to the combinative and contradictory logic of oxymoron. As a conceptual construct, "noble jilt" challenges the very basis of society; as a paradoxical phrase, it threatens fundamental assumptions about language itself. Such names may in fact be "absurd and insignificant," as Hobbes contends, but Trollope also shows that they may change rather than merely confirm behavior. For the Pallisers, as well as the Greys, the act of naming promotes self-analysis and fosters a more general consciousness of words as pragmatic and not merely semantic entities.

Even more than the oxymoron, the rhetorical question engenders contradiction, for it is subject to mutually exclusive interpretations—one literal, one figurative, as Paul de Man has demonstrated.[9] In accounting for the rhetorical question that serves as the title of the novel, Trollope says that he had originally planned to use the title of his unproduced play, *The Noble Jilt*, but that he "was afraid of the name for a novel, lest the critics might throw a doubt on the nobility." He chooses instead a title "more of tentative humility" (*A* 180). His indecisiveness suggests an onomaphobia of the very kind that the novel itself sets out to dispel; furthermore, the title upon which he settles, *Can You Forgive Her?*, may complicate the very fears it is intended to circumvent. Given the narrator's repeated answers to the question of whether Alice is to be forgiven for breaking three engagements (*CYFH* 1:114, 384; 2:311, 418), there would seem to be only one possible answer, exasperatedly supplied by Henry James: "Can we forgive Miss Vavasor? Of course we can, and forget her, too, for that matter."[10] Yet the narrator's compulsive return to the issue of forgiving the jilt signals an interest in this question and in rhetorical questions generally that the formally minded James may have overlooked. Unlike James's celebrated examples of pronominal indeterminacy, Trollope's title is hyperbatonic, delaying the antecedent until the first paragraph of the novel where Alice is identified as the "she, whom you are to forgive" (*CYFH* 1:1). While the "who," therefore, seems comparatively unproblematic, the title simultaneously initiates a process of (pro)nominal slippage: her = Alice = the noble jilt.[11] The pronoun and noun are purely designative; the noun phrase, on the contrary, is descriptive. The question now becomes not who but what is to be forgiven. In substituting a rhetorical question, *Can You Forgive Her?*, for an oxymoron, *The Noble Jilt*, Trollope sustains his focus on the logic of contradiction while significantly complicating the hermeneutic and moral action that lies at the heart of his work. The narrator's repeated assurances that he has forgiven Alice for her less-than-direct journey to marriage suggest that the question posed by the novel's title is purely figurative. If so, it is less an interrogative than a declarative, perhaps even a disguised imperative. But the title may be read literally as well as figuratively. Such a reading transforms the nature of Alice's transgression from a breach of social decorum into a disclosure of linguistic necessity. Viewed in these terms, the answer to "Can you forgive her?" may well be "No"—less because Alice misuses language than because she exposes readers to its inevitable, even when unintentional, unreliability.

Rhetorical questions are connected with promises in that Trollope seems to imply that even an apparently unequivocal and direct question such as "Will you marry me?" is subject to contradictory logic. On the one hand, an explicit proposal is also an implicit promise; it is simultaneously question and contract. On the other hand, this question is clearly rhetorical when used manipulatively, as it is by George Vavasor, or when acceptance is presumed, as it is by John Grey. Irrespective of the speaker's intentions, however, proposals of marriage and their acceptances must be construed as "rhetorical promises." This phrase may appear to be another oxymoron insofar as promises would not seem to admit the contradictory logic of rhetorical questions. But engagement entails a complexity belied by a simple "Yes" or "No." Its significance is clearly social and conventional, yet it should also be personal and figurative—alluding to the emotions and intentions of the co-promisers, in addition to initiating a dialogical process between them. Reconstruing betrothal in these "oxymoronic" terms enables Trollope to suggest why "noble jilt" need not be, as one character believes, "a contradiction in terms" (*ED* 2:109).

A noble jilting does describe some of the political action in the Palliser novels, for instance, Plantagenet Palliser's rejection of a Cabinet post in order to keep a promise to his wife and Phineas Finn's decision to resign from office rather than vote against his conscience and the platform presented to his constituency. In general, however, there is more jilting than nobility in the politics of *Can You Forgive Her?* and politicians are treated with increasing skepticism in successive novels. Nevertheless, the choice of Cicero as the subject of a biography appearing in the same year as the last of the Palliser novels (1880) and Trollope's generally laudatory commentary upon Ciceronian oratory indicate his continuing fascination with public life and speaking. Cicero is the ideal politician because his oratorical skill is dedicated to civic welfare, therein proving that a "silver tongue" can be mightier than the sword.[12] One can scarcely imagine higher praise coming from Trollope than his description of Cicero as "one who might have been a modern gentleman" (LC 2:300).

Although Cicero is an exemplary public figure, his career also manifests one of the dangers inherent in persuasive oratory. Trollope criticizes the separation of oratorical skill from its practical objective, especially when this dissociation allows Cicero to support positions of which he privately disapproves: "The mind rejects the idea that it can be the part of a perfect man to make another believe that which he believes to be false. If it be necessary that an orator should do so, then must the orator be imperfect" (LC 2:317). Imperfect orators transform politics into a self-aggrandizing profession rather than a patriotic pursuit. Trollope sounds rather like Maine in attributing Cicero's occasional failure in this regard to the absence of "that theoretic aversion to a lie which is the first feeling in the bosom of a modern gentleman" (LC 2:355). Thus Cicero is yet another paradoxical figure, a man who both might be and who could not be "a modern gentleman."

The example of Cicero points to a central issue in the Palliser novels encompassing not simply the ethics but the hermeneutics of public speaking. Imperfect oratory detaches the speaker from the spoken, leaving audiences in a quandary. Is character or content to be accorded more weight when responding to a persuasive speaker? In terms of the idiom and issue of Trollope's day, are men or measures to be the fundamental basis for political action? Relying on the former has the effect of denying the objective significance of language and the inherent truth of particular propositions. The latter criterion reinstates both but does so at the cost of disregarding contextual circumstances that may be essential to well-informed judgment. This hermeneutic dilemma is dramatized when the politically inexperienced George Vavasor pursues a careeer in Parliament. Trollope exploits his innocent perspective to characterize and to criticize the modern practice of political oratory.

Just as clearly as the stage demarcates a boundary between art and life, the door to the House of Commons establishes a boundary between radically discrete universes of discourse. Trollope writes that "the outside Briton who takes a delight in politics . . . should not be desirous of peeping behind the scenes. No beholder at any theatre should do so" (CYFH 1:10). But such a backstage glance is precisely what George

Vavasor offers readers when he enters a world as strange as that behind the looking glass. He prepares for this world under the tutelage of an election agent, Mr. Scruby. With the help of this political operative, George devises a bogus platform and fabricates the figures that will make his proposed embankment of the Thames seem plausible. Although he knows that the project is not feasible, George is "able even to work himself into an apparent heat when he was told that the thing was out of the question; and soon found that he had disciples who really believed in him" (*CYFH* 2:39). What the well-paid skeptic Grimes calls "all that gammon about the River Bank" (*CYFH* 2:39) is evidently substantial enough to appease voters' appetites.

While George's becoming an MP is a direct consequence of the strategy of obfuscation, an indirect result is the creation of a new political state, one comprised solely of words detached from any reference point outside of language itself. To dramatize this point, Trollope shows "the whole of the south-western part of the metropolis . . . covered with posters . . . and placards in which the letters are three feet long" (*CYFH* 2:40). The size and quantity of the letters constitute their message, irrespective of the names or slogans emblazoned on them. The Chelsea district is literally transformed into a teeming mass of wandering words: "Vavasor and the River Bank was carried about by an army of men with iron shoulder straps, and huge pasteboard placards six feet high on the top of them. . . . And then sides of houses were covered with that shibboleth, 'Vavasor and the River Bank': the same words repeated in columns down the whole sides of houses" (*CYFH* 2:38). The cityscape becomes a logoscape that speaks, not to urban planning and riparian development, but to the political ambitions of George Vavasor and to the power of language itself.

George's initiation into the practice of oratory within the House of Commons occurs on his first day, when he is greeted by the spectacle of Lord Middlesex addressing the House while "the Members were swarming away through the doors like a flock of sheep. . . . The Speaker sat, urbane and courteous, with his eyes turned towards the unfortunate orator; but no other ears in the House seemed to listen to him" (*CYFH* 2:50). Although Middlesex is an "earnest man, meaning to do well, seeking no other reward for his work than the appreciation of those whom he desired to serve" (*CYFH* 2:49), he is ignored, even by the twenty-three members too lethargic to join the exodus. Neither his subject—the Irish Church—nor his delivery—he "knocked his words together when he talked" (*CYFH* 2:49)—is calculated to retain an audience interested only in those issues directly affecting their political futures or in those speakers capable of showing a red flag to the somnolent bulls of the other party. For instance, before this address, "[t]hree hundred men had hung listening on upon [the] words" of a thoroughly disreputable man, who avoids prison only because of the immunity from prosecution granted members of Parliament. Because Mr. Farringcourt is a notorious bull-baiter, "[c]rowds of Members flocked into the House from libraries and smoking rooms when it was known that this ne'er-do-well was on his legs." His verbal feints are as sensational as mata-dorial capework, his rhetorical thrusts as barbed as a picador's lance. An otherwise indolent audience is thus left both delighted and "breath-less, as the Spaniard sits in the critical moment of the bull-killing" (*CYFH* 2:50).

For all his flourish and violence, however, Farringcourt does not cut off any ears on this day. Such is not his purpose; he counts, rather, upon political payment from the very people he attacks. His verbal skill is rewarded, not with the downfall of the government, but by inclusion in it. Appointment to a well-paid position in the administration neutralizes an otherwise acerbic tongue. Trollope's comparison of politicians to sheep and of political action to bullfighting suggests that there is some-thing subhuman in all of this. Though highly articulate, the occupants of this animal farm are interested primarily in their own amusement and profit.

It is perhaps a somewhat surprising circumstance that speeches inside the House, where the audience consists of fellow orators and not the gullible electorate, do not differ in content and manner from cam-paign speeches. One factor accounting for the unexpected similarity is apparent from this observation concerning Middlesex's speech: the "papers would not report one sentence in twenty of those he uttered." As he speaks, the "corps of reporters had dwindled down to two, and they used their pens very listlessly." Farringcourt, on the contrary, keeps the press "working their fingers wearily till the sweat drops stood upon their brows" (*CYFH* 2:49, 50). The presence of journalists guarantees that the speeches in the House will be directed primarily to the public, only secondarily to fellow members, and not at all to their purported topics. This point is emphasized by Barrington Erle, the Liberal whip who believes that debates

> create that public opinion which was hereafter to be used in creating some future House of Commons; but he did not think it possible that any vote should be given on a great question, either this way or that, as the result of a debate; and he was certainly assured in his own opin-ion that any such changing of votes would be dangerous, revolution-ary, and almost unparliamentary. (*PF* 1:15–16)

Speeches in the House are fundamentally involved in the dynamics of the electoral process and the machinations of party politics. Orations are virtually without an audience until they are edited and amplified by the press for the ostensible benefit of an electorate.

The ultimate effect of parliamentary debate is precisely that of campaign rhetoric: the creation of an exclusively verbal world. Although the medium is more refined—neatly printed columns of newsprint as opposed to gargantuan placards—the legislators, like the candidates, transform *polis* into *logos*. As the newspaper accounts of Middlesex's and Farringcourt's addresses demonstrate, selective reporting and a predilection for verbal pyrotechnics produce a logosphere as remote from actuality as George's platform is from the appearance of the Thames. The play of political speech severs words from referents, freeing language to sustain partisan debate without extralinguistic contraint. As Trollope writes in *The New Zealander* (and in anticipation of George Orwell's *1984*): "If Mr. Smith out of the House states that Black is White he will lose his credit for veracity, and men will gradually know him for a liar. But if he merely votes Black to be White within the House, no one on that account accuses him of untruth."[13] The object of political rhetoric, whether in or out of Parliament, is neither sincerity nor truth, but more words.

Partisan politics maintains the hermetic logocentrism of the House. Just as language is detached from its conventional meaning and use, the two parties become increasingly removed from the philosophies and traditions that have defined them. Whig and Tory can now be recognized only by their automatic antagonism to one another, not by loyalty to any particular issue or cause. Character may count for very little, but party is everything. This philosophy is embodied by "the very model of an English statesman" Lord Brock, who believes "in men rather than measures. As long as he had loyalty around him, he could be personally happy, and quite confident as to the country. He never broke his heart because he could not carry this or that reform" (*PM* 1:102–3). There can be no gray actions here, merely a succession of continually shifting assertions of black or white. Thus the only standard of truth is the party standard.

Understanding this circumstance enables Lady Laura Standish to observe that a "political leader is so sure of support and so sure of attack, that it is hardly necessary for him to be anxious to be right" (*PF* 1:53). This circumstance spares the party in power a degree of anxiety, but it affords opposition speakers complete freedom from worry. Those attacking the government are fully sanctioned in their disregard of accuracy. Mr. Monk, who succeeds Lady Laura as Phineas's political mentor, explains "how great were the charms of that inaccuracy which was permitted to the Opposition" (*PF* 1:163). Although widely respected as a man of integrity and independence, Monk seems to be as ironically

named as Grimes is aptly so, for he prefers the "delights of wild irresponsible oratory" (*PF* 2:263) to rhetorical piety. The adversarial,
bipartite political structure virtually guarantees that even the most
monkish members will succumb to the pleasures of verbal indulgence.

Trollope's critique of this system is obvious, as is his apparent sympathy for an alternative. If voting according to party affiliation results
in an endless cycle of verbiage, then acting on the basis of measures
rather than men would seem to provide the commonsensical escape
from this prison House of language. This philosophy is apparently
embodied by Plantagent Palliser, whom Trollope describes in the same
terms applied to Cicero: he is "a perfect gentleman" (*A* 310). He is "one
of those politicians in possessing whom England has perhaps more reason to be proud than of any other of her resources" (*CYFH* 1:246).
Although very much a party loyalist, he brings his relatively poor oratorical skills to bear only upon those topics in which he believes, and is
respected because of it:

> he was listened to as a laborious man, who was in earnest in what he
> did, who got up his facts with accuracy, and who, dull though he be,
> was worthy of confidence. And he was very dull. He rather prided him-
> self on being dull, and on conquering in spite of his dulness. He never
> allowed himself a joke in his speeches, nor attempted even the smallest
> flourish of rhetoric. . . . He had taught himself to believe that oratory,
> as oratory, was a sin against honesty in politics by which he strove to
> guide himself. He desired to use words for the purpose of teaching
> things which he knew and which others did not know, and he desired
> also to be honoured for his knowledge. But he had no desire to be hon-
> oured for the language in which his knowledge was conveyed. (*CYFH*
> 1:246–47)

When Henry James describes Trollope as "one of the most trustworthy,
though not one of the most eloquent" of writers, he comes close to
describing Palliser as an orator.[14] In addition to sharing a political philosophy of conservative-liberalism, the author and his hero have similar
attitudes to the primary medium of their respective trades, that is, language itself.

This modern Cicero is also a paradoxical figure—one who speaks
well by speaking poorly. Palliser is "listened to in the House, as the
phrase goes" (*CYFH* 1:246), but not because he is actually heard. He
produces a numbing litany of facts and figures that has a soporific effect
upon his audience. George Vavasor, for instance, recalls an occasion
upon which Palliser had spoken "for two hours together, and all the
House had treated his speech with respect—had declared that it was useful, solid, conscientious, and what not; but more than half the House
had been asleep more than half the time that he was on his legs" (*CYFH*

2:125). Even when his audience remains awake, however, there is no evidence that they understand his words and numbers. Palliser's "downright honest figures" about public revenue unintentionally achieve what his nemesis Sir Timothy Beeswax consciously accomplishes with rhetorical flourish and a "pseudo-patriotic conjuring phraseology which no one understood but which many admired" (*DC* 165). Palliser himself senses that his lengthy and detailed fiscal analyses are received with "the delight of one-half the House, and the bewilderment of the other" (*CYFH* 2:285)—exactly the reception of Sir Timothy's performances.

The modern Cicero's paradoxical nature does not stop here. What, for instance, explains the circumstances in which one well-intentioned, carefully researched, but dully presented speech (Palliser's) receives a hearing while another (Middlesex's) does not? On the opening day of the Parliamentary session, for instance, Palliser is greeted with the same exodus prompted by Middlesex: "Members went out gradually, and the House became very thin during this oration; but the newspapers declared, next morning, that his speech had been the speech of the night, and the perspicuity of Mr. Palliser pointed him out as the coming man" (*CYFH* 2:14). One factor in the different interpretations of these mass exits is the press's recognition that, whereas Middlesex is merely a marginal and monogamous player, Palliser is potentially a key figure in the game of switching political partners. The public is evidently as interested in the political seductions and infidelities reported in the papers as in the romantic alliances and misalliances represented in novels. This point is underscored by the fact that when Trollope introduces the political world of *Can You Forgive Her?*, he does so in erotic terms:

> if Parliament were an Olympus in which Juno and Venus never kissed, the thing would not be nearly so interesting. But in this Olympus partners are changed, the divine bosom, now rabid with hatred against some opposing deity, suddenly becomes replete with love towards its late enemy, and exciting changes occur which give to the whole thing all the keen interest of a sensational novel. (*CYFH* 1:10)

Comparing the Houses of Parliament to the mountain of the gods reinforces the notion that politicians are privileged beings, unfettered by the norms of ordinary human discourse. That political action is likened to romantic intrigue also suggests that this remote realm bears some resemblance to life on the human plane. Here, too, partners are changed and interchanged with surprising rapidity. That political action is compared to sensational fiction furthermore indicates to readers exactly what Trollope is not concerned with: "all the keen interest" of erotic intrigue.[15] His mythic metaphor deflects attention from the action of predictably shifting political and erotic alliances to the surprising structural similarities between the languages emanating from the heights of political achievement and the bowers of romantic pursuit.

Alice Vavasor is courted in two distinct styles by George Vavasor, the "Wild Man" (*CYFH* 34), and John Grey, the "Worthy Man" (*CYFH* 20). The technique of the former is indebted to Don Juan and proceeds according to the stereotypical imagery and conventions of romantic poetry and sensational fiction—literature proving to be as serviceable as placards and newspapers in persuading a skeptical audience. As in *Jane Eyre*, success typically depends upon who is being quoted more than on what is said. The technique of the latter is modeled on "plain-spoken John Bull" (*CYFH* 2:313). The language is prosaic and rational; its "downright honest figures" are apt to sound more like a lecture on, than a proposal of, love. Insofar as Alice is concerned, neither strategy would seem to be superior to the other, since she twice accedes to each man's proposals. Thus modes of courtship that appear to be radically distinct and whose chief practitioners seem to have nothing in common (apart from an interest in Alice) prove to be quite similar. The language of romance confirms the lesson of political oratory: contradictory rhetorical assumptions and procedures are likely to have common effects. Alice's betrothals ultimately have less to say about the character of the noble jilt than about the paradoxical effects of courtship discourse and the problematic status of promises of marriage.

Although George never speaks in Parliament, he is a skilled romancer of women, with whom, the narrator tells us, "he could really associate" (*CYFH* 1:162). At first glance, though, he seems as unlikely a Don Juan as Plantagenet Palliser is a Cicero, for as a rule he is not a distinguished conversationalist. In his first courtship of Alice, he is almost taciturn. He uses a simple squeeze of the hand as "his most eloquent speech of love" (*CYFH* 1:148). Proposing a second time, he writes more tellingly of money than of his feelings. It is perhaps not surprising, therefore, that he describes himself as ill adept at "romantic phraseology" (*CYFH* 1:389). In affairs of the heart, he appears to be motivated more by the cool rationality of John Bull than by Don Juan's heated passions. He tells his sister: "If there's anything on earth I hate . . . it is romance. If you keep it for reading in your bedroom, it's all very well for those who like it, but when it comes to be mixed up with one's business it plays the devil" (*CYFH* 1:398). As if to prove this point, he resolves his indecision about proposing to Alice for a second time by tossing a coin. Both act and means—gambling and specie—reveal that George is engaging in a business proposition, not proposing a romantic engagement.

Nevertheless, Squire Vavasor is substantially correct when he tells Alice that his grandson "must be a very clever sort of man . . . when he has talked you out of such a husband as John Grey" (*CYFH* 1:336). George is fully capable of playing the part of Don Juan when he chooses to do so. The roles that he borrows from Byron and ascribes to Burgo, Glencora, and her husband, are equally appropriate to his own romantic drama: "Juan [George himself] and Haidée [Alice] with Planty Pall [Grey] coming after . . . like old Lambro" (*CYFH* 1:303).[16] Hence Grey's joking portrait of George as the romantic hero rescuing Alice from "Paynim foes, . . . the dungeons of oppressors . . . and stray tigers in the Swiss forests" (*CYFH* 1:21) is both less comic than the former supposes and more apt than the latter would admit. George enacts the role of romantic hero/Gothic villain by imprisoning Alice on a balcony overlooking the Rhine River—even if the prison is constructed of nothing more formidable than a strategically placed chair. His Corsair cruelty takes the form of sharp questions about her impending marriage—a "cross-question[ing]" that Alice compares to his "putting a pistol to my ear" (*CYFH* 1:50). The effect of this interrogation is not intimidation but seduction, as is evident from the questions that Alice puts to herself during this scene: "Why should she show such a need [to escape her captor]? . . . Or why, indeed should she entertain it? . . . But why should she wish to escape? . . . Why should she leave it [the balcony]?" (*CYFH* 1:48–49). Alice's questions are purely rhetorical—asked only that their answers might be avoided. The evasive self-examination constitutes an implicit acquiescence to what the narrator calls "something of romance during those days in Switzerland" (*CYFH* 1:112).

This romance is conducted by means of suggestive statement and poetic imagery that are the counterparts of Alice's rhetorical questioning. George proves himself to be not only as honey-tongued but also as calculatedly pragmatic as Sir Timothy Beeswax. This point becomes clear when George explains his theory of poetic beauty, using precisely the theatrical analogy employed by the narrator to describe politics. George contends that poetry and romance are ruined by those who would get "behind the scenes at a ballet, or [make] a conjuror explain his tricks. . . . In this world things are beautiful only because they are not quite seen, or not perfectly understood. Poetry is precious chiefly because it suggests more than it declares" (*CYFH* 1:44). George seems to have modeled his theory upon that of Mr. Flosky, who lectures Miss Marionetta Celestina O'Carroll: "Mystery is the very key-stone of all that is beautiful in poetry, all that is sacred in faith, and all that is recondite in transcendental psychology. I am writing a ballad which is all mystery; it is 'such stuff as dreams are made of'" (*NA* 76). The airy rostrums from which George instructs Alice—a hotel balcony and a bridge over the Rhine—emphasize the ephemeral character of his aesthetics. Nevertheless, when it is time for Alice and Kate to "vote" (*CYFH* 1:46), both cast their ballots for the success of the trip. George's "election" thus proves the Alps are as favorable to romantic divagation as Mt. Olympus.

George utilizes the Rhine for romance as effectively as he does the Thames for politics. The mountain scenery heightens Alice's fears about a flat English existence. Entrapped on the balcony, she thinks: "Nothing could be more lovely than the scene before her." This setting is quite different from "John Grey's flower-beds and shrubs; . . . the river seemed to sing a song of other things than such a home as that,—a song full of mystery, as are all river songs when one tries to understand their words" (*CYFH* 1:49–50). The narrator's irony is lost upon Alice, who is swept away on the currents of romance. She accepts George's characterization of the Vavasors as a poetic family well-suited to lives of Alpine adventure but ill-adapted to the household routine of English country life. He tells Alice that having "grown beyond our sugar-toothed ages," neither she nor he can survive in the gingerbread houses of Victorian domesticity. Life with Grey would be "soft-flowing milk and honey," whereas the Vavasors are "all fire." Marriage to her fiancé would be "as though one who had lived on brandy should take himself suddenly to a milk diet" (*CYFH* 1:53); marriage to him, on the contrary, would be passionate and intoxicating.

To readers such imagery seems meretricious, but Alice's susceptibility to it implies that poetry inheres in the search for it more than in other people and places. George is ironically right: the "poetry and mystery are lost to those who make themselves familiar with their details" (*CYFH* 1:44). Obscurity constitutes the only and the necessary language of romantic illusion. Alice, for instance, savors the "half feeling of danger," which is augmented by the "soft half light" of the moon and the "poetry of half-developed beauty" (*CYFH* 1:49). Her experience is necessarily that of a "half-world" because her feeling is molded of partial sensations and fleeting emotions that cannot survive careful analysis. This world is partial not simply because it excludes the prosaic landscape of flatlands and sunlight, but also because its half-truths are the expressions of a language of suggestive statement and rhetorical question—a discursive mode incompatible with either declaration or interrogation.

The mystification and monologism typifying romance are further apparent in Glencora Palliser's relationship with Burgo Fitzgerald. She transforms a small water color entitled "Raphael and Fornarina" into an idyllic image rivaling Alice's Helvetian fantasy. The locale is different—Italy rather than Switzerland—but the setting is in effect the same.

On a secluded balcony bathed in "pale moonlight," Raphael is "at her knee, hardly speaking to her, but making his presence felt by the halo of its divinity. He would have called upon her for no hard replies" (*CYFH* 2:20). Once again, romance flourishes in subdued light by means of soft tales, whose language is so suggestive that not only is it unnecessary to speak fully and directly but it is also virtually unnecessary to speak at all. Difficult questions are censored from this visionary world, for the rhetoric of romance can withstand neither "hard replies" nor the give and take of dialogical exchange.

Glencora's romantic infatuation, like Alice's, depends upon exotic settings. On another occasion, she is stimulated by the moonlit ruins of a priory to confess her love for Burgo to Alice:

> "Is it not beautiful!" said Glencora. "I do love it so! And there is a peculiar feeling of cold about the chill of the moon, different from any other cold. It makes you wrap yourself up tight, but it does not make your teeth chatter; and it seems to go into your senses rather than into your bones. But I suppose that's nonsense," she added, after a pause.
> "Not more so than what people are supposed to talk by moonlight." (*CYFH* 1:283)

Alice's irony reveals that she sees her friend's situation more clearly than she does her own, for her comment about Glencora's "nonsense" echoes the narrator's remark upon her own appetite for "mystery." The shivers that Glencora denies result from the cold are exactly those felt by Alice as she looks down upon the river and that she too denies are the effect of a physical chill (*CYFH* 1:58). Their shudders are the somatic expression of a romantic fever that distorts both perception and judgment. Such fevers transform the sound of a river into a song of love and induce delirious ramblings amidst appropriately decaying churches. Such loves arise from the images and values of literature, not from life.

The landscape of romance is ridiculed by the subplot involving Mrs. Greenow and her two topographical admirers, Bellfield and Cheeseacre. The wealthy widow likes "a little romance about" her lovers: "just a sniff, as I call it, of the rocks and valleys. One knows that it doesn't mean much; but it's like artificial flowers,—it gives a little colour, and takes off the dowdiness. Of course, bread-and-cheese is the real thing. The rocks and valleys are no good at all, if you haven't got that" (*CYFH* 2:242). There is little doubt about which of her gallant pursuers will be chosen, since Mr. Cheeseacre, as his name suggests, exudes rather more of the literal aroma of his dairy than the metaphorical "sniff" of exotic settings. The forty thousand pounds inherited from her late husband provide Mrs. Greenow with ample means to perfume the effluvia of poverty emanating from the Captain. Bellfield may not be up to the sublime beauty of the Swiss mountains, but he can manage a modest request for rocks and valleys.

Lacking the financial resources to supply romance, George turns to the power of words alone to win love. His indifference to conversation suggests that the poetic speech with which he woos Alice is purely theatrical. Just as George brings himself to believe in his campaign platform when he is haranguing voters, "in the energy of his speaking [to Alice], a touch of true passion had come upon him" (*CYFH* 2:62). The act of speaking itself engenders the emotions that are otherwise absent and that cannot survive the cessation of words. Insisting upon the gestures of a love that neither feels, George repeatedly importunes Alice to "remember the balcony at Basle" (*CYFH* 1:148, 218). This "pretty bit of acting" (*CYFH* 2:57), however, fools George himself only a little and Alice not at all. Like seasoned politicians, both recognize the pretense of their second betrothal, and Alice ultimately cannot even bring herself to perform the part required of her. As in Jane Eyre's counterproposal to St. John Rivers, Alice can offer practical support but not marriage to a man whom she does not love.

The dance of promise and counter-promise between George and Alice demonstrates that men and women are no less enemies in a game of rhetorical seduction than are Conservatives and Liberals. In both contests, the predictable results are bombastic oratory and deceitful action. While the dynamic of political opposition is purely binary, that of gender is triangular, following the pattern traced by René Girard in *Deceit, Desire and the Novel*.[17] For example, when George pursues Alice, he is "keenly alive to the pleasure of taking from John Grey the prize which John Grey had so nearly taken from him" (*CYFH* 1:312, 363). And if George's pursuit of his cousin for a second time is mediated through Grey, Alice's willingness to become engaged to him a second time is no less the function of a third party. Her loveless betrothal is modeled upon Kate's relationship with her brother. Alice "envied Kate. Kate could, as his sister, attach herself on to George's political career, and obtain from it all that excitement of life which Alice desired for herself. Alice could not love her cousin and marry him; but she felt that if she could do so without impropriety she would like to stick close to him like another sister" (*CYFH* 1:112). The triadic structure motivating relationships that are of necessity dual further proves the accuracy of Jeanette's platitude about crying halves. It also guarantees that romantic rhetoric will be characterized by a superfluity of reference. Courtship discourse necessarily says more than it intends. It is unconsciously, as well as consciously, intimative and suggestive, for it speaks indirectly to the absent mediator as well as directly to the present lover.

While Kate may be an object of Alice's envy, she is not perhaps the best object of imitation. For in copying her, not only does Alice confuse sororal and sexual love, but she also identifies herself with one who readily admits to being "not so wedded to truth but what I can look, and act, and speak a few falsehoods" (*CYFH* 1:30). Kate is the paradoxical friend of whom the narrator asks: "What shall we say of a woman who could be as false as she had been and yet could be so true?" (*CYFH* 1:328). Her wanderings between truth and deceit result in an itinerary neither round nor square; indeed, at times she seems uncertain of the basic means of transportation: "I wish I was out of this *boat*," she said to Alice in the *train*" (*CYFH* 2:403, my emphasis). Having tried as assiduously as her brother to get Alice to cross the Rubicon, Kate discovers that the result of her falsehoods, as of his broken promises, is not only vehicular confusion but also an unsatisfactory journey leading to an undesirable destination.

The language of John Bull is no less problematic than that of Don Juan. While no one would mistake John Grey for George Vavasor, their rhetorical practices have a comparable effect. Her vacillation between them is not simply a matter of choosing between a "worthy man" and a "wild man," or between milk and brandy. When Kate implies that her brother is Hyperion to Grey's Satyr (an equation likely to be reversed by readers), Alice's response is only apparently rhetorical, "And which is the Satyr?" (*CYFH* 1:64). Her question must be taken in earnest, for it takes both terms to describe each man.

Like Eliot, Trollope elides those scenes with the greatest potential for poetic language, such as Alice's initial engagement to George and Glencora's falling in love with Burgo. The novel opens well after both women have been launched on the stormy seas of romance and have sailed into at least one Scylla or Charybdis in the form of a more or less mellifluous male. Their circumstances—one is unhappily engaged, the other unhappily married—militate against the poetic excesses of first love, exotic setting, and escapist adventure. The fitful courtship of Alice Vavasor and John Grey provides readers with an extended example of commonsensical romantic rhetoric. Trollope analyzes the workings of a language that seeks to persuade by reasoned argument and direct statement rather than by intimation, figuration, and false promises. When Grey enters the novel, it is to reinforce what he correctly perceives to be Alice's crumbling resolve to go through with the wedding. To accomplish this task, he tells her that he will "still trust to my personal eloquence for success. Or rather not trust,—not trust, but hope" (*CYFH* 1:22). His qualification is perhaps a bit of rhetorical modesty, for Grey has every reason to be confident of his ways with words. The narrator describes him as "a man who knew well how to make words pleasant. . . . No man could be more gracious in word and manner than John Grey" (*CYFH* 1:32). Even his chief rival says that "he talks in the way I like a man to talk" (*CYFH* 1:31). George's praise is not insignificant, for it reveals a common element in the courtship strategies of the worthy and the wild man: their mystification and monologism.

Grey's discourse resembles Sir Timothy's "great hocus-pocus system" (*DC* 165); his methods of courtship owe something to the public life to which he is so opposed but for which he is destined. Kate compares his imperious rhetoric to the wave of the necromancer's hand over a skeptical audience or of the faith healer's over a hypochondriacal follower. Picturing the scene in which Alice tries to break her engagement, Kate says: "I can see him so plainly as he stood up in unruffled self-possession, ignoring all that you said, suggesting that you were feverish or perhaps bilious, waving his hand over you a little, as though that might possibly do you some small good, and then taking his leave with an assurance that it would be all right as soon as the wind changed" (*CYFH* 1:137). Alice also feels that Grey, much less than asking for her hand in marriage, simply "wave[d] his hand over her" (*CYFH* 1:154). His strategy resembles a kind of hypnosis. A flow of reassuring words leaves no option but acquiescence to the speaker's dominant will. Any questions that he might ask—and he asks very few—are of necessity purely rhetorical. Rather like Darcy in *Pride and Prejudice*, Grey treats the proposal of marriage as a mere formality. He expects, not an answer, but an echo, and he tolerates no counterpoint of inquiry or doubt. For all of its rationality, common sense, and apparent justice, his language is in this regard no different from George Vavasor's.

The language of engagement neither poses nor invites questions. It is intolerant of dialogical exchange. For instance, Alice is excluded from considering how and where she will live after her marriage. Grey speaks, the narrator tells us, "as though there could be no question that his manner of life was to be adopted, without a word or thought of doubting, by his wife" (*CYFH* 1:34). Although she would prefer to live in London, he considers this no more seriously than he would residence in central Africa (*CYFH* 2:347). It is presumed that they will reside on his Cambridgeshire estate: "He had never argued the matter with her. He had never asked her to argue with him. He had not condescended so far as that" (*CYFH* 2:233). Grey resembles Cheesacre in his dogged appreciation of a setting and way of life whose romantic value largely escapes others. Nethercoats, after all, is scarcely a more probable or flattering name than Oileymeade, and the comparison between them is made explicit by Kate, who describes Grey's estate as a "flat Eden . . . hemmed in by broad dykes, in which cream and eggs are very plentiful" (*CYFH* 1:138). The world of the gentleman landowner seems to have so insinuated itself into his vision that he treats people like domesticated plants, just as Cheesacre, the gentleman farmer, measures the world at large in terms of the richness of its soil and the sweetness of its butter. A pattern of figurative references to his gardens emphasizes Grey's practical and antiromantic nature. For example: in "speaking of the happiness of his entire life . . . [he] had no more sign of passion in his face than if he were telling his gardener to move a rose tree" (*CYFH* 1:160).

As for taking Alice at her word when she asks to be released from her engagement, Gray "would as soon think of taking the fruit-trees from the southern wall because the sun sometimes shines from the north" (*CYFH* 1:116). He conceptualizes her wish to break the engagement in precisely the terms with which a diseased romantic consciousness might be described. She suffers from the "hallucination of a sickened imagination" and a "melancholy madness" (*CYFH* 1:116–18). The presumption of illness is a self-authorizing diagnosis that allows him to discount what she says: "She might bid him begone in what language she would. . . . But he would not allow a word coming from her in such a way to disturb arrangements made for the happiness of their joint lives" (*CYFH* 1:116). Her request that he "take me at my word" (*CYFH* 1:117) is, of course, ironic, since it entails discounting her previous word, that is, her acceptance of his proposal of marriage. But it is nevertheless ingenuous and serious, since she asks only that she be listened to now as she was then.

Grey's insistence that Alice keep her original promise resembles George Vavasor's (and Willoughby Patterne's) treatment of promises as a matter of convenience. While admitting that he should no longer pursue her after his "dismissal," Grey nevertheless persists, saying, "I don't know that I care much about such rules" (*CYFH* 1:159). He ignores the conventions of courtship when they do not suit his purposes, but insists that Alice honor them when they do. Thus like George, he sometimes treats engagement as if it were marriage. In the midst of trying to make Alice *become* his wife, for example, Grey argues, "You *are* my wife" (*CYFH* 1:117, my emphasis). Of course, the very circumstance in which he makes this claim disproves its validity. George makes the same assertion, seemingly oblivious to grammatical and semantic contradictions of his utterances. He takes heed neither of the confused verb tense of his remark, "Alice, you are my wife now. Tell me that it will make you happy to call me your husband" (*CYFH* 1:361), nor of the contradictory nature of his insistence that he is her "affianced husband" (*CYFH* 2:331). Brontë's Mr. Rochester succeeds for a short time in being the husband of one woman and the fiancé of another, but it is impossible for either Grey or Vavasor to be engaged and married at the same time.

Reinforcing the similarities between Alice's two suitors are their theories of beauty. When Grey follows Alice to Switzerland, he also follows George's example of associating beauty with distance. Prompted by "one of the prettiest spots in that land of beauty" (*CYFH* 1:351), he propounds a theory that, while not identical to George's, has the same practical effect. Both men would banish poetry to penumbral realms impervious to the light of a prosaic day. Grey holds that beauty experienced too frequently loses its impact. He is loyal to the English district possessing "fewer rural beauties than any other county in England" (*CYFH* 1:100) "[p]artly because all beauty is best enjoyed when it is sought for with some trouble and difficulty, and partly because such beauty, and the romance which is attached to it, should not make up the staple of one's life. Romance, if it is to come at all, should always come by fits and starts" (*CYFH* 2:352). Vavasor's conception of the poetic is spatial, Grey's temporal, but both make beauty and romance matters of mystery. The narrator playfully satirizes this idea when he implies that in today's society of world-weary travelers, nearby locales and ordinary scenes are of greater romantic potential than distant and seemingly exotic lands. He declines to write an account of his journey to Switzerland because such books are so common that "[n]o living man or woman any longer wants to be told anything of the Grimsell or of the Gemmi. Ludgate Hill is now-a-days more interesting than the Jungfrau" (*CYFH* 1:44)—as, no doubt, are London to George and Cambridgeshire to John. The larger point is that whatever the attractions of the proximate, defining beauty in terms of the unexamined, on the one hand, or of the infrequent, on the other, is less an aesthetic observation than a rhetorical stratagem. It serves the immediate purposes of the speaker, whatever else it may do to advance the theory of beauty.

These aesthetic theories, like their proponents' selective use of conventional courtship rules, emphasize the antagonistic basis of both kinds of romantic language. Whether in the form of poetic excess or of rational understatement, courtship discourse is meant to coerce Alice into making or keeping engagements about which she has justifiable reservations. Nothing could make this point more clear than the decidedly mixed message that she delivers after having tacitly accepted Grey's second offer of marriage: "'You win everything—always,' she said, whispering to him, as she still shrank from his embrace" (*CYFH* 2:356). Engagement, it seems, is a matter of victory and defeat; surrender—and the silence with which it is indicated—must be unconditional.

When he inquires about their future mode of living, Alice responds, "Oh, John, what right can I have to say anything?" (*CYFH* 2:380). Her question seems to be rhetorical. She has previously stated that as "a fallen creature," she has forfeited the right to criticize him (*CYFH* 2:355). Now she implies that having sinned against propriety in the past, she can have no right to a voice in her future. Her question, then, indicates that she has accepted the terms of surrender. A different reading of the scene, however, is possible. Given Grey's characteristic monologism, his question would seem to be the rhetorical one, and Alice may justifiably ask what her role in this marriage can be. He has heretofore shown very little need of the counselor he claims to seek in her. In this view, her inquiry is actually a statement. Her question is rhetorical, then, only insofar as its articulation is predicated upon its having already been answered—at least by Alice herself. In posing it, she both asserts her own voice and asks that he listen as well as speak.

In this interpretation of the scene, Grey's asking Alice about their future implies that, like Darcy, he has learned that a proposal of marriage is not a mere rhetorical exercise. Even though his response to her question contains the tones of Hyperion that have proven so Satyr-like to her, it also intimates a nascent dialogism in the relationship: "No one else can have so much right, putting aside of course myself, who must be responsible for my own actions" (*CYFH* 2:380). This modest concession to conversation is sufficient to elicit from Alice the kind of verbal enthusiasm that has not previously characterized her speech. It is to be remembered, for instance, that although Vavasor talks her out of an engagement with Grey, he cannot talk her into "speak[ing] to him soft winning words of love" (*CYFH* 1:362). With Grey as well, her love "lacked romance. Its poetry was too hard for romance. There was certainly in it neither fun nor wickedness" (*CYFH* 2:298). But with only this small encouragement, Alice begins to resemble the more exuberant and loquacious Glencora Palliser.[18] Alice's excitement leads to utterances of "more vehemence than discretion" (*CYFH* 2:381). This "out-spoken enthusiasm" is not typical, but it does demonstrate a capacity for romantic expressiveness even within the prosaic limitations of a Cambridgeshire dialect. It also intimates the extent to which Alice's voice will be heard after her marriage.

Glencora Palliser and Alice Vavasor take indirect routes to marriage; each is engaged to a man she does not love. Once married, Glencora narrowly avoids becoming "what she did not dare to name even to herself" (*CYFH* 2:22); four times engaged, Alice does not escape the name that she "called herself . . . with that inaudible voice which one uses in making self-accusations" (*CYFH* 1:336). Ironically, Glencora does not acquire that unmentionable appellation because of Alice's—not her own—belief that a woman "should be true to her marriage-vow, whether that vow when made were true or false" (*CYFH* 1:287). Alice clearly distinguishes between the inviolability of marriage vows and the frangibility of promises to marry. She believes that Glencora ought to be true to a false vow, while she herself must be false to a true promise.

Condemning her own inconstancy, she is nonetheless vindicated by John Grey, who defends her character: "throughout it all you have spoken no word of falsehood" (CYFH 2:355). The paradoxical circumstances of a truthful promise breaker become more clear from an examination of how naming and promising function generally in the world of the Pallisers.

In a novel in which naming plays a pivotal role, the political realm poses several perplexing problems.[19] For one thing, it seems virtually impossible to make a name stick. That is to say, names tend not to refer to the named person; rather, they are moves in a strategic political game. This circumstance is enabled by the "willing suspension of belief" demanded of members when they walk into the House of Commons. It takes George but a short time to learn, for example, "that it means nothing; that Lord This does not hate Mr. That, or think him a traitor to his country, or wish to crucify him; and that Sir John of the Treasury is not much in earnest when he speaks of his noble friend at the 'Foreign Office' as a god to whom no other god was ever comparable in honesty, discretion, patriotism, and genius" (CYFH 2:10). Neither praise nor condemnation carries much meaning, for it is never more that a strategic maneuver in the political game—it does not describe the characters of the players. This circumstance so disillusions Phineas Finn that he laments: "I don't know which are the falser, . . . the mock courtesies or the mock indignations of statesmen" (PR 609). His near execution on a false murder charge forcibly enlightens him about the sad priorities of the political system. Everything is grist for the mill of words—including his life.

An elaborate apparatus for rhetorical justice, which should regulate the excesses to which such histrionic performances are prone, actually functions to promote them. Given the largely verbal existences of the legislators, it is not surprising that there are a fair number of heated exchanges and that most MPs fairly quickly become impervious to insult. Politicians are "generally . . . indifferent to the very hard words that were said of them knowing what they were worth" (PM 2:149). The procedures intended to control the use of "hard words" during debates have become part of the tactical maneuvering employed by one party at the expense of the other. Any statement determined by the Speaker of the House to exceed "the latitude of parliamentary animadversion" (DC 202) can be removed from the official record of the proceedings. Doing so, however, accentuates rather than mutes the remark. Charging a speaker with verbal violence necessarily calls attention to the offending words. Furthermore, since there is no penalty for unacceptable locutions, speakers can savor the impact of verbal battery, knowing all the while that evidence of the crime will be expunged from the record on the condition that their language is sufficiently offensive. The policing of parliamentary language is primarily ornamental; its sole substantive effect is to encourage that which it purportedly regulates. Recognizing this situation, Phineas sarcastically comments: "Turveydrop and deportment will suffice for us against all odds" (*DC* 203). For like Mr. Turveydrop, the parliamentary process of self-regulation is concerned exclusively with the appearance of propriety. Parliamentary deportment is, therefore, consistent with both the prevailing theatricality of political practice and the politicians' investment in language itself. It proves once again that what is said means very little, but the fact of its being said means a great deal.

That is not to say that names are unimportant. Trollope comically illustrates this point by depicting the effort to decide what to call the new coin required by the plan to convert the British economy to a decimal system. "A question, perhaps of no great practical importance, had occurred to Mr. Palliser,—but one which, if overlooked, might be fatal to the ultimate success of the measure. There is so much in a name" (*ED* 2:140). The ensuing debate on farthing or fifthing, quint or semi-tenth, comically rehearses the debate between natural and arbitrary languages, and also recalls the White Knight's attempt in *Through the Looking Glass* to differentiate between a song, its name, the name of the song, and the name of the name (*AW* 186–87). The political veteran, Mr. Gresham, resolves the issue pragmatically rather than philosophically by saying, "Stick to the old word," sentiments reinforced by the Duke of St. Bungay: "We hate new names" (*ED* 2:141). The Liberal ministers' conservative sentiments reveal more than a fear of names, or even of the changing times of which these names are the proof. Their resistance to nominative innovation suggests the pragmatic force of existing labels and categories.

In politics there seems to be only one context is which this inertia is threatened, and that is when names are used self-reflexively. A metalinguistic act, that is, calling a name a name, threatens the verbal structure and procedures of the status quo simply by bringing attention to them. Metanominative categories are not changeable in the way that George Vavasor becomes Gregory Vance or the chancellor of the Exchequer becomes the prime minister. Mr. Bott, for instance, alludes to one such category, speaking more truly than he realizes, when he tells George: "The forms of the House are everything; upon my word they are" (*CYFH* 2:47). Bott's tag phrase, "upon my word," is ironically apt, for it emphasizes the verbal hermeticism of this system. The "forms of the House" can be maintained only so long as their *ad hominem* basis is not publicly named; thus, Barrington Erle speaks off the record when he says that the person who "intended to look to measures and not to men is unstable and dishonest" (*PF* 1:15). This view can neither be known outside the House nor officially articulated within it. The illusion must be sustained that oratory is pragmatic, not merely performative.

The self-reflexive function of naming calls attention to the very element that Trollope the novelist wishes to render invisible and that politicians and lovers would keep cloaked in mystery—language itself. When a specific discursive practice is named, the centrifugal impulse of theatrical modes is checked, and word-use is brought back into the ken of the ordinary. Identifying Parliament as a self-enclosed and self-serving universe of discourse thus endangers its existence. The clearest example of this danger is presented in *Phineas Finn* when the Liberal leader announces that he opposes a Church reform bill (a measure with which the Liberals have been historically and philosophically associated) simply because it is proposed by the Conservatives. In announcing his opposition, Mr. Gresham articulates the widely acknowledged but heretofore unnamed principle of politics:

> It was doubted whether such a political proposition had ever before been made in England. It was a simple avowal that on this occasion men were to be regarded, and not measures. No doubt such is the case, and ever has been the case, with the majority of active politicians. . . . Men and not measures are, no doubt, the very life of politics. But then it is not the fashion to say so in public places. (*PR* 1:275–76)

Mr. Gresham's "men-not-measures" speech is both atypical and dangerous because it invokes the appellative power of language to force the recognition of that which could otherwise be ignored. By naming names, Mr. Gresham creates at least the possibility of modulating, if only to a slight extent, the unregulated linguistic slippage in which Conservatives resemble Liberals and vice versa—whether on the issues, such as Church reform, or in practice, such as placing men above measures. That possibility is not realized on this occasion—as Gresham hoped it would not be. His gamble, therefore, becomes nothing more than another successful political ploy. The Conservative leader is brought down, and the Liberals are returned to power, all at the expense of Church reform. On this occasion the act of naming threatens but is unable to change a political system thoroughly entrenched in its own verbal processes. Neither does the public rebel against this revelation of the de facto functioning of their government, nor do the members acknowledge their primary activity as merely *pro forma* maneuvers in an elaborate game.

Since metanomination is so rarely practiced, virtually all questions raised in the House of Commons will of necessity be rhetorical, at least in the popular sense that they will be a matter of words and little else. The place of promising in politics reinforces this conclusion. For instance, political pragmatism precludes keeping campaign promises, even if they are sincere. George's political success depends upon the failure of his platform, as Mr. Scruby explains: "Of course it won't be done. If it were done, that would be an end of it, and your bread would be taken out of your mouth. But you can always promise it at the hustings, and can always demand it in the House" (*CYFH* 2:38). A basic premise of political rhetoric is withheld from the electors of Chelsea—an audience presumably accustomed to a discursive world in which promises are made in order to be kept. Campaign speeches, on the contrary, function according to the paradoxical proposition that promises are more meaningful when broken than when fulfilled. The ordinary rules of promising are rewritten and reversed in politics. The lesson of promising, therefore, is the same as that of naming: language is performative rather than constative; it is self-referential and entirely self-serving, despite repeated protests to the contrary. Neither is this language spoken anywhere other than in the House and at the hustings nor can it be translated into the language of everyday experience—except, perhaps, when it comes to matters of the heart.

Naming and promising feature prominently in the languages with which lovers as well as voters are wooed. The names with which Trollope is most concerned are those that identify breaches of decorum or convention and that are intended as checks upon behaviors threatening to transgress accepted boundaries of propriety. Names of this kind are not personal but general. To that extent, they are different from those typically coming under the consideration of the Speaker of the House of Commons, who must decide, for instance, whether "bellicose Irishman" (*DC* 202) is an acceptable locution. Social labels, on the contrary, refer to categories of experience, not to personal idiosyncrasy. Their force is conventional but ineluctable. When certain names are applied, individuals have no choice but to respond.

Although infrequently invoked, the nominative function of language is potentially quite disruptive, and its impact may be either divisive or corrective. "Duenna" and "prude" exemplify the unsettling but ultimately corrective effects of naming. Chafing under the propriety of married life and suffering from the absence of romantic love, Glencora calls her husband's observant acquaintances "duennas." Alice Vavasor, who is called a "prude" (*CYFH* 2:224, 289) for her efforts, feels that Glencora "should not have allowed the word duenna to have passed her lips in speaking to any one; but, above all, she should not have done so in the hearing of Mr Palliser's cousin" (*CYFH* 1:287). When the word does slip past Glencora's lips with Plantagenet himself and is subsequently replaced by the even more pointed term, "spies" (*CYFH* 1:90, 2:187), he must confront the realities of his loveless marriage and his wife's desire for Burgo Fitzgerald.[20] Even though he logically disproves the literal correctness of her terms, they possess the painful figurative power needed to initiate the self-examination that will make both husband and wife more clear-sighted.

For her part, Alice resents the label Glencora assigns her, especially when it is implied that in being a prude she is also a duenna. In her own defense, she calls attention to an issue fundamental to naming: "If you consider it prudery on my part to disapprove of your waltzing with Mr Fitzgerald . . . you and I must differ so totally about the meaning of words and the nature of things that we had better part" (*CYFH* 2:224–25). The problematic relation of "the meaning of words" and "the nature of things" lies at the heart of *Can You Forgive Her?*, as Juliet McMaster has recognized.[21] Beyond raising the issues of reference and reality, however, scenes such as this one reveal that the act of naming, irrespective of accuracy, possesses powerful pragmatic force. At stake is less the truth of the name than the nature of the action that follows upon its utterance. In courtship, unlike politics, names do have impact outside of the circumstances of name-calling itself.

"Prude" is a particularly interesting example because of its contrast to the principal label associated with Alice, "jilt." Both terms are pejorative: a prude pays too much attention to social propriety, a jilt too little. But when Glencora insults Alice, the injury is to her own character more perhaps than to Alice's, for in calling her friend a prude, Glencora in effect identifies herself a flirt, or, worse, "what she did not dare to name even to herself." Trollope's readers may have been helped to this conclusion by Richard Chenevix Trench, who offers "prude" as an example of those words that "bear the slime on them of the serpent's tail."[22] Formerly a term of rectitude, "the word 'prude' came to designate one who affected a virtue, even as none were esteemed to do anything more; and in this use of it, which, having once acquired, it continues to retain, abides an evidence of the corrupt world's dislike to and disbelief in the realities of goodness, its willingness to treat them as mere hypocrisies and shows."[23] Glencora evokes the word in a cause, her illicit love of Burgo, of which both Trench and Trollope would surely disapprove. The latter, however, is less concerned with etymological ethics than with discursive practice, and the oxymoronic situations in which he is most interested are disallowed by Trench's diachronic logic.

Throughout the Palliser novels, courtship and marriage are disrupted by the use of single nouns of overdetermined significance, such as "prude" or "jilt." Words of this kind, and the various adjectives associated with them, are the pillars of a highly articulated social structure.

Oswald Chiltern and Violet Effingham, for example, break off their engagement when she suggests "that his life was discreditable,—and, of course, no man would bear such language" (*PF* 2:306). Chiltern misremembers her word as "disreputable" and labels it "the harshest word that you could use in all the language" (*PF* 2:324). This is very much the sentiment of Glencora Palliser when her husband in effect accuses her of vulgarity: "Vulgarity! There was no other word in the language so hard to bear as that" (*PM* 1:177). He uses another "ugly name" (*PM* 1:178) in describing his daughter's surreptitious engagement. Her fiancé protests: "Disgraceful is a violent word, my Lord" (*DC* 1:42), and Mary is equally shocked by her father's language:

> "Then you must conquer your love. It is disgraceful and must be conquered."
> "Disgraceful!"
> "Yes. I am sorry to use such a word to my own child, but it is so."[24] (*PM* 65)

Although the consequences of invoking words like "discreditable," "vulgarity," and "disgraceful" are neither automatic nor invariably consistent with speakers' intentions, they can have an ameliorative impact upon individuals and upon the system of manners itself. Chiltern confronts his recklessness and Glencora reconsiders her ostentatious political parties. Mary Palliser instigates an overhaul, or at least a tune-up, of the social machinery by redefining the situations to which "disgraceful" might apply. In applying "a violent word" (*DC* 40) to his daughter, Palliser painfully discovers the unintended violence of his own utterance. Thus, whether one names or is named, the resulting process may renew rather than reify social relations. It is not simply the case that the world of the Pallisers is obsessed with violations of social codes of behavior. Nor is Trollope's interest in Victorian practice a matter of showing, as Trench attempts to do, that language itself is proof of humankind's fallen state. Rather, against the background of an elaborate system of manners and social practice, language is recognized as a form of action. What is less obvious but nonetheless clear from Trollope's analysis is that words have far-reaching psychological ramifications that go well beyond the social judgments implicit in their use.

In romance as in politics, the most serious names are metanominative, and of these the most potentially explosive is "liar." Lying may be accepted in both worlds, but identifying liars is not. Laurence Fitzgibbon, for example, is a valued political operative and personal confidant precisely because he "tell[s] a lie with good grace" (*CYFH* 2:3). He only slightly stretches the boundaries of acceptable disingenuousness when he includes in the subjects upon which a man may prevaricate "without subjecting himself to any ignominy of falsehood" to "dealing with a tradesman as to his debts, or with a rival as to a lady, or with any man or woman in defence of a lady's character" (*CYFH* 2:3). But, as Mr. Monk counsels Phineas, "men don't call each other liars" (*PR* 1:314). This wisdom is applied to social relations by Glencora Palliser, who observes that "the world tells lies every day,—telling on the whole much more lies than truth,—but the world has wisely agreed that the world shall not be accused of lying" (*PM* 1:178).[25] Even the prudish Alice condones fibs of the kind to which Glencora is prone: "Everyone makes excuses of that kind" (*CYFH* 1:244). The "civility of a lie" (*DC* 577) is preferable to an insulting truth, especially in relation to a lady's, or for that matter, a gentleman's character. The most egregious fault in lying lies not in the doing but in the naming. Beyond simply violating the norms of polite society, naming the lie is a self-reflexive act that redounds upon all language use. It exposes both the fragile structure of language and the deceit upon which society depends.

The Palliser novels contain several examples of the cataclysmic effects of calling someone a liar. Robert Kennedy creates a greater sensation by doing so than by doubting his wife's sexual conduct. When she tells Phineas that her husband has accused her of lying, he is shocked:

> "What!—with that word?"
> "Yes,—with that very word. He is not particular about his words, when he thinks it necessary to express himself strongly. And he has told me since that because of that he could never believe me again."
> (*PF* 2:244)

Kennedy's reaction may be disproportionate to Lady Laura's social fib, but in calling her a liar he provides the justification that she requires in order to leave him. She has, of course, lied to her husband, but that he confronts her with this charge is unsupportable.

Lucy Morris's good-natured innocence of the decorum of misstatement rivals Kennedy's obsessive intolerance of it. She does not understand that the accusation of dishonesty can be more calamitous than lying itself. Her difference of opinion with Lord Fawn is not technically a matter of either's being a liar. They merely disagree as to the character of her fiancé. But in speaking the "terrible words" that indict Lord Fawn, she unwittingly invokes a formula that demands a response: "If you [Fawn] say that he [Greystock] is not a gentleman, it is not true" (*ED* 1:245). Put in these terms, the nexus of their disagreement is shifted from Frank Greystock's character to Fawn's, and, more to the point, from the expressed issue of character to the tacit question of linguistic practice. Even setting aside the perceived disrespect of a governess's contradicting the head of the household, Lucy violates "all rules of good breeding. . . . [U]nder no circumstances could a lady be justified in telling a gentleman that he had spoken an untruth" (*ED* 1:248). Lucy comes to understand only after repeating her crime that its offense to the Fawn household lies not in thought but expression: "Of all this Lucy understood something. The word 'lie' she knew to be utterly abominable. That Lizzie Eustace was a little liar had been acknowledged between herself and the Fawn girls very often,—but to have told Lady Eustace that any word spoken by her was a lie, would have been a worse crime than the lie itself" (*ED* 1:261).

In the absence of an internal mechanism like the judicial system of the House of Commons, social disputants faced with the accusation of lying have few alternatives to courses of action lying outside the boundaries of social propriety, such as dueling or law suits. These options, however, have precisely the effect that they are intended to avoid: exclusion from respectable society. Dueling is neither fashionable nor legal; thus, it is open only to latter-day Corsairs like Chiltern and Ferdinand Lopez, who warns Everett Wharton: "But pray remember that under no circumstances should you call a man a liar, unless on cool consideration you are determined to quarrel with him for lying, and determined also to see the quarrel out" (*PM* 22). The alternative to physical combat, and the only option open to women, is a legal battle. Yet since to be engaged in court action is itself a dishonorable experience, only someone already beyond the pale, like "Lizzie the Liar" (*PR* 2:292), considers the courts when, for instance, her fiancé threatens to break off the engagement. A breach of promise action is in effect the only way of calling a man a liar and "seeing the quarrel out."

The connection between lying and promising is made by Lizzie herself, who calls to Frank Greystock's attention the fact that he has placed himself in an equivocal position by making love to her while being engaged to Lucy Morris. Sensing that her seductive control over her cousin may be weakening, she upbraids him:

> He rose and came to her, and attempted to take her hand, but she flung away from him. "No!" she said—"never again; never, unless you will tell me that the promise you made me when we were down on the sea-shore was a true promise. Was that truth, sir, or was it a—lie?"
> "Lizzie, do not use such a word as that to me." (*ED* 1:289–90)

Frank's discomfort reflects more than Henry Tilney's snobbery about faithful promises. It is partly authentic (he has compromised himself) and partly formulaic (a gentleman cannot tolerate the accusation of lying). Whether or not, as Roger Carbury claims, a man may "break a promise and yet not tell a lie," Frank clearly counts upon the latitude granted men to engage in romantic dalliances.[26] Lizzie, however, forces the issue by invoking the name that cannot be ignored. Her ploy parallels Gresham's political tack, and not surprisingly so, since, in one sense, the promises of lovers resemble those of politicians: no one expects them to be honored.

This attitude is accentuated when Trollope's mechanicals hold an outdoor fête and one of them describes the occasion by alluding to Shakespeare's "Venus and Adonis": "Bid me discourse, I will enchant thine ear, / Or like a fairy trip upon the green, / Or like a nymph, with long dishevell'd hair, / Dance on the sands, and yet no footing seen" (CYFH 1:77, only the final line is cited in the text). This gravity-defying promise does not refer to a future action but is itself a part of the process of enchantment. The promise is not meant to be kept; its premise is pragmatic, not cognitive; its force is figurative rather than literal. As the narrator comments: "It was all very well for Venus to make the promise, but when making it she knew that Adonis would not keep her to her word" (CYFH 1:93). A Victorian Venus like Lizzie, however, may well call in such a promise, and latter-day Adonises should consider themselves forewarned.

Frank Greystock clearly does not expect Lizzie's embarassing, because incisive, question. Nor does George Vavasor expect that he will be held to his promises. He quite facilely breaks the promise implicit in his three-year relationship with Jane—an affair that is probably responsible for his first broken engagement to Alice. "He had not only promised falsely," Alice tells herself, "but he had made such promises with a deliberate, premeditated falsehood" (CYFH 1:25). This recognition demonstrates that Alice refuses the logic of promising that defines George's courtship. She may have condoned Glencora's social fibs, but she cannot take her Adonis's promises so lightly.

This logic, applied to herself, yields a painful conclusion. Alice says that she has "sinned with that sin which especially disgraces a woman. . . . She had sinned against her sex" (CYFH 1:37, also see 74). The power of this acculturated judgment is concentrated in the single word, jilt. When Alice is first confronted with this "grievous reproach" (CYFH 1:353), the narrator writes, "It is hard to explain how heavy a blow fell upon her from the utterance of that word! Of all words in the language it was the one which she now most dreaded" (CYFH 1:336). This is a heinous social offense because it not only includes the charge of dishonesty associated with lying but also reaches to the pillar of Victorian value, marriage. To break a promise to marry is to commit a double crime—one announced, the other hidden. Publicly, the jilt is either deceitful or fickle, but in both cases she is untrustworthy and unworthy. Privately, the jilt is the condemned reminder of the troubled relation between language and reality in general and between courtship and desire in particular.

The spokeswomen of this social conservatism are the kindly but cowed Lady Macleod and her distant and imperious relative, Lady Midlothian. The former expresses shock at the very idea of a broken engagement: "And is not your word pledged to him? . . . I don't see how it is possible you should go back. Gentlemen when they do that sort of thing are put out of society,—but I really think it is worse in a woman" (*CYFH* 1:152). The latter even more pointedly invokes the concept of a woman's honor, lecturing Alice that "[t]here are things in which a young lady has no right to change her mind after it has been once made up; and certainly when a young lady has accepted a gentleman, that is one of them. He cannot legally make you become his wife but he has a right to claim you before God and man" (*CYFH* 1:193). The verdict of social guilt against a jilt is inevitable and unremitting. Whatever Lady Macleod implies about the ethics of broken engagements, such ruptures are practically much worse for women than for men because there is no appealing the charge. Lacking alternatives to the marriage market, the woman judged to be a jilt is apt to receive a life sentence of solitary confinement.[27]

The idea of the jilt is more humorously introduced into *The Eustace Diamonds*. Several characters attend a play of the title that Trollope was afraid to use for *Can You Forgive Her?* The performance prompts this comment from Mrs. Carbuncle, a woman whose credentials as a theater critic are called into question by the mixed metaphor with which her critique is expressed (and whose qualifications as a moral adviser are discredited by her role in enforcing the reluctant Lucinda Roanoke to keep her engagement to Sir Griffin—a coercion that ultimately drives Lucinda insane):

> "A noble jilt, my dears," said Mrs. Carbuncle eloquently, "is a contradiction in terms. There can be no such thing. A woman, when she has once said the word, is bound to stick to it. The delicacy of the female character should not admit of hesitation between two men. The idea is quite revolting. . . . [W]hen she has once given herself there can be no taking back without the loss of that aroma which should be the apple of a young woman's eye." (*ED* 2:109)

One wonders about what this visible scent might be, although perhaps it resembles Mrs. Greenow's sniff of "rocks and valleys." Lizzie Eustace rather unsentimentally responds: "It's all very well to talk of aroma, but to live with a man you don't like—is the devil!" (*ED* 2:110). Her response recalls Glencora's objection to her husband's preoccupation with statistics during their French travels. While he notes the number of eggs consumed daily by Parisians, she "protested that the information was worth nothing unless her husband could tell her how may of the eggs were good, and how many bad" (*CYFH* 68). Palliser's immersion in numbers insulates him from the odor of rotten eggs. What Lizzie and Glencora humorously object to is the detachment of social norms or statistical abstracts from existential circumstances. These comic scenes suggest that neither political principles (men vs. measures) nor social values (women vs. promises) can be construed or applied in absolute terms; they can be evaluated and practiced only in the very tangled circumstances from which they emerge.

Alice Vavasor takes jilting a lover much more to heart than does Lizzie. Foundering under the weight of this charge, she labors to defend herself and at least initially produces an argument worthy of Lizzie herself. She insists that "[s]he had no husband;—not as yet. He [Grey] spoke of their engagement as though it were a betrothal, as betrothals used to be of yore; as though they were already in some sort married. Such betrothals were not made now-a-days" (*CYFH* 1:23–24). Reversing the rhetorical ploys of her suitors, who take betrothal to be tantamount to marriage, Alice attempts to dismiss the significance of engagement altogether. They appeal to the promise, she to the woman. The narrator does not endorse the relativism of this position and calls Alice's reasoning "those very poor arguments which she had used in trying to convince herself that she was still free if she wished to claim her freedom" (*CYFH* 1:32).[28] Trollope presents promises as being neither so frivolous as Alice hopes nor so irrevocable as George and Grey contend. A promise does possess intrinsic significance and meaning, especially a promise so enmeshed in convention and tradition as betrothal. Alice cannot simply take to promising the strategy that Humpty Dumpty applies to semantics: "When *I* use a word . . . it means just what I choose it to mean—neither more nor less" (*AW* 163).

J. Hillis Miller argues that promises are as subjective as Humpty Dumpty believes words are. This relativism is a function of language itself. Performatives like "I promise"

> always exceed the intentions of their performers. They do not depend on intention for their efficacy. A performative always makes something happen, but it by no means always makes happen what the one who utters it intends or expects. The words work on their own, mechanically, impersonally, independently of any conscious, willing subjectivity, just as grammar does.[29]

When Humpty Dumpty tells his Alice, "The question is . . . which is to be master—that's all" (*TLG* 163), he implies that speakers control meaning—a logic apparently not extended to the words of a promise, since he places unquestioned confidence in the King's promise to "send all his horses and all his men" (*AW* 160). Miller, on the contrary, suggests that it is the other way around, or at least that, if language is not quite in control, it nonetheless effectively prevents anything or anyone else from determining or restricting the mechanical production of meaning. From this perspective, Humpty Dumpty's confidence is unjustified, his thinking scrambled.

Trollope's sympathies, however, lie neither with Humpty Dumpty nor with Hillis Miller but with the two Alices. Carroll's Alice rejects both the desirability and the inevitability of subjective and multiple meanings. She tells Humpty Dumpty: "The question is . . . whether you *can* make words mean so many different things" (*AW* 163). Trollope's Alice comes to learn that the same is true of promises. Promises can mean many things, but they cannot be willed to mean anything—not, in any event, without making them a lie. Promising in this regard resembles writing a novel. Both are communicative activities. The novelist, Trollope believes,

> must be intelligible. Any writer who has read even a little will know what is meant by the word intelligible. It is not sufficient that there be a meaning which may be hammered out of the sentence, but that the language should be so pellucid that the meaning should be rendered without an effort to the reader;—and not only some proportion of meaning, but the very sense, no more and no less, which the writer has intended to put into his words. (*A* 235)

Intelligibility is a cooperative and invariably an approximate norm. When used with care, however, the words of the novel (like those of a promise) can establish a dynamic connection between writer and reader (or between lovers). Neither writing nor promising is an intransitive verbal practice; neither is an after-the-fact communication of a preexisting circumstance. Betrothal does not quiescently follow courtship; it is a part of courtship and takes meaning from the contingencies of courtship. The lesson of Alice Vavasor's experience is that lovers both speak and are spoken by their promises.

Promising can be likened to the metanominative use of language. Promises not only label and bring into contact the world of courtship discourse and the world of social reality, but they also bring attention to the use of words themselves. By the action of words alone, lovers assume a new name and a new, albeit transitional, place within an elaborate social structure. The promise to marry should engage the betrothed in an analysis of what they have said in relation to how they must live. The result of that process may be marriage or separation, but it should entail the self-examination that makes either act meaningful. The success of the process can be traced in Alice's perhaps circuitous but ultimately fortuitous path to matrimony.

In leaving *Can You Forgive Her?* for *The Wings of the Dove*, we return to the skeptical vision of *Jane Eyre*—a skepticism heightened by the fact that Kate Croy's circuitous journey is never squared. This return does not spell a failure by Eliot, Meredith, and Trollope to redefine betrothal, but it does reaffirm the difficulty of answering what James calls "the question of our speech."[30] Echoing the Victorian evolutionary concerns expressed by Maine and Müller, James suggests that language is a "living organism, fed by the very breath of those who employ it . . . who carry it with them, on their long road, as their specific experience grows larger and more complex, and who need it to help them to meet this expansion" (*QS* 46). Expanded need not always mean improved, and the civilized speech of James's sophisticates often masks primitive sentiments. James warns that we may "find ourselves emulating the beasts, who prosper as well without a vocabulary as without a marriage-service. It is easier to overlook any question of speech than to trouble about it, but then it is also easier to snort or neigh, to growl or to 'meaow,' that to articulate and intonate" (*QS* 47). The "trouble" of *The Wings of the Dove* is not articulation but silence—secrecy—and not verbal indolence but promissory freedom. Snorting, it turns out, is not confined to the farms of Loamshire; it has a civilized counterpoint in the salons of London.

CHAPTER 8

Dying Promises in
The Wings of the Dove

The preface to *The Wings of the Dove* presents readers with an anomalous entity: a retrospective promise. This promise is actually doubly anomalous because it can be known only by means of its having been broken. Its existence is intimated by James's hope that any sense readers might have of failure in artistic execution will be mitigated by their recognition of his good intentions:

> Yet one's plan, alas, is one thing and one's result another; so that I am perhaps nearer the point in saying that this last strikes me at present as most characterised by the happy features that *were*, under my first and most blest illusion, to have contributed to it. I meet them all, as I renew acquaintance, I mourn for them all as I remount the stream, the absent values, the palpable voids, the missing links, the mocking shadows, that reflect, taken together, the early bloom of one's good faith.[1]

One such shadow, he feels, is his rendering of the Croy family. Readers "were to have been *shown*, with a truth beyond the compass even of one's most emphasised 'word of honour' for it" (*WD* 9–10), the negative effect that Lionel Croy has had upon his daughter. In the wake of the confession that he has not fully realized this objective, James presents readers with what must appear to be another "mocking shadow," an apologetic request that words be accepted in lieu of actions: "One's poor word of honour has *had* to pass muster for the show" (*WD* 10).

Despite acknowledging that a "poor author's" affirmations are "comparatively cold" and his guarantees "thin" (*WD* 12), James surprisingly concludes the preface with another promise: "as to what there may be to note, of this and other supersubtleties, other arch-refinements, of tact and taste, of design and instinct, in 'The Wings of the Dove,' I become conscious of overstepping my space without having brought the full quantity to light. The failure leaves me with a burden of residuary comment of which I yet boldly hope elsewhere to discharge myself" (*WD* 16). The preface like the novel itself, therefore, does not deliver on its promises. In this instance, James does not simply ask readers to take his "poor word" for it; rather, he offers the bold hope of fuller explanation in the future.

The "burden of residuary comment" to which he alludes, however, has been more readily borne by James's critics than it has been discharged by James himself. Readers may well wonder, then, if his promises are at best a polite rationalization and at worst a blatant deception.

A similar suspicion attends Merton Densher's invitation to Milly Theale to visit his rooms in Venice. Her "offer to him of her company" (WD 282) elicits an "almost shamelessly" (WD 283) temporizing response: "a hollow promise. . . . [T]here had been in the prospect from the first a definite particular point at which hollowness, to call it by its least compromising name, would have to begin. Therefore its hour had now charmingly sounded" (WD 283). Hollow words may yield rich tones, but Milly subsequently learns that Densher's promises are both empty and hypocritical. Similarly, the last sentence of the preface, however charmingly it rings in the novel, may leave readers with the haunting impression that James no less than Densher is responding "in a mere time-gaining sense" (WD 283).

While the prefatory references to failed intentions, unsatisfactory or incomplete artistic execution, and unfulfilled promises may arouse skepticism concerning the narrative to follow, they themselves constitute an implicit promise of sorts—a promise that promising itself will feature prominently in the pages to follow. This topic is introduced in the first chapter when James presents the Croy family: "the whole history of their house had the effect of some fine florid voluminous phrase, say even a musical, that dropped first into words and notes without sense and then, hanging unfinished, into no words nor any notes at all" (WD 21). Kate herself identifies this musical "phrase" as the "tune . . . to which we're a failure as a family!" (WD 55). While her father's disgraceful and her sister's insignificant existences seem to constitute a dramatic decrescendo trailing off into sordid silence, she fully intends to deliver on the family promise: "She hadn't given up yet, and the broken sentence, if she was the last word, *would* end with a sort of meaning" (WD 22).[2] Whether "sort of" will be different from "sordid" remains uncertain; however, the contrast between the musical descriptions of the Croys and of Milly Theale is suggestive in this regard. Densher thinks of Milly as having "meanings that hung about [her], waiting upon her, hovering dropping and quavering forth again, like vague faint snatches, mere ghosts of sound, of old-fashioned melancholy music" (WD 286). She is "the American girl," whose "national character [is] so invoked . . . in Milly's chords" (WD 322, 323). Kate, on the contrary, is "the contemporary London female, highly modern" (WD 50); hence, her meanings are florid rather than faint, voluminous rather than ghostly, melodramatic—or perhaps "in the line of old Venetian comedy" (WD 303)—rather than elegiac.

Were she to offer one, Kate's interpretation of the family failure might affect readers in the same way that her conclusions typically impress Densher: "There were moments again—we know that from the first they had been numerous—when he felt with a strange mixed passion the mastery of her mere way of putting things" (*WD* 292). One example of this mastery is the favorable interpretation placed on the "hollow promise" to Milly. Kate "—ready always, as we say, with the last word—had given him the benefit of her righting of every wrong appearance, a support familiar to him now in reference to other phases" (*WD* 284). While "hollow" may be the "least compromising" term for his promise, an even more euphemistic phrase is required for her interpretation of it: Densher's "inward ache was not wholly dispelled by the style, charming as that was, of Kate's *poetic versions*" (*WD* 285, my emphasis). His promises temporize, her poetry dissembles—both, however, in charming fashion.

Such charm is delightful but dangerous. For instance, in considering the effort to insulate Milly from the hard facts of her malady, Densher ponders the "conscious fool's paradise" (*WD* 347) inhabited by the poet: "'The mere aesthetic instinct of mankind—!' our young man had more than once, in the connexion, said to himself; letting the rest of the proposition drop" (*WD* 347). His sentence, like Kate's, is unfinished, and ominously so. For a "*mere* aesthetic instinct," like a "*mere* way of putting things," must raise suspicion about the gap between artistic or rhetorical versions of things and the things themselves. The novel's conclusion questions whether there can be other than a "fool's paradise," conscious or otherwise, in the wake of the "beautiful beneficent dishonesty" (*WD* 154) with which Kate and Merton treat Milly. On the one hand, it is clear that poetry (or in this case, a poetic version) makes nothing happen.[3] Milly will die regardless of how that prospect is presented to her by medical advisers and friends. On the other hand, Milly's final weeks are greatly affected—and her end is perhaps hastened—by their ways of putting things. The "connexion" of which Densher is thinking has to do with the "expensive vagueness made up of smiles and silences and beautiful fictions and priceless arrangements" constructed by Milly's English friends. Their motivations are mixed, as is suggested by the contrasting connotations of terms like "expensive" and "priceless"; their accomplishments are similarly mixed, since Milly's final weeks are both supernal and infernal; their "vagueness," on the contrary, is singularly clear: "poetic versions" and "beautiful fictions," whatever else they may do, carry prosaic, even ugly, meanings.

The last word in the novel is indeed Kate's, though it does not establish a conclusive ending to the broken sentence of the Croys. "We shall never be again as we were!" (*WD* 403) provides terminal punctuation both to the Croy diminuendo and to Kate's (now apparently broken) engagement, but for readers her postmortem is likely to be read as an interrogatory rather than an exclamatory expression. Consistent with the set of discursive values according to which making a "direct . . . appeal" (such as Milly makes in requesting to visit Densher's rooms) is construed as "slightly sinister" and "positively scaring" (WD 283), Kate's closing words are oblique, describing what is not rather than what is.[4] They mark the fact, but neither the nature nor the significance, of change. Thus James's conclusion may itself seem "slightly sinister" because of its indirection and openness. Any promise of closure (or of "residuary comment") is, if not hollow, then at least equivocal. Readers are left to wonder what, if anything, has been promised them and what, if anything, it might have meant.

The note of anomalous promises sounded by the preface emphasizes two aspects of promising figuring prominently in *The Wings of the Dove* and exemplified by the "rich compact" (WD 72) uniting Kate Croy and Merton Densher. The first concerns the status and social function of secret promises. Carole Pateman argues that the "meaning of 'I promise' is not purely subjective and individual but is social and intersubjective. It is 'constitutive of the social matrix in which individuals find themselves and act', and it forms part of the relationship of obligation that is created through the making of a promise."[5] This is all the more true of betrothal, which formalizes and publicizes intentions, situating the co-promisers in a context of established social and legal practice. James poses the possibilities that, on the one hand, secrecy, or what Kate and Merton call "a high level of discretion" (WD 73), may mean deception, but that, on the other hand, it might foster both sensibility and sentience, or what James calls "the whole soft breath of consciousness meeting and promoting consciousness" (WD 282).[6] Milly cannot be certain of the deception until Lord Mark informs her of the true state of Kate's affections, but she senses the possibilities for enhanced consciousness from her earliest introduction to London society. At Mrs. Lowder's dinner party, she quickly discerns that

> nothing was so odd as that she should have to recognise so quickly in each of these glimpses of an instant the various signs of a relation; and this anomaly itself, had she had more time to give to it, might well, might almost terribly have suggested to her that her doom was to live fast. It was queerly a question of the short run and the consciousness proportionately crowded. (WD 105)

This discovery, anomalous in nature and effect, anticipates what Milly learns, or seems to learn, from Sir Luke Strett when she is told to "see all you can" (WD 151). At her London debut, however, the impetus to a full life is social rather than medical. Milly comes to appreciate that "the way they let all phrasing pass was . . . a characteristic triumph of the civilised state" (*WD* 178). Those conversant in and with a society of nuanced expression, expressive silence, and silent promises must of necessity be sentient and perceptive; they must be, as James says in another context, "one of those upon whom nothing is lost."[7]

The second aspect of promising involves the pragmatic effect of promises upon those making them. Kate and Merton's betrothal seems to result less in a commitment to, than a freedom from, the promised act. By giving a promise, individuals incur a specific responsibility and create a certain expectation, but the more dramatic consequence in *The Wings of the Dove* is a general freedom on the part of promisers to do something apart from, often in direct conflict with, the promised act. This freedom is not a matter of intentional deceit, that is, of deliberately making false promises. Nor does this freedom abrogate the obligation to perform the promised act. Rather, in agreeing to the terms of one action, characters find that an unrelated possibility is created. By promising to do one thing, characters are strangely empowered to do something else. The logic of promising, then, is not simply that of a contractual agreement in which, within a particular social economy, services of roughly equal value are exchanged. Instead, a "promissory surplus" is produced, the uses of which become a central issue in the novel.

There is a final turn of the promissory screw: promises, not their makers, have the last word. Lovers may become engaged *by means of* promises, but ultimately they are possessed *by* their promises. Seemingly free to enjoy what Maggie Tulliver might call the "bonus" of promising, they discover that they are likely to get more than they bargained for. Promising, therefore, is characterized by a double paradox: by committing themselves, promisers are set free; having been set free, they are confined by their liberators. Subjected to their word in ways they can neither anticipate nor control, those who make promises are condemned to be free, that is, to experience fully the unknown and unknowable ramifications of their act. Promises, therefore, are like a dove—they "stretch . . . out [their] wings. They cover us" (*WD* 403).

While promising in *The Wings of the Dove* varies in nature from a casual statement of intention or expectation to a causal guarantee of future action, the most common use of the term is figurative. Promising in this informal sense refers to the expectations resulting from a particular set of circumstances or an agreed upon arrangement. For Kate and Densher, "promise" in this context refers to the human spectacle—a panorama whose contours are only partially shaped by actions they initiate. While deeply interested in the scene before them, they also exhibit something of an aesthetic attitude; they are anxious to see what will come of the schemes they have set in motion. So, for example, as Densher is led to consider and engage in an increasingly complex set of social maneuvers, "[s]omething suddenly . . . welled up in him and overflowed—the sense of his good fortune and her [Kate's] variety, of the future she promised, the interest she supplied" (*WD* 219–20). The prospect of interest outweighs the sense of danger that the schemes might run awry. When Densher considers that he must "work" his good relations with Kate, Aunt Maud, Milly, and Susan Stringham, "it crystallized before him in such guise as not only to promise much interest—fairly, in the case of success, much enthusiasm; but positively to impart to failure an appearance of barbarity" (*WD* 225). Readers who recall the description of the two classes of people in London relations, the working and the worked (*WD* 116), will recognize in Densher's thoughts the underlying characteristics of promise as contract, in addition to the overt sense of promise as prediction.

For Milly the panorama is initially natural rather than social. She tells Mrs. Stringham that she "expected, she had frankly promised, to be restless" (82) during their European travels. Thus while walking in the Swiss mountains, she is drawn to a promontory by "the promise" of a "'view' pure and simple" (*WD* 87). This anticipatory sense of promise seems relatively straightforward—"pure and simple"—but it does not remain so for long. Even this general use of "promise" is complicated by the anomalies to which readers have been introduced by James's preface. For they, along with Susan Stringham, must retrospectively construct the nature of the promise that European travel holds for Milly, and only then can they know that it holds very little promise at all.

Having succumbed to the promise of the promontory, Milly grows restless. She is dissatisfied with her desultory wandering and now promises Susan Stringham "to think till supper of where, with all the world before them, they might go" (*WD* 89). The promise to be restless and the promise of scenery give way to the promise of "'people'": "what she wanted of Europe was 'people,' so far as they were to be had, and that, if her friend really wished to know, the vision of this same equivocal quantity was what had haunted her during their previous days, in museums and churches, and what was again spoiling for her the pure taste of scenery" (*WD* 93). With these words, Milly announces a revised travel plan, and Mrs. Stringham guesses that "something of a promise" (*WD* 93) must have been given to Mr. Densher to visit him in London. Although Milly does not say so, Susan surmises that "people" is more accurately "person," and more specifically "Merton Densher."[8] If Milly has, as Susan suspects, made such a promise, it is the first in a sequence of indirect and at best oblique promises whose existence and purpose cannot be known until the sequence is virtually complete.[9]

The problematic status of what Milly may or may not have promised Densher embroils readers in the dynamics of promising first encountered in the preface. Her seeming promise is characterized by several incongruent elements. First of all, we cannot even be sure that a promise has occurred, for Milly tells Mrs. Stringham that she has done nothing "either to impair or to enhance" (*WD* 94) Densher's confidence that she will visit him in England. Second, we have only the promisee's request for, not the promiser's utterance of, the promise. Susan Stringham can only faintly remember Milly's having mentioned "the confidence expressed by the personage in question [Densher] in her never doing so dire a thing as to come to London without, as the phrase was, looking a fellow up" (*WD* 94). Third, the promise is a secret one, and evidence of its existence is only indirectly and belatedly forthcoming. Milly says nothing to her companion about actually looking the fellow up. Susan infers the existence of the promise primarily from the sudden and unexpected change in itinerary.

She should perhaps have anticipated this change, since the European trip itself is sprung upon her with a suddenness and urgency exceeded only by its mystery. Less than a week after visiting Milly in New York, Mrs. Stringham is asked: "Would she start for Europe with her young friend at the earliest possible date, and should she be willing to do so without making conditions? The enquiry was launched by wire; explanations, in sufficiency, were promised; extreme urgency was suggested and a general surrender invited" (*WD* 81). "Explanations, in sufficiency," are exactly what readers expect in the preface, but in neither case is the promised clarification provided. Readers are left in the dark, as is Mrs. Stringham, for despite both "an education in the occult . . . begun the day she left New York with Mildred" (*WD* 76) and a protracted attempt at "applying tests, laying traps, concealing signs" (*WD* 83), she cannot divine the reason for the sudden voyage.[10] In deciphering the mysterious change from natural to social vistas, Susan reverts to logic worthy of Buzfuz and the Red King. She constructs a motivation for the English visit from the absence of evidence for it. Milly's evasive response to mention of Densher's name must mean that he is the reason for the change of plans: "Milly's look had to be taken as representing one of two things—either that she was completely vague about the promise or that Mr. Densher's name itself started no train. But she really couldn't be so vague about the promise, the partner of these hours quickly saw, without attaching it to something; it had to be a promise to somebody in particular to be so repudiated" (*WD* 93–94). Susan now guesses what the narrator has heretofore withheld from readers—and what Milly's "explanations, in sufficiency" have incompletely conveyed—the fact and importance of Merton Densher's three visits to her in New York. Densher's name may be less significant than Dr. Finch's in launching Milly's ship to Europe, but it seems very likely that his name and his name alone "started her train" to England.

This sequence of figurative and literal, of surmised and categorical, promises suggests that promissory expectation may have more to do with retrospection than anticipation. The anachronism inherent in this process does not fit the pattern of a detective story in which current circumstances are clarified when past events are brought to light. In this case, readers, who can only belatedly compose the significance of the promissory chain, cannot know with any certainty if their constructions are accurate. They have additional reason to wonder about the significance of their circuitous interpretive journey because, despite the mystery surrounding who promised what to whom, the existence of a promise seems finally not to make a great difference in what Milly actually does. Mrs. Stringham says that, "at any rate, promise or no promise, Milly would at a pinch be able, in London, to act on his permission to make him a sign" (WD 94–95). Her pragmatic attitude suggests that promises may be less important in themselves than for the heightened consciousness and increased discernment that they demand of all parties directly or indirectly connected with them.

The Wings of the Dove provides other examples of how even relatively simple promises of the kind discussed so far might be fraught with complications. For instance, in addition to the promise of the Swiss Alps, Milly is impressed by the "view" afforded by the setting and the interior of Sir Luke Strett's office. Her reading of the great man and his office is not demonstrably incorrect, but it does raise the specter of unjustifiable expectation. Upon returning to the office for a second visit—the first one having lasted a scant ten minutes—Milly experiences a reassuring sense of promise: "The very place, at the end of a few minutes, the commodious 'handsome' room, far back in the fine old house, soundless from position, somewhat sallow with years of celebrity, somewhat sombre even at midsummer—the very place put on for her a look of custom and use, squared itself solidly round her as with promises and certainty" (WD 146). The echo of Trollope's geometric contradiction suggests that all may not be as settled and secure as the situation promises. Furthermore, the compound phrase, "promises and certainty," underscores that the former do not inevitably lead to the latter—that promises cannot provide certainty however secure they might appear to be or, as Catherine Morland might say, however faithfully they are given. The tension intimated by James's language is strengthened by the contradictions between the physical setting and, on the one hand, the emotional significance attached to it and, on the other hand, the medical condition that brings Millie to the Doctor's door. She has "come forth to see the world, and this then was to be the world's light, the rich dusk of a London 'back,' these the world's walls, those the world's curtains and carpet" (*WD* 146). Milly's prospects may be great, but her view will be severely circumscribed by the "world's walls." Whether in London or in Venice, she finds herself most often amidst the obscure light, muffled sound, and enclosed space of an invalid's quarters.

Milly's confidence derives not only from the place but also from Sir Luke himself, who, she believes, has "found out simply by his genius—and found out, she meant, literally everything" (*WD* 145). She wants him "to see me just as I am" and says that one should "at the start, show the worst" (*WD* 148), which includes the "fraud" (*WD* 145) of hiding these visits from Mrs. Stringham. Despite her trust, Milly suspects that the doctor's genius is fallible and that he himself may be susceptible to the fraud that she practices upon her traveling companion. Milly entertains

> the bold idea that he could really *be* misled; and there actually passed between them for some seconds a sign, a sign of the eyes only, that they knew together where they were. This made, in their brown old temple of truth, its momentary flicker; then what followed it was that he had her, all the same, in his pocket; and the whole thing wound up for that consummation with his kind dim smile. Such kindness was wonderful with such dimness; but brightness—that even of sharp steel—was of course for the other side of the business, and it would all come in for her to one tune or another. (*WD* 148–49)

This scene is nothing if not crepuscular: a brief flicker is marked by a dim smile in a brown temple. But it is further a chiaroscuro of contradiction. Underlying the darkness is an ominous illumination: the gleam of a surgeon's scalpel, a gleam whose intensity is subsequently indicated by Densher's association of Sir Luke's name with "fifty thousand knives!" (*WD* 216). In addition, the entire scene rests on an unlikely foundation: a temple of truth built upon the possibility and the practice of deception. As with her apparent promise about "looking a fellow up," this knowledge does not seem to count for much since she remains "in the doctor's pocket" whatever the acuity of his diagnoses or the reasons, personal or professional, for his medical counsel.

Although she claims to have discovered "everything" on her previous visit, Milly obeys the summons of "her distinguished friend" (*WD* 145) in hopes of an explicit prognosis. Her life, she feels, will be "put into the scales" (*WD* 146) and its weight—if not its value—objectively measured: "the state of being found out about . . . that . . . was truly what she had come for, and that . . . would give her something firm to stand on. She struck herself as aware, aware as she had never been of really not having had from the beginning anything firm. It would be strange for the firmness to come, after all, from her learning in these agreeable conditions that she was in some way doomed" (*WD* 146). Initially, it seems, the "agreeable conditions" portend—and, indeed, produce—beneficent medical advice. Sir Luke's tells her: "to 'live' [is] exactly what I'm trying to persuade you to . . . do" (*WD* 151). Milly, however, wonders why she is being told to live unless it is that she is about to die. She leaves the office with an agreeable impression, but one that upon consideration gives way to an ominous inference.

Her doom, the promise of death, as announced by Sir Luke, is virtually unrecognizable as such. Milly is told, not that she will die, but that she must live. Sir Luke Strett counsels: "Well, see all you can. That's what it comes to. Worry about nothing. You *have* at least no worries. It's a great rare chance" (*WD* 151). Sharon Cameron glosses this advice as follows:

> Since you know what the outcome is, you are free to live. In the most trivial sense, if you did not know what the outcome was, you would worry about it. But as you are—certainly—going to die, that certainty, or your knowledge of that certainty, suggests you therefore have a chance to live. But you have this chance because you realize that, however paradoxical such a formulation, both parts of it are true, and cannot be mitigated.[11]

The promise of death yielding the promise of life is the clearest and the most dramatic example of promissory surplus. Milly is free to live—and to love—because she knows that death is imminent. This formulation is, as Cameron suggests, paradoxical; it expresses the (il)logic with which all promissory acts are invested.

James also dramatizes the liberating effect of death's promise in *The Princess Casamassima*.[12] When Hyacinth Robinson makes the "tremendous, terrible vow" (*PC* 327) to Diedrich Hoffendahl, he in effect accepts a death sentence; as he puts it: "I have put my head in a noose" (*PC* 331). Hyacinth likens his promise to the Jesuits' vow of obedience and describes it as a "consecration" (*PC* 335, 333).[13] Its effect, indeed, seems comparable to that of ordination or conversion, albeit to a pronouncedly secular order. When Hume compares promises in general "to *transubstantiation*, or *holy orders*, where a certain form of words, along with a certain intention, changes entirely the nature . . . of a human creature," he describes in a singularly apt manner the particular force of Hyacinth's promise. What makes this promise even more "mysterious and incomprehensible" than Hume could have envisioned is that Hyacinth's vow transforms his life in ways that he cannot anticipate and that are diametrically opposed to the course of action to which he appears to be committing himself. As a result of his pledge to the terrorists, Hyacinth, sounding rather like Sir Luke, embraces "the great religious rule—to live each hour as if it were to be one's last" (*PC* 335). His promise may entail a commitment to die, but it produces an intensification of life. He believes that he "will have been positively happy," or at the least, as the Princess says, that he will "have had some fine moments" (*PC* 336). Swearing allegiance to the proletariat, he affects the life of an aristocrat; espousing political anarchy, he enters a world of aesthetic pleasure; professing self-denial, he practices self-indulgence.

The fine moments to which the Princess alludes blossom in Paris but date from the moment that Hyacinth agrees to die in the cause of social revolution: "since that terrible night at Hoffendahl's a change had come over the spirit of his dream. He had not grown more concentrated, he had grown more relaxed" (*PC* 382). Even before visiting the Continent, he experiences London in a new way, living "more intensely in the previous six months than in all the rest of his existence" (*PC* 383). Medley provides a further introduction to the finer things of life, and after this interlude of cultural indulgence, Hyacinth discovers in France a "sense of the wonderful, precious things it [society] had produced, of the brilliant, impressive fabric it had raised" (*PC* 382–83). The promise of death awakens him to the knowledge that "since he was destined to perish in his flower he was right to make a dash at the beautiful, horrible world" (*PC* 383). The belief that he is good only for death gives birth to the belief "that he was good enough for anything" (*PC* 384).

When the Princess tells Hyacinth that "your famous engagement, your vow . . . will never come to anything," he replies, "*Vous me rendez la vie!*" (*PC* 485). If not the Princess, then at least the promise *has* given Hyacinth life—paradoxically by committing him to death. The promise of death, therefore, engenders an experience and a consciousness that make fulfilling the promise something quite different from what Hyacinth expects in making it. Whatever the Princess's wish for her friend, and Hyacinth's for himself, his vow does come to something. He does not keep the promise in the terms understood by the four witnesses in the "backroom in Bloomsbury" (*PC* 328), but his suicide fulfills the terms of the pact as Hyacinth understands them: "I gave my life away" (*PC* 327).

In Milly's case, the promise of death is more equivocal, emanating as it does from the kindly Sir Luke Strett rather than the ominous Diedrich Hoffendahl. Its effects are similarly paradoxical, however, as is apparent from Milly's actions upon leaving the doctor's office. She wonders if pity rather than honesty has motivated Sir Luke's advice, therefore, if what she has learned is not another instance of misleading information or fraud.[14] Instead of having her life placed on Sir Luke's scale, Milly finds herself weighing

> questions numerous and strange, but she had happily, before she moved, worked round to a simplification. . . . She had been asking herself why, if her case was grave—and she knew what she meant by that—he should have talked to her at all about what she might with futility "do"; or why on the other hand, if it were light, he should attach an importance to the office of friendship. She . . . either mattered, and then she was ill, or, she didn't matter, and then she was well enough. Now he was "acting," as they said at home, as if she did matter. (WD 154–55)

Milly is left, in short, with a renewed prospect of "dishonesty," probably beneficent but certainly inscrutable, possibly significant but finally irrelevant. Sir Luke tells her to do what she must do in any event: to live until she dies.

Immersed in dusk, Milly is encouraged to see; ensconced in a London "back," she is told, "the world's before you" (WD 257); placed under a sentence of death, she is free to live. Such contradictions and anomalies are emblematic of all promising, even in its figurative and casual senses. As an indication of probability or expectation, "promise" tends to be both ambiguous and uncertain; as an indication of certainty or of commitment, it results in a doubly paradoxical sense of freedom and of free play. Promising in its more literal and conventional usage, to which I now turn, raises this free play, especially in the marriage market, to a "beautiful, horrible" art form.

The more conventional sense of promise-making is also characterized by promissory liberty. Promises in this context tend to be quasi-commercial contracts in which services are exchanged within a highly competitive marriage market. This market is not so much regulated by promises as propelled by them, since giving one's word is characterized by three factors that generate rather than restrict trading activity. The first of these is the promissory equivalent of *caveat emptor*. Irrespective of what is promised, the fact of a promise betokens a free market economy in which anything goes and self-interest rules. Thus promises function partly as Hume describes them, that is, to define instances of interested as opposed to disinterested commerce. According to Hume, promises themselves mark the difference between these two classes of relations and only in case of the former do we need a mechanism to "bind ourselves to the performance of any action." Within the endogamous

economy of these characters, the existence of a promise invariably signifies interested commerce, while its absence cannot always be taken as
proof of the opposite. Giving one's word of honor announces that something is amiss and that the speaker might not be trustworthy; not giving
one's word of honor only occasionally expresses the trust that makes
promises redundant. In these rare instances—and they usually involve
Milly Theale—one's word of honor is implicitly established by its not
being needed.

The second factor promoting the unregulated consequences of
promising is the pragmatism governing two aspects of promissory
behavior. The first is the rather general sense that promises are important for what they do, not for what they mean. The significance of
promises resides less in what is promised than in the activity that the
promises themselves implicitly sanction. In this social economy,
promises function as a negotiable currency rather than as a means to a
specific goal. They are an enabling mechanism, and the bearer of a
promissory note is entitled to unrestricted activity on the marriage market. This freedom, in contradistinction to that discussed in the previous
section, is less the freedom to live, such as Milly experiences after learning that she is doomed, than it is the freedom to live at someone else's
expense. The second pragmatic aspect of promising is somewhat nar-
rower than the first. It refers specifically to the belief that promises
should be judged exclusively in terms of ends, not means—that is, in
terms of actions, not intentions. The result of this principle is that no
behavior or activity, however inconsistent it may seem to be with the
promised action, is definitionally prohibited by that promise. In other
words, traders in the marriage market are subject only to the letter of the
law and may engage in any deception or coercion so long as a promise
is literally kept.

The third factor is an effect of the first two. A kind of promissory
polygamy follows directly from the contractual and pragmatic understanding of promises. The system virtually guarantees, first, that
promises will engender more promises and, second, that successive
promises will tend to cancel or contradict prior ones. Promise and effect
thus tend to be negatively related. It is not just that one thing leads to
another in an increasingly intricate and conflicted social arrangement.
Rather, it is that one thing necessitates another, which is conventionally
prohibited by the first. In practical terms, this means that a marriage
agreement does not remove the plighted from the market but gives them
a license to pursue other prospective spouses under the guidance of marriage brokers like Mrs. Lowder. Hence, Kate, engaged to Densher,
accepts the attentions of Lord Mark, while her intended courts Milly.
Mark, who has reached an understanding with Mrs. Lowder concerning

her niece, nevertheless pursues and proposes to Milly. No one, it seems, would be much troubled by Jeannette's homely observation about "crying halves." Engagements regularly proceed on an inclusive rather than exclusive basis.

Elizabeth Gaskell's *Wives and Daughters* (1866) provides a good introduction to this view of promising marriage. Very early in this novel, Lady Cumnor indicates the extent to which marital customs have changed and the force of marital promises has been vitiated: "I believe that one-third of the engagements I have heard of, have never come to marriages."[15] Her account proves to be, if anything, understated; certainly, it is so with regard to Cynthia Kirkpatrick, who breaks two of her three engagements. The premarital career of this "'Jilting Jessie'" (*WAD* 591) is even more sensational than Alice Vavasor's. Alice may have had more engagements (four), but at least hers are sequential. Cynthia is twice engaged to two men at the same time, or in her own unique marital calculus, has "half-engagements to two men" (*WAD* 535). When the second of Cynthia's fiancés runs off at the sight of the third, she seriocomically proclaims: "Gone. Oh, what a relief! It seems to be my fate never to be off with the old lover before I am on with the new" (*WAD* 656). Cynthia's actions, however, initiate a serious inquiry into courtship practices, especially into the role of secrecy in betrothal. Her secret promises of marriage, and the resulting confusion about who is free to court whom, are particularly relevant to *The Wings of the Dove* since Kate, Merton, and Lord Mark all simultaneously sustain, or appear to sustain, two lovers.

The most problematic of Cynthia's half-engagements is that to Roger Hamley. The fact that she is already engaged at the time of accepting Roger is itself a complicated issue, but when Robert Preston reluctantly agrees to release Cynthia from her prior commitment, that question, at least in terms of its immediate and pragmatic implications, is resolved. More difficult is the status of her understanding with Roger. They seem unable to agree as to whether or not they are actually engaged. He says no, even though he loves her; she says yes, even though she does not love him. Roger provides a novel twist on the idea of the half-engagement when he tells Cynthia, "I will not accept your pledge. I am bound, but you are free. I like to feel bound, it makes me happy and at peace, but with all the chances involved in the next two years, you must not shackle yourself by promises" (*WAD* 419). Roger's counsel is ironically prescient in this case, however, since promissory shackles are precisely what Cynthia is trying to escape—paradoxically by exchanging one loveless betrothal for another. Her second betrothal is motivated less by feeling for Roger than by the need to escape her existing secret engagement to Preston: "It seemed," she says, "a way of assuring myself that I was quite free" (*WAD* 522). The secrecy of her first engagement and the equivocation about her second transform both into half-engagements, during which Cynthia hopes to shop around for a better bargain. For her, promissory freedom is nothing more than the freedom to break promises with impunity. Cynthia's courtships of convenience—the convenience is financial in Preston's case, psychological in Roger's—are manipulative and deceitful, though perhaps less calculated than merely thoughtless. In her mind, a second engagement provides security from the first; it does not seem to suggest to her the fragility of engagements themselves.

Cynthia does not stay half-engaged to two men for very long. Once the imposing solidity of Roger Hamley's class and character banishes her fears of the spectral Preston, she is less eager to acknowledge her betrothal with its restraints upon freedom and flirtation. Thus she reverses her previous position, telling her stepfather, "It's hardly an engagement" (*WD* 432). Finally, she seems unable to bring herself even to say the word: "And, moreover, things are not quite arrived at the solemnity of—of—well—engagement. He would not have it so" (*WD* 483). Her mother also treats promises of marriage as if they were merely currency in an open marriage market. Despite Cynthia's public announcement, Clare does not consider her daughter to be engaged (*WD* 430). She can "afford to call it an 'engagement'" (*WAD* 645) only after learning that a more desirable match with Roger's older brother is not possible. Cynthia's stepfather, on the contrary, refuses the promissory nominalism characterizing the more opportunistic members of his family. He feels that Roger and Cynthia might not "call it an engagement, but of course it is one" (*WAD* 435). For Dr. Gibson, intention and convention are the norms by which promissory behavior is to be judged. Promises of marriage have force no matter what they are called and no matter who knows about them. A promise is a promise, and a secret promise is a means of mischief.

Dr. Gibson appears as the voice of reason in matters of engagement and breach of promise. He upholds the sanctity of promises, but also recognizes situations in which they ought to be dissolved. For example, he encourages Cynthia to keep her promise to Roger, arguing that a promise made by two can only be ended by two: "An engagement like yours cannot be broken off, except by mutual consent. You've only given others a great deal of pain without freeing yourself."[16] Yet upon seeing the state of her affections, he resignedly admits: "Then I do believe it's right for you to break it off" (*WAD* 601). In principle, engagements cannot be unilaterally ended, but practically speaking that should be the case. Thus when Squire Hamley asks about allowing Roger to renege on his agreement with Cynthia, Dr. Gibson says that when one person wants to break an engagement he would advise the other "to be equally willing" (*WAD* 437).

Were Cynthia more interested in keeping than in breaking engagements, she would have every legal right to hold her fiancés to their promises. Neither Roger Hamley nor Mr. Henderson would be justified in breaking his promise to marry solely on the grounds of Cynthia's pre-existing and continuing engagement to other men—an issue decided, as we have seen, in the case of *Beachey* v. *Brown*. In the eyes of the law, despite the fact that the numbers do not seem to add up, a half-engagement is an engagement and a half-cancellation is no cancellation at all. Dr. Gibson, on the contrary, would release Cynthia from her promise only as a last resort, and he holds her responsible for the suffering that her promissory profligacy causes. A half-engagement may turn out not to be an engagement—as those who thought they were betrothed to Cynthia painfully discover—but it cannot be made and abandoned with impunity. Whatever the law might say of Cynthia's case, she is guilty in Gaskell's eyes.

In *Wives and Daughters*, secret and half-engagements sustain an illusory sense of freedom. Cynthia attempts to live as if marriage were something one might cry halves about. She need not withdraw from the marriage market so long as no one knows that she is engaged, just as Osborne Hamley cannot escape that market so long as his marriage is kept a secret—no matter how much he pretends not to be a player in it. Clare and Cynthia indulge one scale of value, social and financial, at the expense of another, personal and moral. *Wives and Daughters* is a case study in promissory freedom of a different sort from that experienced by Hyacinth Robinson or Milly Theale insofar as Cynthia Kirkpatrick escapes from, rather than into, experience. Her experience, however, reflects upon that of Kate and her suitors.

In *The Wings of the Dove*, social promises, which are contractually defined, pragmatically motivated, and polygamously used, are often either unarticulated or, if articulated, secret. They vary from the relatively casual to the exacting. The former are illustrated by the early interactions of Milly and Kate. Their first week together is one of "presents, acknowledgements, mementos, pledges of gratitude and admiration, that were all on one side" (*WD* 115)—Milly's. All that she "would have asked in definite 'return,' as might be said, was to be . . . promised the privilege of a visit to Mrs. Condrip" (*WD* 115). Such a visit might seem to be the stuff of threats rather than promises, but since Milly is wealthy, she can afford not to drive a hard bargain. For a "Britannia of the market Place" (*WD* 37) like Mrs. Lowder, exchanges of the kind between Kate and Milly take on a more serious, and a much more coercive, bent. This point is made clear by Lionel Croy when he learns that

Mrs. Lowder consents to keep Kate only if she will have nothing to do with her father. Lionel's reaction is more practical than paternal: "That's her condition then. But what are her promises? Just what does she engage to do? You must work it, you know" (*WD* 29). Mr. Croy advises his daughter to get all that she can out of his wife's wealthy sister. With mock pathos, he describes this arrangement as "a cruel invidious treaty" and pathetically says, "I'm a poor ruin of a old dad to make a stand about giving up—I quite agree. But I'm not, after all, quite the old ruin not to get something *for* giving up" (*WD* 29). For Lionel Croy, social relations are a kind of commercial "treaty," and his daughter is a bargaining chip of inexplicable but considerable value.[17] Lord Mark obviously thinks this way as well. He tells Milly that Mrs. Lowder will "get back her money" for all that she has done in taking up the two American travelers (*WD* 106); that is to say, she will get a handsome return on her social investment. Milly, however, never fully masters the lesson in social economy provided by Lord Mark: "Nobody here, you know, does anything for nothing" (*WD* 106).

Secret contracts are not unknown among Mrs. Lowder's set, but far more common are tacit agreements between interested parties. Mrs. Lowder herself often dispenses with promises, largely because she trusts to the force of "her wonderful gilded claws" (*WD* 60). Promises are unnecessary, not because the parties involved trust each other, but because of the prehensile power of wealth. For instance, in the early stages of Mrs. Lowder's matchmaking, she summons Densher to Lancaster Gate to warn him off of Kate (as she will subsequently put him on to Milly). Densher is "so pleasantly affected by her asking no promise of him, her not proposing he should pay for her indulgence by his word of honour not to interfere, that he gave her a kind of general assurance of esteem" (*WD* 66). They may, in fact, like one another, but in the competitive marriage market they are clearly adversaries. Assurances of mutual esteem are not only worth very little but also misleading. In this instance, Densher fools himself, apparently thinking that promises can be dispensed with because he and Mrs. Lowder maintain friendly relations. "Friendly rivals" would perhaps be a better description of them than "friends," since Densher is all the while "working Lancaster Gate for all it was worth: just as it was, no doubt, working *him*, and just as the working and the worked were in London, as one might explain, the parties to every relation" (*WD* 116). Aunt Maud goes so far as to tell "the proper lie" (*WD* 224) for him—the lie that allows Milly to think that Densher is free—not because of esteem or concern for Densher but because it suits her own interests. His lie is initially one of omission: allowing Aunt Maud to believe that he won't interfere with her plans for her niece. But it immediately becomes one of commission: he becomes engaged to Kate on the first possible occasion after Mrs. Lowder has made her intentions so unequivocally known to him. The "mutual consent" in the parting of Aunt Maud and Densher is little more than mutual exploitation, and the absence of a pledge between them merely confirms what Mark has said to Milly.

Tacit and unarticulated agreements of this kind can lead to considerable confusion, as Lord Mark discovers when he proposes to Milly. After rejecting—and by way of consoling—him, Milly offers the counterproposal that he marry Kate, who, she believes, does not requite Densher's love. This proposal, like Aunt Maud's for Densher, conveniently coincides with her own romantic aspirations. When Mark informs her that Kate is "very much in love with a particular person" (*WD* 275), Milly claims to have Kate's "word for it" (*WD* 276) that this is not true. Mark, who has reason to believe otherwise, asks,

> "And what do you call her word."
>
> "Why, Lord Mark, what should *you* call her word?"
>
> "Ah I'm not obliged to say. I've not asked her. You apparently have."
>
> "We're very intimate so that, without prying into each other's affairs, she naturally tells me things."
>
> "You mean then she made you of her own movement the declaration you quote?"
>
> "I mean what I say: that when she spoke of her having no private interest—"
>
> "She took her oath to you?"
>
> "She left me in no doubt whatever of her being free."
>
> ". . . That's all very well, but why in the world, dear lady, should she be swearing to you?"
>
> "Because, as I've told you, we're such tremendous friends." (*WD* 276–77)

This brief dialogue clearly illustrates the differences between interested and disinterested commerce. Mark operates on the assumption that no one does anything for nothing, Milly on the belief that a wordless word of honor inheres between "tremendous friends." In addition to raising the issue of when promises are required or desirable ("why in the world . . . should she be swearing to you?"), this scene asks the more fundamental question of what actually constitutes a promise ("What do you call her word?").

With regard to the latter issue, the conversation does little if anything to clarify the problem. Lord Mark's cross-examination yields no explicit evidence of a promise, and the text provides no indication that one exists. That Kate misleads Milly is certain, but that she does so by means of a promise is not. Milly offers as proof of Kate's "word" the intimacy that leads Kate "naturally to tell me things." But telling is not promising, and Milly seems merely to have overstated the case when saying that Kate "has given me her word." This likelihood is reinforced by Milly's subsequent sense "that she had given rather more than she intended or than she should be able, when once more getting herself into hand, theoretically to defend" (*WD* 277). Milly infers from Kate's behavior the promise that would have been consistent with it, a hermeneutic strategy successfully applied to her by Susan Stringham. The interpretive procedure is sound, but Milly's zeal in applying it is excessive, as it was in her reading of Sir Luke Strett. She misleads Mark by invoking the language and concepts of interested commerce to describe a relationship that, as far as she is concerned, is disinterested.

Ironically both Aunt Maud, who believes only in interested social relations, and Milly, who accepts the possibility of disinterested relations between friends, dispense with explicit promises. Each, as it turns out, makes a mistake in doing so. Mrs. Lowder places too much trust in her own power and as a result presumes that she need not extract promises from those weaker than or dependent upon herself. Milly, on the contrary, places too much trust in others and as a result assumes that an implicit word of honor has been given to her by Kate.[18] That she has not asked for Kate's word may be to her credit; it is not, however, in her interest.

With regard to the former issue, that is, the question of when promises are required, Mark may well ask why Kate would swear an oath concerning the state of her affections. Milly's statements make little sense according to the logic of interested commerce and do not correspond to his own sense of things. According to his mores, neither is the state of Kate's affections any of Milly's business nor is it something about which one would swear an oath. Since there is no obvious indication of what Kate is giving and what she expects in return, Mark is likely to think that the oath is given precisely because it is false. Furthermore, if he is "given" to Kate, then Milly is free to pursue Densher. Milly's sense, however, is not of free trade entailing an exchange of men but of free relations among intimates, involving voluntary trust rather than contractual security. She implies that between intimate friends promises are neither requested nor coerced but inhere in unspoken mutual esteem of the kind largely unrecognized by Mrs. Lowder and company.

That Mark "should so catechize" (*WD* 276) Milly is surprising, given what readers are led to believe concerning the state of his own affections, or at least of the publicly pledged state of those affections. After Mark pursues Milly to Venice, Kate is in the unusual situation of justifying her public suitor's behavior to her private fiancé and, as if that were not enough, at the same time of assuring the latter that the former is a prospective husband only in her Aunt's eyes, not in her own:

He's [Mark's] not committed to us—he was having his try. Mayn't an unsatisfied man always have his try?"

"And come back afterwards with confidence in a welcome, to the victim of his inconstancy?"

Kate consented, as for argument, to be thought of as a victim. "Oh but he has *had* his try at *me*. So it's alright."

"Through your also having, you mean, refused him?"

She balanced an instant during which Densher might have just wondered if pure historic truth were to suffer a slight strain. But she dropped on the right side. "I haven't let it come to that. I've been too discouraging. Aunt Maud considers, no doubt, that she has a pledge from him in respect to me; a pledge that would have been broken if Milly had accepted him. As the case stands that makes no difference." (WD 292)

Of course, what Mrs. Lowder considers to be a pledge and what Lord Mark has actually said to her may be quite different, but at the very least it seems misleading for him to question Milly, to whom he has just proposed, about promises made by Kate, whom he has courted in the past and will court again upon returning to England. His inconstancy suggests that of Willoughby Patterne (though Mark's spiteful motivation goes beyond egotism to outright maliciousness) and makes clear that practical rather than romantic concerns govern his proposals of marriage.

Perhaps the most telling aspect of the conversation between Kate and Densher is the notion of promise that it reveals. Kate seems not at all bothered by Lord Mark's courtship of Milly. In her eyes, his pledge to Mrs. Lowder would be broken, not by his proposing to Milly, only by her accepting the offer. This notion, of course, justifies her own behavior to Lord Mark while secretly engaged to Densher. As Kate would have it, promises have nothing to do with intention and everything to do with action. Mark may try to break his pledge to Mrs. Lowder, but because he is prevented from doing so by Milly's rejection, he is faithful.

Densher is understandably troubled by the implications of this view for Kate's promise to him. Mystified by Mark's staying at Lancaster Gate during Christmas, Densher asks Kate for further explanation, and she makes clear that her "discouragement" of Lord Mark has at last led to an explicit "refusal" (WD 390). Densher persists in jealously reading the good relations between Mrs. Lowder and Lord Mark as evidence of a continuing understanding between them concerning Kate, and he is unsure whether he has received the "historic truth" or a "poetic version" of her dealings with her inconstant suitor. At issue between them is less the ugly reality at the center of the swirl of "beautiful fictions" than the impossibility of reconciling the competing claims of interested and disinterested commerce, of action and intention, of promissory polygamy and personal monogamy.

Kate admits that "too discouraging" does not convey the full story of her dealings with Lord Mark:

> "I've been trying to place exactly, as to its date, something that did happen to me while you were in Venice. I mean a talk with him. He spoke to me—spoke out."
>
> "Ah there you are!" said Densher who had wheeled around.
>
> "Well, if I'm 'there,' as you so gracefully call it, by having refused to meet him as he wanted—as he pressed—I plead guilty to being so. Would you have liked me," she went on, "to give him an answer that would have kept him from going?" (*WD* 389–90)

Kate's discomfort with the subject is an indication of her duplicitous actions—actions with regard to Lord Mark that mirror his behavior to her, Densher's to Milly, and—Densher fears—Kate's to him. (Given his own behavior in Venice, Densher may be further troubled by Kate's formulation, "meet him as he wanted." Mark does leave Venice, but what did he want and what did he get?) Having previously said that she discouraged Mark, Kate must now answer a direct question concerning her "encouragement": "Of course I had been decent to him. Otherwise where *were* we?" (*WD* 390). Although decency seems to stop short of a polygamous promise, neither she nor Densher anticipates the disorientation that their double courtships engender. The promissory freedom spawned by their engagement leads to a course of action that ultimately renders their promise of marriage untenable. The "contemporary London female" may be "inevitably battered, honourably free" (*WD* 50), but by the end of the novel, the contemporary London couple has sustained a battering of a degree and nature that severely compromises their freedom and suggests that it is more dubious than honorable. For them, as for all players in the marriage game, promissory freedom has a markedly pejorative connotation. It is more properly called promissory license, or perhaps promissory licentiousness.

The most significant promise in *The Wings of the Dove* is, of course, the secret engagement of Kate Croy and Merton Densher. It is the unseen origin of much of the action that follows, and it instigates a sequence of vows offered, requested, and exchanged by the lovers themselves. Their secret betrothal raises some of the same questions that Cynthia Kirkpatrick's does; however, this "rich compact" engenders a more complicated set of circumstances than do her half-engagements. Central among these questions is the effect of an engagement known to no one but the "plighted pair" (*WD* 284). Their unexpected betrothal seems entirely consistent with an already unpredictable courtship, one which "if it was to be shy or secret . . . might have taken place almost anywhere better than under Mrs. Lowder's windows. . . . The fact was that the relation between these young persons abounded in such oddities as were not inaptly symbolised by assignations that had a good deal more appearance than motive" (*WD* 46–47). Chief among these "oddities" is the engagement itself, which triggers two inversely related but interconnected lines of action: as Kate and Merton become more free in their dealings on the marriage market, they become more enmeshed in a chain of promises to one another.

That chain begins with a meeting that is accidental; a courtship that is unconventional; and an engagement that is spontaneous. It is not five minutes after meeting him at a party that Kate realizes: "something between them had—well, she couldn't call it anything but *come*" (*WD* 49). Densher gives "his word" that had he not met her he would have left the party "but that now he saw how sorry he should have been to miss it" (*WD* 48). That this "something" becomes anything more is due to a "happy hazard six months later" (*WD* 49). They meet on a train, communicating at first by means of "movements, smiles, abstentions" (*WD* 49). As at the party, the intensity of their experience seems disproportionate to its extent. Kate feels that "[n]ever in life before had she so let herself go; for always before—so far as small adventures could have been in question for her—there had been, by the vulgar measure, more to go upon" (*WD* 50). From the outset, then, their relationship is characterized by the dramatic contrast between appearance and motive that the narrator associates with their meetings in the park outside Mrs. Lowder's windows.

James comically portrays their mutual glimpse and traces the uncertain progression from silent acknowledgment across the "choked compartment" (*WD* 49), to Densher's impatient travel from vacant place to vacant place until seated beside her, to their finally leaving the train together. This journey-within-a-journey is an emblem of their travels through courtship: fitful, indirect, with Densher's acquiring his objective at the cost of missing his stop. The emblem is misleading, however, if it implies that the two journeys proceed at uniform rates. While the train's course is regular and predictable, the lovers' progress is random. Kate and Merton "were not in the least meeting where they had left off, but ever so much further on, and that these added links added still another between Hight Street and Notting Hill Gate, and then worked between the latter station and Queen's Road an extension really inordinate" (*WD* 50). The most disproportionate extension or intensification occurs at Lancaster Gate and right under Mrs. Lowder's nose.

From this point on, Kate and Densher appear to all the world as "old friends," but they are, in fact, secret lovers:

> They had accepted their acquaintance as too short for an engagement, but they had treated it as long enough for almost anything else, and marriage was somehow before them like a temple without an avenue. They belonged to the temple and they met in the grounds; they were in the stage at which grounds in general offered much scattered refreshment. . . . [T]hey were lovers; she rejoiced to herself and, frankly, to him, in their wearing of the name; but, distinguished creature that, in her way, she was, she took a view of this character that scarce squared with the conventional. (*WD* 52–53)

One would expect engagement to be that "avenue," but such is not to be the case, even though "Densher had at the very first pressed the question" (*WD* 52). Even at this stage of the journey, he resigns himself to Kate's itinerary, getting off wherever she does whether or not it accords with his own wishes.

Kate would seem to have little reason to make a secret engagement to Densher a stop on her marital journey. While she may be her sister's sister and willing, therefore, to consider an "unnatural marriage" (*WD* 55), she is also her father's daughter and her aunt's niece. Sharing their attitude toward "material things" (*WD* 35), she seems unlikely to succumb to the temptations offered by Densher. His eccentric background, however, provides a seductive alternative to Lancaster Gate. Densher is attractive because of "his history rich, his sources full, his outline anything but common" (*WD* 71). Interested in "what sort of queer creature, what sort of social anomaly" (*WD* 79) he might be, Kate describes him as "having tasted of the tree and being thereby prepared to assist her to eat" (*WD* 72). This reference to the Fall (with the gender roles reversed) might seem an ominous description of those seeking access to a temple, but it is consistent with the many incongruities characterizing the scene and all that leads up to it. The most substantial discrepancy is between Kate's and her aunt's ideas of a suitable spouse. Mrs. Lowder desires "a great man" for her niece; Densher is but "half a Briton" (*WD* 65, 70), and an impoverished one at that. Mrs. Lowder tells Densher to "give up her niece for her and go his way in peace" (*WD* 64)—which he all but promises to do. The direct result of this dismissal, however, is betrothal not banishment.

Kate takes unconventionality to a new extreme in pledging herself to Densher in direct opposition to her Aunt's command. Throughout the courtship, her "constant perception of the incongruity of things" (*WD* 56) and a concomitant attraction to the unconventional have contributed to the "free and humorous colour" (*WD* 55) of their conversations. Their discursive freedoms stand in opposition to the stifling of their social and sexual desire. "[I]n the crucible of their happy discussion" (*WD* 68), frustration is vented by means of verbal displacement:

> it was quite as if they had settled, for intercourse, on the short cut of the fantastic and the happy language of exaggeration. It had come to be definite between them at a primary stage that, if they could have no other straight way, the realm of thought at least was open to them. They could think whatever they liked about whatever they would—in other words they could say it. Saying it for each other, for each other alone, only of course added to the taste. (*WD* 56)

As a result of this intellectual and discursive freedom, their talk is a "small floating island" (*WD* 56); converse with others "a dull desert of the conventional" (*WD* 58). That island yields exotic fruits of conversation as flavorful as they are colorful. Discourse for them takes on a sensuous, even a sexual, character: Kate's speeches "liberally, joyfully, intensely adopted and . . . embraced, drew him again as close to her, and held him as long, as their condition permitted" (*WD* 75). The pleasure of such talk—in Barthes's sense of *plaisir*—reaches its climax in the promise of marriage.[19]

A sudden and secret engagement is the culmination of both the incongruity and the erotic displacement of their courtship—the promise itself being a figure of displacement, since in promising the word is taken for the thing. The language of their betrothal is "fantastic and happy," as before, but also "warm" and "transparent" (transparency, of course, being the invisible sign of Edenic language):

> He saw after a little that she had been following some thought of her own, and he had been feeling the growth of something determinant even through the extravagance of much of the pleasantry. . . . Suddenly she said to him with extraordinary beauty: "I engage myself to you for ever."
> . . . They had exchanged vows and tokens, sealed their rich compact, solemnised, so far as breathed words and murmured sounds and lighted eyes and clasped hands could do it, their agreement to belong only, and to belong tremendously, to each other. They were to leave the place accordingly an affianced couple.[20] (*WD* 72)

Their engagement seems more than is usually the case a matter of words. They have reached a pinnacle of a courtship of and by words. Densher replies to Kate: "And I pledge you—I call God to witness!—every spark of my faith; I give you every drop of my life" (*WD* 72). His exaggeration is typical of the semiotic surplus of the scene. In a novel in which promises are typically oblique, ambiguous, and uncertain, this one is explicit and excessive. Their engagement is established by testimony, vows, an exchange of tokens, a contract, joined hands, a nearly religious solemnity, the invocation of God, and a romantic intensification of "breathed words and murmured sounds and lighted eyes." The redundancy, the excess, seems both a defense against and an acknowledgment of the passional gap between words and action, and of the social gulf between engagement and marriage—to say nothing of the verbal abyss between promise and fulfillment.

Secrecy frees Kate and Densher to act as if they were not engaged and to "work" the social situation in which they are trapped. Immediately after giving his promise to Kate, Densher thinks how lucky it is that Aunt Maud "had demanded of him no promise that would tie his hands[;] they should be able to propitiate their star in their own way and yet remain loyal" (*WD* 73). "Loyal," however, seems exactly what Kate and Densher cannot claim to be. Despite his rationalizations, he cannot maintain that a secret engagement is in keeping with the impression given to Mrs. Lowder. Thus he seems no different from Lord Mark or Mrs. Lowder herself in treating engagement as a promissory note admitting the bearer to Vanity Fair. His own statement reveals a duplicitous contradiction: "I don't see that we deceive her. At a given hour, you see, she must be undeceived" (*WD* 73). Obviously, someone who has not been deceived need not be undeceived. Densher himself is operating under a delusion—one sustained by the promise he has just made to Kate.

Kate sees the promise as but one move in a "prodigious game of patience" (*WD* 68) in which Aunt Maud "must take her risks" (*WD* 73). The engagement establishes Kate and Densher as worthy players in the game since they are now "practically united and splendidly strong" (*WD* 73). Its secrecy counteracts the superior financial and social resources of their opponents. Because the game is one of patience, time is of the essence, and by a secret engagement the lovers, as Kate remarks, will "have gained time" (*WD* 73).[21] In this regard, the engagement has an ironic biblical echo, for time is precisely what Adam and Eve "gain" by tasting the forbidden fruit. Betrothal may have made Kate and Densher "deeper and closer" (*WD* 73), but there is no sense of a fortunate fall in what follows. To modify Milly's remark (when looking at the Bronzino portrait) to suit this circumstance: "They will never be better than this."

The dynamics of play in this game of patience are even more complex than my account has so far suggested. For if the lovers are united against Aunt Maud, they are also divided from each other, and not only in the sense that their engagement commits each to the courtship of someone else. Kate also gains time with regard to Densher because her importunate and impatient lover will now be less likely to "press the question." Even though he himself recognizes that they are "trying to temporize in so special a way" (*WD* 196–97), Densher must still on occasion be exhorted: "don't spoil it: wait for me and give me time" (*WD* 196). In some ways, then, as in *Jane Eyre*, the promise functions to postpone rather than to procure the promised act, although in this case the delay is not an eroticizing one. The stratagem proves to be spectacularly successful—so successful, in fact, that the postponement becomes indefinite.

The time acquired by virtue of their betrothal becomes especially valuable once Milly appears and becomes an unwitting player in the game of patience—a game for which, given her medical condition, she is particularly ill suited. Densher's "permitted and proper and harmless American relation" (*WD* 224) takes a devious twist when both aunt and niece recognize Milly's impact on the marriage market and encourage Densher not to neglect her.[22] Mrs. Lowder summons Densher to her drawing room for a second time, and once again unwisely fails to elicit a promise that he will hold up his end of the tacit agreement. This time she sweetens the deal by offering "the American girl as a distraction for him. . . . The pieces fell together for him as he felt her thus buying him off, and buying him—it would have been funny if it hadn't been so grave—with Miss Theale's money" (*WD* 222–23). By remaining silent, Densher conveys the false impression that he accepts the bargain.

Since Aunt Maud and Kate urge similar courses of action, despite their contradictory objectives, Densher wonders about the status of his "rich compact" with his fiancée. This anxiety prompts him to request a new promise—the second in the promissory chain that binds them:

> He waited again an instant. "Then you swear to it?"
>
> "To 'it'? To what?"
>
> "Why that you do 'like' me. Since it's all for that, you know, that I'm letting you do—well, God knows what with me."
>
> She gave at this, with a stare, a disheartened gesture—the sense of which she immediately further expressed. "If you don't believe in me then, after all, hadn't you better break off before you've gone further?"
>
> "Break off with you?"
>
> "Break off with Milly." (*WD* 237)

Ironically, Densher asks from Kate what Mrs. Lowder does not request from him, that is, a confirming promise. His request indicates that their deception of others has begun to insinuate itself into their own relations. Interested and disinterested commerce, as Hume defines them, seem to have been reversed. Lovers feel compelled to exchange promises, while rivals in the marriage market do not. The effect of this apparent reversal is to de-eroticize promising; in fact, Densher's anxiety drives him to ask something that he knows will be anaphrodisiacal to Kate. His mis-understanding of whom he is to break off with reveals the very fear that the requested promise is intended to alleviate. Densher cannot be entirely consoled by Kate's response because, while his interpretation demonstrates that she is foremost in his mind, hers suggests the plan itself is predominant.

Unlike the semiotic surplus of their plighting, the second scene is characterized by indirection taking the form of understatement. Densher asks that Kate promise only that she likes him—initially that she swear to nothing more than "it." The mode of their previous discourse—"the fantastic and happy language of exaggeration"—ominously gives way to its understated opposite. Densher's request is doubly strange since it seems unnecessary in form (why a promise of liking from someone already sworn to loving) and in fact (why another promise from the per-son he's already engaged to). The incongruities of the scene attenuate rather than intensify erotic potential. Densher neither elicits the requested promise nor quickens Kate's rhetorical pulse. Her response can only confirm his mounting fear about "his deficiency in the things a man of any taste, so engaged, so enlisted, would have liked to make sure of being able to show—imagination, tact, positively even humour" (*WD* 238). Thus he finds himself lacking reassurance about his qualities, her love, and their treatment of Milly. Densher wants to feel that if they are acting badly toward Milly, then at least they do so for each other and in the cause of love. Having begun by asking for a sign of love, he ends by giving a sign of complicity: "Well then, just as you like. I'll stay and do my best for you" (*WD* 237).

In the ensuing conversation, he asks directly that she "swear again you love me" (*WD* 238). Requesting more, he receives even less: "She looked about, at door and window, as if he were asking for more than he said. 'Here? There's nothing between us here,' Kate smiled" (*WD* 238).[23] Her rejoinder is an ironic evasion, and his doubts, now com-pounded by self-doubt, must be heightened. The repeated request for reassurance is greeted with irony, and not "the warm transparent irony, into which their livelier intimacy kept plunging like a confident swim-mer" (*WD* 72) on the occasion of their betrothal. There may be some comfort for him in the fact that Kate's response is consistent with the style that sustained their earliest courtship, but this rhetorical mode now seems distancing not unifying, ominous not erotic. Kate's "violent and unfeminine" (*WD* 56) discourse is now more troubling because it seems less an expressive style than a principle of social conduct. Kate's control of language has "something in it that bent him at once to conviction and to reaction" (*WD* 292). He may not take her comment literally, know-ing full well that the promise of marriage is not site-specific, valid in one house and not in another, but he must take it seriously.

His fears are surely augmented by the "hollow promise" that he subsequently gives to Milly. He makes one promise (to Milly) in order to sustain another one (to Kate), all the while dimly conscious that the latter is called into question by the former. The circumstances of the promises are not equal—inviting someone to tea is not on a par with plighting one's troth—yet there is a link between them. Milly has asked to visit Densher's rooms, a plan to which he falsely professes "happy readiness" (*WD* 283). He tells, therefore, a "proper lie" of his own, which, like Aunt Maud's, gives Milly the impression that he is free to court her. The lie also protects the third promissory link in the lovers' chain: Densher's test of Kate's loyalty in the wake of her failure to repromise herself to him. Because he intends these rooms as the site of his sexual trial, he is squeamish about Milly's proposed visit. His sensitivity is less a sign of conscience than a confirmation of his involvement in the sexual and marital intrigues of this society. His turpitude is confirmed, first, by the sexual bargain that he strikes with his intended, and, second, by the false promise that he gives to Milly to avoid "spoiling, should one put it grossly, his game" (*WD* 283)—a game that by now perhaps should be called "Impatience." Densher is callous enough to subject his fiancée to a sexual ultimatum yet fastidious enough to prevent Milly from entering rooms rented with this assignation in mind. He has reached the nadir of his dealings with both. Seeing that Milly's innocence and beauty (*WD* 283) are incompatible with "his game," he compounds the crime with a false promise rather than alter "the reality of his now mature motive" (*WD* 283).

From the outset, Kate and Densher have had differing expectations of their time and intimacy with one another: "Life might prove difficult—was evidently going to; but meanwhile they had each other, and that was everything. This was her reasoning, but meanwhile, for *him*, each other was what they didn't have, and it was just the point. Repeatedly, however, it was a point that, in the face of strange and special things, he judged it rather awkwardly gross to urge" (*WD* 53–54). Densher feels this disparity all the more acutely while he is in America, during which time "his desires had grown." He now thinks it a mistake to hold out "against an impatience that, prolonged and exasperated, made a man ill" (*WD* 189). His "illness" seems an insignificant malady compared to Milly's, but it makes both poor players of the waiting game. Upon returning to England, Densher laments having "nowhere to 'take' his love" and resents the social mores that keep them apart. She would not, he knows, accept an invitation to come into his apartment, and

> he shouldn't be able to ask her, would feel he couldn't without betraying a deficiency of what would be called, even at their advanced stage, respect for her: that again was all that was clear except the further fact

that it was maddening. . . . [R]espect, in their game, seemed some-how—he scarce knew what to call it—a fifth wheel to the coach. It was properly an inside thing, not an outside, a thing to make love greater, not to make happiness less. (*WD* 188)

This sexual frustration and insecurity reach crisis points in the wake of Kate's continuing elusiveness and her evasiveness about repromising her love. Densher requires physical not verbal assurance, just as he had when he returned from America: "The long embrace in which they held each other was the rout of evasion. . . . It was stronger than an uttered vow. . . . This settled so much, and settled it so thoroughly, that there was nothing left to ask her to swear to. Oaths and vows apart, now they could talk. It seemed in fact only now that their questions were put on the table" (*WD* 196). That talk, of course, leads directly to his current anxiety and to his request of another vow. Densher is no longer quite so fastidious, and Kate's "antidotes and remedies and subtle sedatives" (*WD* 189) are no longer quite so efficacious. He jettisons the fifth wheel, respect, and strikes a sexual bargain with Kate, learning only after it is too late that the coach does not ride very smoothly without this seem-ingly supererogatory wheel.

Their agreement is essentially that Densher will, first, "tell any lie you want, any your idea requires" (*WD* 294) and, second, stay on in Venice after Kate leaves, "if you'll come to me. On *your* honour" (*WD* 311). "Honour," repeated three times in this conversation, is incompat-ible with the circumstances in which is it invoked; the test compromises the engagement whose worth it is designed to prove. Their betrothal, voluntarily made and fully savored, has a liminal status: it exists at a threshold between verbal and erotic experience. It is an embrace, a cou-pling in several senses of the term. This promise, on the contrary, which in itself is neither free nor pleasurable, has a criminal status, not only in the sense of the Victorian euphemism, criminal conversation, but also because of its venal nature. By coercing a sexual union, this compact sev-ers the connection between verbal and erotic experience, and interposes an even greater distance between the lovers.

Densher's motivations, beyond the sexual, are various but uniformly discreditable. The test first and foremost is intended to buttress his crumbling ego. He is suspicious and jealous of Lord Mark (*WD* 292); his masculine authority is cast into doubt by Kate, who, even if she refuses to do "*all* the work for" him (*WD* 308), has certainly done most of it. In part, he demands a sexual favor as a sign of his male power, which is briefly restored after Kate "had come, that once, to stay, as people called it" (*WD* 312). He experiences a sense of exuberance and elation not felt since his betrothal: "It had simply *worked*, his idea, the idea he had made her accept; and all erect before him, really covering the ground as far as he could see, was the fact of the gained success that this represented. . . . [S]o that at present, *with* the help rendered, it seemed to acknowledge its office and to set up, for memory and faith, an insistence of its own" (*WD* 312). This success is short-lived, however, because the sexual contract explicitly articulates what has heretofore been largely unspoken: the plot to deceive Milly. Densher can no longer rationalize his behavior and must now openly acknowledge that he is willing not only "to make up to a sick girl" (*WD* 216) but also "to propose to a dying girl" (310). Sexual satisfaction has come at too dear a price. The loss of respect, as a result of his sexual relation with Kate, and the blow to his self-esteem, as a result of his admittedly deceitful relation with Milly, erase the memory traces of a satisfying sexual union.

Kate's acceptance of Densher's deal has been anticipated by her "surrender" (196) to his embrace after his return from the States. On that occasion, she demonstrated "that she could gratefully take it" (*WD* 196); on this one, she proves her claim to be a person "who can do what I don't like" (*WD* 309). She returns to London with the assurance that Densher will carry out their contract. That the nature of their original promise—freely given and without "consideration"—has changed is evident from Densher's pondering Kate's departure:

> He was giving himself up—that was quite enough—to the general feeling of his renewed engagement to fidelity. The force of the engagement, the quantity of the article to be supplied, the special solidity of the contract, the way, above all, as a service for which the price named by him had been magnificently paid, his equivalent office was to take effect—such items might well fill his consciousness when there was nothing from outside to interfere. (*WD* 313)

Quantity of supply, solidity of contract, service, price, and payment: there is little doubt that this "half-Briton" has become a worthy competitor to the "Britannia of the market Place." The phrase "engagement to fidelity" is a suggestive inversion of "fidelity to an engagement." Densher has twice asked Kate to confirm the latter; what he now does is to assert the former, that is, to activate (to engage) the principle upon which business is transacted, mutual indebtedness (fidelity). Having now received consideration for his promise, that is, sexual services from Kate, he may be counted on to maintain his end of the bargain. His statement, therefore, does not express personal loyalty; rather, it is a metapromissory contract calculated to insure that upon which contracts are based: fidelity. Densher may feel faithfulness anew, but it is less to Kate than to the contractual arrangement by which they are bound. "Consideration" in its legal, not its affective, sense is now the operative principle in their relation. Densher engages "that kind of fidelity of which the other name was careful action" (*WD* 314).

After exacting his price from Kate, Densher discovers that their actions have an unintended consequence: "He had in fine judged his friend's pledge in advance as an inestimable value, and what he must now know his case for was that of a possession of the value to the full. Wasn't it perhaps even rather the value that possessed *him*, kept him thinking of it and waiting on it, turning round and round it making sure of it again from this side and that?" (*WD* 313). Promissory freedom in this instance takes the form of "the oppression of success" (*WD* 313). He may have gotten the satisfaction his wilting ego demanded: "[i]t had simply *worked*, his idea, the ideas he had made her accept." The idea is working him, however, for he now knows "that to be faithful to Kate he had positively to take his eyes, his arms, his lips straight off her" (*WD* 314) and apply them to Milly, to whom he must now "lie with his lips" (*WD* 316). Having engaged one notion of fidelity, interested or contractual, he cannot avoid violating the other, disinterested or personal. Thus, in staying on in Venice and courting Milly, he feels that "at least [he] wasn't disloyal to Kate; that was the very tone of their bargain. So was it, by being loyal, another kind of lie, the lie of the uncandid profession of a motive" (*WD* 320). His lie to Milly in Venice has, like his compact with Kate, an unintended consequence. For having worked Milly, he discovers that in death she is working him, and with a vengeance.

That working is apparent in the final situation of promising that occurs between Kate and Densher. Just at the point of acquiring "the thing for which we worked together" (*WD* 402), Densher changes the terms of the agreement. He has promised that after their sexual liaison he will "do everything." But as with Hyacinth Robinson, the promise engenders an experience, in this case the courtship of Milly, that alters the promiser's circumstances and attitude. Densher, who finds Milly too innocent to breathe the air of his rooms in Venice, is too guilty to accept the money he knows she has left him. His offer of a "formal oath" as to his lack of curiosity about Milly's will is a rejection of deception, an attempt to distance himself from the past, and an expression of fidelity (in the commercial sense) to his engagement. Kate, however, feels that Densher reneges on the conditions upon which their marriage is to take place. The betrothed are now in the "interested" position of negotiating by means of counterpromises the conditions upon which they will keep their original promise. Kate suspects that his refusing the money shows that his fidelity (in the emotional sense) has changed. Thus she will accept his new offer only on the condition that he give his "word of honour that [he's] not in love with her memory" (*WD* 403). This memory, however, fades less easily than that of his sexual success. The time purchased by their engagement cannot outlast the impression that Milly has stamped upon the lovers. Kate sadly is right: they will "never be again as [they] were" (WD 403).

Milly's death has one final unintended consequence. The sentence of death has meant, for her, the freedom to live, but, for Densher, the burden of knowledge. Kate is right that "she died for you then that you might understand her" (WD 402). Densher's knowledge, however, and Kate's awareness of it are ironic. Like Adam and Eve after the fall, they know that their expectations have not been fulfilled and that their lives can never be the same as a result. Kate and Merton painfully learn that promises may be intentional acts, but that their consequences seldom correspond with either intentions or expectations.

AFTERWORD

Cross Your Heart . . .

Paul Klee's *Das Wertpaket* (1939) wordlessly emblematizes the subject and the preoccupations of this study. The embrace of the central figures is orthographically "voiced" by the red "X" that the lovers seem to have and to hold in common. Heart-high, at the center of the image, this sanguine sign—standing out against the blackness common to figures and background alike—chromatically inscribes both the carnal and the communal. "X" literally marks the spot, the place belonging neither to one nor the other of the figures separately, but shared exclusively by them. This conjoint space is symbolically signified, first, by the crossing of lines—of "I's" or separate selves—to make the letter "X," the sign of connected lives; and, second, by the vibrant color of this intersection. The white borders of individuality are transformed into the color of communion.

If, however, "X" marks the spot, then it also seems to occlude the heart—a carmine chiasmus resides where a valentine should be. Expecting a heart, we find, instead, an ambiguous "X." Klee possibly intends no more than an echo of the child's or the lover's "xoxo"—a signature perhaps either studiously but clumsily or hurriedly but fondly appended to the end of a note. In this case, the striking red mark is a sanguine abbreviation for "kiss"—a metonymy of love. Or perhaps this "X" crosses, rather than crosses out, the heart. In this case, it echoes the childlike urgency of "Cross my heart and hope to die"—an assurance of honesty and reliability hyperbolically juxtaposed with the dire consequences of breaking one's word. Keeping a promise, however, usually appears to be a matter of life and death only to a child or a childish adult, for example, a comic figure like Willoughby Patterne, who claims that a "broken pledge [is] a form of suicide," or a pathetic one, like Mr. Boldwood or Mrs. O'Hara (*An Eye for an Eye*), for whom a broken engagement becomes the source of insanity and murder. Unlike these extreme instances, most Victorians resign themselves to the fact that a breach of promise is a matter of "substantial damages" not of dueling and dying, and certainly not of suicide or homicide.

Such dark contingencies, however, are suggested by the encompassing blackness of Klee's painting, which adumbrates a threatening unknown against which lovers clasp one another. And while there is perhaps no more hopeful promise in the course of adult lives than that of love, neither is there a more uncertain one. Klee's couple is framed by a hint of opaque light, a fringe of color behind or around an otherwise stygian setting. This modest intimation of hope is reflected in the tentative gesture of extended forefinger and thumb. This frozen moment is that of the promise: desire is expressed but not fulfilled; fingers reach but do not grasp—the unenclosed space reminding us that promises may be broken. The image is in fact paradoxical: it portends closure but presents only incompletion. Promises carry with them the specter of all that might be involved in their breach—disappointment and suffering or, more dramatically, anarchy and death.

The figures in *Das Wertpaket* turn to one another against a darkness that, significantly, includes even them. As James makes clear in *The Wings of the Dove*, promises against circumambient corruption may lead to corruption. And if Klee's "X" is read, not as heart-high, but as inscribed upon an embracing arm, then it aptly figures Kate and Merton's secret engagement. Rather than "wearing their hearts on their sleeves," these lovers display only a generic signature, a nearly anonymous "X." A "rich compact" engages James's characters not only *to* one another but also *in* a process of contamination. Their promise to marry involves them in exactly what the promise of love professes to defy, the prospect of death. Kate's exaggerated and even childlike, "I engage myself to you forever," unwittingly acknowledges this fact. Her statement is ironically accurate because they will always be engaged with (if not to) each other and always enshrouded by Milly's wings.

Klee's combination of the childlike and the adult (a simple line drawing of a mature embrace), as well as of the playful and the serious, echoes the contradictions of the valentine with which this study begins. Bathsheba Everdene's flippant card has a dual audience: "a chubby-faced child" and a middle-aged farmer. Furthermore, it carries a double message: "The rose is red . . . ," the nursery rhyme intended for Teddy, and "'Marry me,' the extraordinary . . . motto" actually sent to Boldwood (*FMC* 78, 79). In *Far from the Madding Crowd*, ill-considered intentions have tragic consequences: Bathsheba's "insistent red seal" becomes for Boldwood an indelible "bolt of blood on the retina" (*FMC* 81, 80), just as Troy—"a bright scarlet spot" and later "a dim spot of artificial red" (*FMC* 133, 143)—distorts Bathsheba's vision and himself becomes marked by a red spot, the blood of a fatal gunshot wound. Klee's vision, in contrast to Hardy's, is tragicomic. His red emblem is gently humorous, melancholic perhaps, but also heartwarming.

The gentle irony of the painting is accentuated by its title, *Das Wertpaket* or Insured Parcel. Like the stamp of a postal inspector, the red

"X" marks this package for its monetary value rather than its expressive potential. The business of insurance transforms words and gifts into commodities. Communication becomes contractual—as if the fact of delivery could be equated with felicitous expression and understanding. Delivery is promised (or damages will be paid), but can communication be guaranteed? Similarly, promises are a form of insurance—but against what (the future?) and of what (if love, what is its value?). *Das Wertpaket* succinctly represents the problem of promising and the dichotomous understanding of betrothal in Victorian society. Klee's image and title constitute a double-voiced, mildly dissonant chord: erotic and economic, interested and disinterested (in Hume's terms), private and public (in James's). Figuratively, the title is sentimental, describing love, lovers, and the desire for mutual protection. Literally, of course, love and loved ones are not to be replaced like so many insured packages damaged in transit. Klee reminds us, if only obliquely, of the dangers of conveying our love to another, or—in a now familiar Victorian trope—of crossing the Rubicon.

That the boundaries of the marital Rubicon are redrawn after Victoria's reign (a point symbolized by the abdication of Edward VIII and raised by the divorce of Prince Charles) explains why my consideration of betrothal ends well before 1939, the date of Klee's painting. For the Victorians, marriage is still a Rubicon, invariably so ideologically and virtually so legally. The site of contested values and practices, therefore, is betrothal, that "pause" during which minds may be changed and partners exchanged. For post-Victorians, on the contrary, marriage is a significant but not an irreversible event. Divorce effectively bridges what is now a modest river and establishes two-way traffic across it. Jove has no choice but to smile—perhaps sardonically—at lovers' perjuries because they are no longer a cause for trial either by combat or by jury. The tragicomic tone of *Das Wertpaket* echoes that of W. H. Auden's comparison of the law to love: "Like love we don't know where or why / Like love we can't compel or fly / Like love we often weep / Like love we seldom keep."[1] Auden, here and in "Lay your sleeping head, my love, / Human on my faithless arm," decriminalizes broken promises and forgives errant lovers—a leniency for which Victorians are unprepared and which makes betrothal a less significant moment in twentieth- than in nineteenth-century narratives.

Victorian fiction, however, does prepare for the decriminalization of broken engagements. It anticipates the eventual elimination of breach of promise laws, not in the manner of *The Pickwick Papers* by satirizing them, but by ignoring them. In effect—and in one final promissory paradox—the narratives of Victorian novelists enable legal change by presenting a conservative social narrative. The fictions of Charlotte Brontë,

George Eliot, Anthony Trollope, George Meredith, and Henry James all imply that affairs of the heart are not properly the concern of litigation. Disputes between lovers should not be resolved in public and certainly not by the adversarial legal system. That these arguably conservative views do not serve conservative ends, however, is explained by the writers' resistance to traditional conceptions of language and verbal practices. The tendency of Victorian linguistics to relativism, skepticism, and empiricism is translated by novelists into a view that language may and ought to work contextually rather than merely textually. By anchoring language and language practices in quite specific social interactions, novelists from Brontë to James suggest that words and promises are significant for their performative, in addition to—if not more than—their constative or contractual force. Their redefinitions of the process of promising propose a range of alternatives to arbitration as a means of resolving disputes and suggest possibilities for social change more radical than simply abolishing breach of promise laws. We might change who we are by changing how we speak.

The novels discussed here play out individually and with each other a dialectic of promissory rejection and revival, of linguistic apprehension and appreciation. In each case, however, this process is registered on a metafictional level insofar as the act of writing (the promise of narrative) itself counterpoints, without entirely countermanding, the subject of writing (the narrative of promise). These novels warn of words and about promises—in words and with promises. Thus, no matter how dire the warning, its expression constitutes an act of faith in the resources of language and fulfills the implicit promise that writers necessarily make to their audiences. As a consequence, readers are inevitably reminded that, in various ways and for many reasons, ours is indeed a promising language.

NOTES

FOREWORD

1. George Eliot, *Middlemarch* (Harmondsworth, England: Penguin, 1975), 276. All future references are to this edition and are cited as *M*. Thomas Hardy, *The Mayor of Casterbridge* (New York: Norton, 1977), 73. All future references are to this edition and are cited as *MC*.

2. Plato, *The Symposium*, trans. Walter Hamilton (Harmondsworth, England: Penguin, 1980), 49.

INTRODUCTION

1. Max Müller, *Lectures on the Science of Language* (London: Longman, Green, Longman, and Roberts, 1861); Sir Henry Sumner Maine, *Ancient Law* (London: Oxford Univ. Press, 1959). Maine explicitly recommends that historical jurisprudence follow the methods of comparative philology (101). Peter Stein suggests that Maine's approach "seems to have been the result of the contemporary interest in comparative philology." *Legal Evolution: The Story of an Idea* (Cambridge: Cambridge Univ. Press, 1980), 91.

2. Müller, 354.

3. Maine, 141.

4. *Orley Farm* (Oxford: Oxford Univ. Press, 1985), 23. Serial publication of the novel begins in 1861 and is completed the following year. Hereafter abbreviated as *OF*.

5. *An Essay on the Origin of Language* (London: John Murrary, 1860), 3.

6. "The Law of Breach of Promise," *The Examiner*, January 21, 1871, in *The Woman Question: Papers Reprinted from "The Examiner"* (London: R. H. Lapham, 1872), 57.

7. Farrar, 115. Max Müller, *The Science of Language. Second Series* (London: Longman, Green, Longman, Roberts, & Green, 1864), 588.

8. *The Notebooks of Samuel Taylor Coleridge*, ed. Kathleen Coburn (New York: Bollingen, 1957–1973), 1016.

9. Cited by Richard Stang, *The Theory of the Novel in England: 1850–1870* (New York: Columbia Univ. Press, 1959), 50.

10. William Wordworth, "Preface" to *Lyrical Ballads*, in *Selected Prose*, ed. John O. Hayden (Harmondsworth, England: Penguin, 1988), 281.

11. M. M. Bakhtin, *The Dialogic Imagination*, trans. Caryl Emerson and Michael Holquist (Austin: Univ. of Texas Press, 1981), 3. See also his comment on Pushkin (49).

12. On the former, see Hans Aarsleff's *The Study of Language in England, 1780–1860* (Minneapolis: Univ. of Minnesota Press, 1983); on the latter, see Elisabeth K. M. Murray's *Caught in the Web of Words: James Murray and the Oxford English Dictionary* (New Haven: Yale Univ. Press, 1977).

13. *Biographies of Words* (London: Longmans, Green, and Co., 1888), x, 5. The identical image is used by Richard Chenevix Trench. See *On Some Deficiencies in Our English Dictionaries*, Second Edition (London: John W. Parker, 1860), 41; *On the Study of Words & English Past and Present* (London: Dutton, n.d.), 11.

14. See J. L. Austin, *How to Do Things with Words*, ed. J. O. Urmson and Marina Sbisà (Cambridge: Harvard Univ. Press, 1975); John R. Searle, *Speech Acts: An Essay in the Philosophy of Language* (Cambridge: Cambridge Univ. Press, 1969); Shoshana Felman, *The Literary Speech Act: Don Juan with J. L. Austin, or Seduction in Two Languages*, trans. Catherine Porter (Ithaca, N.Y.: Cornell Univ. Press, 1983); and Judith Butler, *Excitable Speech: A Politics of the Performative* (London and New York: Routledge, 1997).

15. *Allegories of Reading: Figural Language in Rousseau, Nietzsche, Rilke, and Proust* (New Haven: Yale Univ. Press, 1979), 269.

16. de Man, 273.

17. Friedrich Nietzsche, *On the Genealogy of Morals* in *Basic Writings of Nietzsche*, trans. and ed. Walter Kaufmann (New York: Modern Library, 1968), 668.

18. Samuel Taylor Coleridge, *Biographia Literaria*, ed. James Engell and W. Jackson Bate, *The Collected Works of Samuel Taylor Coleridge*, vol. 7, Bollingen Series LXXV (Princeton, N.J.: Princeton Univ. Press, 1983), II:134.

19. Jacques Derrida, *Memoires for Paul de Man* (New York: Columbia Univ. Press, 1986), 93.

20. Wordsworth writes of *Lyrical Ballads*: "I will not take upon me to determine the exact import of the promise which, by the act of writing in verse, an Author, in the present day makes to his readers: but it will undoubtedly appear to many persons that I have not fulfilled the terms of an engagement thus voluntarily contracted" (281). Coleridge makes a related point in *Biographia Literaria* (II, 66–67).

21. A. J. Greimas, *On Meaning: Selected Writings in Semiotic Theory* (Minneapolis: Univ. of Minnesota Press, 1987). For more on this point, see Bernard S. Jackson, *Semiotics and Legal Theory* (London: Routledge, 1985); *Law, Fact and Narrative Coherence* (Liverpool: Deborah Charles, 1988); and "Narrative Models in Legal Proof," in *Narrative and the Legal Discourse: A Reader in Storytelling and the Law*, ed. David Ray Papke (Liverpool: Deborah Charles, 1991): 158–78.

22. Peter Brooks, *Reading for the Plot: Design and Intention in Narrative* (New York: Random House, 1985), 12, 52.

23. George Eliot, *Adam Bede* (New York: New American Library, 1961), 174. All future references are to this edition and are cited as *AB*.

24. The metaphor neatly glosses over the fact that, while the novel may not be an arbitrary picture, it is necessarily and only a picture. For more on this point, see George Levine, *The Realistic Imagination: English Fiction from Frankenstein to Lady Chatterley* (Chicago: Univ. of Chicago, 1981), 15–18.

25. *The Rise of the Novel* (Berkeley: Univ. of California Press, 1957), 31.

26. Watt, 31, 32.

27. See Stanley Fish, *Doing What Comes Naturally: Change, Rhetoric, and the Practice of Theory in Literary and Legal Studies* (Durham, N.C.: Duke Univ. Press, 1988); and Peter Goodrich, *Reading the Law: A Critical Introduction to Legal Method and Techniques* (Oxford: Basil Blackwell, 1986), and *Legal Discourse: Studies in Linguistics, Rhetoric and Legal Analysis* (New York: St. Martin's, 1987).

28. Hayden White, "The Value of Narrativity in the Representation of Reality," in *The Content of the Form: Narrative Discourse and Historical Representation* (Baltimore: Johns Hopkins Univ. Press, 1987), 20, 24. Also see White's *Tropics of Discourse: Essays in Cultural Criticism* (Baltimore: Johns Hopkins Univ. Press, 1978), 125; and Lawrence Stone, *The Past and the Present Revisited* (New York: Routledge & Kegan Paul, 1987): 74–96.

29. See Michael Riffaterre, *Fictional Truth* (Baltimore: Johns Hopkins Univ. Press, 1990).

30. *The Pursuit of Signs: Semiotics, Literature, Deconstruction* (Ithaca, N.Y.: Cornell Univ. Press, 1981), 174, 178.

31. See, for example: Ronald Dworkin, "How Law Is Like Literature," rpt. in *Law and Literature: Text and Theory*, ed. Lenora Ledwon (New York: Garland, 1996): 29–60; Sanford Levinson, "Law as Literature," rpt. in *Interpreting Law and Literature: A Hermeneutic Reader* (Evanston, Ill.: Northwestern Univ. Press, 1988): 229–49; and Richard Posner, *Law and Literature: A Misunderstood Relation* (Cambridge: Harvard Univ. Press, 1988).

32. Dworkin, "How Law Is Like Literature," 31. A similar account of the "chain of law" is posited by Dennis M. Patterson in "Law's Pragmatism: Law as Practice and Narrative," in *Wittgenstein and Legal Theory*, ed. Dennis M. Patterson (Boulder, Colo.: Westview Press, 1992), 116–17.

33. "On 'Narrative Coherence' in Legal Contexts," in *Reason in Law: Proceedings of the Conference Held in Bologna, 12–15 December 1984*, III, ed. Carla Faralli and Enrico Pattaro (Milan: A. Giuffrè, 1988), 169.

34. Robert Cover, "Foreword: *Nomos* and Narrative," *Harvard Law Review* 97 (1983), 53.

35. For a study of this practice, see Samuel Pyeatt Menefee, *Wives for Sale: An Ethnographic Study of British Popular Divorce* (Oxford: Basil Blackwell, 1981); and Stephen Parker, *Informal Marriage, Cohabitation and the Law, 1750–1989* (London: Macmillan, 1990).

36. Joseph Conrad, *Lord Jim* (New York: Norton, 1968), 129.

37. Thomas Hardy, *Far from the Madding Crowd* (New York: Norton, 1986), 79, 94. All future references are to this edition and are cited in the text as *FMC*.

38. See Lawrence Stone, *The Road to Divorce: England 1850–1987* (Oxford: Oxford Univ. Press, 1990).

1. LANGUAGE AND THE VICTORIANS

1. Cited by Aarsleff, *The Study of Language*, 210.

2. See Hans Aarsleff's "Locke's Reputation in Nineteenth-Century England" in *From Locke to Saussure* (Minneapolis: Univ. of Minnesota Press, 1982), 120–145.

3. Tooke, for example, suggests that grammarians have been misled "by the useful contrivances of language . . . and supposed many imaginary differences of things: and thus added greatly to the number of parts of speech, and in consequence to the errors of philosophy." *The Diversions of Purley* (Menston, England: The Scolar Press, 1968), 22, 37. All future references are to this edition and are cited in the text as *DP*. In the "Essay on Language," Bentham defines a fictitious entity as "an object, the existence of which is feigned by the imagination,—feigned for the purpose of discourse, and which, when so formed, is spoken of as a real one." *The Works of Jeremy Bentham*, ed. John Bowring (New York: Russell & Russell, 1962), 8:325. Unless otherwise noted, all references to Bentham's writings are to this edition and are cited as *CW*. In "A Fragment on Ontology," he writes: "A fictitious entity is an entity to which, though by the grammatical form of the discourse employed in speaking of it, existence be ascribed, yet in truth and reality existence is not meant to be ascribed" (*CW*, 8:197).

4. *The Science of Language. Second Series* (London: Longman, Green, Longman, Roberts, & Green, 1864), 337–38.

5. Michel Foucault, *The Order of Things* (New York: Random House, 1970), 282.

6. Max Müller, *Lectures on the Science of Language* (London: Longman, Green, Longman, and Roberts, 1861), x; Foucault, 297. Foucault adds that the "grammatical arrangements of a language are the *a priori* of what can be expressed in it" (297), anticipating the first step of de Man's argument about promising.

7. Peter Goodrich, *Legal Discourse: Studies in Linguistics, Rhetoric and Legal Analysis* (New York: St. Martin's, 1987), 19.

8. Cambridge: Harvard Univ. Press, 1992, 20.

9. Müller, *Second Series*, 334.

10. All references to *An Essay Concerning Human Understanding* are from the Clarendon Edition (1975) and are cited in the text.

11. Foucault, 298.

12. See *Essay*, III.iv.20 and III.v.10.

13. This point is stressed by Talbot J. Taylor in *Mutual Misunderstanding: Skepticism and the Theorizing of Language and Interpretation* (Durham: Duke Univ. Press, 1992), 32.

14. Condillac writes: "We need only to have a short acquaintance with a person, in order to learn his language: I say, *his language*, for every man according to his passions has a particular one of his own." *An Essay on the Origin of Human Knowledge* (London: J. Nourse, 1756), 284.

15. "The Natural History of German Life," in *Essays of George Eliot*, ed. Thomas Pinney (London: Routledge & Kegan Paul, 1963), 114–15.

16. Cited by Lynda Mugglestone, *'Talking Proper': The Rise of Accent as Social Symbol* (Oxford: Clarendon Press, 1995), 83.

17. Laurence Sterne, *The Life and Opinions of Tristram Shandy, Gentleman*, ed. James Aiken Work (Indianapolis: Odyssey Press, 1940), 218. All references are to this edition and are cited in the text as *TS*.

18. "Preface" to *Lyrical Ballads, Selected Prose*, ed. John O. Hayden (Har-

mondsworth: Penguin, 1988), 381, 379. This objective, Wordsworth continues, "has cut me off from a large portion of phrases and figures of speech which from father to son have long been regarded as the common inheritance of Poets. I have also thought it expedient to restrict myself still further, having abstained from the use of many expressions, in themselves proper and beautiful, but which have been foolishly repeated by bad Poets, till such feelings of disgust are connected with them as it is scarcely possible by any art of association to overpower" (285).

19. "Preface" to *Lyrical Ballads*, 299. Stephen K. Land describes what he calls Wordsworth's "antipathy to words" and claims that the poet's "general attitude to language is consistently suspicious." "The Silent Poet: An Aspect of Wordsworth's Semantic Theory," *University of Toronto Quarterly* 42 (1972–73): 162–63.

20. "Essay on Epitaphs, III," *Selected Prose*, 361.

21. Ibid.

22. Bentham, "Essay on Language," *CW*, 8:331.

23. Tooke is rebutted by a number of people throughout the Victorian period, among them: J. W. Donaldson, *The New Cratylus* (1839), F. W. Farrar, *Essay on the Origin of Language* (1860), and E. B. Tylor, *Primitive Culture: Researches into the Development of Mythology, Philosophy, Religion, Language, Art, and Custom* (1871). See J. W. Burrow, "The Uses of Philology in Victorian England," in *Ideas and Institutions of Victorian Britain: Essays in Honour of George Kitson Clark*, ed. Robert Robson (New York: Barnes and Noble, 1967), 180–204.

24. Cited in *The Study of Language in England*, 71.

25. *The Politics of Language: 1791–1819* (Oxford: Clarendon, 1984), 131.

26. See his letter to William Godwin, September 22, 1800. *Collected Letters of Samuel Taylor Coleridge*, ed. Earl Leslie Griggs, 6 vols. (Oxford: Oxford Univ. Press, 1956–1971), 1:625–26. Coleridge criticizes Tooke, who "in writing about the formation of words only, thought he was explaining the philosophy of language, which is a very different thing." *Specimens of the Table Talk of the Late Samuel Taylor Coleridge*, ed. H. N. Coleridge (London, 1835), II, May 7, 1830. Also see James C. McKusick, *Coleridge's Philosophy of Language*. Yale Studies in English 195 (New Haven and London: Yale Univ. Press, 1986).

27. *Collected Letters*, 4:701. A summary of Coleridge's plans for the *Logic* is provided by J. R. de J. Jackson in his introduction to *The Collected Works of Samuel Taylor Coleridge*, 13 (Princeton: Princeton Univ. Press, 1981). All references are to this edition of *Logic* and are cited in the text as *L*.

28. *Biographia Literaria* in *The Collected Works of Samuel Taylor Coleridge*, ed. James Engell and W. Jackson Bate, vol. 7, Bollingen Series LXXV (Princeton: Princeton Univ. Press, 1983), II:31. Future references are to this edition and are cited in the text as *BL*.

29. Cited by Joshua H. Neumann, "Coleridge on the English Language," *PMLA* 63 (1949), 646. Neumann goes on to say, "This faith of Coleridge's in the power of words anticipates by almost a century the attitude of contemporary non-linguistic semanticists toward the 'tyranny' of symbols" (646).

30. *Collected Letters*, 2:698.

31. Neumann, 647. Michael Kent Havens argues that Coleridge's "relation to the project of an English dictionary on historical principles is unclear, but the evidence available suggests a close connection between his thought and the eventual masterwork, the *Oxford English Dictionary*." "Coleridge on the Evolution of Language," *Studies in Romanticism* 20 (1981), 165.

32. *Aids to Reflection*, ed. Thomas Fenby (Liverpool: Edward Howell, 1877), xiii.

33. *The Notebooks of Samuel Taylor Coleridge*, ed. Kathleen Coburn (New York: Bollingen, 1957–1973), III, no. 3954.

34. See Havens, "Coleridge on the Evolution of Language" (163–83).

35. Coleridge writes: "Επεα πτροευτα, winged words: or language, not only the vehicle of thought but the wheels. With my convictions and views, for επεα I should substitute λογοι, that is, words select and determinate, and for πτροευτα Ζωουτεζ, that is, living words. The wheels of the intellect I admit them to be: but such as Ezekiel beheld in *the visions of God* as he sate among the captives by the river of Chebar. *Withersoever the Spirit was to go, the wheels went, and thither was their Spirit to go; for the Spirit of the living creature was in the wheels also.*" Author's Preface to *Aids to Reflection* (1825), 114.

36. Cited by J. A. Appleyard, *Coleridge's Philosophy of Literature: The Development of a Concept of Poetry, 1791–1819* (Cambridge: Harvard Univ. Press, 1965), 85.

37. *The Notebooks of Samuel Taylor Coleridge*, 1016.

38. John Stuart Mill, *A System of Logic Ratiocinative and Inductive* in *The Collected Edition of the Works of John Stuart Mill* (Toronto: Univ. of Toronto Press, 1963), VII:19. All references are to this edition and are cited in the text as *SL*.

39. *Utilitarianism*, in *Collected Works*, X, 245.

40. "Thoughts on Poetry and Its Varieties," *Collected Works*, 1:345.

41. Another example of this trope is "The Novel-Reading Disease" published in 1871: "This dropsical habit of body finds its exact analogue in the species of mental dropsy which is produced by over-indulgence in three-volumed novels." *The Woman Question: Papers Reprinted from "The Examiner"* (London: R. H. Lapham, 1872), 64.

42. Linda Dowling, *Language and Decadence in the Victorian Fin de Siècle* (Princeton: Princeton Univ. Press, 1986), 62. This is a highly illuminating study, and one from which I have learned a great deal.

43. "Introduction," *On the Study of Words & English Past and Present*, ix.

44. *On Some Deficiencies in our English Dictionaries*, Second Edition (London: John W. Parker, 1860), 4. He defines a dictionary as "an inventory of the language" and "an historical monument" (6).

45. *Deficiencies*, 4–5.

46. *Words*, 40. For more on this point see, Olivia Smith, *The Politics of Language: 1791–1819*; Tony Crowley, *Standard English and the Politics of Language* (Urbana and Chicago: Univ. of Illinois Press, 1989); and Dennis Taylor, *Hardy's Literary Language and Victorian Philology* (Oxford: Clarendon, 1993).

47. *On the Study of Words*, 13, 46. For example, "Language is the amber in which a thousand precious and subtle thoughts have been safely embedded and preserved" (22).

48. *Words*, 38.

49. *Words*, 13–14.

50. The published lectures went through fourteen printings by 1886. See Kurt R. Jankowsky, "F. Max Müller and the Development of Linguistic Science," *Historiographica Linguistica* 6.3:339–59.

51. *Lectures on the Science of Language*, 12.

52. *Lectures on the Science of Language*, 36, 23

53. Müller, *Second Series*, 1; *First Series*, 25.

54. Müller, *Second Series*, 368.

55. Cited by Burrow, 200. Müller resoundingly concludes that "no process of natural selection will ever distill significant words out of the notes of birds or the cries of beasts" (*Second Series*, 340). Trench explicitly rejects the "'ourang-outang'" theory of the origin of language in favor of the account of Genesis (*Words*, 17). This theory, suggested by Lord Monboddo's late eighteenth-century work, *Of the Origin and Progress of Language*, challenges the notion that language is a Rubicon. In Monboddo's view, speech is an artificial, not a natural, acquisition, and humans are distinguished from monkeys not so much by language as by the ability to develop language. This theory is mocked by Thomas Love Peacock in *Melincourt* (1807), a new edition of which appears in 1856 with an added subtitle, *Melincourt, or, Sir Oran Haut-ton*. Another, more serious, consideration of animals and language is Lord Brougham's *Dissertations on Subjects of Science Connected with Natural Theology* (1839).

56. *The Descent of Man*, 138–39. Lyell uses the same image in *The Geological Evidence of the Antiquity of Man* (New York: Dutton, n.d.), 360. For more on this point, see Gillian Beer, "Darwin and the Growth of Language Theory," in *Nature Transfigured: Science and Literature, 1700–1900*, ed. John Christie and Sally Shuttleworth (Manchester and New York: Manchester Univ. Press, 1989).

57. Müller, *First Series*, 384–85.

58. "Victorian Oxford and the Science of Language," 161. Maurice Olender argues that Müller's "theological presuppositions determined his approach to linguistics and religious history" (87).

59. Müller, *Second Series*, 548, 375–76.

60. Müller, *Second Series*, 544.

61. Müller, *First Series*, 36–37.

62. New Haven: Yale Univ. Press, 1980, 100–101.

63. "Introduction," *The Mill on the Floss* (Harmondsworth, England: 1986), 13. All citations are from this edition and are cited in the text as *MF*. Eliot is well versed in linguistics and describes *The Science of Language* as a "great and delightful book." *The George Eliot Letters*, ed. Gordon S. Haight, 7 vols. (New Haven: Yale Univ. Press, 1954–55), 8. Müller's name comes up several times in Eliot's correspondence, usually in reference to her reading. She records meeting Müller at Oxford in 1873.

64. Cited by Irene Tayler and Gina Luria, "Gender and Genre: Women in

British Romantic Literature," in *What Manner of Woman*, ed. Marlene Springer (New York: New York Univ. Press, 1977), 100. Ong's comment reaffirms the gendered nature of promising previously discussed in *Far from the Madding Crowd*.

65. This passage is also discussed by Mary Jacobus in "The Question of Language: Men of Maxims and *The Mill on the Floss*," *Critical Inquiry* 8 (1981): 207–22.

2. VICTORIAN PROMISES

1. Jane Austen, *Northanger Abbey* (Harmondsworth, England: Penguin, 1985), 198. Mary Smith, the narrator of *Cranford*, also reports having "promised faithfully." Elizabeth Gaskell, *Cranford/Cousin Phillis* (Harmondsworth, England: Penguin, 1986), 64.

2. Samuel Smiles, *Self-Help; with Illustrations of Conduct and Perseverance* (London: John Murray, 1882), 401–2. Smiles repeatedly emphasizes that "[i]ntegrity in word and deed is the backbone of character" (387, 398).

3. *A Treatise of Human Nature*, ed. L. A. Selby-Bigge (Oxford: Clarendon Press, 1960), 546. All references are to this edition and are cited in the text.

4. Maine, 140. Also see J. W. Burrow, *Evolution and Society: A Study in Victorian Social Theory* (Cambridge: Cambridge Univ. Press, 1966).

5. *Ancient Law*, 258.

6. Friedrich Nietzsche, *The Genealogy of Morals* in *The Philosophy of Nietzsche* (New York: Modern Library, 1954), 668.

7. *Ancient Law*, 258, 312.

8. Carleton Kemp Allen, "Introduction" to *Ancient Law*, xvi. Even Allen must acknowledge that Maine's narrative of the evolution of promising among the Romans "leans a little towards the romantic" (xxiv). For more on Maine's relation to Darwin, see Roger Cotterell's *The Politics of Jurisprudence: A Critical Introduction to Legal Philosophy* (London: Butterworths, 1989), 45. Maine's "comparative jurisprudence" is explicitly linked to the comparative method of philology by R. C. J. Cocks in *Sir Henry Maine: A Study in Victorian Jurisprudence* (Cambridge: Cambridge Univ. Press, 1988), 19–23, 35–36. Cocks notes that Maine was very much interested in the methods of Müller's comparative philology (101).

9. Elizabeth Longford, *Wellington: The Years of the Sword* (London: Weidenfeld and Nicolson, 1969), 113.

10. Cited by Longford, 100. In addition to this work, see Elizabeth Longford, *Wellington: Pillar of State* (London: Weidenfeld & Nicolson, 1972); Arthur Bryant, *The Great Duke or The Invincible General* (London: Collins, 1971); and Neville Thompson, *Wellington after Waterloo* (London: Routledge & Kegan Paul, 1986).

11. George Meredith, *The Amazing Marriage* (New York: Charles Scribner's Sons, 1895). All references are to this edition and are cited in the text as *AM*. For a summary of critical skepticism about the novel, see Judith Wilt, *The Readable People of George Meredith* (Princeton: Princeton Univ. Press, 1975), 225–26.

12. Cited by Longford, 122.

13. He writes: "That task of breeding an animal which can make promises, includes, . . . as its condition and preliminary, the more immediate task of first *making* man to a certain extent, necessitated, uniform, like among his like, regular, and consequently calculable. The immense work of what I have called, 'morality of custom.'" *The Genealogy of Morals*, 670.

14. *The Rise and Fall of Freedom of Contract* (Oxford: Clarendon, 1979), 283.

15. William Paley, *Principles of Moral and Political Philosophy* (Canandaigua: J. D. Bemis, 1822), 88. Paley does, however, warn that to "gird the obligations so tight, as to make no allowances for manifest and fundamental errors, would in many instances be productive of great hardship and absurdity" (88).

16. Paley, 84.

17. Adam Smith, *The Theory of Moral Sentiments*, ed. D.D. Raphael and A. L. MacFie (Oxford: Clarendon, 1976), 331.

18. Smith, 332.

19. P. S. Atiyah, *Promises, Morals, and Law* (Oxford: Carendon, 1981), 77.

20. John Fowles, *The French Lieutenant's Woman* (New York: New American Library, 1969), 324. All references are to this edition and are cited in the text as *FLW*.

21. Anthony Trollope, *Kept in the Dark* (Oxford: Oxford Univ. Press, 1992), 19. All subsequent references are to this edition and are cited in the text as *KD*. When Boldwood learns that Bathsheba loves Sergeant Troy, he expresses a similar sentiment, albeit in a more bathetic manner (*FMC* 160).

22. This phrase, which the *OED* cites as first appearing in 1858, is traced by Atiyah to a court case of 1821 (*The Rise and Fall of Freedom of Contract*, 402).

23. Anthony Trollope, *Lady Anna* (Oxford: Oxford Univ. Press, 1984), 231. All future references are to this edition and are cited in the text as *LA*.

24. Anthony Trollope, *Phineas Finn* (Harmondsworth, England: Penguin, 1985), 181.

25. George Eliot, *Daniel Deronda* (Harmondsworth, England: Penguin, 1986), 626.

26. *An Eye for an Eye* (London: Trollope Society, 1993), 63. Future references are cited in the text as *EE*.

27. See Elie Halévy, *The Growth of Philosophical Radicalism*, trans. Mary Morris (New York: Augustus M. Kelley, 1949).

28. Anthony Trollope, *The Eustace Diamonds*, 2 vols. (Oxford: Oxford Univ. Press, 1973), 2:39.

29. Cited by W. J. Brockelbank, "The Nature of the Promise to Marry—A Study in Comparative Law," *Illinois Law Review*, 41.1 (May–June 1916), 4.

30. Jacques Derrida, *Memoires for Paul de Man* (New York: Columbia Univ. Press, 1986), 94.

31. *Hansard's Parliamentary Debates*, third series, vol. 245 (London: Cornelius Buck, 1879), 1867.

32. *Hall* v. *Wright* (1859), Q. B. El. Bl. & E., 789.

33. Crowder, J., *Hall* v. *Wright* (1859), Q. B. El. Bl. & E., 787.

34. In this regard, betrothal is different from many other contractual obligations. One of the judges in *Hall* v. *Wright* argues that, were any connection between marriage and other contracts to be admitted, it would be with contracts for personal services, "which can be performed only during the lifetime of the party contracting [and] are subject to the implied condition that he shall be alive to perform them: and, should he die, his executor is not liable to an action for the breach of contract occasioned by his death." In *Finlay* v. *Chirney* (1888), the plaintiff unsuccessfully sues the estate of her deceased fiancé for breach of promise.

35. *Hansard's Parliamentary Debates*, third series, vol. 245, 1884.

36. *Hansard's Parliamentary Debates*, third series, vol. 245, 1878.

37. See Mary Lyndon Shanley, *Feminism, Marriage, and the Law in Victorian England* (Princeton: Princeton Univ. Press, 1989).

38. *Hansard's Parliamentary Debates*, third series, vol. 245, 1876, 1878.

39. *Hansard's Parliamentary Debates*, third series, vol. 245, 1876–77.

40. William Makepeace Thackeray, *Vanity Fair* (Harmondsworth, England: Penguin, 1985), 220. All future references are cited in the text as *VF*.

41. *Hall* v. *Wright* (1859), Q. B. El. Bl. & E., 794, 781.

42. *Hall* v. *Wright* (1859), Q. B. El. Bl. & E., 796.

43. *Hansard's Parliamentary Debates*, third series, vol. 245, 1870.

44. *Hansard's Parliamentary Debates*, third series, vol. 245, 1871–72.

45. Ibid., 1881.

46. Ibid., 1880–81.

47. Ibid., 1886. In commenting on the stressful marriage of Thomas Carlyle and Jane Welsh, Samuel Butler opines: "It was very good of God to let Carlyle and Mrs. Carlyle marry one another and so make only two people miserable instead of four, besides being very amusing." Cited by G. B. Tennyson, "Introduction," *A Carlyle Reader* (Cambridge: Cambridge Univ. Press, 1984), xiii–xiv.

48. Bills to abolish all actions for breach of promise to marry were introduced in 1883, 1884, 1888, and 1890, but on no occasion did they receive a second reading.

49. Peter Goodrich, *Reading the Law: A Critical Introduction to Legal Method and Techniques* (Oxford: Basil Blackwell, 1986), 188.

50. *Ancient Law*, 260.

51. William Vitek discusses Eliot as an example of the intentional model of promising in *Promising* (Philadelphia: Temple Univ. Press, 1993). Here and throughout the discussion of promising I am indebted to Professor Vitek's insightful study.

52. Peter J. Wilson, *Man, the Promising Primate* (New Haven: Yale Univ. Press, 1983), 107.

53. For more on this point, see Robert Polhemus, *Erotic Faith: Being in Love from Jane Austen to D. H. Lawrence* (Chicago: Univ. of Chicago Press, 1990).

54. Tony Tanner, *Adultery in the Novel: Contract and Transgression* (Baltimore: Johns Hopkins Univ. Press, 1979), 68–70.

55. Willes, J., *Hall* v. *Wright* (1859), Q. B. El. Bl. & E., 786.

3. LEGAL FICTIONS

1. Charles J. MacColla, *Breach of Promise: Its History and Social Considerations* (London: Pickering, 1879), 35.

2. Anthony Trollope, *The Eustace Diamonds* (Oxford: Oxford Univ. Press, 1989), 2:148. All references are to this edition and cited in the text as *ED*.

3. See Rosemary J. Coombe, "'The Most Disgusting, Disgraceful and Inequitous Proceeding in Our Law': The Action for Breach of Promise of Marriage in Nineteenth-Century Ontario," *University of Toronto Law Journal* 38.1 (Winter 1988): 64–108. For a study of fictional portrayals of women and the law, see Lynne Marie DeCicco, *Women and Lawyers in the Mid-Nineteenth Century Novel* (Lewiston, N.Y.: Edwin Mellen, 1996).

4. "Damages for Breach of Promise of Marriage," rpt. in *The Albany Law Journal* 10 (1874): 342–43.

5. *Hansard's Parliamentary Debates*, third series, vol. 245, 1874, 1882.

6. For another example, see Miss Witherfield's concern about the near "duel in Ipswich" between Peter Magnus and Mr. Pickwick (*PP* chapter 24).

7. George Meredith, *Diana of the Crossways*. *The Works of George Meredith*. *Memorial Edition*, vol. 16 (New York: Charles Scribner's Sons, 1910), 207. All future references are to this edition and are cited in the text as *DCW*.

8. *Hansard's Parliamentary Debates*, third series, vol. 245, 1886.

9. *Black's Law Dictionary*, Sixth Edition (St. Paul, Minn.: West Publishing, 1990), 623.

10. *An Old Man's Love* (Oxford: Oxford Univ. Press, 1992), 111. All references are to this edition and are cited as *OML*.

11. *Beachey v. Brown*, El. Bl. & El., 804.

12. *Beachey v. Brown*, El. Bl. & El., 804.

13. *Beachey v. Brown*, El. Bl. & El., 804.

14. For an analysis of promises and vows, see Michael H. Robins, *Promising, Intending, and Moral Autonomy* (Cambridge: Cambridge Univ. Press, 1984).

15. There are comparatively few instances of men suing women for breach of promise. In cases like *Leeds v. Cook and Wife* (1803) and *Baddeley v. Mortlock and Wife* (1816), the courts maintain the letter of the law, according to which a promise is promise, but counteract its effect by awarding token damages of one shilling.

16. *Beachey v. Brown*, El. Bl. & El., 798.

17. *Beachey v. Brown*, El. Bl. & El., 805.

18. *Beachey v. Brown*, El. Bl. & El., 797.

19. *Beachey v. Brown*, *The All England Law Reports Reprint: 1843–1860*, ed. G. F. L. Bridgman, Esc., O.B.E. (London: Butterworth, 1860), 507.

20. *Beachey v. Brown*, El. Bl. & El., 803.

21. *Beachey v. Brown*, El. Bl. & El., 798, 799.

22. See Percy Fitzgerald: "The verdict was clearly a wrong one—no sufficient evidence had been furnished either of a promise, or a breach." *Bardell v. Pickwick* (London: Elliot Stock, 1902), 98–99. For an opposed opinion, see P. S. Atiyah, *Introduction to Law of Contract* (London: Clarendon, 1971).

23. Brown, 474; MacColla, viii.

24. One hears a similar argument from a Member of Parliament scandalized by breach of promise settlements: "But even in cases where some sort of promise had been given, it was impossible for a man to obtain justice, for it was always difficult to get the facts fairly weighed by a jury. If he attempted, in the course of the case, to suggest that the woman was anything but an angel in temper—a very embodiment of all female virtues—so that there would be some reason to justify a man in not marrying her, the mere suggestion was enough to bring down upon him a whole torrent of invective." *Hansard's Parliamentary Debates*, third series, vol. 245, 1869.

25. The last point explains the ironic instructions to the jury in Gilbert and Sullivan's *Trial by Jury* (1875): "Oh, listen to the plaintiff's case: / Observe the features of her face— / The brokenhearted bride. / Condole with her distress of mind: / From bias free of every kind, / This trial must be tried!" *The Complete Plays of Gilbert and Sullivan* (New York: Modern Library, n.d.), 44.

26. *Hansard's Parliamentary Debates*, third series, vol. 245, 1882. This position is opposed by the claim that the "Courts were open to all, and it was at the option of parties to have recourse to them. Besides, Parliament did not legislate for high-minded or low-minded people. It legislated on the justice of the case, and the evils which it was predicted would arise from its removal were not found to exist in those classes." *Hansard's Parliamentary Debates*, third series, vol. 245, 1874–75, 1879.

27. "Breach of Promise Suits," *University of Pennsylvania Law Review* 77 (February 1929), 494.

28. Cited by Jane W. Stedman, "'Come, Substantial Damages!'" in *Victorian Scandals: Representations of Gender and Class*, ed. Kristine Ottesen Garrigan (Athens: Ohio Univ. Press, 1992), 84.

29. Mary Elizabeth Braddon, *Lady Audley's Secret* (New York: Dover, 1974), 285.

30. This sentiment is echoed by Herschell, who sarcastically apologizes to lawyers for "tak[ing] away that class of cases from them especially at a time of so much depression of trade." *Hansard's Parliamentary Debates*, third series, vol. 245, 1875. Also note Sam Weller's testimony at the trial (*PP* 574).

31. *The Methods of Ethics* (London: Macmillan, 1907), 304, 308–9.

32. *The Methods of Ethics*, 304.

33. Charles Dickens, *Bleak House* (New York: Norton, 1977), 113. Guppy elaborates upon the meaning of his legalism, "without prejudice": "It's one of our law terms, miss. You won't make any use of it to my detriment, at Kenge and Carboy's, or elsewhere. If our conversation shouldn't lead to anything, I am to be as I was, and am not to be prejudiced in my situation or worldly prospects" (*BH* 113).

34. *Hansard's Parliamentary Debates*, third series, vol. 245, 1883.

35. Cited by J. Dundas White, "Breach of Promise of Marriage," *The Law Quarterly Review* 10 (1894), 141. This view seems to be the typical one. According to W. J. Brockelbank, "In particular the courts have turned a deaf ear to defenses based on incompatibility of tastes and temperament or the defendant's opinion that the marriage could not be a success, that the parties fail to

respect or have ceased to love each other. . . . In short, all the facts may point realistically to the near certainty that, if the marriage were ever solemnized, it would either be very unhappy or end in divorce, yet the courts do not bar the action." *Illinois Law Review* 41 (1946), 9.

36. Charles Dickens, *Great Expectations* (Harmondsworth, England: Penguin, 1965), 427.

37. *Honyman* v. *Campbell*, II D & C, 282.

38. For a discussion of this incident, see J. Hillis Miller, *Topographies* (Stanford: Stanford Univ. Press, 1995).

39. Stanley Fish, *Doing What Comes Naturally*, 138. Earlier he writes: "rules *are* texts. They are in need of interpretation and cannot themselves serve as constraints on interpretation" (121).

40. *Short* v. *Stone*, Q. B. 8 Q. B., 369. Also see *Caines* v. *Smith* (1847), 15 M. & W., 189–90.

41. *Wild* v. *Harris*, C. P. 7 C. B., 1002.

42. *Wild* v. *Harris*, C. P. 7 C. B., 1005–6. Legal and moral opinion agree in this instance. See Paley, 84.

43. *Millward* v. *Littlewood*, 5 Ex., 775.

44. *Millward* v. *Littlewood*, 5 Ex., 776.

45. *Millward* v. *Littlewood*, 5 Ex., 778.

46. *Millward* v. *Littlewood*, 5 Ex., 777.

47. *Millward* v. *Littlewood*, 5 Ex., 778.

48. *Hansard's Parliamentary Debates*, third series, vol. 245, 1887, 1880.

49. See Michael Grossberg, *Governing the Hearth: Law and the Family in Nineteenth-Century America* (Chapel Hill and London: Univ. of North Carolina Press, 1985).

50. *Bessela* v. *Stern*, *The Law Reports. Common Pleas Division*, vol. 2 (London: Clowes, 1877), 271–72.

51. Cover, 9.

52. London: Henry S. King, 1874, 55. Blackstone notes: "these fictions of law, although at first they may startle the student, he will find upon further consideration to be highly beneficial and useful." *Commentaries on the Laws of England* (Oxford: Clarendon, 1765), III, 43. William S. Holdsworth writes that common law procedures at the beginning of Victoria's reign are "perhaps the most artificial and the most encumbered with fictions that any legal system has ever possessed." *Charles Dickens as a Legal Historian* (New Haven: Yale Univ. Press, 1929), 117.

53. Jeremy Bentham, *The Theory of Fictions*, in C. K. Ogden, *Bentham's Theory of Fictions* (New York: Harcourt, Brace, 1932), 143.

54. Cited by Ogden, 30.

55. *CW*, 8:198. In considering the relation between thought and language, Bentham alludes to "the discoveries, half-concealed or left unperfected" by Horne Tooke and comments on the importance of distinguishing real and fictitious entities: "Almost all names, employed in speaking of the phenomena of the mind, are names of fictitious entities. . . . Lamentable have been the confusion and darkness produced by taking the names of *fictitious* for the names of *real* entities." *CW*, 8:120.

56. Lewis Carroll, *Alice in Wonderland* ed. Donald J. Gray (New York: Norton, 1971), 95. All future references are to this edition and are cited in the text as *AW*.

57. *The Theory of Fictions*, 143.

58. *The Theory of Fictions*, 148.

59. Bentham writes that in legal usage "appearance" takes on "at least half a score different meanings; but that which it has in the language of common sense is not of the number." *The Theory of Fictions*, 143.

60. James Boyd White, *Heracles' Bow* (Madison, Wis.: Univ. of Wisconsin Press, 1985), 36.

61. *Law, Fact, and Narrative Coherence*, 2. Hayden White makes a related point concerning historians: "the process of fusing events, whether imaginary or real, into a comprehensible totality capable of serving as the *object* of representation is a poetic process. Here the historians must utilize precisely the same tropological strategies, the same modalities of representing relationships in words, that the poet or novelist uses." "The Fictions of Factual Representation," 125.

62. *Aristotle's Theory of Poetry and Fine Art*, trans. S. H. Butcher (New York: Dover, 1951), 107. Aristotle addresses the issue of probability in legal argument in his *Rhetoric*. See Goodrich, 181–82 and 189–90.

63. Bernard S. Jackson, "Narrative Models in Legal Proof," in *Narrative and the Legal Discourse: A Reader in Storytelling and the Law*, ed. David Ray Papke (Liverpool: Deborah Charles, 1991), 165. Jackson draws upon the research of W. Lance Bennett and Martha S. Feldman in *Reconstructing Reality in the Courtroom* (New Brunswick, N.J.: Rutgers Univ. Press, 1981). Also see Stephen C. Yeazell, "Convention, Fiction, and Law," *NLH* (1981): 89–102.

64. William M. O'Barr and John M. Conley, "Litigant Satisfaction versus Legal Adequacy in Small Claims Court Narratives," in Papke, 87.

65 *Foulkes* v. *Selway*, *Reports of Cases Argued and Ruled at Nisi Prius in the Court of King's Bench and Common Pleas*, III (Philadelphia: P. Byrne, 1805), 236.

66 *Leeds* v. *Cook & Wife* (1803), *Reports of Cases Argued and Ruled at Nisi Prius in the Courts of King's Bench and Common Pleas*, IV (Philadelphia: P. Byrne, 1807), 258.

67. C. P. Holt 151.

68. *Irving* v. *Greenwood* (1824), 1 Car. & P., 350–51. The jury believes the plaintiff and awards Irving £500 damages. Also see *Wharton* v. *Lewis* (1824), N. P. 1 C. & P., 529–30.

69. Cited in *Bench* v. *Merrick*, 1 Car. & K., 464.

70. *Bench* v. *Merrick*, 1 Car. & K., 464.

71. Thomas Hardy, *Tess of the d'Urbervilles* (Harmondsworth, England: Penguin, 1978), 37. All future references are to this edition and are cited in the text as *TD*.

72. One witness reports telling the defendant of the plaintiff's past and then carrying a message from him to her: "I told the plaintiff, that the defendant said he could never think of marrying her unless she cleared up her character; and she replied, that he ought not to be so particular, as he had kept company with several girls, whom he had deceived." *Bench* v. *Merrick*, 1 Car. & K., 466–67.

73. *Bench* v. *Merrick*, 1 Car. & K., 466.

74. *Bench* v. *Merrick*, 1 Car. & K., 467–68.

75. El. Bl. & El, 802–3.

76. *Atchinson* v. *Baker* (1796), Peake Add. Cas., 103.

77. *A Treatise on the Law of Contracts and upon Defences to Actions Thereon* (8th ed. 1868), cited by Coombe, 88.

78. "The Nature of the Promise to Marry—a Study in Comparative Law," *Illinois Law Review* 41:1 (1946), 7–8.

79. *Hall* v. *Wright*, Q. B. El. Bl. & E., 796.

80. *Hall* v. *Wright*, Q. B. El. Bl. & E., 759–60. This view is supported by the claim that "canon law is clear upon the point, that only impotence, permanent and incurable, such as that which results from the loss of one of the necessary organs of generation, constitutes an impediment to marriage, and not that which may be temporary or curable." *Hall* v. *Wright*, Q. B. El. Bl. & E., 785.

81. *Hall* v. *Wright*, Q. B. El. Bl. & E., 779–80.

82. *Finlay* v. *Chirney*, Queen's Bench Division, 20, 494, 502

83. *The Melodramatic Imagination: Balzac, Henry James, Melodrama, and the Mode of Excess* (New Haven: Yale Univ. Press, 1976), 31. Frost writes: "Like putting on a large-scale theatrical production, suing for breach of promise in the nineteenth century was a long and complicated process. . . . That script closely resembles a domestic melodrama, with an innocent young woman as the victim of a scheming villain, high-flown discourse, and a triumphant final vindication in court" (26).

84. These terms are coined by Jackson to differentiate between the narrative told during the trial and the story of the trial itself. *Law, Fact, and Narrative Coherence*, 35.

85. Percy Fitzgerald, *Bardell v. Pickwick*, 53.

86. Cited by William S. Holdsworth, 68. This material is also available in Fitzgerald.

87. The rationale for this course of argument is framed in these terms: "although courtship, or intention, will not supply the place of a promise, yet they come so near, that if these are once made out, we get on a good way toward our journey's end." *Honyman* v. *Campbell*, II Dow & Clark, 282.

88. *Vineall* v. *Veness*, 4 F. & F., 344–46.

89. "Breach of Promise Suits," *University of Pennsylvania Law Review* 77 (1929), 496.

90. Caroline Norton, *Caroline Norton's Defense: English Laws for Women in the Nineteenth Century*, intro. Joan Huddleston (Chicago: Academy Chicago, 1982), 91.

91. *The Methods of Ethics*, 304.

92. *The Literary Speech Act*, 68.

4. ENGAGING LIES IN *JANE EYRE*

1. Charlotte Brontë, *Jane Eyre*, ed. Q. D. Leavis (Harmondsworth, England: Penguin English Library, 1966), 309. All references to the novel are cited in the text as *JE*.

2. For an analysis of how contemporary readers would have interpreted Brontë's autobiographical pose, see Jerome Beaty, *Misreading* Jane Eyre: *A Postformalist Paradigm* (Columbus: Ohio State Univ. Press, 1996).

3. Of the many excellent readings of the novel, I would like to acknowledge three in particular that have been especially helpful to me and to which I am more than a little indebted: Rosemarie Bodenheimer, "Jane Eyre in Search of Her Story," *Papers on Language and Literature* 16 (1980): 387–402; Mark M. Hennelly, Jr., "Jane Eyre's Reading Lesson," *ELH* 51 (Winter 1984): 693–717; and John Kucich, "Passionate Reserve and Reserved Passion in the Works of Charlotte Brontë," *ELH* 52 (Winter 1985): 913–37.

4. For discussions of Byron's influence on Brontë, see Harold Bloom, "Introduction," *Charlotte Brontë's Jane Eyre* (New York: Chelsea House, 1987); Mark Schorer, "*Jane Eyre*," in *The World We Imagine: Selected Essays by Mark Schorer* (New York: Farrar, Strauss, & Giroux, 1968): 80–96; and Donald D. Stone, *The Romantic Impulse in Victorian Fiction* (Cambridge: Harvard Univ. Press, 1980).

5. Jane alludes to the limits of childhood perception and expression that she experiences but overcomes: "Children cannot analyse their feelings; and if the analysis is partially effected in thought, they know not how to express the result of the process in words" (*JE* 56, also see 66).

6. Brontë's interest in phrenology has been well documented by her biographers. For its importance in the novel, see Karen Chase, *Eros & Psyche: The Representation of Personality in Charlotte Brontë, Charles Dickens, and George Eliot* (New York and London: Methuen, 1984); and Doreen Roberts, "*Jane Eyre* and 'The Warped System of Things,'" in *Reading the Victorian Novel: Detail into Form*, ed. Ian Gregor (London: Vision, 1980), 131–49.

7. There is ample evidence of Rochester's parallel abuse of spoken language. He is particularly adept at using words to mystify rather than to enlighten. It is relatively easy to do so with Mrs. Fairfax, who admits that she "cannot be always sure whether he is in jest or earnest, whether he is pleased or the contrary" (*JE* 136, 274). Although Jane is much more adept at deciphering "what sort of talk this was" (*JE* 154), even she is confused by Rochester's "queer question[s]" (*JE* 163) and "jargon" (*JE* 230). She refuses either to take part in "a discourse that was all darkness" (*JE* 169) or to "talk nonsense" (*JE* 231). In general, she mistrusts any form of circumlocution, such as riddles (*JE* 226), that places an interlocutor at a disadvantage. Rochester nevertheless regularly speaks "like a sphinx" (*JE* 169) and twists genres to suit his secretive purposes. In fact, all rhetorical forms tend to be reduced to a single genre, the riddle. The game of charades is one example; others are parable, which to him is not a means of explanation but of mystification (*JE* 248) and fairy tale. His fantastic story about life on the moon encodes a private wish-fulfillment dream that Jane calls "badinage" and Adèle calls lies (*JE* 296).

8. For an analysis of the difference between promises and threats, see John Searle, "What Is a Speech Act?", in *Readings in the Philosophy of Language*, ed. Jay F. Rosenberg and Charles Travis (Englewood Cliffs, N.J.: Prentice-Hall, 1971): 614–28.

9. The question is asked by a rat of a mouse that seeks the protection of

the League of Rats against a voracious cat. The choice of this particular fable is ominous since the rats, who in self-interest agree to help, arrive too late to prevent the cat from eating a mouse.

10. Miss Temple may be an exception; she displays only "round curls" (*JE* 79).

11. Robert Bernard Martin also makes this point: "Brusqueness, teasing, and plain speaking throughout the novel have always been the mark of sincerity." *The Accents of Persuasion: Charlotte Brontë's Novels* (London: Faber & Faber, 1966), 91. Martin does not, however, question the adequacy of such discursive modes.

12. Tony Tanner argues that the dream "of some impossible realm of freedom" is a recurrent element in the novel of adultery. *Adultery in the Novel*, 34. Of related interest is his "Passion, narrative and identity in *Wuthering Heights* and *Jane Eyre*," in *Teaching the Text*, ed. Susanne Kappeler and Norman Bryson (London: Routledge & Kegan Paul, 1983): 109–25.

13. The phrase "verbal fencing" is also used by Philip Momberger in "Self and World in the Works of Charlotte Brontë," *ELH* 32 (September 1965), 364. In describing the relationship that she herself desires with a prospective husband, Brontë says that she must be free to "laugh, and satirise, and say whatever came into my head first." Letter to Ellen Nussey, 12 March 1839, in *The Brontës: Their Lives, Friendships, and Correspondence*, ed. T. J. Wise and J. A. Symington (Oxford: Shakespeare Head, 1932), 1:174. This combat is usually discussed with a sexual rather than a rhetorical emphasis. See Nina Auerbach, *Romantic Imprisonment: Women and Other Glorified Outcasts* (New York: Columbia Univ. Press, 1985); and Terry Eagleton, *Myths of Power: A Marxist Study of the Brontës*, Second Edition (London: Macmillan, 1988).

14. Compare this method with Blanche Ingram's "meretricious arts and calculated manoeuvres": "Arrows that continually glanced off from Mr Rochester's breast and fell harmless at his feet" (*JE* 216).

15. The possible and improbable exception is the call that summons Jane from Moor House to Ferndean. Ruth Bernard Yeazell interprets the call as expressing "the truth of the psyche." See "More True than Real: Jane Eyre's 'Mysterious Summons,'" *Nineteenth-Century Fiction* 29 (September 1974), 128. Several critics discuss the call as indication of Brontë's "natural supernaturalism." See Lawrence Jay Dessner, *The Homely Web of Truth: A Study of Charlotte Brontë's Novels* (The Hague and Paris: Mouton, 1975); and Barry V. Qualls, *The Secular Pilgrims of Victorian Fiction: The Novel as Book of Life* (Cambridge: Cambridge Univ. Press, 1982). Another way in which Jane and Rochester exhibit the desire for transcendent language can be seen in their appropriation of spiritual language for carnal topics. See Valentine Cunningham, *Everywhere Spoken Against: Dissent in the Victorian Novel* (Oxford: Clarendon, 1974). For more on this topic, see Cynthia A. Linder, *Romantic Imagery in the Novels of Charlotte Brontë* (London: Methuen, 1978), and M. H. Scargill, "Poetic Symbolism in *Jane Eyre*," in *Charlotte Brontë: Jane Eyre and Villette: A Casebook*, ed. Miriam Allot (London: Macmillan, 1973), 175–81.

16. Kucich, 916.

17. See John Maynard, *Charlotte Brontë and Sexuality* (Cambridge: Cambridge Univ. Press, 1984).

18. Feminist critics in particular have emphasized the connections between Jane and Bertha. See Linda Kaufmann, *Discourses of Desire: Gender, Genre, and Epistolary Fiction* (Ithaca, N.Y.: Cornell Univ. Press, 1986).

19. Jane often silently criticizes the Reeds but shares with readers the suppressed sentiments. See, for example, her silent thoughts about her "feeble-minded" cousin (*JE* 269).

Although these hyperbolic "three minutes" have been read as the exaggeration of youthful perception and articulation, it seems more likely that this and similar expressions are the sarcastic accounts of a mature voice. Thus temporal exaggerations are used in the narrative when Jane is older, for example, in her account of the dilatory postmistress at Lowton (*JE* 119). Such passages typically appear either in broad caricatures of figures like John Reed, Brocklehurst—whose public denouncement of Jane as a liar is punctuated with a dramatic silence of a full ten minutes (*JE* 98)—and Blanche Ingram. Brontë signals the natural exaggeration of a child, as opposed to the deliberate irony of an adult. For instance, she contradicts Jane's sense that the journey to Lowood is of a "preternatural length," requiring "travel over hundreds of miles of road" (*JE* 74), by informing us that the school is fifty miles from Gateshead. Indeed, the child-like perception of her journey is accentuated by Brontë's prosaic summary of her next trip, which is from Lowood to Thornfield and is taken eight years later when she has matured (*JE* 125). Of her next journey, from Thornfield to Gateshead, nothing at all is said (*JE* 255).

20. Mary Poovey discusses this scene in terms of Jane Eyre's rage. See *Uneven Developments: The Ideological Work of Gender in Mid-Victorian England* (Chicago: Univ. of Chicago Press, 1988).

21. Annette Tromly, *The Cover of the Mask: The Autobiographers in Charlotte Brontë's Fiction*, ELS Monograph Series, 26 (Victoria, B.C.: Univ. of Victoria Press, 1982), 48. The extent to which the narrator misleads readers is discussed by Hennelly. He concludes that as a narrator Jane is neither "'relatively reliable' like Moll Flanders nor 'relatively unreliable' like Molly Bloom. She is somewhere in between the two, but more like Molly than has been acknowledged" (704). The opposing view is presented by Earl A. Knies, *The Art of Charlotte Brontë* (Athens: Ohio Univ. Press, 1969), 112.

22. Charlotte Brontë, "A Word to *The Quarterly*," in *Jane Eyre: An Authoritative Text, Backgrounds, Criticism*, ed. Richard J. Dunn (New York: Norton, 1971), 444.

23. A similar scene of including the forbidden or the foreclosed occurs when Jane contemplates Rochester's illicit proposal after she learns Bertha's identity. She imagines the "fount of rapture [that] would spring to my lips" (*JE* 347) were she to express her love to him.

24. Jane's need to tell her tale is evident, for example, when she flees from Thornfield. After two days in the coach, she worries about the hardships that she must endure "before my tale could be listened to, or one of my wants relieved" (*JE* 350).

25. The similarities between Richardson's and Brontë's novels have been

traced by Janet Spens, "Charlotte Brontë," *Essays and Studies by Members of the English Association*, 14 (1929): 53–70.

26. "What Is a Text? Explanation and Understanding," in *Twentieth-Century Literary Theory: An Introductory Anthology*, ed. Vassilis Lambropoulos and David Neal Miller (Albany: State Univ. of New York Press, 1987), 332.

27. An intermediary form of story—somewhere between ecstatic and interrogated narrative—is exemplified by Rochester's pseudo-interrogatory tactics, for example, when he disingenuously cross-examines Jane upon first seeing her (*JE* 164) and again after Bertha tears the wedding vale (*JE* 311–13). On another occasion, he assumes both dialogical roles, not only questioning Jane but also answering ventriloquially for her (*JE* 327).

28. See Sylvère Monod, "Charlotte Brontë and the Thirty 'Readers' of *Jane Eyre*," in *Jane Eyre*, ed. Richard J. Dunn, 503.

29. Julia Kristeva, *Tales of Love*, trans. Leon S. Roudiez (New York: Columbia Univ. Press, 1987). All references are to this edition and are cited in the text as *TL*.

30. "Criminals, Idiots, Women, and Minors," in *'Criminals, Idiots, Women, and Minors': Nineteenth-Century Writing by Women on Women*, ed. Susan Hamilton (Peterborough, Ontario: Broadview, 1995), 122.

5. RIGHT SPEAKING IN *ADAM BEDE*

1. A comparable example is to be found in Hardy's description of the residents of Casterbridge who speak "in other ways than by articulation. Not to hear the words of your interlocutor in metropolitan centres is to know nothing of his meaning. Here the face, the arms, the hat, the stick, the body throughout spoke equally with the tongue." Thomas Hardy, *The Mayor of Casterbridge*, 47.

2. George Eliot, "The Natural History of German Life," in *Essays of George Eliot*, ed. Thomas Pinney (London: Routledge & Kegan Paul, 1963), 114–15.

3. Richard D. Altick alludes to changing attitudes to slang during this time in *The Present of the Past: Topics of the Day in the Victorian Novel* (Columbus: Ohio State Univ. Press, 1991): 757–98.

4. "The Natural History of English Life," 109.

5. Dennis Taylor, *Hardy's Literary Language and Victorian Philology* (Oxford: Clarendon, 1993), 88. Taylor writes that the "1860s was the decade when two major traditions came into conflict: one the tradition of prescriptive grammars and usage books, the other that tradition of historical scholarship which saw the standard language as a momentary construct, one dialect among many" (3).

6. "The Natural History of German Life," 115. Eliot's views are similar to Rousseau's in "Essay on the Origin of Languages." See *The First and Second Discourses together with the Replies to Critics and Essay on the Origin of Languages*, ed. and trans. Victor Gourevitch (New York: Harper & Row, 1986), 249.

7. "The Natural History of German Life," 128.

8. During her research for the novel, Eliot notes Tooke as one of the "*Remarkable Persons*, living in 1799." *George Eliot: A Writer's Notebook: 1854–1879 and Uncollected Writings*, ed. Joseph Wiesenfarth (Charlottesville: Univ. of Virginia Press, 1978), 30.

9. Cited by Olivia Smith, *The Politics of Language: 1791–1819* (Oxford: Clarendon, 1984), 123.

10. "The Natural History of German Life," 128.

11. "Preface" to *Lyrical Ballads, Selected Prose*, 299. In the "Essay, Supplementary to the Preface" of 1815, Wordsworth describes language as "a thing subject to endless fluctuations and arbitrary associations" (411).

12. My argument resembles in several important particulars that of James Eli Adams in "Gyp's Tale: On Sympathy, Silence, and Realism in *Adam Bede*," in *Dickens Studies Annual: Essays on Victorian Fiction*, 20 (New York: AMS Press, 1991): 227–41. Unlike Adams, I do not want to claim that this skepticism places the realistic novel as a genre in the anomalous position of "constantly trying to write itself into silence" (229).

13. According to this view, language expresses the essence of a people or a nation. For more on the influence of romantic philology in England, see Linda Dowling, *Language and Decadence in the Victorian Fin de Siècle*.

14. See Margaret Homans, "Dinah's Blush, Maggie's Arm: Class, Gender, and Sexuality in George Eliot's Early Novels," *Victorian Studies* 36.2 (Winter 1993): 155–78.

15. For a discussion of her sermon in relation to Wesleyan practice and "the Methodist Way," see Valentine Cunningham, *Everywhere Spoken Against: Dissent in the Victorian Novel*. John Goode discusses the sermon in "Adam Bede" in *Critical Essays on George Eliot*, ed. Barbara Hardy (London: Routledge & Kegan Paul, 1970): 19–41. For a comment on Dinah's sermon as drama, see Nina Auerbach, *Romantic Imprisonment: Woman and Other Glorified Outcasts* (New York: Columbia Univ. Press, 1985), 261–63. Also see Elsie Holmes, "George Eliot's Wesleyan Madonna," *The George Eliot Fellowship Review* 18 (1987): 53–59.

16. Adam imagines that she "must look as if she'd come straight from heaven, like th' angels in the desert" (*AB* 374). Lisbeth tells Dinah: "ye comed in so light, like the shadow on the wall, an' spoke i' my ear, as I though ye might be a sperrit" (*AB* 114). Another point of comparison between Dinah and Wesley is their voices. Dinah remembers Wesley's voice as "not like any voice I had ever heard before" (*AB* 35), and her own "mellow treble tones" (*AB* 37) are frequently commented on.

17. This mistake is also made by Mrs. Poyser, who takes the dirt left in the corners by Molly as proof of her having "never been brought up among Christians" (*AB* 82). Just as Dinah exaggerates Bessy's remorse on this occasion, she later misreads Hetty's tears (*AB* 161).

18. A similar view is expressed by Christopher Herbert. I would stop short, however, of comparing Dinah to a kind of Christian "vampire" (416). See "Preachers and the Schemes of Nature in *Adam Bede*," *Nineteenth-Century Fiction*, 29.4 (1975): 412–27.

19. Lisbeth compares Dinah to "snow-drop flowers" (*AB* 124), and Adam

says she is "a lily" (*AB* 125). For a discussion of Eliot's own wishes to remain invisible, despite her public role as author, see Nina Auerbach, *Woman and the Demon: The Life of a Victorian Myth* (Cambridge: Harvard Univ. Press, 1982). Also see Rosemarie Bodenheimer, "Ambition and its Audiences: George Eliot's Performing Figures," *Victorian Studies* 34.4 (1991): 7–33.

20. Ben also teases Seth on this point (*AB* 20). Even Lisbeth comments on Dinah's attractiveness, contrasting her with other "Methody women" of her acquaintance (*AB* 117).

21. Adam's views are seconded by Bartle Massey (*AB* 407).

22. Some of George Eliot's views on preaching are to be found in her essay, "Evangelical Teaching: Dr. Cumming." *Essays of George Eliot*, ed. Thomas Pinney.

23. The significance of the biblical tale of Rachel and Jacob is discussed by Joseph Wiesenfarth in *George Eliot's Mythmaking* (Heidelburg: Carl Winter, 1977), 91–93.

24. This passage among others is the subject of Dianne Sadoff's deconstructive reading of the novel. See "Nature's Language: Metaphor in the Text of *Adam Bede*," *Genre* 11.3 (1978): 411–26.

25. What we do hear is the language with which he seduces himself into believing that this dalliance is merely "flirting" or "trifling" (*AB* 288). The narrator mocks the language of sentimental romance by associating its heroines with velvet or downy peaches (*AB* 134, 153).

26. Joseph Wiesenfarth suggests that insofar as Adam is a latter-day Christ figure, "Dinah is, at the mythical level, correct in finally refusing to distinguish between her love for Jesus and her love for Adam" (*Mythmaking*, 90).

27. See M. M. Bakhtin, *The Dialogic Imagination*, ed. Michael Holquist, trans. Caryl Emerson and Michael Holquist (Austin: Univ. of Texas Press, 1981).

28. These views are echoed in "The Natural History of German Life," where Eliot tries to correct an idealized picture of the peasantry: "That delicious effervescence of the mind which we call fun, has no equivalent for the northern peasant, except tipsy revelry; the only realm of fancy and imagination for the English clown exists at the bottom of the third quart pot" (109).

29. Bakhtin, 25–26.

30. A fuller version of these lines appears in "The Natural History of German Life" (109), as has been noted by several commentators. See Mary Jean Corbett, "Representing the Rural: The Critique of Loamshire in *Adam Bede*," *Studies in the Novel* 20.3 (1988): 288–301; Suzanne Graver, *George Eliot and Community: A Study in Social Theory and Fictional Form* (Berkeley: Univ. of California Press, 1984); and A. G. van den Broek, "*Adam Bede* and Riehl's 'Social-Political Conservatism,'" *The George Eliot Fellowship Review* 17 (1986): 42–61.

31. The quatrain reads: "Here's a health unto our master, / The founder of the feast; / Here's a health unto our master / and to our mistress!" (*AB* 491).

32. In the agricultural community the sky is also a frequently consulted text. Despite the claim "to ha' studied the look o' the clouds" (*AB* 201), Mr. Craig is not shown to be a reliable meteorologist. He appears to miss the irony

of his own explanation for an incorrect prediction: "the weather, you see, 's a ticklish thing, an' a fool 'ull hit on't sometimes when a wise man misses; that's why the alamecks get so much credit. It's one o' them chancy things as fools thrive on" (*AB* 203).

33. A minor example arises in the discrepancy between personal appearance, on the one hand, and musical accomplishment, on the other (*AB* 197).

34. Sally Shuttleworth is more optimistic about the possibility of reading nature. See *George Eliot and Nineteenth-Century Science* (Cambridge: Cambridge Univ. Press, 1984), 48.

35. U. C. Knoepflmacher also makes this point in *Religious Humanism and the Victorian Novel: George Eliot, Walter Pater, and Samuel Butler* (Princeton, N.J.: Princeton Univ. Press, 1965).

36. *Lectures on the Science of Language*, 340.

37. For a discussion of performative language and George Eliot's theory of narrative discourse, see J. Hillis Miller, *The Ethics of Reading* (New York: Columbia Univ. Press, 1987).

38. Shuttleworth, 36.

39. Cunningham, 124–25.

6. PROMISING MARRIAGE

1. "Rough Truth: Synecdoche and Interpretation in *The Egoist*," *Nineteenth-Century Fiction* 31 (1976), 324. Also see, J. Hillis Miller, "'Herself Against Herself': The Clarification of Clara Middleton," in *The Representation of Women in Fiction, Selected Papers from the English Institute, 1981*, ed. Carolyn G. Heilbrun and Margaret R. Higonnet, New Series, no. 7 (Baltimore: Johns Hopkins Univ. Press, 1983): 98–123; and Michael Sprinker, "'The Intricate Evasions of A': Meredith's Theory of Figure," *The Victorian Newsletter* 53 (Spring 1978): 9–12.

2. Emma Dunstane attributes Redworth's initial failure to win Diana to his inability to "woo . . . in a poetic style, or the courtly by prescription" (*DCW* 474), but ultimately it is his "poverty in the pleading language [that] melted her" (*DCW* 482). Redworth's character, Diana's fate, and the resolution of the novel are discussed by Penny Boumelha in "'The Rattling of her Discourse and the Flapping of her Dress': Meredith Writing the 'Women of the Future,'" in *Feminist Criticism: Theory and Practice*, ed. Susan Sellers (Toronto: Univ. of Toronto Press, 1991): 197–208.

3. Jonathan Culler, *The Pursuit of Signs: Semiotics, Literature, Deconstruction* (Ithaca, N.Y.: Cornell Univ. Press, 1981), 202.

4. *The Pursuit of Signs*, 204.

5. This theme has been earlier sounded in Clara's comments about his love letters: "You are able to express yourself to men as your meaning dictates. In writing to . . . to us it is, I suppose, more difficult" (*E* 1:76, Meredith's ellipsis). What is meant by the phrase "lady's tongue" is made transparently clear by Dr. Middleton: "I have not the 'lady's tongue'. My appeal is always to reason" (*E* 2:35).

6. This is Ted Cohen's description of metaphor, a term I take him to use figuratively to refer to figurative language in general. "Figurative Speech and Figurative Acts," *The Journal of Philosophy* 72 (1975), 671.

7. Further evidence of their questionable accuracy is Mrs. Mountstuart's naive method of analysis: "Her directions for the reading of Miss Middleton's character were the same that she practised in reading Sir Willoughby's, whose physiognomy and manners bespoke him what she presumed him to be, a splendidly proud gentleman" (*E* 1:51). Presumption verified by appearance seems a questionable interpretive method. Vernon recognizes that Mrs. Mountstuart's brilliant epithets serve primarily to "dazzle the penetration of the composer" (*E* 2:77). The capacity of language to blind its speaker is discussed by Gary J. Handwerk in "Linguistic Blindness and Ironic Vision in *The Egoist*," *Nineteenth-Century Fiction* 39 (1984): 163–85.

8. The failure to accept this mixed nature is also characteristic of Willoughby, whose "notion of women was the primitive black and white. . . . Women of mixed essences shading off the divine to the considerably lower, were outside his vision of woman" (*E* 1:129–30). They are also, if the narrator of *Diana of the Crossways* is to be believed, outside English vision in general: "The English notion of women seems to be that we are born white sheep or black; circumstances have nothing to do with our colour. They dread to grant distinctions, and to judge of us discerningly is beyond them" (*DCW* 158).

9. The issue of gender and voice is discussed by Carolyn Williams in "Unbroken Patternes: Gender, Culture, and Voice in *The Egoist*," *Browning Institute Studies* 13, ed. Adrienne Auslander Munich (New York: The Browning Institute, Inc., and the Graduate School and University Center, CUNY, 1985): 45–70. Also see Rachel M. Brownstein, *Becoming a Heroine* (New York: Viking, 1982).

10. For a discussion of the figurative impenetrability of the opening chapter of the novel, see Gayla McGlamery, "In His Beginning, His Ends: The 'Preface' to Meredith's *Diana of the Crossways*," *Studies in the Novel* (1991): 470–89.

11. The association of language and eating recurs throughout the novel. In aristocratic settings, wit is figured as salt (*DCW 147*, 192); in rural environments, bacon and volubility are linked (*DCW* 99).

12. It is further implied that she offends the masculine authority of her husband: "What is the husband of a vanward woman? He feels himself but a diminished man. The English husband of a voluble woman relapses into a dreary mute" (*DCW* 122).

13. The narrator later uses an extended metaphor for London as "the head of the British giant, and if not the liveliest in bubbles, it is past competition the largest broth-pot of brains anywhere simmering on the hob." The metaphor may not be superobese, but it is somewhat contrived, and the narrator defensively comments, "Let grander similes be sought" (*DCW* 191).

14. Diana herself, for instance, is occasionally "guilty of a little whiff of blarney" (*DCW* 79). She is subject to "seizures of iridescent humor" (*DCW* 120). From the English perspective, the Irish are characterized by their poetic,

therefore, irresponsible nature—hence the stereotype of "the iridescent Irishman, whose remembered repartees are a feast" (*DCW* 191).

15. See, too, Clara's image of "an obelisk lettered all over with hieroglyphs" (*E* 1:115).

16. Meredith criticizes academic discourse in "On the Idea of Comedy and of the Uses of the Comic Spirit" (Memorial Edition, vol. 23). The academics are the adjudicators of word usage. For instance, Dr. Middleton criticizes Willoughby for combining "judicial" and "abhor" in a single sentence (*E* 2:207).

17. Smirlock also discusses this passage. He concludes: "In fine, figurative language is rough truth, and *The Egoist* is a revel of it" (317).

18. The image of women as changeable and inconsistent is seen throughout the novel. Clara is herself very much aware of it: "She had heard women abused for shallowness and flightiness: she had heard her father denounce them as veering weather-vanes, and his oft-repeated quid femina possit: for her sex's sake, and also to appear an exception to her sex, this reasoning creature desired to be thought consistent" (*E* 1:211–12).

19. Although he does not win this war, De Craye seldom loses a skirmish. Adept at contests of wit, he is also a skilled and calculating raconteur. For example, his "tales of youngest Cupid upon subterranean adventures" (*E* 2:14) exemplify what they relate; that is, they are themselves part of an amorous subterfuge that diverts Willoughby and allows Clara to escape from Patterne Hall. His courtship is carried on by glib performances, such as his "essay on Honeymoons" (*E* 1:253), that reveal both his superior rhetoric and his own purely "oratorical" existence.

20. Mrs. Mountstuart makes a similar proposal to Willoughby on his twenty-first birthday: "Were I . . . twenty years younger, I think I would marry you to cure my infatuation" (*E* 1:16).

21. Shoshana Felman, *The Literary Speech Act: Don Juan with J. L. Austin, or Seduction in Two Languages*, trans. Catherine Porter (Ithaca, N.Y.: Cornell Univ. Press, 1983), 27.

22. Felman, 28.

23. Felman, 35. Of the conditions necessary to the act of promising, Don Juan clearly violates what John Searle calls "the sincerity condition," and Willoughby fails to fulfill a "preparatory condition," specifically, that the thing promised be something the promisee wants done and that the promiser know this. What Willoughby knows, however, is that, whatever Laetitia may once have felt, neither she nor Clara wants to marry him. His promise to marry, then, is actually a threat to marry. John Searle, "What Is a Speech Act?", in *Readings in the Philosophy of Language*, ed. Jay F. Rosenberg and Charles Travis (Englewood Cliffs, N.J.: Prentice Hall, 1971): 614–28.

24. Talk in the drawing room often functions as "noise" does in communication theory. See Ross Chambers, *Story and Situation: Narrative Seduction and the Power of Fiction* (Minneapolis: Univ. of Minnesota Press, 1984).

25. Lionel Stevenson calls this Meredith's "trick of dodging a key scene." *The Ordeal of George Meredith* (New York: Scribner's, 1953), 225.

26. Miller, 115.

27. Felman, 34.

7. QUESTIONING RHETORIC

1. Thomas Hobbes, *Leviathan* (London: Pelican), 4:17.

2. Anthony Trollope, *Can You Forgive Her?* (Oxford: Oxford Univ. Press, 1989), 2:383. Unless otherwise noted, all references to the works of Anthony Trollope are from The World's Classics Series of Oxford University Press and are cited parethetically in the text: *The Small House at Allington* (*SHA*), *Can Your Forgive Her?* (*CYFH*), *He Knew He Was Right* (*HKHWR*), *Phineas Finn* (*PF*), *The Eustace Diamonds* (*ED*), *Phineas Redux* (*PR*), *The Prime Minister* (*PM*), *The Duke's Children* (*DC*), *The Way We Live Now* (*WWLN*), *Autobiography* (*A*).

3. The same locution is used in *Bleak House*. Dickens calls attention to its inherent contradiction: "'I had confident expectations that things would come round and be all square,' says Mr. Jobling, with some vagueness of expression, and perhaps of meaning, too" (*BH* 248). It should be noted that Alice herself threatens to go to her lawyer, Mr. Round, to make things square with her cousin George (*CYFH* 2:211).

4. Alice at one point denies her initial engagement to George Vavasor (*CYFH* 1:18), but the general consensus seems to be that there was an engagement (chapters four and thirty-one), and Alice herself refers to jilting three lovers, which would mean that George has been jilted twice.

5. *Nightmare Abbey, The Works of Thomas Love Peacock*, vol. 3 (New York: AMS Press, 1967), 74. All references are to this edition and are cited in the text as *NA*.

6. John W. Clark, *The Language and Style of Anthony Trollope* (London: Andre Deutsch, 1975), 18. Also see Walter M. Kendrick, *The Novel Machine: The Theory and Fiction of Anthony Trollope* (Baltimore: Johns Hopkins Univ. Press, 1980).

7. C. P. Snow, *Trollope* (London: Macmillan, 1975), 113.

8. The two suitor theme is discussed by Jean E. Kennard, *Victims of Convention* (Hamden, Conn.: Archon, 1978). Also see, Deborah Denenholz Morse, *Women in Trollope's Palliser Novels* (Ann Arbor and London: UMI Research Press, 1987).

9. Paul de Man, "Semiology and Rhetoric," *Diacritics* 3 (Fall 1973): 27–33.

10. Review article, *Nation* (New York: 28 September 1865), reprinted in *Trollope: The Critical Heritage*, ed. Donald Smalley (London: Routledge & Kegan Paul, 1969), 249–50.

11. This point would not be conceded by Robyn Warhol, who argues that "her" could refer to any of the following: Alice, Glencora, Mrs. Greenow, the jilt, or the flirt. See *Gendered Interventions: Narrative Discourse in the Victorian Novel* (New Brunswick: Rutgers Univ. Press, 1989), 135–36.

12. Anthony Trollope, *Life of Cicero*, 2 vols. (London: Chapman and Hall, 1880), 2:272. All references are to this edition and are cited in the text as (*LC*). Ruth apRoberts has previously noted the importance of the *Life of Cicero* to Trollope's thought, and she cites Edith Hamilton's remark: "the English gentleman, who has meant much to many generations, may well have

had his beginnings, in, certainly he was fostered by, the English schoolboy's strenuous drilling in Cicero." *The Moral Trollope* (Athens: Ohio Univ. Press, 1971), 63. Also see George Butte, "Trollope's Duke of Omnium and 'the Pain of History': A Study of the Novelist's Politics," *Victorian Studies* 24 (1981): 209–27. Cicero and Trollope's concern with "the ethics of advocacy" are touched upon by R. D. McMaster in *Trollope and the Law* (London: Macmillan, 1986). Also see Mary Rosner, "The Two Faces of Cicero: Trollope's *Life* in the Nineteenth Century," *Rhetoric Society Quarterly* 18 (1988): 251–58.

13. Anthony Trollope, *The New Zealander*, ed. N. John Hall (Oxford: Oxford Univ. Press, 1972), 122. Among the terms to be found in the Newspeak of *1984* is "blackwhite": "Applied to an opponent, it means the habit of impudently claiming that black is white, in contradiction of the plain facts. Applied to a Party member, it means a loyal willingness to say that black is white when Party discipline demands this." George Orwell, *1984* (Harmondsworth, England: Penguin, 1954), 169–70.

14. Cited by Snow, p. 115.

15. In the *Autobiography*, Trollope says that "love and intrigue" are thrown in for the benefit of readers who cannot take too much unalleviated political discussion (*A* 317).

16. The allusion is to Byron's *Don Juan*, Canto III. For a discussion of Trollope's indebtedness to Byron, see Donald D. Stone, *The Romantic Impulse in Victorian Fiction* (Cambridge: Harvard Univ. Press, 1980). For related discussions, see L. J. Swingle, *Romanticism and Anthony Trollope: A Study in the Continuities of Nineteenth-Century Thought* (Ann Arbor: Univ. of Michigan Press, 1990); John Christopher Kleis, "Passion vs. Prudence: Theme and Technique in Trollope's Palliser Novels," *Texas Studies in Literature and Language* 11 (1970): 1405–14; and David R. Eastwood, "Romantic Elements and Aesthetic Distance in Trollope's Fiction," *Studies in Short Fiction* 18 (1981): 395–405.

17. René Girard, *Deceit, Desire and the Novel* (Baltimore: Johns Hopkins Univ. Press, 1965).

18. On Glencora's and Alice's habits of speaking, see George Levine, "Can You Forgive Him?: Trollope's *Can You Forgive Her?* and the Myth of Realism," *Victorian Studies* 18 (1974): 5–30.

19. For a study of naming in the sense of applying proper names, see Michael Ragussis, *Acts of Naming: The Family Plot in Fiction* (Oxford: Oxford Univ. Press, 1986).

20. The same issue arises between Emily Trevelyan and her husband. Lady Milborough is shocked at Emily's description of Louis as a spy: "My dear, how could you bring yourself to use the word spy to your husband?" (*HKHWR* 101).

21. Juliet McMaster, *Trollope's Palliser Novels* (London: Macmillan, 1978), 26.

22. *On the Study of Words*, 35.

23. *On the Study of Words*, 35.

24. The duke later mitigates his opinion of this romance: "It had never seemed to him that she had disgraced herself by loving Tregear—but that a great

misfortune had fallen upon her" (*DC* 528). The same term becomes an issue between Emily and Louis Trevelyan (*HKHWR* 257).

25. Plantagenet Palliser says, "I never yet gave the lie to a gentleman, and I hope I never may be driven to do so" (*DC* 39).

26. *The Way We Live Now* (London: Trollope Society, 1992), 223.

27. See Mary Lyndon Shanley, *Feminism, Marriage, and the Law in Victorian England, 1850–1895* (Princeton, N.J.: Princeton Univ. Press, 1989).

28. In announcing the "play, as a play was a failure" because the central "character afforded no scope for sympathy" (*ED* 2:109), Mrs. Carbuncle, however mistaken her values, echoes the criticism that Trollope received from the actor to whom he first sent *The Noble Jilt* for a reading. Her criticism also expresses Trollope's fear about critics' acceptance of Alice as noble. See Michael Sadleir's "Preface" to *The Noble Jilt* (Arno Press, 1981).

29. *Topographies* (Stanford, Calif.: Stanford Univ. Press, 1995), 124–25.

30. *The Question of Our Speech, The Lesson of Balzac: Two Lectures* (Boston and New York: Houghton Mifflin, 1905). All references are to this edition and are cited as *QS*.

8. DYING PROMISES

1. Henry James, *The Wings of the Dove*, ed. J. Donald Crowley and Richard A. Hocks (New York: W. W. Norton, 1978), 9. All references to the novel are from this edition and are cited in the text as *WD*.

2. Kate later tells Densher: "we're such a failure as a family!" She alludes to "the dishonour [of] her father," "the wounded state of her mother, abandoned despoiled and helpless," "the extinction of her two young brothers," and to her sister's "unnatural marriage" (*WD* 55).

3. I am paraphrasing W. H. Auden's "In Memory of W. B. Yeats."

4. The indirect and secretive nature of social interchange in the novel is often commented upon. For an insightful discussion of this theme, see Mary Cross, *Henry James: The Contingencies of Style* (New York: St. Martin's, 1993).

5. Carole Pateman, *The Problem of Political Obligation: A Critical Analysis of Liberal Theory* (Chichester: John Wiley & Sons, 1979), 27. Pateman is quoting H. Pitkin in *Wittgenstein and Justice: On the Significance of Ludwig Wittgenstein for Social and Political Thought* (Berkeley: Univ. of California Press, 1972).

6. This argument bears some relation to that of Lee Clark Mitchell, "The Sustaining Duplicities of *The Wings of the Dove*," *Texas Studies in Literature and Language* 29:2 (1987): 187–214.

7. "The Art of Fiction," in *Theory of Fiction: Henry James*, ed. James E. Miller, Jr. (Lincoln: Univ. of Nebraska Press, 1972), 35.

8. That such is the case is implied by Milly's reaction to her London debut, a dinner at Aunt Maud's: "To have made their pilgrimage all for the sake of such society as Mrs. Lowder might have in reserve for them—that didn't bear thinking of at all, and she herself had quite chosen her course for curiosity about other matters" (*WD* 99).

9. The apparent promise between Densher and Milly concerning her looking him up in London initiates a second promissory sequence. Having fulfilled the first promise, Milly is presented with a request for a second one. Densher asks that Milly return to London after visiting Venice (*WD* 232), and she requests that he invite her to his rooms after he has followed her to Venice (*WD* 283). This, in turn, elicits the "hollow promise" discussed in this chapter.

10. Of Milly's restiveness, we are told, "it was not Milly's unpacified state, in short, that now troubled her—though certainly, as Europe was the great American sedative, the failure was to some extent to be noted: it was the suspected presence of something behind the state—which, however, could scarcely have taken its place there since their departure. What a fresh motive of unrest could suddenly have sprung from was in short not to be divined" (*WD* 82).

11. Sharon Cameron, *Thinking in Henry James* (Chicago: Univ. of Chicago Press, 1989), 141–42.

12. All references are to the Penguin edition (Harmondsworth, England: 1986) and are cited in the text as *PC*.

13. Deborah Esch compellingly argues that *The Princess Casamassima* represents "a mise-en-scene of the 'case' of promising," a case subsequently and succinctly described as that of "the illocutionary act that cannot be bound once and for all to its 'original' context." "Promissory Notes: The Prescription of the Future in *The Princess Casamassima*," *American Literary History* 1.2 (Summer 1989), 319, 330. In "Words and Deeds in *The Princess Casamassima*," Taylor Stoehr notes: "Perversely, in typical Jamesian fashion, the result is freeing, and things begin to happen to Hyacinth immediately upon his swearing his oath." *ELH* 37.1 (1970), 119–20.

14. This pity is described in terms that are also used in *The Princess Casamassima*: "when pity held up its telltale face like a head on a pike, in a French revolution, bobbing before a window, what was the inference but that the patient was bad" (*WD* 148). The narrator speculates that Madame Poupin's "grandmother, in Paris, in the Revolution, must certainly have carried bloody heads on a pike" (*PC* 468).

15. Elizabeth Gaskell, *Wives and Daughters* (Harmondsworth, England: Penguin, 1969). All references are to this edition and are cited in the text as *WAD*.

16. This is Preston's view as well. He says that Cynthia has "made promises which she will find it requires the consent of two people to break" (*WAD* 530). His willingness to coerce Cynthia into a loveless marriage, however, discredits this claim.

17. The source, nature, and quantity of Kate's value are repeated themes in the novel. Kate, for instance, ponders her value to her aunt (*WD* 51) and clearly recognizes that to her family: "'My position's a value, a great value, for them both'—she followed and followed. Lucid and ironic, she knew no merciful muddle. 'It's *the* value—the only one they have'" (*WD* 59, also see 65).

18. Milly ought to remember the scene in which she does ask Kate for a promise. Visiting Sir Luke Strett for the first time, she enlists Kate's help, but does so on the condition that Susan Stringham be kept in the dark. She does

this despite feeling that secrecy implies that there is something "wicked and false" (*WD* 140) about her request for a "promise of absolute silence" (*WD* 141). As is typically the case in the novel, the giving of requested promises is not recorded in the text, which invariably leaves some uncertainty about the circumstances, even the existence, of the promise. In this case, readers must infer Kate's promise from her accompanying Milly to Sir Luke's. The only concrete evidence of the promise is negative and is found in Milly's speculation that perhaps Kate has broken the promise and confided in Mrs. Stringham (*WD* 156).

19. *The Pleasure of the Text*, trans. Richard Miller (New York: Hill and Wang, 1975).

20. James's idea for the nature of this engagement is suggested by his notebook entry: "But the young man is entangled with another woman, committed, pledged, 'engaged' to one—and it is in that that a little story seems to reside." *The Notebooks of Henry James*, ed. F. O. Matthiessen and Kenneth Murdock (New York: Oxford Univ. Press, 1947), 169.

21. Promising often functions in this way, as we have seen with Densher's hollow promise to Milly. Time is gained by Kate's subsequent plotting, which, she tells Densher, "helps you . . . to serve *me*. It gains you time" (307).

22. See the advice of Kate (*WD* 211) and Mrs. Lowder (*WD* 222). Densher now actively misleads Milly as do they. For instance, he tells Milly that he doesn't know Kate: "I don't feel as if I knew her—really to call know." He may tell himself "during a silence that ensued for a minute he had time to recognise that his own [words] contained after all no element of falsity" (*WD* 233), but his acquital on a technicality merely convinces readers of his guilt. Kate is, of course, a complex person, whom Densher cannot fully know; however, that limitation is a function of Kate's complexity not of their lack of intimacy. Densher's statement is false.

23. "Here" is Milly's hotel, where Densher and Kate arrive independently of one another to visit their friend. This scene anticipates Milly's exclusion from Densher's rooms in Venice since, in a sense, "there's everything between Kate and Densher there."

AFTERWORD

1. *Collected Poems*, ed. Edward Mendelson (New York: Vintage, 1979), 91.

WORKS CITED

Aarsleff, Hans. *The Study of Language in England,* 1780–1860. Minneapolis: Univ. of Minnesota Press, 1983.

——. *From Locke to Saussure: Essays on the Study of Language and Intellectual History.* Minneapolis: Univ. of Minnesota Press, 1982.

Adams, James Eli. "Gyp's Tale: On Sympathy, Silence, and Realism in *Adam Bede.*" *Dickens Studies Annual: Essays on Victorian Fiction,* 20 (1991): 227–41.

Allen, Carleton Kemp. "Introduction," *Ancient Law.* London: Oxford Univ. Press, 1959, ix–xxviii.

Altick, Richard D. *The Present of the Past: Topics of the Day in the Victorian Novel.* Columbus: Ohio State Univ. Press, 1991.

Amos, Sheldon. *The Science of Law.* London: Henry S. King, 1874.

Appleyard, J. A. *Coleridge's Philosophy of Literature: the Development of a Concept of Poetry,* 1791–1819. Cambridge: Harvard Univ. Press, 1965.

apRoberts, Ruth. *The Moral Trollope.* Athens: Ohio Univ. Press, 1971.

Aristotle, *Aristotle's Theory of Poetry and Fine Art.* Trans. by S. H. Butcher. New York: Dover, 1951.

Atiyah, P. S. *Introduction to Law of Contract.* London: Clarendon, 1971.

——. *Promises, Morals, and Law.* Oxford: Clarendon, 1981.

——. *The Rise and Fall of Freedom of Contract.* Oxford: Clarendon, 1979.

Auden, W. H. *Collected Poems.* Ed. by Edward Mendelson. New York: Random House, 1968.

Auerbach, Nina. *Romantic Imprisonment: Women and Other Glorified Outcasts.* New York: Columbia Univ. Press, 1985.

——. *Woman and the Demon: The Life of a Victorian Myth.* Cambridge: Harvard Univ. Press, 1982.

Austen, Jane. *Northanger Abbey.* Harmondsworth, England: Penguin, 1985.

Austin, J. L. *How to Do Things with Words.* Ed. by J. O. Urmson and Marina Sbisà. Cambridge: Harvard Univ. Press, 1975.

Bakhtin, M. M. *The Dialogic Imagination.* Ed. by Michael Holquist and trans. by Caryl Emerson and Michael Holquist. Austin: Univ. of Texas Press, 1981.

Barthes, Roland. *The Pleasure of the Text.* Trans. by Richard Miller. New York: Hill and Wang, 1975.

Beaty, Jerome. *Misreading* Jane Eyre: *A Postformalist Paradigm.* Columbus: Ohio State Univ. Press, 1996.

Beer, Gillian. "Darwin and the Growth of Language Theory." In *Nature Transfigured: Science and Literature,* 1700–1900. Ed. by John Christie and Sally

Shuttleworth, 152–70. Manchester and New York: Manchester Univ. Press, 1989.

Bennett, Lance and Martha S. Feldman. *Reconstructing Reality in the Courtroom.* New Brunswick: Rutgers Univ. Press, 1981.

Bentham, Jeremy. *Theory of Fictions.* In Ogden, C. K. *Bentham's Theory of Fictions.* New York: Harcourt, Brace, 1932.

———. *The Works of Jeremy Bentham.* Ed. by John Bowring. New York: Russell & Russell, 1962.

Blackstone, Sir William. *Commentaries on the Laws of England.* Oxford: Clarendon, 1765.

Bloom, Harold. "Introduction," *Charlotte Brontë's Jane Eyre.* New York: Chelsea House, 1987, 1–6.

Bodenheimer, Rosemarie. "Jane Eyre in Search of Her Story." *Papers on Language and Literature,* 16 (1980): 387–402.

———. "Ambition and its Audiences: George Eliot's Performing Figures." *Victorian Studies,* 34:4 (1991): 7–33.

Boumelha, Penny. "'The Rattling of her Discourse and the Flapping of her Dress': Meredith Writing the 'Women of the Future.'" In *Feminist Criticism: Theory and Practice.* Ed. by Susan Sellers, 197–208. Toronto: Univ. of Toronto Press, 1991.

Braddon, Mary Elizabeth. *Lady Audley's Secret.* New York: Dover, 1974.

Brockelbank, W. J. "The Nature of the Promise to Marry—A Study in Comparative Law." *Illinois Law Review.* vol. 41, no. 1 (May–June 1916): 2–26.

Brontë, Charlotte. *Jane Eyre.* Ed. by Q. D. Leavis. Harmondsworth, England: Penguin, 1966.

———. "A Word to *The Quarterly.*" In *Jane Eyre: An Authoritative Text, Backgrounds, Criticism.* Ed. by Richard J. Dunn. New York: Norton, 1971.

Brooks, Peter. *The Melodramatic Imagination: Balzac, Henry James, Melodrama, and the Mode of Excess.* New Haven: Yale Univ. Press, 1976.

———. *Reading for the Plot: Design and Intention in Narrative.* New York: Random House, 1985.

Brown, Robert C. "Breach of Promise Suits." *University of Pennsylvania Law Review.* vol. 77 (1929): 474–97.

Brownstein, Rachel M. *Becoming a Heroine.* New York: Viking, 1982.

Bryant, Arthur. *The Great Duke or The Invincible General.* London: Collins, 1971.

Burrow, J. W. *Evolution and Society: A Study in Victorian Social Theory.* Cambridge: Cambridge Univ. Press, 1966.

———. "The Uses of Philology in Victorian England." In *Ideas and Institutions Of Victorian Britain: Essays in Honour of George Kitson Clark.* Ed. by Robert Robson, 180–204. New York: Barnes and Noble, 1967.

Butler, Judith. *Excitable Speech: A Politics of the Performative.* London: Routledge, 1997.

Butte, George. "Trollope's Duke of Omnium and 'the Pain of History': A Study of the Novelist's Politics." *Victorian Studies,* 24 (1981): 209–27.

Cameron, Sharon. *Thinking in Henry James.* Chicago: Univ. of Chicago Press, 1989.

Carlyle, Thomas. *A Carlyle Reader*. Ed. by G. B. Tennyson. Cambridge: Cambridge Univ. Press, 1984.

Carroll, Lewis. *Alice in Wonderland*. Ed. by Donald J. Gray. New York: Norton, 1971.

Chambers, Ross. *Story and Situation: Narrative Seduction and the Power of Fiction*. Minneapolis: Univ. of Minnesota Press, 1984.

Chase, Karen. *Eros & Psyche: The Representation of Personality in Charlotte Brontë, Charles Dickens, and George Eliot*. New York and London: Methuen, 1984.

Clark, John W. *The Language and Style of Anthony Trollope*. London: Andre Deutsch, 1975.

Cobbe, Frances Power. "Criminals, Idiots, Women, and Minors." In *'Criminals, Idiots, Women, and Minors': Nineteenth-Century Writing by Women on Women*. Ed. by Susan Hamilton, 108–31. Peterborough, Ontario: Broadview, 1995.

Cocks, R. C. J. *Sir Henry Maine: A Study in Victorian Jurisprudence*. Cambridge: Cambridge Univ. Press, 1988.

Cohen, Ted. "Figurative Speech and Figurative Acts." *The Journal of Philosophy*, 72 (1975): 670–82.

Coleridge, Samuel Taylor. *Aids to Reflection*. Ed. by Thomas Fenby. Liverpool: Edward Howell, 1877.

———. *Biographia Literaria. The Collected Works of Samuel Taylor Coleridge*, vol. 7. Ed. by James Engell and W. Jackson Bate. Princeton, N.J.: Princeton Univ. Press, 1983.

———. *Logic. The Collected Works of Samuel Taylor Coleridge*, vol. 13. Intro. by J. R. de J. Jackson. Princeton, N.J.: Princeton Univ. Press, 1983.

———. *The Notebooks of Samuel Taylor Coleridge*. Ed. by Kathleen Coburn. New York: Bollingen, 1957–1973.

Condillac, Etienne Bonnot de. *An Essay on the Origin of Human Knowledge*. Trans. by Thomas Nugent. London: J. Nourse, 1756.

Conrad, Joseph. *Lord Jim*. New York: Norton, 1968.

Coombe, Rosemary J. "'The Most Disgusting, Disgraceful and Inequitous Proceeding in Our Law': The Action for Breach of Promise of Marriage in Nineteenth-Century Ontario." *University of Toronto Law Journal*, 38:1 (Winter 1988): 64–108.

Corbett, Mary Jean. "Representing the Rural: The Critique of Loamshire in *Adam Bede*." *Studies in the Novel*, 20:3 (1988): 288–301.

Cotterell, Roger. *The Politics of Jurisprudence: A Critical Introduction to Legal Philosophy*. London: Butterworths, 1989.

Cover, Robert. "Forward: *Nomos* and Narrative." *Harvard Law Review*, 97 (1983): 4–68.

Cross, Mary. *Henry James: The Contingencies of Style*. New York: St. Martin's, 1993.

Crowley, Tony. *Standard English and the Politics of Language*. Urbana and Chicago: Univ. of Illinois Press, 1989.

Culler, Jonathan. *The Pursuit of Signs: Semiotics, Literature, Deconstruction*. Ithaca, N.Y.: Cornell Univ. Press, 1981.

Cunningham, Valentine. *Everywhere Spoken Against: Dissent in the Victorian Novel.* Oxford: Clarendon, 1974.

"Damages for Breach of Promise of Marriage." *The Albany Law Journal,* 10 (1874): 341–42.

Darwin, Charles. *The Descent of Man and Selection in Relation to Sex.* New York: D. Appleton, 1896.

DeCicco, Lynne Marie. *Women and Lawyers in the Mid-Nineteenth Century Novel.* Lewiston, NY: Edwin Mellen, 1996.

de Man, Paul. *Allegories of Reading: Figural Language in Rousseau, Nietzsche, Rilke, and Proust.* New Haven: Yale Univ. Press, 1979.

———. "Semiology and Rhetoric." *Diacritics,* 3 (Fall 1973): 27–33.

Derrida, Jacques. *Memoires for Paul de Man.* New York: Columbia Univ. Press, 1986.

Dessner, Lawrence Jay. *The Homely Web of Truth: A Study of Charlotte Brontë's Novels.* The Hague and Paris: Mouton, 1975.

Dickens, Charles. *Bleak House.* New York: Norton, 1977.

———. *Great Expectations.* Harmondsworth, England: Penguin, 1965.

———. *The Pickwick Papers.* Harmondsworth, England: Penguin, 1972.

Dowling, Linda, *Language and Decadence in the Victorian Fin de Siècle.* Princeton, N.J.: Princeton Univ. Press, 1986.

Dworkin, Ronald. "How Law Is Like Literature." In *Law and Literature: Text and Theory.* Ed. by Lenora Ledwon, 29–60. New York: Garland, 1996.

Eagleton, Terry. *Myths of Power: A Marxist Study of the Brontës.* Second Edition. London: Macmillan, 1988.

Eastwood, David R. "Romantic Elements and Aesthetic Distance in Trollope's Fiction." *Studies in Short Fiction,* 18 (1981): 395–405.

Eliot, George. *Adam Bede.* New York: New American Library, 1961.

———. *Daniel Deronda.* Harmondsworth, England: Penguin, 1986.

———. "Evangelical Teaching: Dr. Cumming." In *Essays of George Eliot.* Ed. by Thomas Pinney. London: Routledge and Kegan Paul, 1963.

———. *The George Eliot Letters,* 7 vols. Ed. by Gordon S. Haight. New Haven: Yale Univ. Press, 1954–55.

———. *George Eliot: A Writer's Notebook: 1854–1879 and Uncollected Writings.* Ed. by Joseph Wiesenfarth. Charlottesville: Univ. of Virginia Press, 1978.

———. *Middlemarch.* Harmondsworth, England: Penguin, 1975.

———. *The Mill on the Floss.* Harmondsworth, England: Penguin, 1986.

———. "The Natural History of German Life." In *Essays of George Eliot.* Ed. by Thomas Pinney. London: Routledge & Kegan Paul, 1963.

Esch, Deborah. "Promissory Notes: The Prescription of the Future in *The Princess Casamassima.*" *American Literary History,* 1:2 (Summer 1989): 317–38.

Farrar, Frederick. *An Essay on the Origin of Language.* London: John Murrary, 1860.

Felman, Shoshana. *The Literary Speech Act: Don Juan with J. L. Austin, or Seduction in Two Languages.* Trans. by Catherine Porter. Ithaca, N.Y.: Cornell Univ. Press, 1983.

Fish, Stanley. *Doing What Comes Naturally: Change, Rhetoric, and the Practice of Theory in Literary and Legal Studies.* Durham, N.C.: Duke Univ. Press, 1988.

Fitzgerald, Percy. *Bardell v. Pickwick.* London: Elliot Stock, 1902.

Foucault, Michel. *The Order of Things.* New York: Random House, 1970.

Fowles, John. *The French Lieutenant's Woman.* New York: New American Library, 1969.

Frost, Ginger S. *Promises Broken: Courtship, Class and Gender in Victorian England.* Charlottesville: Univ. Press of Virginia, 1995.

Gaskell, Elizabeth. *Cranford/Cousin Phillis.* Harmondsworth, England: Penguin, 1986.

———. *Wives and Daughters.* Harmondsworth, England: Penguin, 1969.

Girard, René. *Deceit, Desire and the Novel.* Baltimore: Johns Hopkins Univ. Press, 1965.

Goode, John. "Adam Bede." In *Critical Essays on George Eliot.* Ed. by Barbara Hardy, 19–41. London: Routledge & Kegan Paul, 1970.

Goodrich, Peter. *Legal Discourse: Studies in Linguistics, Rhetoric and Legal Analysis.* New York: St. Martin's, 1987.

———. *Reading the Law: A Critical Introduction to Legal Method and Techniques.* Oxford: Basil Blackwell, 1986.

Graver, Suzanne. *George Eliot and Community: A Study in Social Theory and Fictional Form.* Berkeley: Univ. of California Press, 1984.

Greimas, A. J. *On Meaning: Selected Writings in Semiotic Theory.* Minneapolis: Univ. of Minnesota Press, 1987.

Grossberg, Michael. *Governing the Hearth: Law and the Family in Nineteenth-Century America.* Chapel Hill: Univ. of North Carolina Press, 1985.

Halévy, Elie. *The Growth of Philosophical Radicalism.* Trans. by Mary Morris. New York: Augustus M. Kelley, 1949.

Handwerk, Gary J. "Linguistic Blindness and Ironic Vision in *The Egoist.*" *Nineteenth-Century Fiction,* 39 (1984): 163–85.

Hansard's Parliamentary Debates. Third Series. vol. 245, London: Cornelius Buck, 1879.

Hardy, Thomas. *Far from the Madding Crowd.* New York: Norton, 1986.

———. *The Mayor of Casterbridge.* New York: Norton, 1977.

———. *Tess of the d'Urbervilles.* Harmondsworth, England: Penguin, 1978.

Havens, Michael Kent. "Coleridge on the Evolution of Language." *Studies in Romanticism,* 20 (1981): 163–83.

Hennelly, Mark M., Jr. "Jane Eyre's Reading Lesson" *ELH,* 51 (Winter 1984): 693–717.

Herbert, Christopher. "Preachers and the Schemes of Nature in *Adam Bede.*" *Nineteenth-Century Fiction,* 29:4 (1975): 412–27.

Hobbes, Thomas. *Leviathan.* London: Pelican, 1970.

Holdsworth, William S. *Charles Dickens as a Legal Historian.* New Haven: Yale Univ. Press, 1929.

Holmes, Elsie. "George Eliot's Wesleyan Madonna." *The George Eliot Fellowship Review,* 18 (1987): 53–59.

Homans, Margaret. *Bearing the Word: Language and Female Experience in Nineteenth-Century Women's Writing.* New Haven: Yale Univ. Press, 1989.

———. "Dinah's Blush, Maggie's Arm: Class, Gender, and Sexuality in George Eliot's Early Novels." *Victorian Studies*, 36:2 (Winter 1993): 155–78.

Hume, David. *A Treatise of Human Nature*. Ed. by L. A. Selby-Bigge. Oxford: Clarendon, 1960.

Jackson, Bernard S. *Law, Fact and Narrative Coherence*. Liverpool: Deborah Charles, 1988.

———. "Narrative Models in Legal Proof." In *Narrative and the Legal Discourse: A Reader in Storytelling and the Law*. Ed. by David Ray Papke, 158–78. Liverpool: Deborah Charles, 1991.

———. *Semiotics and Legal Theory*. London: Routledge, 1985.

Jacobus, Mary. "The Question of Language: Men of Maxims and *The Mill on the Floss*." *Critical Inquiry*, 8 (1981): 207–22.

James, Henry. "The Art of Fiction." In *Theory of Fiction: Henry James*. Ed. by James E. Miller, Jr., 28–44. Lincoln: Univ. of Nebraska Press, 1972.

———. *The Notebooks of Henry James*. Ed. by F. O. Matthiessen and Kenneth Murdock. New York: Oxford Univ. Press, 1947.

———. *The Princess Casamassima*. Harmondsworth, England: Penguin, 1986.

———. *The Question of Our Speech, The Lesson of Balzac: Two Lectures*. Boston and New York: Houghton Mifflin, 1905.

———. *The Wings of the Dove*. Ed. by J. Donald Crowley and Richard A. Hocks. New York: Norton, 1978.

Jankowsky, Kurt R. "F. Max Müller and the Development of Linguistic Science." *Historiographica Linguistica*, 6:3 (1979): 339–59.

Kaufmann, Linda. *Discourses of Desire: Gender, Genre, and Epistolary Fiction*. Ithaca, N.Y.: Cornell Univ. Press, 1986.

Kendrick, Walter M. *The Novel Machine: The Theory and Fiction of Anthony Trollope*. Baltimore: Johns Hopkins Univ. Press, 1980.

Kennard, Jean E. *Victims of Convention*. Hamden, Conn.: Archon, 1978.

Kleis, John Christopher. "Passion Vs. Prudence: Theme and Technique in Trollope's Palliser Novels." *Texas Studies in Literature and Language*, 11 (1970): 1405–14.

Knies, Earl A. *The Art of Charlotte Brontë*. Athens: Ohio Univ. Press, 1969.

Knoepflmacher, U. C. *Religious Humanism and the Victorian Novel: George Eliot, Walter Pater, and Samuel Butler*. Princeton, N.J.: Princeton Univ. Press, 1965.

Kristeva, Julia. *Tales of Love*. Trans. by Leon S. Roudiez. New York: Columbia Univ. Press, 1987.

Kucich, John. "Passionate Reserve and Reserved Passion in the Works of Charlotte Brontë." *ELH*, 52 (Winter 1985): 913–37.

Land, Stephen K. "The Silent Poet: An Aspect of Wordsworth's Semantic Theory." *University of Toronto Quarterly*, 42 (1972–73): 157–169.

"The Law of Breach of Promise." *The Examiner*, January 21, 1871. In *The Woman Question: Papers Reprinted from "The Examiner."* London: R. H. Lapham, 1872.

Levine, George. "Can You Forgive Him?: Trollope's *Can You Forgive Her?* and the Myth of Realism." *Victorian Studies*, 18 (1974): 5–30.

———. *The Realistic Imagination: English Fiction from Frankenstein to Lady Chatterley*. Chicago: Univ. of Chicago Press, 1981.

Levinson, Sanford. *"Law as Literature."* In *Interpreting Law and Literature: A Hermeneutic Reader*. Ed. by Sanford Levinson and Steven Mailloux, 229–49. Evanston, Ill.: Northwestern Univ. Press, 1988.

Linder, Cynthia A. *Romantic Imagery in the Novels of Charlotte Brontë*. London: Methuen, 1978.

Locke, John, *An Essay Concerning Human Understanding*. Oxford: Clarendon, 1975.

Longford, Elizabeth. *Wellington: Pillar of State*. London: Weidenfeld & Nicolson, 1972.

———. *Wellington: The Years of the Sword*. London: Weidenfeld and Nicolson, 1969.

Lyell, Charles. *The Geological Evidence of the Antiquity of Man*. New York: Dutton, n. d.

MacColla, Charles J. *Breach of Promise: Its History and Social Considerations*. London: Pickering, 1879.

Maine, Sir Henry Sumner. *Ancient Law*. London: Oxford Univ. Press, 1959.

Martin, Robert Bernard. *The Accents of Persuasion: Charlotte Brontë's Novels*. London: Faber & Faber, 1966.

Maynard, John. *Charlotte Brontë and Sexuality*. Cambridge: Cambridge Univ. Press, 1984.

McGlamery, Gayla. *"In His Beginning, His Ends: The 'Preface' to Meredith's Diana of the Crossways."* *Studies in the Novel* (1991): 470–89.

McKusick, James C. *Coleridge's Philosophy of Language*. Yale Studies in English 195. New Haven: Yale Univ. Press, 1986.

McMaster, Juliet. *Trollope's Palliser Novels*. London: Macmillan, 1978.

McMaster, R. D. *Trollope and the Law*. London: Macmillan, 1986.

Menefee, Samuel Pyeatt. *Wives for Sale: An Ethnographic Study of British Popular Divorce*. Oxford: Basil Blackwell, 1981.

Meredith, George. *The Amazing Marriage*. New York: Charles Scribner's Sons, 1895.

———. *Diana of the Crossways*. *The Works of George Meredith. Memorial Edition*, vol. 16. New York: Charles Scribner's Sons, 1910.

———. *The Egoist*. *The Works of George Meredith. Memorial Edition*, vols. 13–14. New York: Charles Scribner's Sons, 1910.

———. *"On the Idea of Comedy and of the Uses of the Comic Spirit."* *The Works of George Meredith. Memorial Edition*, vol. 23. New York: Charles Scribner's Sons, 1910.

Mill, John Stuart. *A System of Logic Ratiocinative and Inductive. The Collected Edition of the Works of John Stuart Mill*, vols. 7–8. Toronto: Univ. of Toronto Press, 1963.

———. *"Thoughts on Poetry and Its Varieties."* *The Collected Edition of the Works of John Stuart Mill*, vol. 1. Toronto: Univ. of Toronto Press, 1963.

———. *Utilitarianism. The Collected Edition of the Works of John Stuart Mill*, vol. 7. Toronto: Univ. of Toronto Press, 1963.

Miller, J. Hillis. *The Ethics of Reading*. New York: Columbia Univ. Press, 1987.

———. *"'Herself Against Herself': The Clarification of Clara Middleton."* In *The Representation of Women in Fiction, Selected Papers from the*

English Institute, 1981. Ed. by Carolyn G. Heilbrun and Margaret R. Higonnet, 98–123. New Series, no. 7. Baltimore: Johns Hopkins Univ. Press, 1983.

———. *Topographies.* Stanford: Stanford Univ. Press, 1995.

Mitchell, Lee Clark. "The Sustaining Duplicities of *The Wings of the Dove.*" *Texas Studies in Literature and Language,* 29:2 (1987): 187–214.

Momberger, Philip. "Self and World in the Works of Charlotte Brontë." *ELH,* 32 (September 1965), 349–69.

Monod, Sylvère. "Charlotte Brontë and the Thirty 'Readers' of *Jane Eyre.*" In *Jane Eyre: An Authoritative Text, Backgrounds, Criticism.* Ed. by Richard J. Dunn. New York: Norton, 1971.

Morse, Deborah Denenholz. *Women in Trollope's Palliser Novels.* Ann Arbor and London: UMI Research Press, 1987.

Mugglestone, Lynda. *'Talking Proper': The Rise of Accent as Social Symbol.* Oxford: Clarendon, 1995.

Müller, Max. *Biographies of Words.* London: Longman, Green, and Co., 1888.

———. *Lectures on the Science of Language.* London: Longman, Green, Longman, and Roberts, 1861.

———. *Lectures on the Science of Language. Second Series.* London: Longman, Green, Longman, Roberts, & Green, 1864.

Murray, Elisabeth K. M. *Caught in the Web of Words: James Murray and the Oxford English Dictionary.* New Haven: Yale Univ. Press, 1977.

Neumann, Joshua H. "Coleridge on the English Language." *PMLA,* 63 (1949): 642–61.

Nietzsche, Friedrich. *On the Genealogy of Morals.* In *Basic Writings of Nietzsche.* Trans. and ed. by Walter Kaufmann. New York: Modern Library, 1968.

Norton, Caroline. *Caroline Norton's Defense: English Laws for Women in the Nineteenth-Century.* Intro. by Joan Huddleston. Chicago: Academy Chicago, 1982.

O'Barr, William M. and John M. Conley. "Litigant Satisfaction versus Legal Adequacy in Small Claims Court Narratives." In *Narrative and the Legal Discourse: A Reader in Storytelling and the Law.* Ed. by David Ray Papke. 65–89. Liverpool: Deborah Charles, 1991.

Ogden, C. K. *Bentham's Theory of Fictions.* New York: Harcourt, Brace, 1932.

Olender, Maurice. *The Languages of Paradise: Race, Religion, and Philology in the Nineteeth Century.* Cambridge: Harvard Univ. Press, 1992.

Orwell, George. *1984.* Harmondsworth, England: Penguin, 1954.

Paley, William. *Principles of Moral and Political Philosophy.* Canandaigua, N.Y.: J. D. Bemis, 1822.

Parker, Stephen. *Informal Marriage, Cohabitation and the Law, 1750–1989.* London: Macmillan, 1990.

Pateman, Carole. *The Problem of Political Obligation: A Critical Analysis of Liberal Theory.* Chichester: John Wiley & Sons, 1979.

Patterson, Dennis M. "Law's Pragmatism: Law as Practice and Narrative." In *Wittgenstein and Legal Theory.* Ed. by Dennis M. Patterson. Boulder: Westview Press, 1992.

Peacock, Thomas Love. *Nightmare Abbey*. *The Works of Thomas Love Peacock*, vol. 3. New York: AMS Press, 1967.

Plato, *The Symposium*. Trans. by Walter Hamilton. Harmondsworth, England: Penguin, 1980.

Polhemus, Robert. *Erotic Faith: Being in Love from Jane Austen to D. H. Lawrence*. Chicago: Univ. of Chicago Press, 1990.

Poovey, Mary. *Uneven Developments: The Ideological Work of Gender in Mid-Victorian England*. Chicago: Univ. of Chicago Press, 1988.

Posner, Richard. *Law and Literature: A Misunderstood Relation*. Cambridge: Harvard Univ. Press, 1988.

Qualls, Barry V. *The Secular Pilgrims of Victorian Fiction: The Novel as Book of Life*. Cambridge: Cambridge Univ. Press, 1982.

Ragussis, Michael. *Acts of Naming: The Family Plot in Fiction*. Oxford: Oxford Univ. Press, 1986.

Ricoeur, Paul. "What Is a Text? Explanation and Understanding." In *Twentieth-Century Literary Theory: An Introductory Anthology*. Ed. by Vassilis Lambropoulos and David Neal Miller, 331–49. Albany: State Univ. of New York Press, 1987.

Riffaterre, Michael. *Fictional Truth*. Baltimore: Johns Hopkins Univ. Press, 1990.

Roberts, Doreen. "*Jane Eyre* and 'The Warped System of Things.'" In *Reading the Victorian Novel: Detail into Form*. Ed. by Ian Gregor, 131–49. London: Vision, 1980.

Robins, Michael H. *Promising, Intending, and Moral Autonomy*. Cambridge: Cambridge Univ. Press, 1984.

Rosner, Mary. "The Two Faces of Cicero: Trollope's *Life* in the Nineteenth Century." *Rhetoric Society Quarterly*, 18 (1988): 251–58.

Rousseau, Jean Jacques, *First and Second Discourses together with the Replies to Critics and Essay on the Origin of Languages*. Ed. and trans. by Victor Gourevitch. New York: Harper & Row, 1986.

Sadleir, Michael. "Preface." *The Noble Jilt*. Intro. by Robert H. Tayler. Arno Press, 1981.

Sadoff, Dianne. "Nature's Language: Metaphor in the Text of *Adam Bede*." *Genre*, 11:3 (1978), 411–26.

Scargill, M. H. "Poetic Symbolism in *Jane Eyre*." In *Charlotte Brontë: Jane Eyre and Villette: A Casebook*. Ed. by Miriam Allot, 175–81. London: Macmillan, 1973.

Schorer, Mark. "*Jane Eyre*." In *The World We Imagine: Selected Essays by Mark Schorer*, 86–90. New York: Farrar, Strauss, & Giroux, 1968.

Searle, John. *Speech Acts: An Essay in the Philosophy of Language*. Cambridge: Cambridge Univ. Press, 1969.

———. "What Is a Speech Act?". In *Readings in the Philosophy of Language*. Ed. by Jay F. Rosenberg and Charles Travis, 614–28. Englewood Cliffs, N.J.: Prentice Hall, 1971.

Shanley, Mary Lyndon. *Feminism, Marriage, and the Law in Victorian England*. Princeton, N.J.: Princeton Univ. Press, 1989.

Shuttleworth, Sally. *George Eliot and Nineteenth-Century Science*. Cambridge: Cambridge Univ. Press, 1984.

Sidgwick, Henry. *The Methods of Ethics*. London: Macmillan, 1907.

Smalley, Donald. Ed. *Trollope: The Critical Heritage*. London: Routledge & Kegan Paul, 1969.

Smiles, Samuel. *Self-Help; with Illustrations of Conduct and Perseverance*. London: John Murray, 1882.

Smirlock, Daniel. "Rough Truth: Synecdoche and Interpretation in *The Egoist*." *Nineteenth-Century Fiction*, 31 (1976): 313–328.

Smith, Adam. *The Theory of Moral Sentiments*. Ed. by D. D. Raphael and A. L. MacFie. Oxford: Clarendon, 1976.

Smith, Olivia. *The Politics of Language: 1791–1819*. Oxford: Clarendon, 1984.

Snow, C. P. *Trollope*. London: Macmillan, 1975.

Spens, Janet. "Charlotte Brontë." *Essays and Studies by Members of the English Association*, 14 (1929): 53–70.

Sprinker, Michael. "'The Intricate Evasions of A': Meredith's Theory of Figure." *The Victorian Newsletter*, 53 (Spring, 1978): 9–12.

Stang, Richard. *The Theory of the Novel in England. 1850–1870*. New York: Columbia Univ. Press, 1959.

Stedman, Jane W. "'Come, Substantial Damages!'" In *Victorian Scandals: Representations of Gender and Class*. Ed. by Kristine Ottesen Garrigan, 69–96. Athens: Ohio Univ. Press, 1992.

Stein, Peter. *Legal Evolution: the Story of an Idea*. Cambridge: Cambridge Univ. Press, 1980.

Sterne, Laurence. *The Life and Opinions of Tristram Shandy, Gentleman*. Ed. by James Aiken Work. Indianapolis and New York: Odyssey Press, 1940.

Stevenson, Lionel. *The Ordeal of George Meredith*. New York: Scribner's, 1953.

Stoehr, Taylor. "Words and Deeds in *The Princess Casamassima*." *ELH*, 37 (1970): 95–135.

Stone, Donald D. *The Romantic Impulse in Victorian Fiction*. Cambridge: Harvard Univ. Press, 1980.

Stone, Lawrence. *The Past and the Present Revisited*. New York: Routledge & Kegan Paul, 1987.

———. *The Road to Divorce: England 1850–1987*. Oxford: Oxford Univ. Press, 1990.

Sullivan, Sir Arthur and W. S. Gilbert. *Trial by Jury*. In *The Complete Plays of Gilbert and Sullivan* (New York: Modern Library, n. d.).

Swingle, L. J. *Romanticism and Anthony Trollope: A Study in the Continuities of Nineteenth-Century Thought*. Ann Arbor: Univ. of Michigan Press, 1990.

Tanner, Tony. *Adultery in the Novel: Contract and Transgression*. Baltimore: Johns Hopkins Univ. Press, 1979.

———. "Passion, narrative and identity in *Wuthering Heights* and *Jane Eyre*." In *Teaching the Text*. Ed. by Susanne Kappeler and Norman Bryson, 109–25. London: Routledge & Kegan Paul, 1983.

Tayler, Irene and Gina Luria. "Gender and Genre: Women in British Romantic Literature." In *What Manner of Woman*. Ed. by Marlene Springer, 98–123. New York: New York Univ. Press, 1977.

Taylor, Dennis. *Hardy's Literary Language and Victorian Philology.* Oxford: Clarendon, 1993.

Taylor, Talbert J. *Mutual Misunderstanding: Skepticism and the Theorizing of Language and Interpretation.* Durham: Duke Univ. Press, 1992.

Thackeray, William Makepeace. *Vanity Fair.* Harmondsworth, England: Penguin, 1985.

Thompson, Neville. *Wellington After Waterloo.* London and New York: Routledge & Kegan Paul, 1986.

Tooke, John Horne, *Winged Words, or the Diversions of Purley.* Menston, England: Scolar Press, 1968.

Trench, Richard Chenevix. *On Some Deficiencies in our English Dictionaries.* Second Edition. London: John W. Parker, 1860.

———. *On the Study of Words & English Past and Present.* (London: Dutton, n.d.).

Trollope, Anthony. *An Autobiography.* Oxford: Oxford Univ. Press, 1987.

———. *Can You Forgive Her?.* Oxford: Oxford Univ. Press, 1989.

———. *An Eye for an Eye.* London: Trollope Society, 1993.

———. *The Eustace Diamonds.* Oxford: Oxford Univ. Press, 1989.

———. *Kept in the Dark.* Oxford: Oxford Univ. Press, 1992.

———. *Lady Anna.* Oxford: Oxford Univ. Press, 1984.

———. *Life of Cicero.* 2 vols. London: Chapman and Hall, 1880.

———. *The New Zealander.* Oxford: Oxford Univ. Press, 1972.

———. *An Old Man's Love.* Oxford: Oxford Univ. Press, 1992.

———. *Orley Farm.* Oxford: Oxford Univ. Press, 1985.

———. *Phineas Finn.* Harmondsworth, England: Penguin, 1985.

———. *Phineas Redux.* Oxford: Oxford Univ. Press, 1988.

———. *The Prime Minister.* Oxford: Oxford Univ. Press, 1987.

———. *The Small House at Allington.* Oxford: Oxford Univ. Press, 1980.

———. *The Way We Live Now.* London: Trollope Society, 1992.

Tromly, Annette. *The Cover of the Mask: The Autobiographers in Charlotte Brontë's Fiction.* ELS Monograph Series, 26. Victoria, B.C.: Univ. of Victoria Press, 1982.

van den Broek, A. G. "*Adam Bede* and Riehl's 'Social-Political Conservatism.'" *The George Eliot Fellowship Review*, 17 (1986): 42–61.

Van Roermund. Bert C. "On 'Narrative Coherence' in Legal Contexts." In *Reason in Law: Proceedings of the Conference Held in Bologna, 12–15 December 1984*, III, Ed. by Carla Faralli and Enrico Pattaro, 150–70. Milan: A. Giuffrè, 1988.

Vitek, William. *Promising.* Philadelphia: Temple Univ. Press, 1993.

Warhol, Robyn. *Gendered Interventions: Narrative Discourse in the Victorian Novel.* New Brunswick: Rutgers Univ. Press, 1989.

Watt, Ian. *The Rise of the Novel.* Berkeley: Univ. of California Press, 1957.

White, Hayden. *Tropics of Discourse: Essays in Cultural Criticism.* Baltimore: Johns Hopkins Univ. Press, 1978.

———. "The Value of Narrativity in the Representation of Reality." In *The Content Of the Form: Narrative Discourse and Historical Representation.* Baltimore: Johns Hopkins, Univ. Press, 1987.

White, J. Dundas. "Breach of Promise of Marriage." *The Law Quarterly Review*, 10 (1894): 135–42.

White, James Boyd. *Heracles' Bow: Essays on the Rhetoric and Poetics of Law.* Madison, Wis.: Univ. of Wisconsin Press, 1985.

Wiesenfarth, Joseph. *George Eliot's Mythmaking.* Heidelburg: Carl Winter, 1977.

Williams, Carolyn. "Unbroken Patternes: Gender, Culture, and Voice in *The Egoist,*" *Browning Institute Studies*, vol. 13. Ed. by Adrienne Auslander Munich, 45–70. New York: The Browning Institute, Inc., and the Graduate School and University Center, CUNY, 1985.

Wilson, Peter J. *Man, the Promising Primate: The Conditions of Human Evolution.* New Haven: Yale Univ. Press, 1983.

Wilt, Judith. *The Readable People of George Meredith.* Princeton, N.J.: Princeton Univ. Press, 1975.

Wise, T. J. and J. A. Symington. Eds. *The Brontës: Their Lives, Friendships, and Correspondence.* Oxford: Shakespeare Head, 1932.

Wordsworth, William. *Selected Prose.* Ed. by John O. Hayden. Harmondsworth: Penguin, 1988.

Yeazell, Ruth Bernard. "More True than Real: Jane Eyre's 'Mysterious Summons.'" *Nineteenth-Century Fiction*, 29 (September 1974): 127–43.

Yeazell, Stephen C. "Convention, Fiction, and Law." *NLH* (1981): 89–102.

CASES CITED

Atchinson v. *Baker* (1796). Peake Add. Cas., 103–5.

Baddeley v. *Mortlock and Wife* (1816). C. P. Holt, 151–53.

Beachey v. *Brown* (1860). El. Bl. & El., 796–805; *All England Law Reports Reprint: 1843–1860*. Ed. by G. F. L. Bridgman, Esq., O.B.E. London: Butterworth, 1860, 506–8.

Bench v. *Merrick* (1844). 1 Car. & K., 463–68.

Bessela v. *Stern* (1877). *The Law Reports. Common Pleas Division*, vol 2. Ed. by James Redfoord Bulwer, Q.C. London: William Clowes, 1877, 265–72

Caines v. *Smith* (1847). 15 M. & W., 189–90.

Finlay v. *Chirney* (1888). *The Law Reports. Queen's Bench Division*, vol. 20. Ed. A. P. Stone. London: William Clowes, 1888, 494–508.

Finney v. *Garmoyle* (1884). Stedman, Jane W. "'Come, Substantial Damages!'" In *Victorian Scandals: Representations of Gender and Class*. Ed. by Kristine Ottesen Garrigan. Athens: Ohio Univ. Press, 1992.

Foulkes v. *Selway* (1805). *Reports of Cases Argued and Ruled at* Nisi Prius *in the Court of King's Bench and Common Pleas*, vol 3. Ed. by Isaac Espinasse. Philadelphia: P. Byrne, 1805, 236–37.

Hall v. *Wright* (1858, 1859). Q. B. El. Bl. & E. 746–64; Ex. Ch. El. Bl. & El., 765–95; 120 *All England Law Reports Reprint. Exchequer Chamber*, 735–37.

Harbert v. *Edgington* (1844). Cited in *Bench* v. *Merrick* (1844). 1 Car. & K., 466.

Honyman v. *Campbell* (1831). 2 Dow & Clarke, 265–87.

Irving v. *Greenwood* (1824). 1 Car. & P., 350–51.

Leeds v. *Cook & Wife* (1807). *Reports of Cases Argued and Ruled at* Nisi Prius *in the Courts of King's Bench and Common Pleas*, vol 4. Ed. by Isaac Espinasse. Philadelphia: P. Byrne, 1807, 256–58.

Millward v. *Littlewood* (1850). 5 Ex., 775–78.

Short v. *Stone* (1846). Q. B. 8 Q. B., 361–72; *Queen's Bench Reports*. New Series, vol. 3. Ed. by John Leycester Adolphus and Thomas Flower Ellis. Philadelphia: T. & J. W. Johnson, 1859, 358–69.

Vineall v. *Veness* (1865). 4 F. & F., 344–46; 176 *English Reports*, 593–94.

Wharton v. *Lewis* (1824). N. P. 1 C. & P., 529–30; 171 *English Reports*, 1303–4.

Wild v. *Harris* (1849). C. P. 7 C. B., 999–1006.

INDEX